Humana Festival '95
The Complete Plays

Humana Inc. is one of the nation's largest
managed health care companies
with more than 1.6 million members in its health care plans.

The Humana Foundation was established in 1981
to support the educational, social, medical and cultural development
of communities in ways that reflect
Humana's commitment to social responsibility
and an improved quality of life.

D0962887

Humana Festival '95
The Complete Plays

Edited by Marisa Smith

Contemporary Playwrights Series

SK

A Smith and Kraus Book

A Smith and Kraus Book
Published by Smith and Kraus, Inc.
One Main Street, PO Box 127, Lyme, NH 03768

Copyright © 1995 by Smith and Kraus
All rights reserved

Manufactured in the United States of America

Cover and Text Design by Julia Hill

First Edition: September 1995
10 9 8 7 6 5 4 3 2 1

Library of Congress Cataloguing-in-Publication Data

Humana Festival '95 : the complete plays / edited by Marisa Smith. --1st ed.
p. cm. --(Contemporary playwrights series)   ISBN 1-880399-92-X
1. American drama--20th century. I. Smith, Marisa. II. Series.
PS634.H862   1995
812'.5408--dc20   95-37497
CIP

Contents

Introduction

What I always love about good theatrical writing is how it finds room for the personal and passionate amidst the crowding practical necessities of writing for the stage. Once again the American theatre is tightening its belt and making soup from its shoes.

> Dear Playwright:
>   Only one set, dear playwright, and preferably no walls, inexpensive costumes, very little furniture, less than six actors, go easy on the special effects, no wigs, simple sound, but other than that feel free to be as expansive as you like.
>   Yours Sincerely,
>   Budget and Management

To which the playwright ordinarily replies, "Sure, no problem, anything else?" And the theatre continues its marginal life in the culture as it has always done. And yet…and yet the playwrights take these strictures and explode then outward as if they were delicious opportunities to pour their passionate politics, social observation, personal pain, and ribald satire into and over the economically denuded circumstance. If this isn't valor, I don't know what is!

Seems like the windmill these works collectively tilt at has something to do with that moment when you look up and see the tidal wave a hundred miles away and oncoming. These plays embody the "what-the-hell-do-we-do-now?!" response. There's a kind of desperate energy in many of them that sense there is little time and much to do. In

Donald Margulies' *July 7, 1994* there's a physician trying to staunch an entire society's wounds while she bleeds herself. In Jane Martin's *Middle-Aged White Guys* three perpetrators in a junk yard try to find a single gesture that will make amends for a lifetime of exploitation. And in Regina Taylor's *Between the Lines* driven women try to heal the schism between public and private lives that are spinning out of control.

Control. It's a collected works of losing the old control and trying to hold onto the wall with your nails.

So here they are, those valorous playwrights, singing like canaries in the mine for those who have the head and the heart to listen.

Where are the medals for these people? Don't tell me we forgot to bring the medals?

Jon Jory
Producing Director
Actors Theatre of Louisville

Humana Festival '95

The Complete Plays

Tough Choices for the New Century:

A SEMINAR FOR RESPONSIBLE LIVING

by Jane Anderson

BIOGRAPHY

Ms. Anderson grew up in northern California and after two years in college, dropped out to move to New York City to train as an actress. In 1975 she appeared in the New York premiere of David Mamet's *Sexual Perversity in Chicago.* She began writing in 1979 when she founded the New York Writers Bloc with playwrights Donald Margulies and Jeffery Sweet. She developed a series of characters and performed as a comedienne in New York clubs and cabarets. In 1982, her act was discovered by Billy Crystal, and she was brought to Los Angeles to be a regular on *The Billy Crystal Comedy Hour* which was taken off the air after three weeks. Ms. Anderson continued to perform in Los Angeles, receiving critical acclaim for her one-woman show, *How to Raise a Gifted Child.*

For several years she worked as a television writer, working on staff for several series, including *Wonder Years* and creating a short-lived show for Grant Tinker called *Raising Miranda.*

Her playwriting career began in 1986 with *Defying Gravity,* which premiered in L.A. and later received a W. Alton Jones Grant for a production at the Williamstown Theatre Festival. Her plays to follow were *Food & Shelter, The Baby Dance, The Pink Studio, Hotel Oubliette* (recipient of the Susan Smith Blackburn Prize) and several short plays, including *Lynette at 3 AM* and *The Last Time We Saw Her,* both winners of the Heideman Award. Her works are published and have been widely produced off-Broadway and in theatres around the country, including Long Wharf, The McCarter, Williamstown Theatre Festival, The Pasadena Playhouse, ACT, and Actors Theatre of Louisville.

In 1993, Ms. Anderson received an Emmy Award and Writer's Guild Award for her H.B.O. movie, *The Positively True Adventures of the Alleged Texas Cheerleader-Murdering Mom.*

Her film work includes: *Cop Gives Waitress $2 Million Tip,* renamed for release to *It Could Happen to You* (Tristar). Currently in production is her film adaptation of *How To Make An American Quilt* from the novel by Whitney Otto. It will be released in winter of 1995 by Amblin/Universal.

Ms. Anderson is a member of the Dramatists Guild.

Author's Note

I live in Los Angeles. My city has had too many full-color disaster spreads in *Newsweek*. We've survived fires, riots, floods, mud slides, and earthquakes. All those calamities can wear a population down. I've noticed that we're getting the flu a lot. Marriages are falling apart. And seemingly rational people are buying guns. Some of us have fled for more stable parts of the earth only to realize that there are no guarantees that you won't be harmed by some random act of nature or an angry man with a bomb. But we'll never stop trying to control the uncontrollable. And sometimes our attempts to do so are what will kill us in the end.

Original Production

Tough Choices for the New Century was first produced at Actors Theatre of Louisville as part of the Humana Festival 1995. It was directed by Lisa Peterson with the following cast:

Bob Dooley . . . . Kenneth L. Marks
Helen Dooley, Arden Shingles . . . . Susan Knight

TIME

Present (whatever time curtain goes up.)

PLACE

A seminar room.

OUR SEMINAR SPEAKERS:

BOB AND HELEN DOOLEY: Bob has been giving his very popular preparedness seminars all around the country. Helen has recently joined the team and is an experienced volunteer for the Red Cross. They originally hail from Columbus, Ohio, and currently reside in the Southern California area where Bob is a construction consultant.

ARDEN SHINGLES: Ms. Shingles is author of the best-seller, *Armed For Life*. She has been teaching seminars and workshops in self-defense for the past eleven years and was twice-named Business Woman of the Year by the Austin Business Women's Association.

(Note: Arden and Helen may be played by the same actress.)

What people are saying after taking our seminars!

"I used to live my life in fear. Now I know that I have control over what happens to me."
—*Grace Larkin, Michigan*

"I thought I was prepared before. Now I'm *really* prepared for whatever happens. And I feel great about it."
—*Ron Held, Florida*

"I've turned my losses into gains. I learned a lot about positive thinking."
—*Douglas Uley, Indiana*

TOUGH CHOICES FOR THE NEW CENTURY

*As we enter the theater, we are given handouts [see Choices Itinerary &
Questionnaire] with a small stubby pencil and urged to fill them out
while we wait for the seminar to begin. On the stage is a screen with a
slide thrown up: Tough Choices for the New Century. There's a chair
and a table with a plastic pitcher of water and plastic cups for the
speakers to use.*

    *Bob and Helen are already on stage setting up, going over notes,
handing last-minute slides to someone on the seminar staff [can be
played by the stage manager or one of the backstage persons]. Bob and
Helen are a nicely groomed, middle-class white couple. Bob's manner is
energetic and folksy, a user-friendly kind of guy. Helen is maintaining
a pleasant expression on her face but seems slightly cut off.*

    *When the seminar begins, the lights in the audience should dim
only slightly because we should feel that we're in lecture space rather
than a theatre.*

BOB: *(to audience)* Everybody here who's supposed to be here?
Everybody in the right seminar? This is Tough Choices for the
New Century. Now's your chance to escape! Terrific. My name is
Bob Dooley and this is my wife Helen.

HELEN: Hello.

BOB: This is Helen's first time up here. I've been giving workshops for
several years now and I've always bounced my ideas off Helen

while we're sitting around the dinner table. And a few weeks ago, I finally said to her, "Honey, I think you'd have a heck of a lot to share with people, why don't you come up and help me lead this seminar?" And it didn't take much convincing after that to get her to agree.

HELEN: I'm just here to keep an eye on him.

BOB: Well, I wish I were that handsome that you had to worry. Anyway, we're real lucky to have Helen with us and if you take a look at the schedule—everyone get one?, terrific—if you glance through your schedules you'll see that we have a really full weekend ahead of us. But you'll also have time to use the great facilities here. There's a beautiful pool, tennis courts, putting green, computer center, a jacuzzi—Helen, I bet that's where you'll be headed for some quiet time.

HELEN: Oh, you bet, Honey.

BOB: Oh and Sunday afternoon, after the last talk, there will be a barbecue. So if you don't have to rush back home, we'd love you to stay and wind down with us, have some great food, chat about the weekend...Super. Let's get started. Helen?

(Helen changes the slide. We see a map of America with large areas marked in red.)

HELEN: This is a government map showing every region that's been declared a national disaster zone in the past five years. Which means that by the year 2000, one out of every five Americans can expect to be directly impacted by a natural catastrophe.

BOB: Helen has family all over the United States and all of them have had their homes devastated in one form or another. Helen you want to tell us a little bit about that?

(Helen clicks to a slide of hurricane destruction.)

HELEN: Well, first my sister Renée and her husband lost their home in hurricane Andrew. Their roof was ripped off and everything inside their house was scattered and blown into the ocean—all of their papers, family pictures, everything was gone. Then my brother and his family, they live in Iowa. *(Helen clicks to a slide of a flooded farm in the midwest.)* When the floods came, they lost all their livestock—cows, chickens, pigs, they all drowned. Their house was under water for a month. Everything in the house—all their furniture, tax returns...family pictures, it all had to be thrown away. And then, oh gosh, my parents had just moved to Altadena,

California, where they bought their retirement home. And they had just finished doing five months of work on the house—new carpeting, new wallpaper, new cabinets in the kitchen...

BOB: They found out that they had to put in new pipes...

HELEN: ...all new pipes, that's right—and finally when the last workman had left, and everything was new and clean and just the way they wanted it, my mother said to my father, "Now wasn't that all worth it," and they went to bed that night, as my mother put it, with big smiles on their faces. But then around five in the morning, they were woken up by someone pounding on their door—

BOB: It was a fireman telling them that the hills were on fire.

(Helen clicks to a slide of the California hills on fire.)

HELEN: My parents were told that they had to evacuate. The fire was coming so fast, my mother didn't even have time to put in her teeth. She said that when they ran outside, they saw a giant wall of flames coming down from the hills—

BOB: She said it looked like a tidal wave from hell.

HELEN: I can tell it, Honey. *(to audience)*—and in less than a minute the house caught fire like it was a cardboard box. They had to put my father in a wheelbarrow because he couldn't run from the fire fast enough.

BOB: *(to audience)* Actually, what happened was—*(to Helen)*...sorry, Honey.

HELEN: Go ahead.

BOB: Helen's father wanted to stay and hose down their roof—

HELEN: Which was stupid.

BOB: —sure, that's not something we recommend in a situation like this, but Helen's dad is actually a pretty neat guy. Listen to this— after the fire, at age *seventy-six,* he took the insurance money they got for the house and bought a boat. He's already sailed to Hawaii twice. Now don't you wish we all had that kind of positive attitude on life? *(to Helen)* Go ahead, Honey.

HELEN: Well, I was going to say that just the year before, my mother's sister who lives in Northern California had her house destroyed by the fire up there. And she had all the other family pictures...we had some pictures, but I couldn't find the album after the earthquake. So there are no more family pictures left.

BOB: OK, what is Helen saying here? If family pictures mean something to you, know where they are, keep them in a box that you can easily locate and slip into a backpack or the front seat of your car. What Helen is saying is, *be prepared.* Honey?

(Helen changes the slide to a photo of the famous casts of the victims of Pompeii.)

BOB: *(Addressing the slide.)* These are not statues. These are casts of actual people who were killed by the famous Volcano of Pompeii almost twenty centuries ago. As they ran back to their homes to collect their possessions, they were overwhelmed by sulfurous fumes and their bodies were covered by ash and burning lava, leaving this record of their agonizing struggle with death. Yes, this was tragic, yes this was awful, but the people of Pompeii *knew* they were living under an active volcano. They knew what was coming. Every morning when they woke up, they could look out their bedroom windows and see that mountain smoking. *What* was going through their heads? Were they just sitting there at their breakfast tables, saying, "Well, Helena, looks like that volcano is going to give us another smoggy day," you know? I'm not putting them down, but the people of Pompeii just didn't want to bother themselves with preparedness. And that's why half the population ended up in a museum case.

(Helen changes the slide to another map of America, the regions marked in red, orange, and yellow.)

BOB: Now some people have said to me, "Bob, my idea of preparedness is to not live in a place where I know disaster will hit." Good idea. But where? Take a look at this map. The red shows us where disasters are expected to occur at least once a year. The orange shows areas where disasters are expected every five years and the yellow shows where disasters are expected to occur every ten years. Let's take a look at where there aren't any colors—the Mojave Desert, gee, I'd sure like to move there, wouldn't you, Helen?

HELEN: Well, it would be restful.

BOB: But it wouldn't be home, would it? Would it, Helen?

HELEN: No, it wouldn't, Bob.

BOB: *(to audience)* Everybody, if we look at this map you'll see that there's no point in running when there's nowhere to go. I don't want to see any of you pulling up stakes and moving to the so-called "safe zones." That's living your life out of fear. But I also don't want to see any of you living your life in denial. What's the middle ground here? How do we cope? Once again, it's that word again. I know you're going to get real sick of hearing me say it, but let's hear it, the P-word…

HELEN & BOB: *(with audience)* Preparedness.

BOB: One more time, louder, come on. *(with audience)* Preparedness. Terrific. Helen?

(Helen changes the slide to: 1) Securing Your Castle; 2) Securing the Family Jewels; 3) Securing Your Identity; 4) Securing the Right Perspective.)

BOB: These are the four points of preparedness that we'll be covering this weekend. *(using the pointer) Securing Your Castle*—if you live in a fire area, replace your shake roof with tile, if you live in an earthquake zone, retrofit your foundation, if you live in flood country, add another story, live on the top floor. *(pointing) Securing the Family Jewels*—how do you protect your irreplaceables—birth certificates, tax returns, computer disks, pets.

HELEN: Family pictures.

BOB: Family pictures, one of Helen's favorite losses. We'll go over all of that later. Moving on, we have—*(pointing) Securing your Identity*—this has to do with making sure that no matter where you are when a disaster hits, even if you're stepping out of the bathtub in your birthday suit, that you'll always have some form of identification on you. One of the biggest problems after any catastrophe is identifying the victims. If you're unable to communicate because of injury or death, you'll want relief workers to know who you are. *(Bob pulls his socks down. Helen looks away, clearly disturbed by this.)* I had my name and social security number tattooed on my ankle—any tattoo artist can do this for a reasonable fee, just make sure they're licensed and the needles are clean. Some people prefer to have the tattoo placed on a spot on their torso because sometimes limbs can get separated. But that's up to you. Helen can tell us another reason why I.D.'s are so important. After the quake, Helen stood in line for eight hours to apply for emergency relief and when she finally got to the head of the line, they wouldn't give her an application because she didn't have any identification. Helen, what does FEMA stand for?

HELEN: Few Enlightened, Many Assholes.

BOB: *(laughs)* Excuse her French, but Helen had quite a time wrestling with the red tape. OK, let's look at number four: *(pointing) Securing the Right Perspective.* I'd like to spend the rest of this time talking about this point. How do we keep our perspective on disaster? How do we not let a disaster depress us, or make us feel like a victim? Helen, what did your mother say after she lost her house in the fire?

HELEN: She said, "Well, I guess God didn't mean us to move to California."

BOB: *(to audience)* All right, how many people here believe that God sends down disasters to punish us? Come on, let's have a show of hands. It's all right if you believe it, it's something we've all been taught—Helen change that slide for me please?

(Helen changes the slide to a blow-up of a section of a contract with a particular sentence highlighted.)

BOB: Look at this, how many of you have ever signed a contract that had this clause in it? *(reading the slide)* "…the undersigned will not be held responsible in the event of war, civil disturbance, fire, earthquake, flood or any other *Act of God*." Act of God. Isn't that wild? Helen, what do you think about this?

HELEN: Well, I do believe there is a God.

BOB: But do you think he's out to punish us?

HELEN: No. *(laughs)* Well, I hope not.

BOB: *(to audience)* Do you know what I think? I think that blaming God, is just another excuse that people make for not preparing, "Well, if God's going to send an earthquake my way, I guess there's nothing I can do about it." Sorry, but I have to get tough here, that's just a bunch of you-know-what. I want all your minds to take a giant U-turn and start thinking in another direction—Honey?

(Helen changes the slide that shows in large letters: A CATASTRO-PHE IS NOTHING PERSONAL.)

BOB: *(Addressing the slide.)* A catastrophe is nothing personal. I want this to become your mantra. I want you to print this on a T-shirt and wear it around for all your friends and neighbors to see. Come on, let's all say it together—*(with audience)* A CATASTROPHE IS NOTHING PERSONAL. Helen?

HELEN: I never said it was, Bob.

BOB: But I think it helps us all to say it. You want to say it with us?

HELEN: All righty. *(Helen pours herself some water.)*

BOB: Come on, let's all say it again with Helen and me. One more time. A CATASTROPHE IS NOTHING PERSONAL.

(Helen deliberately drinks her water through this. Bob sees this.)

BOB: *(flatly)* Terrific. *(Bob goes over to the table, pours himself a cup of water so he can check on Helen. Quietly:)* How're you doing, Honey? *(Back to audience.)* Let's try something. *(Bob puts his cup of water down next to the pitcher.)* According to the laws of gravity, if I put this cup of water down on the table next to this pitcher...and I take a walk way over to here, I can be pretty sure that the pitcher and cup will stay where they are until I come back. The pitcher and cup are held there by gravity. Gravity is what keeps the world around us in place. Gravity is what gives humankind security. But what happens if I do this? *(Bob walks back to the table, puts his hands on the sides and jiggles it very slightly.)* This is what would happen during a three point earthquake. Nothing much is going on, I notice some vibrations in the water but no big deal. All right, let's try a four point earthquake. *(Bob jiggles the tables even more. He glances at Helen who's watching him suspiciously.)* Well, that was kind of disturbing. I see that the pitcher has moved an inch or two and there's a little spillage. Oh well, but I guess I could still live with that. All right, here's a five point earthquake. *(Bob jiggles the table until the pitcher just slides to the edge.)* Wow, close call. That will teach me never to leave something on the edge of the table. *(He slides the pitcher back to the middle of the table.)* How about a six point earthquake? *(Bob rocks the table until the pitcher and cup fall off. Water spills all over the floor.)*

(Helen is splashed by the water, stands up. She's trying very hard not to react.)

BOB: And here's a seven point. *(Bob picks up the table and throws it on the ground.)* And here's an eight point. *(Bob picks up the table and hits it over and over again on the floor until it breaks.)*

(Helen winces but doesn't move.)

BOB: *(laughs, winded)* Well, I guess it wouldn't have done me any good to duck and cover under that piece of furniture. *(To Helen)* How are you doing?

HELEN: Just fine and dandy.

BOB: *(Calling back stage:)* Could we get some paper towels...? Thanks. *(to Helen)* Honey, you did great. You really did.

(Someone on the Seminar Staff hands Helen a stack of brown paper towels. She starts mopping up the spilled water.)

BOB: Honey, that's OK, they can do that.

HELEN: That's all right.

BOB: *(back to audience)* Let's talk a little about earthquakes. We'll be covering other disasters later on, but I like to start with earthquakes because they're the least predictable, the least controllable, and, seemingly, the most impossible to escape.

(Helen is obsessively drying a part of the floor with a paper towel making a skishing noise.)

BOB: Thank you, Honey, that's terrific, thank you. *(Bob helps Helen gather up the paper towels. He hands them to a Seminar Staff person.)* Thank you. *(back to audience)* Helen and I have lived in the southern California area for fifteen years and have been through several quakes. But in the last one, which was pretty wild, we had quite a lot of damage. *(to Helen)* Honey, can we have those slides of the house?

(Helen forwards through a couple of disaster slides and stops at a slide of a kitchen destroyed by an earthquake.)

BOB: This is what happened to our kitchen. As you can see everything that was in the cupboards, on the walls, the counters, just flew out.

HELEN: *(flatly)*...the blender, the coffee maker, the knives on the rack—

BOB: The knives on the rack, that's right—they ended up clear across the kitchen.

(Helen clicks to a slide of kitchen knives stuck in the wall.)

BOB: Thank God this happened at four in the morning. Can you imagine if Helen was standing there preparing a meal? We have a lot to be thankful for.

HELEN: Yes indeedy, we do. *(Helen snaps to the next slide—a dining room destroyed by the earthquake.)*

BOB: Here's our dining room. I don't know if you can tell in this picture, but we had a big china cabinet that fell down and all of Helen's knickknacks were broken to bits.

HELEN: My Hummels.

BOB: And of course you have to keep reminding yourself that these are only things.

HELEN: My mother gave me my Hummels. I'd been collecting them since I was a girl. There weren't even any pieces left that were big enough to glue.

BOB: But we're still in one piece, and that's what's important.

HELEN: The piano flipped over. On top of my Hummels.

BOB: The piano, that's right, and the dining room table, marble-topped, you couldn't move it if you tried, but it flipped right over like it was made of balsa wood.

HELEN: The cat was hiding under the table. She thought it was safe. Our cat Marmalade. She got her tail crushed.

BOB: —the table fell on her tail, that's right.

HELEN: She thought it was safe. That's where she went, under the table. We found her in the morning with her tail caught. The vet had to cut it off...*(Helen stops at a slide of Marmalade with the stub of her tail bandaged.)*

BOB: But here's something interesting—Honey, could you show us the next slide?

(Helen changes to a slide of a water heater.)

BOB: The one thing that didn't move was the water heater. We had it strapped to the wall as a precaution. So preparedness really does pay off. We'll be talking later about wall-securing all your major appliances.

HELEN: If there are any walls left, you can't strap something to a wall that's going to come down.

BOB: No, you're absolutely right.

HELEN: My God, look what just happened in Japan.

BOB: OK, Helen.

HELEN: "Oh, the Japanese aren't scared of earthquakes. They've built everything to code."

BOB: Fine, let's talk about Japan. *(to Helen and audience)* First of all, Kobe was not a prepared city, all right? They don't have earth-quakes in the western part of Japan. If this had happened in Tokyo, it would have been a completely different story.

HELEN: You don't know that.

BOB: Just wait a minute. *(to audience)* I'm glad Helen has brought this up. This is a very important point. The other mistake that the Japanese have made, is that in their drive to become leaders in the world economy, they gave up the flexibility of the reed for the hardness of steel. You see, traditionally, houses in Japan were con-structed of light materials—paper, wood, bamboo poles—and all activities—eating, sleeping, cooking—were done low to the ground. Pillows, instead of chairs, futons instead of beds, hibachis instead of stoves. The previous generations of Japanese were very smart. By tradition, they kept things very spare. They might have one small, pretty little vase with a single flower. If there was an earthquake, it might fall over but they could easily dodge it because they weren't running away from a hundred other things that were falling off the walls.

HELEN: No one lives like that, Bob.

BOB: That's right, and isn't that a shame. *(to audience)* What I'm saying is, simple living is safe living. There was a couple in Northridge who were killed in the quake by their fifteen hundred piece collection of depression-era ceramics. Now what's the point of that? Helen loved her Hummel figurines. But how often would she really look at them? Honey, how often would you say you actually looked at them, maybe once a year?

HELEN: It was more than that.

BOB: All right, once a month? The point being, after they were gone— well, this was months after, when we finally moved back into our house—I asked Helen one day, "Honey, do you miss your Hummels?" *(to Helen)* And what did you say?

HELEN: I don't remember.

BOB: You said no. You said you didn't even remember what they looked like.

HELEN: I was still in shock.

BOB: But do you really need your Hummel figurines? Are they something you need every day to survive, like you would need a blanket or a jug for water or a bowl to eat your food in?

HELEN: We're not cave dwellers, Bob, there are certain things I like to have around.

BOB: So do I, but I'd feel pretty bad if you got clobbered on the head by one of my soft ball trophies. *(laughs, to audience)* All right, I think you all get my point. Let's move on. *(a beat)* Let's take a look at the chair Helen is sitting on. Now according to the laws of gravity, a chair is a stable and safe place to rest. *(Bob grasps the back of Helen's chair.)* This is a three point earthquake. *(Bob jiggles the chair slightly. Helen starts to look tense.)*

BOB: Helen, did you feel much?

HELEN: Yes, I felt the chair shaking.

BOB: But you didn't feel like you were going to fall.

HELEN: No, Bob, I didn't.

BOB: All right, now let's try a four point earthquake. *(Bob shakes the chair a little more.)*
(Helen tries not to react.)

BOB: How are you doing, Helen, you feel like you're falling off?

HELEN: *(flatly)* No, I don't.

BOB: OK, here comes a five point earthquake. *(Bob shakes the chair harder.)*

(Helen grabs the sides.)

BOB: And here's a six point earthquake. *(Bob violently rocks the chair back and forth while Helen grasps the sides.)*

HELEN: Bob, please stop it.

BOB: All right, Helen wanted me to stop because she felt like she was about to topple over. That's because furniture of Western cultures have a high center of gravity. They aren't designed for earthquakes. Now let's look at the Japanese-style chair. *(Bob calls to someone on the Seminar Staff.)* Could I have one of our pillows? *(The staff member hands him an upholstered pillow.)* *(to audience)* Later, we'll be showing you how to save your life in a hurricane with something as simple as a cushion from your couch. Anyway. How many of you have gone to one of those traditional Japanese restaurants that have a tatami room, you know, where you have to take your shoes off and sit on the floor on these funny little pillows, and your more adventurous friends are saying, "Come on, let's try it," and you're saying to yourself, "Geez, how am I gonna get through this meal without wrecking my back?" Well, I'm here to tell you that sitting Japanese-style is the best thing you can do for your posture, but more importantly it's the best thing you can do to save your life. *(Bob drops the pillow on the floor.)* Helen is going to try out this tatami pillow.

(Helen gives Bob a panicked look. Bob gently takes her arm, gets her to sit on the pillow. He kneels behind Helen, massages her shoulders.)

BOB: Boy, Helen is like a rock. That's from sitting in those Western chairs. *(quietly to Helen)* Honey, breathe, it's OK.

(Helen shuts her eyes.)

BOB: All right this is what would happen during a seven point quake. *(Bob grasps the sides of the pillow, violently shakes it back and forth.)*

HELEN: BOB STOP! FOR GOD'S SAKE, JUST STOP!

(Bob stops, puts his arms around Helen. She starts to sob.)

BOB: OK, that was scary for Helen, but there was no way that she was going to get hurt because she was so low to the floor. Helen, did you feel like you were going to fall over?

HELEN: Don't do that to me again, I don't want you to do that again...

BOB: *(hugging her)* Shhh, it's OK.

HELEN: *(over him)*…this is not helping me, this is not what I need. It's not working, I don't like it, Bob…

BOB: *(over her)* Shhh, OK, OK, everything's OK, we're all OK…*(to audience)* You see, for Helen, and many people, it's the fear of getting hurt that makes an earthquake so upsetting. But with the right preparation—and this is what I keep telling Helen…

(Helen throws Bob's arms off, gets up from the pillow, and looks for her purse.)

BOB: Honey, you need my hankie?

(Helen shakes her head, finds a Kleenex in her purse.)

BOB: *(back to audience)*…what I've been trying to do for Helen is to help her separate her fear from the reality. Her fear is that there will be another earthquake and that she'll get hurt. The reality is, yes, there will be another earthquake, but no, she will not get hurt.

HELEN: You don't know that! How can you say you know that!?

BOB: Okay, Helen has brought up another good point. What Helen is saying, is that there are no guarantees. Honey, is that what you're saying?

(Helen won't answer.)

BOB: OK, but let's take a for-instance. There is no guarantee that anyone here won't be killed crossing the street. But your chances are better if you look both ways. And that's preparedness. You see what I'm saying? Honey?

HELEN: I get it, Bob, I understand. Thank you.

BOB: Great. Could you change the slide for me please? *(a beat)* Helen?

(Helen ignores him, wipes her nose with the tissue.)

(Bob picks up the slide remote, changes the slide to a text book rendering of Indians around a teepee.)

BOB: Two hundred years ago, our own native Americans witnessed one of the biggest earthquakes ever to occur on this continent. But reports say that the Indian tribes did not experience any damage. That's because the Indians had a very simple life style. Their teepees, which were made of hide and flexible poles, didn't collapse on their heads but gently swayed with the tremors. And, being nomadic, they didn't collect a lot of breakables. So instead of feeling terror when the ground started shaking, they felt wonder and awe and they all ran out and did a dance with mother earth.

HELEN: Well aren't they special and aren't I the poor sport.

BOB: That's not what I'm saying.

HELEN: Oh, I think it is.

BOB: No, listen to what I'm saying. What I'm saying is, that we should look at disasters as a learning opportunity. If you can let it change you in a positive rather than a negative way, then you're way ahead of the game. I mean, look at your father learning to sail in his 70s. *(to the audience)*—He loses his home in a fire, now he's off following a dream.

HELEN: Oh please, my father is running away.

BOB: From what? He has nothing left.

HELEN: He has my mother, Bob.

BOB: Fine, but if she wants to shut herself up in a dark apartment, feeling sorry for herself that's up to her.

HELEN: I don't want to have this discussion right now.

BOB: No, this is very useful. *(to audience)* This is important. Excuse my French, but Shit Happens. That's just a fact of life. So we might as well face the music, practice our preparedness, and get on with our lives.

HELEN: He's a real trooper, my husband. *(to Bob)* What did you say to me during the quake?

BOB: I don't remember.

HELEN: *(to audience)* This is at four in the morning and the bed is shaking and I'm yelling at Bob to help me find my glasses. What did you say to me, Bob?

BOB: OK, Honey.

HELEN: "Helen don't let me die, please make it stop, I don't want to die. Make it stop. Oh Mommy make it stop."

BOB: I think to be fair, I was woken up from a dead sleep. Heck, we all got rattled, that's normal, but then you go on. You can't start sobbing every time you think you feel an aftershock.

HELEN: If you'd let me sob, if you'd let me just goddamn sob then maybe I'd be all right.

BOB: Fine, but there comes a point when it turns into just plain whining and self-indulgence.

HELEN: You're a horrible man. You're a fool. I hate you. Go to hell. *(Helen kicks her chair over, walks off.)*

BOB: Helen? *(a beat)* Honey? *(A beat. Bob sets the chair upright again.)* Guess that was a seven point eight. OK. I'm going to bring out the next speaker, but what I'd like you to do while we set up is for you to take a little mental tour of your house or apartment. In your mind's eye, look at all the things you have on your shelves—picture frames, souvenirs from your vacation, that set of commemorative dishes that you never eat on, trophies, the clay dog your child made in kindergarten, that glass jar filled with pennies, that jumbo bottle of scotch your office chums gave you on your birthday. *Now imagine all these objects being hurled across the room at your head at sixty miles per hour.* Or imagine a wave of fire tearing through your bedroom, spreading over your bed, the blankets the bed spread, all those dopey little frou-frou pillows that you have to throw off to get to the real pillows—imagine all of it starting to smoke in the terrible heat then Whoosh, exploding into flames! And all those crappy plastic knickknacks you keep throwing in the drawer of your bedside table—imagine it all melting into a bubbling, black ooze. And what about that guitar in the closet you never play, that stupid walking stick someone brought you back from Scotland and *baskets,* how many of you keep collecting *baskets*—Whoosh! Or imagine being Noah sailing across the flood-swollen earth. Imagine the miles and miles of muddy, garbage-choked water, people's jetsam floating up, banging up against the side of the ark— KACHUNK, KACHUNK, KACHUNK—spooking all the animals inside, driving you nuts! Or imagine millions and millions of locusts swarming into your living room, devouring everything in their path, slip covers, curtains, all those coffee table books you never read—*The Cat Lover's Handbook, (he makes eating sounds) Hawaii from the Air, (more devouring eating) The World of Hummel, (he makes extra vicious eating sounds)* Imagine everything you own or love or *thought* you loved being destroyed in countless other ways. Imagine it all gone. Then ask yourself, "What would I really miss?" *(a beat)* What would I really miss? *(Bob takes his hankie out, wipes his mouth.) (quietly)* OK, terrific.

(Arden enters, a smartly groomed woman, dressed in a short-skirted business suit and heels. She's carrying a metal briefcase. Bob perks up when she comes on, is clearly attracted to her.)

BOB: Super. Everybody, say hello to Arden. *(with audience)* Hello, Arden.

ARDEN: Hello, everybody. *(Arden looks around for the table, sees it smashed on the floor.)*

BOB: Oh, sorry. *(looks backstage)* Can we get another table out here, please?

(Someone on the Seminar Staff comes out with a new table, cleans up Bob's mess. Arden puts her case on the new table, opens it up, starts laying out a couple of hand guns, a can of mace, some other equipment.)

BOB: *(part of their routine)* Arden, not to get personal, but you were married once, weren't you?

ARDEN: That's right.

BOB: You and your husband ever have fights?

ARDEN: Like cats and dogs.

BOB: All part of a marriage, I guess.

ARDEN: Part of some.

BOB: Especially if there's been a lot of outside stress, wouldn't you say?

ARDEN: I'd say that.

BOB: But wouldn't you say that the stronger we become as individuals, the stronger the bonds become in marriage?

ARDEN: Strong minds make strong hearts, Yessir.

BOB: You bet. OK. *(to audience)* I think the best introduction for Arden is to read this passage from her book: *(reading)* "There is no time when we're more vulnerable than during a disaster when resources are scarce and the police force is stretched to its limits. We must make sure that we aren't victims a second time around." Arden is one of the most knowledgeable people I know in the security business, and she's also a really, really super lady. I think you're going to get a lot out of her.

ARDEN: Thank you, Bob.

BOB: I'm going to stick around and give Arden a hand. Her partner Rudy had a little family emergency. His son Brad—*(to Arden)* Is Bradley all right?

ARDEN: They got his finger back on, yeah.

BOB: Thank God. Well, give him our best. Terrific.

ARDEN: Aren't we supposed to have water here?

BOB: Sorry. *(Bob runs backstage.)*

(Arden takes the slide remote, changes the slide to Protecting Your Life.*)*

ARDEN: *(to audience)* Hello everybody, I'm Arden Shingles and protecting your life is not just a privilege…it's your right. But it's more than just a right…*(She changes the slide:* Your Responsibility.*)*…it's your responsibility.

(Bob comes back with another pitcher of water and cups, pours some water for Arden.)

BOB: Sorry. Here you go.

(Arden takes the water, gives Bob the slide remote. She takes her time drinking the water, lets everyone wait. She hands the cup back to Bob, turns back to the audience.)

ARDEN: I'd like to tell you a story. There was a successful saleswoman who lived outside of Austin. She was headed for a sales meeting in Fort Worth. Instead of flying she decided to drive. She wanted to test out the brand new Lexus that her company had awarded her just that week. She had her fuzz buster on, the cruise control set at eighty, Garth on the tape deck…as she was driving, she started to notice that the air was getting kind of dusty. After about a mile she slowed down because she felt her car being rocked by a very strong wind. And there in the distance, heading in her direction, she saw a giant black funnel. It was a tornado. She stopped the car, knowing enough to open the windows a crack so they wouldn't explode. She then lay down on the front seat, shielding her face and praying to God that the twister would pass without doing her harm. Suddenly out of nowhere, a gigantic object falls out of the sky, lands on the car, shatters the windshield. The woman screams. Cut to, an hour later. The woman is now standing by the side of the road with an entire tree laying across the hood of her new car. She tries her car phone, it doesn't work. Great, so here she is, in the middle of nowhere, no phone, no help, it's starting to get dark, what is this woman going to do? She sees another car coming up the road. It pulls over, it's a Cadillac Seville. A nice-looking man gets out, early fifties, business suit, tie, grey at the temples—he reminds her of her boss. She glances through the window of his car, sees a briefcase on the front seat, a *Business Week,* a take-out coffee in the cup holder, the steam rising up over the dash—the sight is so comforting, she almost cries. He asks if she needs help. She says, Yessir, yes, she certainly does. The man walks around to the back of his car and opens up his trunk. He pulls out a knife, holds it at her throat and tells her to get in. For two hours she's trapped in the trunk of his car while the man drives her around. She can hear him screaming obscenities at her from the front seat, telling her all the things he's going to do to her when they reach their destination—taking off her breasts with a hack saw being the least of it, OK? Finally the

car comes to a stop. The motor is turned off. She can hear him walking around to the back. She hears him putting his key in the lock of the trunk—"Are you ready to die like the bitch you are?" he says—and as he opens the trunk, she's ready with the .38 handgun she keeps in her purse. She shoots him twice through the chest and the man falls over dead. She climbs out of the trunk, her hands still shaking, and she uses the man's car phone to call the highway patrol—fully expecting that she might be put on trial for killing a seemingly innocent businessman. When the police arrive, they tell her that they had been trying to track down the suspect of a string of gruesome murders. They said that not only did she save herself, but she saved dozens of other women from a prolonged and horrible death. That woman is alive today because she was not afraid to take responsibility for her own protection. That woman is alive because she practiced aggressive long-term thinking. That woman is alive. That woman is me. *(Arden goes over to a table picks up a .38 revolver.)* During this talk, I'm going to give those of you who've never touched a gun before an opportunity to familiarize yourself with this piece of equipment. *(She snaps open the cylinder of the gun, holds it up and spins it to show that there are no bullets in the gun.)* This is a .38 double-action revolver, which is used and recommended by most police officers. I prefer a .38 to a .22 because it has guaranteed stopping power. Many women and also men are drawn to .22s for a first gun because they feel that a .22 might be easier to handle. Which is fine, but if you have an assailant who's on crack or any of your other substances, he might not even notice that he's been hit until he's back on the road, pondering what to do with your credit cards. But again, this is a personal choice.
(Arden hands the gun to Bob who takes it over to the audience and gives it to a member to pass around.)
[Note: the gun should be real and not a prop gun. But for safety's sake, a part of it should be made inoperable.]

ARDEN: Pass it around, get to know it. This gun is not loaded, there are no bullets in the chamber. It doesn't have a mind, it doesn't have a will, it doesn't even have batteries. It is just a piece of metal, a collection of movable parts that do not move until you make them do so. Pull the trigger if you like. It will not hurt you. The devil is not hiding in the barrel. It is not "bad." Bad things are done by people, not guns. Good people do not do bad things with guns. And conversely, good people do not turn bad if they have a gun, OK? By the year 2000, a firearm will be as common a piece of equipment as your car phone or pocket calculator. This should not scare you and this should not cause you despair. I'm a historian; I like to compare the Then with the Now; I like to let the past be my path to the future. Here's an example: When they first started putting electricity into homes, some people said, "Oh, no we can't do that, it's too dangerous, someone's gonna kill themselves." They painted these scenarios of entire families laying dead on the floor, with their fingers in the sockets and their eyeballs fried. We can look back on that now and say, "Oh, that was alarmist thinking." Hindsight is easy, I agree, but before we make an instant value judgment on something, it's good to first lay a grid on it. I'm an optimist-realist. What that means is that I look at what could potentially be bad and then figure out a way to make it good. Bob? *(Bob changes the slide to a line graph chart on the projected crime rate up to the year 2000.)*

ARDEN: Take a look at this chart. This is the reality, folks. I wish I could say that things in our country were getting better but sweet people, all you have to do is look at the numbers. And with all the riots, floods, fires, earthquakes, droughts—with all this happening, more and more people are saying, "Hey, the world's coming to an end, I don't give a blankety-blank about the law." You know? And the rest of us, the good people, the ones who, as Bob said, practice preparedness—we're going to have our little supply boxes with our batteries and canned goods, whatever, that we so carefully put together, and what's going to stop someone from walking up to us and saying, "Gimme"? And I hear, "Oh, I know it's really bad out there but there's nothin' I can do about it. Boo-hoo," you know? And I meet so many people, especially women who support this nondefense kind of attitude. They say, "Oh, I don't want to have a gun, my boyfriend says it's not feminine." Well what's feminine? *(pause)* You know? What's feminine—to look at me, I think you'd say that I was "feminine." Bob, would you say I was feminine?

BOB: I sure would.

ARDEN: There you go. I know a lot of women who are ready to take responsibility for their own protection, but they say to me, "Arden, I just can't get behind using a gun." And that's a very natural reaction. As women, our traditional role has been to be life giver, not

life taker. Yes, I agree with all of that. But as life giver, what am I going to do when there's been a hurricane, all lines of communication are down, my husband has gone off to find supplies, and a strange man has just kicked down my door? *(Arden picks up a ring of keys from the table, fits them between her fingers.)*
(Bob joins her for a demonstration.)

ARDEN: Here's a good one. How many of you have thought of this? "OK, I'm now going to defend myself with a bunch of keys sticking out of my knuckles."

BOB: "Watch out, I'm going to kill you, Lady." *(Bob does a simulated attack, disarms Arden then holds her in a grip.)*

ARDEN: *(to audience)* Now what? I am now free to be raped, disfigured, and killed. *(Arden taps Bob to let him know to release her. Arden picks up a can of mace.)* OK, that didn't work, what if I keep a can of mace in my emergency supply box. Here goes.

BOB: "I'm going to kill you, Lady."
(Arden holds up the can of mace, pretends to spray. Bob coughs twice then grabs Arden, holds her in the same grip.)

ARDEN: Oops, guess no one told me that most mace sold on the market is so diluted that it's about as effective as a baby peeing on a rabid dog. Again, I am now free to be raped, disfigured, and killed.
(Arden taps Bob. He releases his grip. Arden picks up a stun gun.)

ARDEN: OK, that was fun, now that all my broken ribs are healed and I've got most of my face back, I think I'll buy myself a stun gun. Now this is a great weapon. It won't penetrate a heavy coat or a leather jacket and in order for it to work at all you have to hold it against the struggling body of your two-hundred-pound assailant for a full three seconds.

BOB: "Bitch! I'm going to kill you, Bitch."
(Arden looks a bit surprised by Bob's acting, then continues the demonstration, tries to zap Bob. Bob grabs her arms holds the gun away from his body then throws Arden in to a grip, holding the stun gun next to one of her nipples.)

ARDEN: Once again, it's open season on me. All right. *(Arden taps Bob. Arden starts to walk back to his chair. Bob suddenly rushes back at Arden. Arden grabs a gun from the table, and whips around taking a stance.)*

ARDEN: "Stop right there. Advance any further and I'll shoot."
(Bob immediately stops.)

ARDEN: "Slowly back away with your hands up. If you make any other movement I will kill you."

BOB: "Don't hurt me, Lady, please don't hurt me."

(Arden backs Bob up and makes him sit in the chair. She lowers the gun and walks back to the table, puts the gun back down.)

ARDEN: Which method of defense involved no physical contact between you and your assailant? Which method of defense protected your dignity as well as your life? And which method of defense involved the least amount of violence? It's like when we used to have nuclear weapons between us and the Russians, which I believe was one of the biggest deterrents to war ever. In other words: The more effective your weapon is, the less likely you will have to use it. What we're talking about is deterrence, Folks. Not death, deterrence.

BOB: It's like preparedness.

ARDEN: That's right. See, I get crazy when people just make these blanket assumptions that all guns kill. That's like saying, oh, let's get rid of all cars because of all the highway deaths. Hey, fine with me— did you know that there are twenty times more fatalities caused by cars than by guns? And you don't see Car Control lobbies out there in Washington. You don't see anyone instituting a ten-day waiting period before you can purchase your new VW. What do you drive, Bob?

BOB: A Ford Bronco.

ARDEN: You like to buy American?

BOB: Wouldn't buy anything else.

ARDEN: Where are all our guns manufactured, Bob?

BOB: The good ol' U.S. of A.

ARDEN: There you go. *(to audience)* But it all comes down to this: Deterrence equals power, power equals choice, choice equals life. By the way, the first thing Hitler did when he came into power? He took the guns away from the Jewish people. All things to think about. Whoever has the gun, would you mind holding it up so Bob can collect it?

(Bob walks down to the audience. Arden sits on the edge of the table.)

ARDEN: Isn't life funny? Lemme tell you one last story. I remember when I was a little girl, my family and I took a trip to the New York World's Fair. Anybody remember going to that? Anyway, there was this one exhibit called The City of Tomorrow. We stood in this long line that went into a room where you stood on a catwalk and looked down at a giant model of what a city would look like in fifty years. There were all these dome-shaped houses and weird-looking towers and monorails. And all the little people in the city looked kind of sealed in…and I don't know, it all looked so strange to me that I got a sick feeling in my stomach. I started to cry and my mother asked me what the problem was. I told her my stomach hurt and she said that was because I'd been eating junk all day. And I said, no, my stomach hurt because the model of the City of Tomorrow scared me, that I didn't ever want to have to live like that. And my father looked down at me, and you know what he said? He said, "Don't worry, Girl, by the time the future gets here, you won't know the difference."

(Bob hands Arden the .38 and a case of bullets. She slowly starts loading bullets into the gun.)

ARDEN: One last point. What would happen if I put bullets in this gun and passed it back around? *(a beat)* Maybe that gun would just continue to be passed from hand to hand. Or maybe it would stop with that one bad apple who's sitting among you. He or she would hold on to that loaded gun, cock the hammer and take advantage of us one by one. *(a beat)* OK, but what if I gave everyone a loaded gun? You see how it all makes sense? *(Arden hands the loaded gun back to Bob. She exits.)*

BOB: OK, folks. A lot to think about. We're going to take a short break. Stretch your legs, there's drinks in the lobby. We'll see you back in fifteen. *(Bob puts the loaded gun in the case and snaps it shut. He picks it up and exits.)*

END OF PLAY

TOUGH CHOICES FOR THE NEW CENTURY
WEEKEND ITINERARY

Friday, [appropriate date]
5:00-6:00 PM—Cocktail Hour and Mixer (Frontier Room, Main
    Lodge) Please wear your name tags!
6:30 PM—Dinner (Dining Room, Main Lodge)
8:00 PM—Introduction to Getting prepared (Elk Seminar Room)
9:00 PM—Nightcap (pay bar in Frontier Room)

* * *

Saturday, [appropriate date]
7:00 AM-9:00 AM—Buffet breakfast (Dining Room, Main Lodge)
10:00 AM—Home Preparedness (Elk Seminar Room)
11:00 AM—Duck & Cover Workshop (Elk Seminar Room)
12:30 PM—Lunch (Dining Room, Main Lodge)
2:00 PM—Fire (Elk Seminar Room) *optional*
2:30 PM—Floods and Mudslides (Evergreen Seminar Room) *optional*
3:00 PM—Earthquakes (Elk Seminar Room) *optional*
3:30 PM—Civil Disturbance (Evergreen Seminar Room) *optional*
4:00 PM—Tornadoes and Hurricanes (Santa Fe Seminar Room)
    optional
4:30 PM—Locusts (Elk Seminar Room) *optional*
5:00-6:00 PM—Cocktail Hour (Frontier Room, Main Lodge)
6:30 PM—Dinner (Dining Room, Main Lodge)
8:00 PM—Film—"Back Draft" (Evergreen Room) *optional*

* * *

Sunday, [appropriate date]
7:00 AM-9:00 AM—Buffet breakfast (Dining Room, Main Lodge)
9:30-11:30 AM—Defense Workshop (Fitness Center) Please wear com-
    fortable clothing
12:30 PM—Lunch (Dining Room, Main Lodge)
2:00-3:00 PM—FEMA and Insurance Workshop (Santa Fe Seminar
    Room)
3:00-4:30 PM—Building a New Life (Elk Seminar Room)
5:00-7:00 PM—Barbeque and Cocktails (picnic area)

TOUGH CHOICES FOR THE NEW CENTURY
QUESTIONNAIRE

1) Have you ever experienced one of the following (please circle):
   a) Earthquake   b) Fire   c) Tornado   d) Hurricane
   e) Flood   f) Landslide   g) Riots   h) Locusts
   i) Other _____

2) If yes to #1, What kind of damage did you experience to your personal property?
   a) none   b) slight   c) moderate   d) severe
   e) total devastation

3) Have you lost any family or loved ones to a natural or man-made catastrophe (please do not include wars).
   Please specify _____

4) Have you recently moved because of a disaster. If yes, from where to where: _____

5) Which one do you feel you would be most prepared to face?
   a) Earthquake   b) Fire   c) Tornado   d) Hurricane
   e) Flood   f) Landslide   g) Riots   h) Locusts

6) Why are you taking this seminar?

7) What do you hope to get out of it?

Your Obituary is a Dance
by Benard Cummings

*Lovingly dedicated to the memory of Mr. James R. Carroll
and Mr. Dennis Scott*

Biography

Benard Cummings recently made his playwriting debut in *Your Obituary is a Dance* in the Humana Festival of New American Plays at the Actor's Theatre of Louisville. He has recently completed a commissioned full-length play for ATL, entitled *Us Was We Around The Grandmama Tree: A Fable.* As an actor, Mr. Cummings has performed at many regional theatres, including the Hartford Stage, Philadelphia Theatre Co., Arena Stage, the N.J. Shakespeare Festival, and Actors Theatre of Louisville. He is a graduate of Tyler Junior College, Southern Methodist University, and the Yale School of Drama.

Author's Note

Your Obituary is a Dance is a play about life, in spite of the specter of AIDS. Primarily it is the story of a friendship forged out of adversity and bonded by mutual respect. Though Tommy comes home to say "good-bye" he learns, through his childhood friend, Nella Rae, an appreciation of his past that is woven in the complex fabric of African-American identity. Above all, it is a play that seeks—in its short time—to celebrate life and its dance.

Original Production

Your Obituary is a Dance was first performed in March 1995 at the 1995 Humana Festival of New American Plays, Actors Theatre of Louisville. It was directed by Lorna Littleway with the following cast:

Nella Rae . . . . Marcella Lowery
Tommy . . . . Jacinto Taras Riddick

CHARACTERS

TOMMY: Age 30. Effeminate black man. Has AIDS. Quick wit. Dark-complexioned. Sincere and honest spirit.

NELLA RAE: Age 30. Heavy-set black woman. Dark-complexioned. Full of zest and fire.

TIME

Now.

PLACE

Small East Texas town.

YOUR OBITUARY IS A DANCE

Nella Rae sits listening to a jambox that sits on the kitchen table. The song, "You've Got the Best of My Love" by The Emotions, plays. She sits rubbing her feet, singing along. She wears a pair of faded jeans and a T-shirt with the logo "Big Junior's Rib Joint" across the front.

Tommy enters carrying a duffle bag. He knocks. She turns to the door and has to catch her breath at this sight.

NELLA: Tommy? *(She crosses to the door)* Tommy, is that you?

TOMMY: Un un…oh no, Miss Thang…you gotta be a little more surprised to see me than that. Start acting like you real happy to be seeing me, woman.

NELLA: Wait a minute, Negro. You know damn well I'm happy to be seeing you after all these years! Now, chill and let me create some atmosphere of suspense here. Damn. Now shut up and let me start over. *(She crosses back to the kitchen table. Pause)* Well, knock!
(He plays along)

NELLA: Tommy?!

TOMMY: Nella Rae! I'm home!

BOTH: Aaahhh!!!!

NELLA: Look what the wind done blowed in! How you doing, baby?

TOMMY: Better now that I'm laying these tired eyes of mine on you.

NELLA: Lord, chile, it's been forever and a couple of days since I done last laid eyes on you. Not to mention heard from your triflin' self.

What's the matter? Whatn't no telephones were you was? Postman didn't come by your house or something?

TOMMY: Girl, don't come for me. You know you been on my mind, and definitely with me in spirit.

NELLA: Spirit, my ass! I ain't known no sucha thing; so, don't you come for me either.

TOMMY: Look, Diva, don't go there. I already done been read once today, and I ain't trying for another one.

NELLA: You musta' stopped by your Mu'dear's house first?

TOMMY: Simple as that was, yes. She threw me so much shade that I thought I was deep in the heart of the Amazon Jungle. I could just whip my own black ass for stopping by there first.

NELLA: Oooooo, sister-girl read you, huh?

TOMMY: And burned down the library! Chile, break out that Jack Daniels I know you got chilling up in your freezer. I sho' could use a stiff drink.

(She crosses to refrigerator and takes out a chilled bottle of Jack Daniels, and a bag of homegrown marijuana. She gets two glasses.)

NELLA: Un. You should've had a stiff drink before you went and saw that "holy-hallelujah-amen corner-kneel at the cross" Mu'dear of yours. Chile, please…you don't have to tell this girl no more. *(tosses him the homegrown)* Here, roll us up a couple of good friends to keep Mr. Daniels company.

TOMMY: HOMEGROWN! Girl, you still a mess. I ain't had none of this stuff in a long time. I see you still keep your reefer and liquor in the freezer. You just as country as a dozen eggs sitting on top of a bale of hay.

NELLA: You damn skippin'. And proud of it. So, cock-a-doodle doo!

TOMMY: Where's your man at, Nella? Thought Otis was too jealous to ever leave you alone.

NELLA: Chile, please. Otis is way down by Galveston roughnecking on some oil rig. Wanted me to pack up and go down there with him. Huh! I told him to g'on down there by hisself and to send me the paycheck come paydays and everything would be just fine.

TOMMY: Oooo, girl, don't you miss that lovin' he be throwin' on you?

NELLA: Chile, I can do without the lovin' for awhile. Just as long as he don't mess with the income. He do that and he got to get to steppin'.

TOMMY: Well, now, I don't mean to be dippin' all up in ya'll's business and whatnot, but how do you know that Otis ain't doing a little "foot shakin'" way down there?

NELLA: What I don't know don't concern me. 'Sides, ain't no ring on this finger.

TOMMY: Aw, looka' here, Diva, don't come for me. You probably got somebody slippin' in your back door anyway.

NELLA: First thang, only men are dogs enough to go sniffin' after strays. And second thang, even if I was slippin', he damn sho' wouldn't have to come through my back door.

TOMMY: Ooooo, you better work, bitch.

NELLA: I know that's right. 'Sides, in this day and age, you better keep it if you don't want to loose it. 'Cause… *(Long pause)* Tommy?
(Long pause)

TOMMY: All day and all night, Nella Rae. Twenty-four seven.
(Pause. In which she takes his hands into her and kisses them. She kisses up his arms, shoulders, his neck, his cheeks, all over his face, and finally his lips. She takes him into her arms and holds him.)

NELLA: Tell your girl how you doing, baby.

TOMMY: That train is pulling into that station, girlfriend. Truth is, when I consider this little ol' life that is mine, I realize that this shit coursing through my veins is par for the course. Nella, I ain't gonna lay up in no hospital bed with tubes and wires and shit coming all out of me. I have no need or desire for that. Understand?

NELLA: Baby, knowing you like I do I truly do understand. That why you home?

TOMMY: Peace to be made. Ghosts to set free. To just see this place where I grew up. To say goodbye, and to finally, finally, let go of it all. Girlfriend, this life has been one tough row to hoe. You know what I mean?

NELLA: Chile, if you told me this was a drama I'd laugh in your face and tell you it was a comedy. Yes, I know what you mean. Being a Black woman in this neck of the woods ain't been no day at the racetrack either.

TOMMY: It's a cryin' shame that I should even think about all these tongues that will be waggin' around here once they find out that…

NELLA: Oh no no no…you can stop that noise right there. Chile, please. Self-appointed Righteous Folks love imagining God sitting up somewhere with nothing better to do than to cause folks they don't like misery and grief. Makes 'em feel safe in believing that a

God actually exists. Now, baby, look, I can understand you wanting to bury ghosts and everything. But take it from me you don't owe these folks around here a thing. See, most of them talked about me like I had a tail hanging off my ass. As you know, I was called every 'fat', 'black', 'nappy headed', 'big nosed', 'African Ju-Ju', name there was when we were growing up...

TOMMY: ...chile, I remember all that grief...

NELLA: ...I know damn well you do. We caught hell, baby. That's why you and I was as tight as we was. But let me say this: Folks had me so wound up with hatred for myself that I became lost. You hear me? Lost. Would drop my little drawers and screw quicker than I could draw my little ass back. Thought that that was gonna make me feel beautiful or something. Like someone wanted me. And on top of all that folks still stood righteous and shit, telling me I was gonna' burn in hell. 'Oh yeah,' I said, 'well, your husbands, sons, brothers and lovers gonna' be right down there with me.' Can I get an "amen?"

TOMMY: 'men!

NELLA: But, baby, when the Truth finally shined its light down on me, and I saw just how SWEET my blackness was—SWEET, do you hear me now?...

TOMMY: ...I hear you...

NELLA: ...I got all those tired asses up off this pussy. When Otis finally came into my life all them years ago...you remember...

TOMMY: ...sho' do...

NELLA: ...and told me, "Man can't live on your pussy alone, but by every word of love that proceedeth out of your mouth", I thought that he was crazy as hell. But he LOVED me, baby. And I'm still with his big ol' rusty ass 'cause he showed me 'the darker the night, the brighter the day.' See...my people, my people...folks used to make fun of my berry-black blackness when I was growing up. And now you can't seem to turn around without Black folks acting like the last dark African on God's green earth. Folks wearing more Kente cloth and beads and shit than anybody from Africa wears. All of a sudden it's politically fashionable to be what they tortured me about as a child. And all of it because folks NOW talkin' 'bout some "Afro-American" identity and "reclaiming our roots" and whatnot. Makes me want to scream "Hell, everybody knows we from Africa 'cept us!" I'll just be damned...

TOMMY: You better PREACH, girl!

NELLA: Whatchu' SAY?

TOMMY: I said PREACH!

NELLA: Whatchu' SAY now?

TOMMY: Preach ON!

NELLA: Witness then like you know how to, baby. 'Cause we may be the outcasts of an outcast race, but we dotted the 'I' and crossed the 'T' in 'identity.'

TOMMY: Oooo, you go, girl. You certainly are philosophical and shit this evening. I stopped by the right place.

NELLA: Speaking of stopping by the right place, what on earth possessed you to stop by you Mu'dear's first? I mean, did you think things might've changed or something?

TOMMY: Well, no. 'Cause when she and Papa threw me out of the house all them years back, I was told in no uncertain terms that I had no home there anymore. But, you know, Nella Rae, in some odd way I was hoping that I'd tell Mama that I've got the 'Big A,' that she'd take me into her arms and hold me, tell me she loved me and that everything would be alright. Was I wrong in hoping for that?

NELLA: Un huh…I see…well, come here, Jesus. If that ain't about some of the most sentimental crap I done heard in a long time. Here, pour yourself some more of my good friend, Mr. J.D. I personally feel you and I gon' have to get a little ripped.

TOMMY: Well, it ain't over yet. I'll see her again and next time I'll just speak the Truth…see what happens…

NELLA: You KNOW what's gon' happen: Miss sister-girl gon' read you again and send you on your merry way…with her proslytizing self…sometimes she makes me just want to slap the taste out of her mouth. Forgive me for saying that, baby. Liquor startin' to get hold of my tongue here.

TOMMY: Don't lie on that liquor. You liable to say anything anyway. *(pause)* Sad to see the house and to know Papa wasn't there anymore. He died about…what was it…five years ago, huh?

NELLA: Yeah, that's about right. I even showed up at the funeral hoping you'd surprise us all and be there.

TOMMY: No. That funeral was the last place I wanted to be…which brings me to a point. *(He opens his duffle bag and takes out a notebook and pen, and sits them on the table.)*

NELLA: What's this for?

TOMMY: We gon' write my obituary together...

> *(Overlap dialogue)*

>> NELLA: ...aw, hell, Tommy...un uh...naw...we'll have none of
>> this...

>> TOMMY: ...now wait a minute, Nella Rae...

>> NELLA: ...here we is having a good time getting high, and me
>> up in here on a roll preaching and all like I done lost
>> my ever-loving mind...

>> TOMMY: ...Nella Rae, hush and let me...

>> NELLA: ...and here you is wanting to bring us all down with
>> something crazy like this. I ain't gonna' do no such
>> thing. I don't like this—no way and no how...

> *(He stuffs a joint in her mouth.)*

TOMMY: I don't like okra. But if I was starving I'd thank God for it and eat it. Now you listen to me: I am alive to do this. ALIVE. This way...we let go. Let go. *(Pause)* C'mon my fat, black, nappy-headed, and beautiful Waitutsi woman. Me. You. And these words. *(He hands her the notebook. Pause)*

> *(She finally takes it.)*

NELLA: I must be high to let you talk me into some simple shit like this. *(Pause)* Well, don't be lookin' at me. What you wanna say here?

> *(Pause. They look at the paper like it's a foreign object.)*

NELLA: Well, we can start by writing that 'He was once a fierce drag queen...'

TOMMY: ...un uh...don't you come for me. I never did that tired Patti LaBelle, Judy Garland thang. I personified performance art.

NELLA: Chile, please! You couldn't be Judy Garland even if you had Michael Jackson's money and plastic surgeon; and looka' here, I came to Dallas that time you was living there, and I saw that show you did at that cabaret. If that wasn't drag you was doing then I must've been blind, cripple and crazy.

TOMMY: Oh, girl, 'bye! I did lot's of confused things in those days 'fore I discovered that that wasn't my cup of tea.

NELLA: Cup?! You had a POT! Chile, who was it you was up there imitating?

TOMMY: ...lipsynching...

NELLA: ...whatever...

TOMMY: ...Diana Ross!

NELLA: Yea! That was it! And you had the nerve to sing…

TOMMY: …lipsynch…

NELLA: …whatever…some "Sweetest Love Hangover"! Come here, Jesus!

TOMMY: Wasn't that a big ol' mess!

NELLA: You know, I used to love it when we were kids and you'd put on your Mu'dear's stuff and do me a little show.

TOMMY: You reaching waaaayyy back now.

NELLA: Remember that time she caught us up in ya'll's attic? Who was you imitating?

TOMMY: Donna Summer, girl.

NELLA: That's right! That's right! "Toot toot…ahhhh, beep beep. Bad girls, talkin' bout those bad girls…"

TOMMY: And the look on Mama's face when she caught us!

NELLA: Yeah! She looked like she didn't know whether to cry, faint, shit or holler. All she could do was do: "Tommy! agh ugh vvv rrr zzz what you doin? Stop that!" Miss sister-girl lost her mind.

TOMMY: Then she ran your little fat ass outta' there…

NELLA: …un huh…accusing me of making you do that. As if she hadn't already noticed you was a big ol' sissy. Chile, please…

TOMMY: Did I ever tell you what happened after that?

NELLA: Naw, you never did.

TOMMY: Well, honey, she whipped me right out of that page-boy wig and them hot pants. Then she said that she just had to tell Papa so that he could put a stop to my foolishness. Well, Papa came into my room that night, mad as hell, and made Mama put that wig and hot pants on me. And some eyeshadow. That's right, eyeshadow. Chile, bye. Funny, Nella Rae, but the one clear thing I remember in that moment was that Mama was putting some ugly-ass dark purple eye shadow on me, and I was thinking that she had very little taste to be putting that dark-ass purple on my chocolate skin. But she was crying and shit, begging Papa not to make her do it. Now, Papa was never a violent man. Just as sweet as he could be. Didn't like me much, but a very sweet man. But he had this look in this eye like, Bitch, if you don't put it on him and r-a-t now, rat now, I'm gonna slap the taste out of you and this little sissy. Mama wasn't no fool: she put it on me. Then he made me start doing whatever it was I was doing up there in the attic. And, honey, he made that belt talk across my behind. All the while he kept saying that he was beating the deviance out of me. Truth is, I never hated him for that, Nella. I felt sorry for him. *(pause)* But in a lot of ways that whippin' prepared me well for life: if you think I caught hell from Black folks, white folks are truly another story.

NELLA: …chile, say no more. *(Pause)* So, now what do we put in this obituary?

TOMMY: Look, here it is: I have lived. I have learned. I have lost and won. Done cried. Done lied. And, yes, there were times when I witnessed the Truth. But no regrets 'cause now I rest. *(Pause)* The end. *(Pause)* Funny, but me and Papa will be buried side by side. Someday Mama will join us. And finally death will let us be together like life never could.

NELLA: Amen, baby. You is one sentimental bitch. Damn. *(She puts another tape into the jambox. Closes the notebook. Cheryl Lynn's "Got To Be Real" blasts from the speakers.)* Let's party, baby. Your obituary is a dance.

(They groove. Lights fade)

END OF PLAY

Head On
by Elizabeth Dewberry

Biography

Elizabeth Dewberry is the author of two novels, two plays, and numerous articles and reviews. Her first novel, *Many Things Have Happened Since He Died,* (originally released under the name Elizabeth Dewberry Vaughn), was published by Doubleday in 1990 and reprinted by Vintage Contemporaries in 1992. She co-adapted it for the stage with Tom Key, who directed its premiere at the Horizon Theater in Atlanta in 1994. It garnered Individual Artist grants for her from the Georgia and Alabama State Arts Councils. Her second novel, *Break the Heart of Me,* (also originally released under Elizabeth Dewberry Vaughn), published by Nan A. Talese/Doubleday in 1994, was a Literary Guild Alternate Selection. She has published several articles on Hemingway and some creative nonfiction, and she was a regular reviewer of literary novels for the *Atlanta Journal-Constitution* in 1990 and '91. *Head On,* her first short play, was commissioned by and premiered at the Actors Theatre of Louisville's 1995 Humana Festival of New Plays, and her second, a full-length play called *This Is My Body,* was commissioned for the 1996 Humana Festival. She is working on a new play, commissioned by the Birmingham Festival Theatre, and a novel, *Touch Me, Touch Only Me.*

Ms. Dewberry holds a Ph.D. in twentieth-century American literature from Emory University and a B.S. in English from Vanderbilt. She has taught creative writing and American literature at Emory, the University of the South, Ohio State, the University of Southern California, Stanford, and at the Bread Loaf, Wesleyan, and Sewanee Writers' Conferences.

She lives in Lake Charles, Louisiana, with her husband, Pulitzer Prize–winning author Robert Olen Butler.

Author's Note

When Jon Jory and Michael Dixon at Actors Theatre asked me to write a short play for the 1995 Humana Festival, I had just come from a gathering of Southern writers in Mississippi. Several of us had been promoting our books on talk shows, most of us on local cable Oprah knock-offs, and all our most interesting stories had to do with what went on in the greenrooms before and after our brief television appearances.

I'd been thinking it might be fun to do a play set in such a greenroom with people moving in and out, preparing themselves to go on, warning each other about what to say and what not to say, then dealing with whatever had happened on camera. So when Michael asked me to limit myself to two characters, a therapist with a book to promote and her client immediately volunteered themselves in my mind, and *Head On* was begun. Why it went where it went from there, I have no idea.

ORIGINAL PRODUCTION

Head On was originally produced in March 1995 at the Humana Festival 1995, Actors Theatre of Louisville. It was directed by Shirley Jo Finney with the following cast:

Anne . . . . Adale O'Brien
Anne's Therapist . . . . Dee Pelletier

CHARACTERS

ANNE: A robust woman in her early sixties.
ANNE'S THERAPIST: A slender, intelligent woman in her mid-forties.

TIME

The present.

PLACE

The greenroom of the Oprah Winfrey show.

Head On

The greenroom of the Oprah Winfrey show, ten minutes before taping. The therapist paces anxiously, looking at her watch. Anne enters, in shock, and the therapist runs over to her.

THERAPIST: Oh, thank God you're here. *(Doubletake.)* Anne? What are *you* doing here?

ANNE: I'm sorry I'm late. I saw a wreck.

THERAPIST: But you're not multiorgasmic.

ANNE: No. I'm fine.

THERAPIST: Oh God.

ANNE: I wasn't *in* the wreck. I just saw it happen. I was so afraid I was going to be late. I've wanted to be on *Oprah Winfrey* forever, it's my most recurrent fantasy, and now here I am.

THERAPIST: *Are* you?

ANNE: What?

THERAPIST: Multiorgasmic.

ANNE: I don't think so.

THERAPIST: Who told you to come here?

ANNE: Your receptionist. Do I look bad? I brought another outfit if you don't like this one. This all happened so fast I didn't have time to buy anything. If it hadn't been for the wreck…

THERAPIST: What did she tell you?

ANNE: You were going on Oprah to talk about your book and the client you had coming on with you canceled and would I go on instead.

THERAPIST: Oh God.

ANNE: What? I know I just started seeing you, but you've already been a big help to me, dealing with Jerry's death. I have a lot to say.

THERAPIST: It has to be somebody who's multiorgasmic.

ANNE: Jerry had a bad heart.

THERAPIST: Were you ever multiorgasmic, even by yourself?

ANNE: I never had *one* orgasm. I can't say that on TV. I've never told anybody that before.

THERAPIST: We go on in eight minutes. I can't replace you.

ANNE: It's not my fault. There was a wreck, a head-on collision. But I can do this.

THERAPIST: I know it's not your fault.

ANNE: Two people died. Traffic's still backed up for miles.

THERAPIST: I'm not blaming you. I'm sorry.

ANNE: I'm an official witness, in the police reports. That takes time. Everybody was late to everywhere they were going. Have you ever witnessed a wreck?

THERAPIST: Yes. I have. Can we talk about this later? Right now...

ANNE: Of course. I'm sorry.

THERAPIST: I mean, there's nothing we can do about the wreck.

ANNE: Of course not.

THERAPIST: This was such a great opportunity, *Oprah Winfrey*. I could have been a best-seller. I had this client who was perfect, at age fifty-seven after three months of therapy with me she became multiorgasmic.

ANNE: Why isn't she here?

THERAPIST: She broke her hip.

ANNE: You can break your hip?

THERAPIST: No, she fell in the bathtub.

ANNE: That's too bad.

THERAPIST: It's not the same if you don't have somebody, a real person, to say it works.

ANNE: I'm sorry I haven't read your book, but tell me what to say, and I'll say it. What's the book about?

THERAPIST: Postmenopausal sex.

ANNE: I just wanted to meet Oprah Winfrey. I wanted to talk to her. Sometimes in my imagination I think of her as my daughter—not by Jerry, of course—and I just wanted to shake her hand. I thought maybe after the show we'd hug. Is that asking too much?

THERAPIST: No.

ANNE: I bid on a dress of hers once at a charity auction. Somebody else outbid me, though. I wanted to go twenty dollars higher but Jerry said it's a used dress, we can get you a new one for less than that. Then, of course, we didn't. That's how things went with him.

THERAPIST: And he never brought you to orgasm.

ANNE: Well, I don't know about that.

THERAPIST: Yes you do.

ANNE: I might have had one and forgotten.

THERAPIST: You wouldn't forget.

ANNE: I think sex is overrated anyway. I can't imagine writing a whole book about it. What did you say?

THERAPIST: Have you ever just wanted to ram yourself into something?

ANNE: You know I have. Maybe I could read a chapter real fast. If only that wreck hadn't happened. Look, I'm still trembling.

THERAPIST: You can't read it in six minutes.

ANNE: Right, so tell me. I once heard my mother say it feels like a sneeze between your legs. Should I say that?

THERAPIST: Why don't you focus on the spiritual dimension of sex? Two human beings coming together, each giving their body over to the other, moving out of themselves into the other...

ANNE: It sounds like a head-on collision. *(Beat.)* I'm sorry. I'm wrong.

THERAPIST: No, you're right. It does.

ANNE: Both drivers died. The debris was so bad the ambulances almost hit each other. *(Beat.)* What was the wreck you saw?

THERAPIST: My husband and his girlfriend.

ANNE: Oh.

THERAPIST: He was sitting in the car on a country road waiting for her and she plowed into him at sixty miles an hour.

ANNE: Did they die?

THERAPIST: No, they both had airbags.

ANNE: Those things are amazing. I wish I could go through life wearing airbags in my clothes. I don't think they had airbags this morning. I don't have them, my car doesn't.

THERAPIST: Right after she hit his car she jumped out of hers screaming, "You can't do this to me. I love you. I thought you loved me." Can you imagine?

ANNE: Amazing.

THERAPIST: I can still hear her saying that. I remember thinking that was what I wanted to yell at him, and she'd taken that too.

ANNE: *(Touching the doctor gingerly.)* I'm sorry.
 (Short silence.)
THERAPIST: Five minutes. This is awful.
ANNE: Tell me something to say. I wish I'd read the book. I really ought to read more.
THERAPIST: It has exercises you can do with your partner.
ANNE: But Jerry's dead!
THERAPIST: Maybe you could do them with Oprah.
ANNE: Sex exercises?
THERAPIST: No, it's just ways of developing intimacy, touching each other's inner selves.
ANNE: I already know her inner self. I watch her every day. I know every outfit she owns. I wonder if she's ever going to sell any more of her dresses.
THERAPIST: Why do you want one?
ANNE: Because I want to know what it feels like to be her. Maybe I'll never know what it's like to be rich or famous, but I could know what it feels like to step into the dress of a woman who's beautiful, who knows how to talk to people and how to listen to them. I'd zip her zipper up my back and feel her sleeves on my arms and close my eyes and just for a minute, I'd let myself pretend I was not just in her dress, I was in *her* and I'd become her and she'd become me. I want to do that before I die. *(Short silence.)* I think they died instantly. They would've had to. They were completely smashed together. You couldn't tell one car from the other.
THERAPIST: I would imagine.
ANNE: Jerry took several days. He went into a coma. He had tubes hooking him up to every kind of machine there is. It was awful. And then the trial lasted for months.
THERAPIST: Can we try to put that off for an hour, talk about it as soon as the show is over? Would you do that for me?
ANNE: I'm sorry, you're right, I'm obsessing.
THERAPIST: That's not what I said.
ANNE: You actually saw your husband's wreck happen?
THERAPIST: I told you.
ANNE: My heart was pounding so hard and so fast I could feel it all the way through my body and my skin went tight and hot and I had to fight to keep my eyes open and it was coming and coming, I knew what was going to happen, I knew. And then it did and I felt the

impact in my teeth and the whole world was crashing noises and echoes of crashing noises and spinning and then I heard my voice, my own voice above all the clatter, and I realized I'd been screaming and I stopped. *(Beat.)* Is that how it was for you?

THERAPIST: I was hiding behind a tree. I had a camera with me and I was going to take pictures of them having sex and then I was going to divorce him, and when I saw her car coming, I saw what she was going to do, and I hoped he'd die.

ANNE: You were lucky.

(Therapist looks at her in a question.)

ANNE: I think if Jerry's girlfriend had tried to kill him, even if she'd failed, I could have gotten what I needed from that. Then I wouldn't have had to do it myself.

(Pause while therapist looks at her watch.)

THERAPIST: We can't talk about this right now. In two minutes...

ANNE: I know, I'm sorry.

THERAPIST: Don't talk about Jerry on the show.

ANNE: I promise.

THERAPIST: Not a word.

ANNE: Nothing.

THERAPIST: He never existed. You're just beginning therapy...

ANNE: I had therapy in jail.

THERAPIST: No, you never went to jail. You're a widow beginning private therapy and you're a typical postmenopausal woman in the sense that you have deep longings for human connection inside you that you don't know how to address because you haven't read my book, and I'm going to tell you what you should do, and you're going to sit there and say I'm right, okay?

ANNE: Okay.

THERAPIST: And after the show, right after you hug Oprah, we'll get in our cars and go to my office and we'll have a long session.

ANNE: We'll get in our cars.

THERAPIST: And go to my office.

ANNE: I don't have airbags.

THERAPIST: It's time to go.

ANNE: Do I look okay?

THERAPIST: You look beautiful. Right now, you're wearing the dress of a beautiful woman.

ANNE: Jerry was killed in a car crash. I ran into him with my car in the yard before I hit the house.

THERAPIST: It's okay.

ANNE: I wasn't trying to kill him. I was just trying to get him to listen to me. Afterwards I got out of the car and my head was bleeding so bad I could hardly see but I made my way over the bricks to him and I held him in my arms, my blood dripping on his face, and I said, "When this is all over, can we talk?"

THERAPIST: You and I, we'll talk.

ANNE: What did you do after the girlfriend yelled at your husband?

THERAPIST: I took pictures of them. Then I told them to go fuck themselves and filed for divorce.

ANNE: You look beautiful, too.

THERAPIST: Come on.

ANNE: Do you have airbags?

THERAPIST: Yes.

END OF PLAY

Below the Belt
By Richard Dresser

BIOGRAPHY

Richard Dresser's plays have been widely produced nationally and in New York and are published by Samuel French. They include *The Downside, Alone at the Beach* (which premiered at Actors Theatre of Louisville in the 1988 Humana Festival), *Better Days, Splitsville, The Road to Ruin,* and *At Home.* He was twice chosen for the Eugene O'Neill National Playwrights Conference and is a former member of New Dramatists. For television he has written and produced for *The Days and Nights of Molly Dodd* for which he won an ACE award, *Smoldering Lust,* HBO's acclaimed *Vietnam War Stories* and *Bakersfield P.D.*

AUTHOR'S NOTE

In the course of supporting myself as a writer over the past few decades, I've had occasion to work at a series of jobs ranging from a plastics factory in Central Falls, Rhode Island, where I made G. I. Joe's thighs with a molding machine, to Hollywood, California, where I wrote sitcoms with a group of other writers. And as I reflect on it, those two jobs were remarkably similar. This play is about the deep loneliness of men working together. The need to connect with fellow workers does furious battle with the perceived need to protect one's tenuous position on the food chain. Welcome to the workplace.

ORIGINAL PRODUCTION

Below the Belt was first performed at the 1995 Humana Festival of New American Plays, March 1995. It was directed by Gloria Muzio with the following cast:

Hanrahan	William McNulty
Dobbitt	V. Craig Heidenreich
Merkin	Fred Major

CHARACTERS

HANRAHAN: A man.
DOBBITT: A man.
MERKIN: A man.

PLACE

The play takes place in an industrial compound in a distant land. We see a room with two beds, an office, a little bridge over a stream, and a bit of the surrounding area.

BELOW THE BELT

ACT ONE

In darkness we hear Hanrahan attempting to type. He responds to each keystroke, which echoes in the silent room.

HANRAHAN: Excellent. *(Another keystroke.)* Good. Very good. *(Five quick keystrokes.)* Beautiful. *Beautiful.* Keep it up. Nice and steady. *(Three quick ones.)* Damn you! Damn you to hell! Bastard! *(The sound of paper being viciously crumpled and another piece of paper being put in the typewriter. A pause, then a hesitant keystroke.)* Okay, alright, that's the idea. Easy does it.

(The lights slowly come up on Hanrahan's room, which is small and makeshift, with two small beds, a simple cooking arrangement, an old radio, and a door to the bathroom. Hanrahan is laboriously typing at a desk with a large, old fashioned typewriter. Dobbitt enters, carrying a suitcase. He stands there a moment, not wanting to interrupt. Hanrahan doesn't acknowledge him.)

DOBBITT: I'm Dobbitt. *(Pause, then louder.)* I'm Dobbitt.

HANRAHAN: *(Not looking up.)* Can't you wait 'til I'm done?

(Hanrahan stares at the typewriter. Dobbitt puts his suitcase down as quietly as possible, barely making a sound. Hanrahan turns and glares at him.)

HANRAHAN: What's all this ruckus? I'm busy. I'm looking for the "y."

(Dobbitt goes over and hits the "y" on the typewriter which makes a loud echoing sound. Hanrahan stares at Dobbitt.)

HANRAHAN: Well, well, well. Very impressive. He knows just where they keep the "y." *(Hanrahan stands up, takes the paper from the typewriter, puts it in an envelope, seals the envelope, puts the envelope in a manila folder, puts the folder in a large envelope which he seals, then puts the large envelope in a drawer, which he locks. He puts the key in his pocket, which he buttons.)*

DOBBITT: I was just trying to help.

HANRAHAN: I don't like people looking over my shoulder, passing judgment. There's going to be trouble if you pry into my affairs. Who are you, anyway?

DOBBITT: I'm Dobbitt. You must be Hanrahan.

HANRAHAN: I *must* be Hanrahan? I don't have a choice?

DOBBITT: Are you Hanrahan?

HANRAHAN: Who are you to barge into my room and tell me who I must be?

DOBBITT: You're not Hanrahan?

HANRAHAN: As it turns out, I *am* Hanrahan, but not because it happens to suit your purposes.

DOBBITT: I'm sorry. It was an endless flight and then we drove for hours through the desert. This is where they told me to stay.

HANRAHAN: You're staying here? In my room?

DOBBITT: It's a two-person room. They told me there was someone in here before.

HANRAHAN: Haney. He left early.

DOBBITT: Why did he leave? Did something happen?

HANRAHAN: *(A long look at Dobbitt.)* Which bed?

DOBBITT: Oh, it doesn't matter.

HANRAHAN: Yes it does. This one in the corner gets an icy wind off the desert snapping right through it. The window doesn't close. A man could freeze to death in this bed.

DOBBITT: If it's all the same to you, I'll take the other bed.

HANRAHAN: Suit yourself.

(Dobbitt throws his suitcase down on the bed and starts unpacking. Hanrahan pours himself a mug of coffee.)

HANRAHAN: That one's a sweatbox. Right next to the radiator, which clangs in your ear like a train wreck all night long. You'll be begging for mercy by morning.

DOBBITT: Why don't we move the beds?

HANRAHAN: That's an idea. That should solve everything.

(Dobbitt tries to move the bed.)

HANRAHAN: Except they're bolted to the floor. Lots of thievery on the compound.

DOBBITT: They're stealing beds?

HANRAHAN: Not since the bolts went in.

DOBBITT: Which bed do you sleep in?

HANRAHAN: Both. I start in the one next to the window. When I start to freeze I climb in the other one. Then, when I can't breathe I get up and start the day. I guess that's all gone now that *you're* here.

DOBBITT: I seem to have caught you at a bad time.

HANRAHAN: Oh?

DOBBITT: I fear I've upset you.

HANRAHAN: *You've* upset me? That's a bit grandiose, don't you think?

DOBBITT: You seem disgruntled.

HANRAHAN: Gruntled or disgruntled, it has nothing to do with you.
    (Dobbitt watches Hanrahan sipping from a cup. He yawns.)

DOBBITT: Is that coffee?

HANRAHAN: Yes. *(Hanrahan doesn't move.)*

DOBBITT: I feel as though I've been traveling forever. I should either sleep or try to revive myself. If there's any more coffee.

HANRAHAN: There's plenty more coffee. *(Hanrahan still doesn't move.)*

DOBBITT: I could get it myself.

HANRAHAN: Are you asking for coffee?

DOBBITT: Only if it's no bother.

HANRAHAN: Well of course it's a bother! *(Hanrahan angrily starts clattering around the coffee pot.)*

DOBBITT: Then please, forget it.

HANRAHAN: Now that I'm knee-deep in it you don't want any?

DOBBITT: If it's easier to continue…

HANRAHAN: *(Turning on him.)* See here. I'm not a puppet on a string. You'll have to make up your mind and you'll have to do it right now.

DOBBITT: No coffee. I don't want to put you out.

HANRAHAN: I'm already put out. The only question is whether or not you want coffee.

DOBBITT: Everything else being equal, I would say yes to coffee.

HANRAHAN: Very well. *(He pours a cup of coffee.)* It just means I have to make a whole new pot for myself.
    (He hands it to Dobbitt who tries to refuse the coffee.)

DOBBITT: Then you take this, please—

HANRAHAN: No!

DOBBITT: I insist!

(As they struggle, the coffee spills on Hanrahan, who bellows.)

DOBBITT: My God! I'm terribly sorry—

HANRAHAN: Look what you've done!

DOBBITT: It was an accident—

HANRAHAN: If you'd made up your mind this never would have happened. *(Hanrahan dries himself with a towel. There's a beep from a small intercom on the wall. Hanrahan stops and glares at it.)* Well. That's Merkin. And he sounds upset. *(Grimly.)* Come on, Dobbitt, it's time to meet the boss.

(Hanrahan hurries from the room with Dobbitt following as lights fade.)

(Lights up on Merkin's office, which contains a desk, a desk chair, and one other chair, which looks none too comfortable. A window with drawn blinds looks out on the compound. Merkin peers out through the blinds. Dobbitt and Hanrahan enter. Dobbitt comes forward and shakes hands with Merkin.)

MERKIN: Welcome, Dobbitt. I'm Merkin.

DOBBITT: I'm thrilled to be here, Merkin.

MERKIN: Thrilled? That seems a bit extreme.

DOBBITT: It's my very first off-country assignment. I've had extensive experience in-country, however—

MERKIN: Yes, yes, we've read your file. We frankly know more about your life than we'd like. Make yourself comfortable.

(Hanrahan quickly sits in the one chair. Merkin sits at his desk. Dobbitt looks in vain for another chair, then assumes what he hopes is a casual stance.)

MERKIN: We're in a fix and there's no time to waste. On November fifth we're delivering the largest order this company has ever received. The work must be meticulously checked if we're to avoid penalties and crippling lawsuits and a tarnished reputation that could bring the corporation to its knees. Unfortunately, until this moment, we've been short one Checker.

DOBBITT: What happened to the last Checker?

MERKIN: Why don't you ask your friend Hanrahan?

DOBBITT: *(Turning to Hanrahan.)* Well?

HANRAHAN: He's no friend of mine.

MERKIN: It's enough to say we need you, Dobbitt. You come highly recommended.

DOBBITT: My assignments have been serendipitous to date, and I have no reason to believe this will be any different.

(A sudden laugh from Hanrahan. Dobbitt turns but Hanrahan is staring at the floor.)

MERKIN: All three plants are operational twenty-four hours a day. You'll tour the compound and see. We turn out seven thousand one hundred and eighty-six units per eight hour shift. Which means with all three shifts we do—

HANRAHAN: Twenty-one thousand five hundred and fifty-eight units a day.

MERKIN: So over a six-day work week we do—

HANRAHAN: One hundred twenty-nine thousand three hundred and forty-eight units.

MERKIN: Factor in a loss of 3 percent based on our checking—feel free to jump in, Dobbitt.

DOBBITT: Uh, let's see…I'm just so tired from my trip…

HANRAHAN: Twenty thousand nine hundred and eleven units a day, one hundred twenty-five thousand four hundred and sixty-six units per week.

MERKIN: Thank you. I'm glad *someone* is paying attention. Our delivery date is November fifth, which means at our current rate when will we be done? Dobbitt?

DOBBITT: Oh…I think we'll make it in plenty of time.

HANRAHAN: We'll finish November third at 10:30 PM.

MERKIN: Why do I have November second?

HANRAHAN: Aren't you forgetting the holiday?

MERKIN: Quite right, quite right. Human error. In any event, we have a gun aimed at our head and without a system our brains will be trickling down the wall when November rolls around. While Hanrahan is out checking, Dobbitt will be typing his reports. While Dobbitt is out checking, Hanrahan will be typing his reports. Any questions?

DOBBITT: It sounds like a perfect arrangement.

MERKIN: That's not a question. This is where you're allowed to ask questions.

DOBBITT: I have none. Thank you.

MERKIN: No questions?

DOBBITT: Most people would have a question here?

MERKIN: Frankly, I'm surprised.

DOBBITT: Alright, alright…my question—

MERKIN: Don't ask a question just for the sake of asking a question. Ask only if you want to know the answer.

DOBBITT: I'm fine with no questions.

MERKIN: On the other hand, there's no such thing as a stupid question.

DOBBITT: Tell me, what exactly are those units you spoke of?

MERKIN: Pardon me?

DOBBITT: The units would be…what? What are we making in these factories?

MERKIN: Hear that, Hanrahan?

(Merkin and Hanrahan laugh.)

DOBBITT: I'm just very—

MERKIN: We're well aware of how tired you are. I'd like the two of you to function as a team. Personalities—such as they are in this case—rank a distant second.

DOBBITT: That's my philosophy. I'll do anything I can for the team. While I may not be quite as quick with figures as some, I'm an excellent typist.

MERKIN: Which is to say?

DOBBITT: It might speed things up if Hanrahan helped me with the calculations and I pitched in on his typing.

HANRAHAN: That's not necessary, Dobbitt.

DOBBITT: I just meant in the heat of battle—

HANRAHAN: I said it's not necessary, Dobbitt!

MERKIN: Hanrahan, you're free to go on your merry way. I'd like to tell Dobbitt how we do things on the compound.

(Hanrahan gets up to leave.)

DOBBITT: Thanks, Hanrahan.

HANRAHAN: *(Turning on him.)* For what? For what, Dobbitt?

MERKIN: Alright, Hanrahan, that's enough.

HANRAHAN: I demand to know why Dobbitt is thanking me.

MERKIN: Dobbitt, why are you thanking Hanrahan?

DOBBITT: For welcoming me to the compound.

HANRAHAN: I never did that.

DOBBITT: For sharing your room.

HANRAHAN: I did it under duress.

DOBBITT: For what I just know will be a wonderful partnership.

HANRAHAN: If the platitudes have abated, I'll take my leave.

(Hanrahan leaves. Merkin gives Dobbitt a long look.)

MERKIN: So. What has Hanrahan said about me?

DOBBITT: Nothing at all.

MERKIN: I'm not worthy of mention?

DOBBITT: He *mentioned* you. There hasn't been time for more than that.

MERKIN: Does he hate me?

DOBBITT: Please! Of course not!

MERKIN: How do you know?

DOBBITT: To be honest, I don't *know.*

MERKIN: Then there's a possibility he hates me?

DOBBITT: I am completely unfamiliar with the situation, and after all that time in the air—

MERKIN: I've heard all I can stomach about your damnable flight!

DOBBITT: Well...I suppose technically there's a possibility...

MERKIN: Of what?

DOBBITT: That Hanrahan...

MERKIN: What?

DOBBITT: Hates you.

MERKIN: Dear God.

DOBBITT: Although I have no reason to believe it's true.

MERKIN: If you have no reason to believe it's true then why do you dangle it in front of me, like some terrible carcass rotting on a meat hook? Why, Dobbitt, why?

DOBBITT: I...I don't know...

MERKIN: There's something you should know. Hanrahan and I have served here together for nearly one year. In that time we have grown to be close friends. I trust you'll respect that.

DOBBITT: Of course. No harm was intended.

MERKIN: It never is. Do you know, I am responsible for everything that happens in this entire department? It's a lonely and treacherous job. *(He gets a large, imposing stamp from a desk drawer.)* I make the hard decisions. The people decisions. Who goes up, who goes down. And who stays locked in place, shackled in bureaucratic leg irons until all hope is lost. *(Merkin slams the stamp on a piece of paper. It echoes ominously. He turns the paper to Dobbitt.)*

MERKIN: What does that say?

DOBBITT: "Void."

MERKIN: Exactly. I expect we'll get along fine, Dobbitt.

(Merkin starts going through papers. Dobbitt is unsure what to do.)

DOBBITT: Am I...dismissed?

MERKIN: You may come and go as you please. You're a highly skilled professional and that's exactly how you'll be treated.

DOBBITT: Thank you. *(Dobbitt starts for the door.)*

MERKIN: Oh, Dobbitt? Entre nous, I'd be careful, razzing old Hanrahan about his typing.

DOBBITT: I wasn't razzing!

MERKIN: Sounded like razzing to me. You razzed him up and down and back and forth. You're quite the razzer, Dobbitt.

DOBBITT: I'm no razzer! I wouldn't know how to razz!

MERKIN: He's damned sensitive about his typing. Hell, you might as well have razzed him about his *dancing*. I'd hate to have you discover that the hard way. Consider yourself dismissed.
(Lights fade as Dobbitt leaves.)

(Lights up on a little bridge over a stagnant, polluted river. Dusk. Hanrahan is standing on the bridge, smoking a cigar. Dobbitt comes up wearing a name tag and carrying a brochure.)

DOBBITT: I just finished my tour! What an exhilarating glimpse at modern industry!

HANRAHAN: Will you be standing there long?

DOBBITT: Here?

HANRAHAN: Yes, there. That's exactly what I meant when I said "there."

DOBBITT: Is there someplace else I should stand?

HANRAHAN: This is my favorite time of the whole day. Night coming on. Having a smoke. Looking at the river. All by myself.

DOBBITT: I don't know where else to go. There are limited vistas for observing the sunset.

HANRAHAN: But this is *my* view. It cheapens it if you're looking at the exact same thing as me.

DOBBITT: I'd be happy to look at something else. Over there, for instance.

HANRAHAN: You won't know what *I'm* looking at so how will you know what's safe for *you* to look at?

DOBBITT: I'll look over this way and you look that way.

HANRAHAN: But some of my favorite things are over on your side. You look upstream. It's the only solution if you're to remain here.

DOBBITT: Alright. *(Dobbitt goes to the other side of the bridge and looks upstream, his back to Hanrahan.)* Is the river always like this? I don't believe I've ever encountered such a color in nature before.

HANRAHAN: The colors vary according to our manufacturing schedule. By Thursday it positively glows.

(They watch in silence.)

DOBBITT: Look, Hanrahan, I'm sorry for anything I might have said about your typing.

HANRAHAN: What did Merkin say about my typing?

DOBBITT: He said you were…sensitive about it.

HANRAHAN: Well I'm not! He's feeding you garbage like you're some kind of barnyard animal. Now he's having a good laugh, watching you root and snort in his rancid trough.

DOBBITT: But why would he say something like that if it isn't true?

HANRAHAN: You'll learn that Merkin's brain has a mind of its own.

DOBBITT: In any event, I never would have brought it up if I'd known.

HANRAHAN: Do I seem sensitive to you? Do I?

DOBBITT: I think it's best not to discuss it.

HANRAHAN: But we *are* discussing it, Dobbitt. My penmanship was an inspiration to Checkers of every stripe. Then word comes down our reports must be typed. *Typed!* Why did you bring it up in front of Merkin, anyway?

DOBBITT: Hanrahan, I'm a world-class typist. I can help you.

HANRAHAN: But then you'd get the credit.

DOBBITT: Oh, no, I wouldn't take credit.

HANRAHAN: If you didn't take credit you'd be a fool. Are you a fool?

DOBBITT: I'm nobody's fool.

HANRAHAN: You'd by *my* fool if you did my work for no credit. Are you my little fool, Dobbitt?

DOBBITT: No!

HANRAHAN: Then you're trying to steal credit for my good work. You're either a fool or a thief, which is it, Dobbitt?

DOBBITT: Are those my only choices?

HANRAHAN: And still, not a word of apology.

DOBBITT: I'm sorry.

HANRAHAN: For what?

DOBBITT: I'm not entirely sure. But I feel it's necessary to clear the air.

HANRAHAN: Unless your apology is false, in which case it only muddies the waters. Is this contrition or cowardice, Dobbitt?

DOBBITT: I'm not a coward.

HANRAHAN: Or maybe you're too scared to admit it. Are you brave enough to admit you're a coward?

DOBBITT: Yes!

HANRAHAN: Aha!

DOBBITT: But that makes me strong!

HANRAHAN: It also makes you a coward.

DOBBITT: Why can't I be brave enough to admit I'm a coward without actually being a coward?

HANRAHAN: Because then you'd be boasting about something that isn't true, which would make you a liar.

DOBBITT: I'm certainly not a liar!

HANRAHAN: But we've already established you're a coward, and cowards will lie when they don't have the courage to tell the truth. By insisting on your bravery, you have admitted you're a coward and a liar. Maybe you weren't entirely honest about your so-called bravery. That would let you off the hook.

DOBBITT: I might have stretched it a bit.

HANRAHAN: Which means you know you're a liar and a coward but you aren't brave enough to come out and admit it. You're living in a sad little dream world, Dobbitt.

DOBBITT: What about you, Hanrahan? Are you so perfect?

HANRAHAN: Of course not. But I'm an honest man and precious few can say that.

DOBBITT: I can say that. Usually.

HANRAHAN: And I don't go boasting about all my wonderful qualities.

DOBBITT: I wasn't boasting!

HANRAHAN: Chatter chatter chatter chatter chatter, for God sakes, Dobbitt, this is why I enjoy the river alone!
(They watch in silence.)

HANRAHAN: Merkin's light just went off. He has to throw it in my face every time he works late.

DOBBITT: Will he be joining us at the river?

HANRAHAN: Hah! Merkin wouldn't know how to look at a river.

DOBBITT: He has a great deal of authority here, doesn't he?

HANRAHAN: Is that what he told you?

DOBBITT: He said he makes decisions for the entire department.

HANRAHAN: You and I are the entire department. We're his fiefdom.

DOBBITT: He said the two of you were great friends.

HANRAHAN: What a grotesque parody of friendship *that* would be!

DOBBITT: Then you…dislike him?

HANRAHAN: Oh, I can see there's a fox in the henhouse, a snake in the grass, a monkey on my back, a wolf in sheep's clothing—

DOBBITT: I just thought—

HANRAHAN: You just thought you'd put words in my mouth! Well I choke on your words and I spit them out because I won't be stained by your calumny! If you ever try to put another word in my mouth I'll bite your fingers off.

DOBBITT: I'm sorry, Hanrahan. It won't happen again.

(Dobbitt is staring off in the distance. We can just make out several pairs of dim yellow eyes in the darkness.)

DOBBITT: Hanrahan, look! What are those eyes out by the fence?

HANRAHAN: *(Not turning around.)* Animals.

DOBBITT: Yes, I know they're animals. *(Looks over his shoulder at Hanrahan not looking.)* You're not even looking!

HANRAHAN: I've seen them before.

DOBBITT: What species do they belong to?

HANRAHAN: I believe they're free agents. It's nothing to worry about, Dobbitt, they're outside the fence.

DOBBITT: What do they do?

HANRAHAN: They huddle in the dark and they stare at us. *(Hanrahan starts off.)*

DOBBITT: Hanrahan? Are you going to the room?

HANRAHAN: I was going to.

DOBBITT: I could walk with you.

HANRAHAN: That's not necessary. If you'd like to go to the room, go now.

DOBBITT: If you'd like to go first, that would be fine—

HANRAHAN: Go, Dobbitt! Go and be done with it!

(Dobbitt leaves. Hanrahan is alone on the bridge as lights fade.)

(Lights up on the room. Dobbitt is in his pajamas kneeling by the bed praying. Hanrahan enters.)

HANRAHAN: Ah, the evening prayer. What an oddly touching sight. And what are you praying for, Dobbitt?

DOBBITT: It's personal.

HANRAHAN: Of course. Between you and your deity. So sorry to overstep my bounds with this small gesture of friendship.

DOBBITT: If you must know, I was praying for the happiness of my wife.

HANRAHAN: And you think kneeling on the floor of a hut in the desert will in some way contribute to her happiness?

DOBBITT: Yes, I do.

HANRAHAN: What would make your wife happy?

DOBBITT: My safe return home.

HANRAHAN: So you're really praying for yourself.

DOBBITT: I'm praying for what would make my wife happy.

HANRAHAN: Do you know what *I* think would make your wife happy? If her car started making an odd knocking sound and she pulled into a gas station and the mechanic put the car up on the lift and then led her into the back room and unbuttoned her blouse and caressed her milky-white breasts with his rough, blistered hands until her nipples stood at attention like recent graduates of the Military Academy.

DOBBITT: You don't know my wife well enough to talk about her that way.

HANRAHAN: Don't I?

DOBBITT: I won't have you make a mockery of her happiness!

HANRAHAN: Let's just assume for a moment that the sudden, savage groping of an auto mechanic *would* make her happy. Would you still pray for her happiness?

(Dobbitt starts praying to obliterate what Hanrahan is saying.)

DOBBITT: Our father, who art in heaven, hallowed be thy name...

HANRAHAN: Would you pray that the auto mechanic tears off her dress and throws her down on a dirty pile of blankets underneath an outdated pornographic calendar and has his mechanic's way with her while her car is perched high on the lift for a close inspection by the other auto mechanic who hears the faint sounds of lust emanating from the back room and thinks maybe he'd like to have a little visit with your nude, flushed, panting, all-too-compliant wife as well? Would you pray for that, Dobbitt? Or are you just one more goddam hypocrite?

(Dobbitt stops praying, stands, and faces Hanrahan.)

DOBBITT: Alright, Hanrahan. What have you got against me?

HANRAHAN: You're alive on this planet at the same time I am.

DOBBITT: People have always liked me.

HANRAHAN: People also like chocolate bunnies and Hallmark cards and warm baths. Being liked is no great achievement.

DOBBITT: I treat people fairly and I expect the same in return. Haven't I been fair with you, Hanrahan?

HANRAHAN: You've been a perfect little gentleman.

DOBBITT: Then why don't you like me?

HANRAHAN: Why does it matter?

DOBBITT: Because...I don't want to be alone.

HANRAHAN: We're all of us alone, from our first hopeful breath to the last horrible death rattle rising in our parched throats. We're alone, Dobbitt, regardless of how I treat you!

DOBBITT: Why can't you just meet me half-way?

HANRAHAN: *(Sizing him up.)* I'll meet you a third of the way.

DOBBITT: Alright. That's a start. My only request is, no more gutter talk about my wife.

(Hanrahan goes into the bathroom and is heard gargling.)

DOBBITT: No matter how far apart we are, she makes me feel I'm not alone.

HANRAHAN: *(Offstage.)* She's made many a man feel he's not alone.

DOBBITT: What?

HANRAHAN: *(Offstage.)* Nothing. *(Hanrahan comes back.)*

DOBBITT: I thought you said something about my wife.

HANRAHAN: Catherine?

DOBBITT: Oh, Lord.

(Hanrahan casually prepares for bed as Dobbitt watches him.)

DOBBITT: That was a lucky guess. You've never seen my Catherine.

HANRAHAN: Tell me, does she still wear her hair long, so it cascades in all its coal-black glory over her alabaster shoulders? Or perhaps she's cut it to look more businesslike and severe.

DOBBITT: Stop it.

HANRAHAN: I hope she didn't cap her tooth. I always felt that little chip gave her a rather wild and eccentric kind of beauty.

DOBBITT: I demand to know how you know this.

HANRAHAN: I once had a brief stop-over at the Tampa plant, doing mop-up work with the Elite Checkers—

DOBBITT: That's where I met her. During a routine audit.

HANRAHAN: And there was lovely, lonely Catherine, getting her feet wet in the typing pool.

DOBBITT: You could have gotten all this from looking at my file.

HANRAHAN: Quite possible.

DOBBITT: Hanrahan, you must be honest with me. Did you know my Catherine?

HANRAHAN: *Know* her?

DOBBITT: Please.

HANRAHAN: Relax. I know for a fact she honored you completely from the moment she accepted your marriage proposal.

DOBBITT: Oh, excellent. Excellent. I've never had reason to doubt her virtue, but, well, thank you.

(The men get in their respective beds. Hanrahan turns off his light. Dobbitt is about to.)

DOBBITT: Hanrahan? What about *before* she accepted my proposal? When I was courting her?

HANRAHAN: She didn't do anything a healthy, spirited young woman on her own in the city for the first time wouldn't do.

DOBBITT: Thank you. *(Dobbitt turns out his light.)*

HANRAHAN: Yes, she got it all out of her system so she could be true to you. You can rest easy, Dobbitt, she won't feel the need to go off and try something she's never done. You're a very lucky man.

(They lie there in the darkness.)

DOBBITT: Hanrahan? *You* never—I mean your relationship with my Catherine was—

HANRAHAN: My relationship with your wife was no different from the relationship she enjoyed with many young men. Now let's get some sleep, Dobbitt, tomorrow's a big day.

(In darkness we hear the radiator clanging and the wind whistling through the window which won't close.)

(Lights up on the room. Hanrahan, in the bed next to the window, is shivering, wrapped up in several blankets. Dobbitt, in the bed by the radiator, has kicked off all his blankets and is lying there sweating. They slowly get out of bed and start to get dressed. A single beep from the intercom. They both glare at it. Lights fade.)

(Lights up on Merkin's office. Merkin is peering out through the blinds and eating dry cereal from a bowl. He returns to his desk. Dobbitt and Hanrahan enter. Hanrahan quickly slides into the chair. Dobbitt stands.)

MERKIN: So. You're both here.

DOBBITT: Would you prefer just one of us?

MERKIN: This time I want both of you. But there will be times when I want one of you, or perhaps, the other.

HANRAHAN: How are we supposed to know which one you want?

MERKIN: This is why I wanted to see you both. This affects everyone in the Checking Department. When I want to see Dobbitt, there will be a single beep. Like this. Beep. When I want to see Hanrahan, there will be two beeps. Like this. Beep beep. Is that understood by all parties?

HANRAHAN: Is there a God above us!

MERKIN: What is it, Hanrahan?

HANRAHAN: Why don't you just lop off my arms and be done with it?

MERKIN: That's a separate discussion.

HANRAHAN: I've had that one beep for nearly a year! I as much as own one beep and you simply give it to him!

DOBBITT: I don't mind. I'll happily be two beeps.

HANRAHAN: Your happiness is of no consequence in this matter. *(To Merkin.)* I don't believe you, Merkin. How can you look at yourself or anyone else in the mirror?

MERKIN: What if I were to give Dobbitt two beeps? Mightn't you feel a bit slighted? This Dobbitt fellow blows in from the country and all of a sudden he has twice as many beeps as you.

HANRAHAN: I could accept that. I'm not a crybaby.

MERKIN: You're certainly acting like one.

HANRAHAN: I am not!

MERKIN: You are too!

HANRAHAN: Let's ask Dobbitt.

MERKIN: Dobbitt, Hanrahan's acting like a little crybaby, isn't he?
(Merkin and Hanrahan glare at Dobbitt.)

DOBBITT: Well...I think he feels misunderstood—

MERKIN: See? Crybaby!

HANRAHAN: What an equivocating ball of putty.

MERKIN: What about it, Hanrahan? If Dobbitt is acquiescent, would you like your one beep back?

DOBBITT: "Acquiescent" is my middle name.

HANRAHAN: It's too late. My beep has been tainted. I know in your mind's eye it belonged to Dobbitt, however briefly. I couldn't hear my own beep without thinking maybe it was Dobbitt you wanted.

MERKIN: Well, this is a fine pickle. While we stand here bellyaching about our beeps, the work isn't getting checked.

(Merkin and Dobbitt watch Hanrahan pout.)

HANRAHAN: Oh, give Dobbitt my beep. I'll settle for the two.

MERKIN: That's the spirit!

DOBBITT: I know how much that beep meant to you, Hanrahan. I'll honor it as best I can.

MERKIN: Dobbitt, you've been allocated your beep and it's put the entire department in a tizzy. I suggest you go on your merry way.
(Dobbitt leaves.)

MERKIN: I'm a little wary of Dobbitt. He doesn't say enough.

HANRAHAN: Urge him to say more.

MERKIN: I couldn't do that. Often when he does say something I don't like it.

HANRAHAN: Are you sorry he's here?

MERKIN: Dobbitt does fine checking. I just wish he wouldn't sit in judgment. I wish he could loosen up and be more like us.

HANRAHAN: Do you think we're alike?

MERKIN: We have our differences. But I'd say we're more alike than we are different.

HANRAHAN: And Dobbitt?

MERKIN: He's more different than alike. I think being Dobbitt would be a terrible thing. *(Pause.)* Do you agree?

HANRAHAN: He seems happy.

MERKIN: Are you siding with him?

HANRAHAN: I side with no one.

MERKIN: But you don't seem to think it would be terrible to be Dobbitt and that saddens me.

HANRAHAN: I think it would be terrible to be anyone but me.

MERKIN: It's not terrible being me, I can assure you.

HANRAHAN: Not for you. For me it would be ghastly.

MERKIN: Ghastly? Why?

HANRAHAN: If I found myself you, I'd only remain you for the time it took to jam a loaded pistol in my mouth.

MERKIN: But if you were me then it wouldn't be you being me it would be me being me, which, as I've said, is far from ghastly. And I am a greater authority on being me than you could ever hope to be.

HANRAHAN: I'll have to take your word for it, not being you.

MERKIN: I'm disappointed in you, Hanrahan. I thought if we both felt contempt for Dobbitt it could bring us closer together.
(Lights fade on Hanrahan and Merkin.)

(Lights up on the room. Dobbitt is reading a letter. Hanrahan comes in whistling with a sheaf of notes and sits down at the typewriter. The whistling stops. Hanrahan sees a scone next to the typewriter.)

HANRAHAN: What the devil is this?

DOBBITT: A scone.

HANRAHAN: What is it doing here? This is my time to typewrite.

DOBBITT: I put it there. For you.

HANRAHAN: Get it away. Remove the scone.

DOBBITT: I've seen you eat scones, Hanrahan.

HANRAHAN: My scone consumption has nothing to do with you, Dobbitt. It's a personal matter.

DOBBITT: I thought it would make you happy.

HANRAHAN: No, it was to make *you* happy. To buy me, body and soul, with a pitiful scone so I'd be one more dreary hopeless cipher who "likes" you. What rubbish.

DOBBITT: It was a small act of kindness, which you don't understand.

HANRAHAN: I was a hideous, craven attempt to purchase me like a bolt of chintz or patio furniture for the niggardly price of a wretched little scone. Is that all you think I'm worth? A scone? A scone? A scone?

DOBBITT: I never thought that, Hanrahan.

HANRAHAN: Then tell me, oh great and godlike Dobbitt, what am I worth?

DOBBITT: In scones?

HANRAHAN: Since that is your currency, yes. In scones.

DOBBITT: I don't know you well enough to give an exact figure. I'm sure you're worth many many scones.

HANRAHAN: Thousands?

DOBBITT: Yes, thousands!

HANRAHAN: Not millions?

DOBBITT: Millions! Millions of scones!

HANRAHAN: Do you know why Merkin gave us separate beeps? Because you make him uncomfortable.

DOBBITT: No! It's because there's only one chair and you always take it!

HANRAHAN: I knew you were storing it up, all the venom, all the hate. Well let me tell you, I've earned the right to sit in that chair and if you ever sit there while I'm in the room I'll bloody your face.

DOBBITT: He wanted to give me a chance to sit down. That's why I have my own beep.

HANRAHAN: You don't have your own beep. You have *my* beep which is on loan out of the goodness in my heart until you're gone.

DOBBITT: You can't drive me away. You drove the last one away but I'll outlast you. I'm a survivor.

HANRAHAN: Survivors are the first ones to go.

DOBBITT: Not me! I've moved steadily up through this company.

HANRAHAN: Until now. He's not happy with you.

DOBBITT: What did he say?

HANRAHAN: It's the way you just stand there, Dobbitt.

DOBBITT: I stand there because there's only one chair!

HANRAHAN: It's the things you say, not to be overshadowed by the things you don't say. You might reverse the two. Say the things you wouldn't say and hold back on the things you would say.

DOBBITT: And you think that might help?

HANRAHAN: I'm just reporting what was said. It seems Merkin would prefer that you be a slightly different person than you are.

DOBBITT: I see. Thank you. I'll do what I can.

HANRAHAN: Look, Dobbitt, you can use the typewriter for a while if you like.

DOBBITT: Where will you be?

HANRAHAN: Out here. I'll show you.

(They go out into the sunshine. Hanrahan sits down in a tire from a tractor. He pulls a letter from his pocket.)

HANRAHAN: I'll just sit here and read this letter from my wife.

DOBBITT: And she writes you, I had no idea!

HANRAHAN: Every week, like clockwork. If she ever missed a week I'd assume she was dead in a pool of blood at the bottom of the cellar stairs. *(Leans back.)* Ahhh, this is all it takes, a ray of sunshine, a letter from my one true love, a stolen hour that's all mine—

DOBBITT: Unless Merkin beeps.

HANRAHAN: That's the beauty of it, Dobbitt. I'm just far enough away so I can't hear the beep. This spot is perfectly safe.

DOBBITT: So if you don't hear your beep—

HANRAHAN: I can't be expected to go, can I? I've got that bastard by the balls! This is where his system breaks down. A man has to have a little freedom, doesn't he? Go on, Dobbitt, go peck away at your silly reports. Peck peck peck, Dobbitt, peck peck peck!

(Dobbitt starts off, then stops.)

DOBBITT: What should I do if I hear your two beeps?

HANRAHAN: It's only important that *I* don't hear.

DOBBITT: But then I'm enmeshed in your conspiracy. You sit out here, innocent, while I'm sullied by your chicanery. I won't have it, Hanrahan. You must sit close enough to hear your beeps.

HANRAHAN: That defeats the whole purpose! As an honest man, if I hear my beeps I have to go!

DOBBITT: And if *I* hear your beeps I have to tell you. Why don't you be honest about your deceit and ignore the beeps?

HANRAHAN: The day is ruined.

(Hanrahan and Dobbitt go back inside. They look at the intercom.)

HANRAHAN: He'd better not beep unless he's got a damn good reason.

DOBBITT: It's been a while since he beeped.

HANRAHAN: So?

DOBBITT: Shouldn't we be concerned?

HANRAHAN: Fat lot of good that will do us.

DOBBITT: I think he's punishing us. Why would he punish us?

HANRAHAN: He's a malignant, two-faced bottom-feeder! He's out to get me.

DOBBITT: For what?

HANRAHAN: I need a perfect recommendation from Merkin. My life is in his hands. My temper has ruined me in this company, Dobbitt. One more bad report and I'll be through—

DOBBITT: And then what?

HANRAHAN: Exactly. These days a man without a company is a corpse. But you, Dobbitt, you have no excuse for being such a toady.

DOBBITT: I'm no toady!

HANRAHAN: Toady, toady, toady!

DOBBITT: Stop that! I wish he'd beep.

HANRAHAN: He will. He has to. Sometime.

DOBBITT: Our checking has been acceptable.

HANRAHAN: Our checking has been excellent! This isn't about checking. This is about the criminal abuse of authority. Our only defense is to stop caring.

(Hanrahan tries to busy himself, although his attention is on the intercom. Dobbitt follows suit.)

HANRAHAN: Look at you, Dobbitt. If you're so anxious, why don't you just scamper over and see your master?

DOBBITT: I've drawn the line with Merkin. If he wants to see me then he has to beep.

HANRAHAN: So you're *demanding* to be treated like a dog.

DOBBITT: Yes, but everything after that is gravy.

   (They wait. A muffled beep. They both spring to attention.)

DOBBITT: Wait! Did you hear…

   (Another muffled beep.)

HANRAHAN: One or two?

DOBBITT: One.

HANRAHAN: I could have sworn there were two, Dobbitt.

DOBBITT: One and then one again. That doesn't equal two.

HANRAHAN: I'm not sure about the first one.

DOBBITT: It was there. And unconnected to the second.

HANRAHAN: Then it's you.

DOBBITT: How do you think he sounds today?

HANRAHAN: Not unhappy. But certainly not happy, either. I'm sure you
   have nothing to worry about. *(Calls after him.)* Just don't be yourself!
   (Dobbitt heads off as lights fade.)

   *(Lights up on Merkin's office. He's wielding the "void" stamp, slam-
   ming it down on one document after another. Dobbitt comes in trying
   to be more the way Merkin would like him to be.)*

MERKIN: Happy, Dobbitt?

DOBBITT: For the most part. Although I miss my wife and—

MERKIN: Is this small talk?

DOBBITT: I suppose it is. Yes.

MERKIN: Let's have none of that. Make yourself comfortable.

   (Dobbitt starts to sit.)

MERKIN: No need to sit. This won't take but a minute.

   (Dobbitt stands.)

MERKIN: Do you like parties?

DOBBITT: Pardon me?

MERKIN: Surely you've been to a party.

DOBBITT: Yes. I quite enjoy parties.

MERKIN: On Friday there will be a holiday gala for the entire compound to celebrate Economic Recovery and Realignment Day. I
   trust you'll attend?

DOBBITT: I'd be thrilled! I'll finally get a chance to meet some of the
   workers.

MERKIN: Will you be seeing Hanrahan?

DOBBITT: We live in the same room. We work the same job.

MERKIN: Will you be talking to him?

DOBBITT: Of course.

MERKIN: So you two talk, you and Hanrahan?

DOBBITT: Well…yes.

MERKIN: And what do you talk about?

DOBBITT: Different things. Day-to-day things.

MERKIN: It sounds like the kinds of things that friends talk about. Are you two friends?

DOBBITT: In a manner of speaking.

MERKIN: Is he the best friend you ever had?

DOBBITT: No.

MERKIN: So you find him a hard man to get along with? A bit on the nasty side?

DOBBITT: I suppose there's some of that.

MERKIN: A vitriolic, contentious son of a bitch? A scurrilous pus-muncher?

DOBBITT: Well…

MERKIN: I hear what you're saying. It's a wonder you've stood it so long. He drove the last one mad. Haney.

DOBBITT: What happened?

MERKIN: Day after day with Hanrahan, the poor fellow had enough. One lunch hour he found a tub of glue in the supply shed.

DOBBITT: What did he do?

MERKIN: Drank it down. Glued all his innards together. They needed a hammer and chisel to complete the autopsy. Quite a testimony to the glue but a dark day on the compound. Pity it wasn't Hanrahan. I'm not sure I'll put him on our guest list.

(Dobbitt leaves as lights fade.)

(Lights up on Hanrahan on the bridge at dusk, smoking his cigar. Dobbitt joins him, taking his customary position looking upstream, his back to Hanrahan. A few more pairs of yellow eyes in the distance.)

DOBBITT: Hanrahan? I feel that we may be in prison.

HANRAHAN: Why would we be in prison?

DOBBITT: Perhaps we're guilty.

HANRAHAN: Of what?

DOBBITT: It's just a feeling I have.

HANRAHAN: You think perhaps we've done something?

DOBBITT: Sometimes things happen and you hardly even know it. You rush out of a store forgetting something's in your pocket. You add the numbers wrong on your taxes. You're coming home on a foggy night and there's a sudden thumping sound and the next morning you notice what might be blood on the fender so you wash the car and play eighteen holes and fall asleep in front of the TV with a mug of beer—I mean these are things we've all done but how many of us ever get caught?

HANRAHAN: If we were in prison, wouldn't there be walls all around us?

DOBBITT: There are walls all around us. With barbed wire on top and patrolled by armed guards.

HANRAHAN: If we were in prison we wouldn't be free to leave.

DOBBITT: Do you know anyone who has left this compound?

HANRAHAN: That's by choice.

DOBBITT: Then you think we *could* leave?

HANRAHAN: If we got by the guards.

DOBBITT: Why are they there if not to keep us inside?

HANRAHAN: Maybe to protect us from what's outside.

DOBBITT: And what's outside?

HANRAHAN: It must be much worse than what's in here to justify all the guards. Let's say this *is* a jail, Dobbitt. How are the conditions?

DOBBITT: If it's a jail, I have to admit it's not bad. It's really pretty decent.

HANRAHAN: And what if it's a workplace?

DOBBITT: Then it's entirely unacceptable.

HANRAHAN: And being a rational man, you'd rather be in a place that's pretty decent rather than one that's unacceptable, true?

DOBBITT: But that makes me a prisoner.

HANRAHAN: Exactly! Because you believe you're better off as a prisoner. Face it, Dobbitt, you've made yourself a prisoner in what is quite clearly not a jail—

DOBBITT: How can you be so sure?

HANRAHAN: For one thing, you wouldn't survive in a real jail.

DOBBITT: Yes I would! I'd be a model prisoner!

HANRAHAN: But you'd never figure out what was really going on.

DOBBITT: I'd obey all the rules. I'd keep my nose clean—

HANRAHAN: Whereas I would understand the Byzantine system of power and intimidation and I would thrive—

DOBBITT: Why must you always be the best, Hanrahan? Why can't I be the better prisoner?

HANRAHAN: Actually, Dobbitt, you'd do fine. You'd be a much-desired jailhouse wife. Especially among the older convicts who'd sown their wild oats and just wanted a clean cell and a little cuddling at day's end—

DOBBITT: Hanrahan! Stop!

(Hanrahan turns and sees Merkin approaching with a memo.)

DOBBITT: Good evening, Merkin.

MERKIN: Is it? I can't tell with all these damn bugs. *(He swats and scratches.)* How can you stand it? *(Accusingly.)* Or don't they bother you?

HANRAHAN: They're quite an annoyance, right, Dobbitt?

DOBBITT: A damn nuisance alright.

(Dobbitt and Hanrahan swat and scratch like Merkin.)

MERKIN: Did you tell Hanrahan about the Economic Recovery and Realignment Day Party?

DOBBITT: I thought you might want to tell him yourself.

HANRAHAN: A party? And I wasn't told?

MERKIN: Dobbitt kept it to himself.

HANRAHAN: Didn't want to invite me, Dobbitt?

DOBBITT: I thought Merkin would do the inviting.

MERKIN: Are you saying I have nothing to do but ruminate on galas!

HANRAHAN: That's a cheap shot at Merkin, Dobbitt.

DOBBITT: I didn't mean that!

MERKIN: He was supposed to tell you.

HANRAHAN: I think Dobbitt's a little gadfly.

DOBBITT: I'm not a little gadfly!

HANRAHAN: Buzz buzz buzz, up the social ladder. Didn't want me at his party.

DOBBITT: I want you at my party.

MERKIN: Now he thinks it's *his* party.

HANRAHAN: It's not *your* party, Dobbitt!

MERKIN: You're a slippery snake, Dobbitt. A short-timer with a long reach.

DOBBITT: I hope you'll come to the party, Hanrahan.

HANRAHAN: The party's been tarnished for me.

MERKIN: I'm sorry to report it's been tarnished for our entire Department. Read this. From our Regional Director. *(Merkin hands them the memo.)*

DOBBITT: This sounds spectacular! Skits, fireworks, games of chance—

MERKIN: Read the bottom.

HANRAHAN: "Checkers welcome from 5:30 to 6:15."

DOBBITT: That's an outrage! They're making us leave before the buffet dinner with sing-a-long to follow!

HANRAHAN: I won't be a part of it.

MERKIN: I'm not going.

(They both turn on Dobbitt.)

DOBBITT: Well *I'm* not going!

MERKIN: Then we'll stand together as a department. There will be no Checkers at the Party this year.

DOBBITT: That'll show the bastards!

MERKIN: We'll have our own party!

HANRAHAN: Do you mean it, Merkin?

MERKIN: Of course I mean it! A giant gala for Checkers only! Get out your party clothes, men! *(Starts off, then turns.)* Don't worry, Hanrahan, there won't be any dancing.

(Merkin hurries away. Dobbitt and Hanrahan stop swatting and scratching.)

DOBBITT: Don't like to dance, Hanrahan?

HANRAHAN: There's a lot you don't understand, Dobbitt. I'd like to keep it that way.

(Lights fade on Dobbitt and Hanrahan on the bridge.)

(Lights up on Merkin. He's standing on a chair in his office putting up crepe paper. Lights fade.)

(Lights up on the room. Hanrahan is getting ready for the party in front of a tiny mirror. The sound of a shower. A yell from the bathroom, where the door is partly open.)

DOBBITT: *(Offstage.)* What the devil is wrong with this shower!

HANRAHAN: What happened?

DOBBITT: *(Offstage.)* I just got a blast of cold water!

HANRAHAN: That's not as bad as what happened to me.

DOBBITT: *(Offstage.)* What happened to you?

HANRAHAN: I was in the shower when the water suddenly turned ice-cold.

DOBBITT: *(Offstage.)* That's exactly what happened to me!

HANRAHAN: No, Dobbitt, this was far worse because it happened to *me.*

(Hanrahan is pleased with himself as he gets ready to go.)

DOBBITT: *(Offstage.)* I suppose you're going to rush over and get the only chair.

HANRAHAN: You'll be on your feet for hours! I can hardly wait.

DOBBITT: *(Offstage.)* It's a party, Hanrahan. You'll look like a fool, planted in your chair while the rest of us are mingling and carrying on. *(Two beeps from the intercom.)*

HANRAHAN: Well, there's *my* invitation. *(Pause.)* Don't hear any invitation for *you*. Looks like you won't be going to the party after all, Dobbitt. *(Hanrahan makes loud footsteps toward the door to sound as if he's leaving.)* Still no beep for you, little man. Don't wait up! *(Dobbitt comes out, shirtless, his face covered with shaving cream, brandishing a straight razor.)*

HANRAHAN: The typewriter's all yours tonight.

DOBBITT: You bastard. You're behind this, Hanrahan, you've poisoned Merkin against me. Well I won't have it. You're a pathetic, lonely, friendless malcontent but you won't find me glued together like Haney. I'm going to fight you to the death.

HANRAHAN: Stop it, Dobbitt, stop it.

DOBBITT: You've taken everything else but you can't take this party away from me! *(Dobbitt chases Hanrahan, taking a wild swipe with the razor, which Hanrahan eludes. Then, as Dobbitt prepares for another assault, Hanrahan trips while moving away. He's helpless on the floor. Dobbitt is about to cut his throat with the razor when there's a single beep from the intercom. They both stop and look at it.)*

HANRAHAN: There's your invitation, Dobbitt. Better get dressed.

DOBBITT: My God, Hanrahan, my God. I tried to kill you.

HANRAHAN: It's the first honest emotion you've expressed since you got here. I'd say you're making excellent progress.

DOBBITT: What if I'd cut your throat?

HANRAHAN: You'd have gotten the chair. *(Dobbitt slumps on the bed.)*

DOBBITT: We have to do something, Hanrahan. Or we won't make it out of here.

HANRAHAN: What do you suggest we do?

DOBBITT: It's Merkin. He's playing us off each other.

HANRAHAN: Merkin is Merkin. And never the twain shall meet.

DOBBITT: But we must do something about him!

HANRAHAN: Perhaps we'll outlast him. He's angling to get out.

DOBBITT: Where to?

HANRAHAN: Anywhere but here. It's the company motto, no matter where you're stationed.

DOBBITT: He always calls us over separately. What if we tell each other the truth of whatever is said in his office?

HANRAHAN: The truth?

DOBBITT: Yes. The truth.

HANRAHAN: I don't think you're up to the truth, Dobbitt. The truth doesn't come in a little gift box with a colorful bow.

DOBBITT: I can handle the truth.

HANRAHAN: The truth is a wound in your heart that won't heal. The truth is the last nail in the coffin. The truth is a cold hand reaching up and turning out the light forever. That's the truth.

DOBBITT: The truth is he didn't want to invite you to the party.

HANRAHAN: No?

DOBBITT: The truth is, he thinks you're a nasty, contentious son of a bitch.

HANRAHAN: I see.

DOBBITT: The truth is, he thinks you poison every room you walk into.

HANRAHAN: Go on.

DOBBITT: The truth is, he wishes *you* had drunk the glue, Hanrahan. He wishes you were dead.

HANRAHAN: Beautiful. I'm proud of you, Dobbitt.

DOBBITT: *(Extending his hand.)* You and me, Hanrahan?
(They shake hands. Blackout.)

END OF ACT ONE

Act Two

In darkness we hear the sounds of a boisterous party with laughter, songs, and music. Then lights up on Merkin's office. Merkin, Hanrahan, and Dobbitt are looking out the window at the party. They're in their party clothes sipping punch. There's a plate of cookies on Merkin's desk and a few tired party decorations.

MERKIN: I wouldn't set foot in that party for all the money in the world.

DOBBITT: It looks a bit desperate, don't you think?

HANRAHAN: It makes a mockery of merrymaking.

MERKIN: As if something's missing. Like the heart and soul of this compound.

HANRAHAN: *(Raising his glass.)* Long live the Checkers!

DOBBITT: Why don't they like us?

MERKIN: The high moral ground we walk makes them dizzy. They think we'd judge them.

HANRAHAN: We would! We'd check their party the way we check their work. Anyway, it's best not to fraternize. Our judgments must be cold and impartial.

DOBBITT: But must we always be outside, our noses pressed to the window?

HANRAHAN: They're the ones outside, Dobbitt.

DOBBITT: But we're always here and everyone else is always there. I never knew how lonely it would be when I chose to be a Checker.

MERKIN: You don't choose checking, checking chooses you. My Daddy was a Checker and his Daddy checked before him. He'd say, "Any man can work, it takes an extraordinary man to check work."

HANRAHAN: My Daddy was a worker. Loathed Checkers, thought they were maggots, bloated with the blood of honest workers. I only became a Checker to cause him pain and disappointment. Then it grew inside me until that's who I am. A Checker.

DOBBITT: Here here!

(They raise their glasses.)

DOBBITT: I may be a neophyte, but there isn't a man alive who loves checking as I do.

HANRAHAN: I love it more than you, easy. It's my whole life.

DOBBITT: It's *my* whole life. It's who I am.

MERKIN: We all love checking. But none has given up more for the calling than me.

DOBBITT: I've only seen my wife eleven weeks in the three years of our marriage.

HANRAHAN: Good God, what a holiday you've had! I love my wife more than life itself, but I wouldn't even recognize her if she walked in that door.

MERKIN: Don't talk about sacrifices. I was a continent away when my daughter was born. And it was a damn difficult delivery, let me tell you.

HANRAHAN: With all due respect, Merkin, I believe the birth of my son was worse than anything your wife might have gone through—

DOBBITT: When *my* son was born the umbilical cord was tight around his neck—

HANRAHAN: Piece of cake, Dobbitt. When *my* son was born it was a breach delivery and my wife was in horrible screaming agony for weeks—

DOBBITT: Maybe *my* wife simply handled it better—

MERKIN: When *my* wife gave birth she died. Beat that, boys, death!

(Dobbitt and Hanrahan are stopped in their tracks.)

HANRAHAN: Merkin, I'm sorry, I had no idea...

MERKIN: Oh, yes. I had an off-country assignment, Thailand. I get the telegram that she died in childbirth. The company gave me Domestic Tragedy Leave for the funeral.

DOBBITT: Three days per death per family member?

MERKIN: I'm talking *paid* Domestic Tragedy Leave, if you can believe that!

HANRAHAN: Beautiful!

MERKIN: I walk up the little path to my house feeling like a slug for missing her death like I missed everything else in her life and who should greet me at the door but my wife. Damnedest thing. They managed to bring her back, she hadn't been dead long—

HANRAHAN: Long enough for them to write a telegram—

MERKIN: Which they forgot about when the next shift came in. Human error. So we had a high old time that night, let me tell you, I mean my God, what a gift.

DOBBITT: What was she like after she died?

MERKIN: Quite similar. Except she sang differently. I'd hear her doing the dishes, puttering around the house, and she'd start to sing. But it was possessed, not like any human voice you ever heard. Like someone else was singing through my wife. It gave me the chills. I'd go outside, rake leaves, wherever I was I'd hear that voice, moving through the house like a ghost. She knew something I didn't know and she couldn't tell me. That's when I took the assignment down here. There wasn't room in that house for both of us.

(The phone on Merkin's desk rings.)

HANRAHAN: They're probably wondering if we'll come to their party.

DOBBITT: Tell 'em we can't tear ourselves away from our own party!

MERKIN: *(On phone.)* Hello? Yes, yes. I see.

(Hanrahan and Dobbitt move together to talk. Merkin covers the phone.)

MERKIN: Don't talk among yourselves, I'll only be a minute. *(Back on phone.)* I'll attend to it immediately.

(Merkin hangs up. Outside, the festive sounds of the celebration continue.)

MERKIN: The river is on fire.

DOBBITT: *Our* river?

MERKIN: With everything we've poured into it, all it took was an errant firecracker and it burst into flames. I don't quite know what to do.

HANRAHAN: Isn't that up to the Regional Director?

MERKIN: The Regional Director is temporarily incapacitated by the soiree. I'm the ranking officer and I don't know what to do.

DOBBITT: Convention would seem to call for putting out the fire.

MERKIN: I wish it were that simple. Drinking water on the compound is in short supply. The only water I'm authorized to use is from the river.

HANRAHAN: Which would quite literally add fuel to the fire.

MERKIN: Exactly. It could turn an accident into an incident. Or an incident into a disaster. Or a disaster into a tragedy.

DOBBITT: Then we can rule that out.

MERKIN: Except the alternative is to do nothing. Which will be perceived as weakness and could cripple me in the company. Crisis management is quite a stepping-stone around here. This is my hour to shine.

DOBBITT: Is there some middle ground?

HANRAHAN: Between doing nothing and doing something that makes the situation infinitely worse?

DOBBITT: Some decisive action that is without consequence. Can't you issue a strong statement condemning the fire?

HANRAHAN: It's best to do nothing, Merkin. Let it burn itself out.

MERKIN: But this is my fire and I must put my stamp on it. Fire units are awaiting orders, I have to tell them *something!*
(The phone rings. Merkin stares at it, paralyzed.)

HANRAHAN: Do nothing, Merkin, nothing at all.

MERKIN: But they're all in a dither! Something must be done!

DOBBITT: Hanrahan's right. Do nothing.
(Merkin looks from the ringing phone to Dobbitt and Hanrahan.)

MERKIN: Look at you, the innocent bystanders, trying to ruin me with your help. *(Picks up phone.)* This is Merkin. I want all non-burning water from the river pumped onto the fire. Now!
(Merkin hangs up the phone. Dobbitt and Hanrahan look out the window.)

DOBBITT: It's cast quite a pall on the other party.

HANRAHAN: That's the good news.

MERKIN: What's the bad news?

HANRAHAN: Now the river is burning out of control.

MERKIN: Without leadership skills I'll be stuck in this compound forever. I've got my eyes on Spain, boys, and this could be my ticket out.
(Dobbitt and Hanrahan stare out the window as lights fade.)

(Lights up on the bridge. Dusk. Dobbitt enters carrying a guidebook. He stares off in the distance. More pairs of yellow eyes peer out of the darkness. Hanrahan takes his customary position looking off the other side of the bridge.)

DOBBITT: There's more of them, you know. By the fence. I saw them up close. They have sharp little teeth and insolent yellow eyes. They're not in my guidebook to local flora and fauna, Hanrahan.

HANRAHAN: You won't find them in any book.

DOBBITT: For God sakes, what are they?

HANRAHAN: Would you feel better if they had a name? Would that make them go away?

DOBBITT: If they had a name I'd know who was staring at me, watching every move I make, waiting…

HANRAHAN: What do you imagine they're waiting for?

DOBBITT: I don't know! I'm not inside their horrid little heads. But I know what waiting looks like and they are waiting!

HANRAHAN: They're on the other side of the fence.

DOBBITT: No, they've burrowed under the fence. I've been watching them, Hanrahan, every night they're a few inches closer. Something must be done!

HANRAHAN: What would you do?

DOBBITT: Someone should set a trap. Catch one and study it in a laboratory and find out what it is, for God sakes!

HANRAHAN: How would we lure it into a trap? If we don't know what they are how can we be expected to know what they like? Perhaps they're workers who took a plunge in the river.

DOBBITT: Merkin must take it up with the Regional Director. I look into their eyes and I am very concerned.

HANRAHAN: Merkin can't even requisition another typewriter. What do you think he'd do with a real problem?

(They stand in silence.)

DOBBITT: Hanrahan? I miss the river.

HANRAHAN: I miss it too.

DOBBITT: All I see is the blistered bank where it used to be.

HANRAHAN: *(Looking more intently.)* It looks as if something has started to grow.

DOBBITT: Already?

HANRAHAN: Look for yourself.

DOBBITT: Do you mean that, Hanrahan?

HANRAHAN: Turn around. Have a look.

(Dobbitt turns around and the two men look in the same direction.)

DOBBITT: Flowers are starting to bloom. I always admired your view.

HANRAHAN: It's something, isn't it? Look wherever you like.

DOBBITT: Thank you.

(Night-time sounds. Dobbitt shivers.)

DOBBITT: This reminds me of home. The terror I can't quite see.

HANRAHAN: Do you miss Catherine?

DOBBITT: I miss the idea of Catherine. I miss the future I used to dream about with Catherine. I miss missing Catherine.

HANRAHAN: I've had a mistaken impression of your marriage.

DOBBITT: The company values a solid family life and I'm lucky enough to have one. We both love to be at home. Just not at the same time.

HANRAHAN: Ah.

DOBBITT: Too much time together, well, if things get out of whack, that hurts me in the company. Don't get me wrong, in every other way we're perfect. It's just this one issue of proximity. It's quite a risk.

HANRAHAN: It's not that way with my wife and me, Dobbitt. For us the risk is being apart. I sense it in her letters, she's slipping away, like a ship easing silently off into the fog. I can just make out the dim outline of what was there, but soon that will be gone, too.

DOBBITT: I'm sure it will all work out when you see her—

HANRAHAN: *(Strange intensity.)* I would like to be needed, Dobbitt. I would like my existence to truly matter to someone else in the world.

(Lights fade on Dobbitt and Hanrahan.)

(Lights up on Merkin at his desk. A trophy—a silver fireman's helmet—is on his desk. Dobbitt enters.)

MERKIN: Ah, Dobbitt. Make yourself comfortable.

(Dobbitt starts to sit.)

MERKIN: No need for that! I don't imagine this will be a long meeting. If it is, well, feel free to sit down.

DOBBITT: How will I know the length of the meeting until it's over?

MERKIN: I suppose you won't.

DOBBITT: And then it will be too late.

MERKIN: Quite right. Human error. If you feel the meeting starting to elongate, well, the chair will be waiting.

DOBBITT: Perhaps I should just sit now. To be on the safe side.

MERKIN: No need to jump the gun. I'll have you out of here in a jiffy, if all goes well. I'm expecting a call from the Regional Director, maybe even a personal visitation, for God sakes! There's an open assignment in Spain.

DOBBITT: Excellent!

MERKIN: So to have you sitting here, well, it wouldn't do. *(Briskly gets out memo.)* I received your memo concerning unidentified animals outside the fence.

DOBBITT: Inside the fence! That's my point! They're in the compound with us and we don't have a clue as to what they are.

MERKIN: They're outside the fence until someone at the appropriate level says they're inside the fence. I've memoed the Regional Director. I'll expect a prompt memo back, at which point you will be the first to be memoed.

DOBBITT: I could ask for nothing more.

MERKIN: Well, I'd say we made the right call on the chair.

(Dobbitt starts for the door.)

MERKIN: Oh, Dobbitt? There's one more matter of a rather unfortunate nature. Hanrahan's wife has left him, poor bastard.

DOBBITT: My God! I'm—

MERKIN: Yes, you're shocked, of course. I know exactly how you feel. No need to drag us both through it.

DOBBITT: Why did she leave him?

MERKIN: All that time alone, seems she got a little too close to the Lord. Joined an Order, now she's off to a convent. Took an oath of celibacy. Solitude. Silence. Eventually she hopes to give up breathing.

DOBBITT: He never mentioned it.

MERKIN: He doesn't know. *(Holds up letter.)* He received—or will receive—a Dear Hanrahan letter. You can imagine my discomfort when I read it.

DOBBITT: How can you read his mail, Merkin?

MERKIN: I make time for it, Dobbitt, just as I make time for yours. No one's getting slighted here.

DOBBITT: And you've kept it to yourself?

MERKIN: With regards to his marriage, Hanrahan is out of the loop.

DOBBITT: Doesn't he belong in that loop?

MERKIN: Do you know what he'd do if he knew? He'd go roaring back to the country, and all he's worked for would be out the window. With his history of malfeasance, bad temper, and petty chicanery the company would have no choice but to freeze him out. There he'd be with no wife and no company to boot.

DOBBITT: You're not even going to show him this letter?

MERKIN: I'll show him the letter next week when the work is done and I've written him a glowing report.

DOBBITT: If he doesn't hear from her this week he'll assume she's dead, he told me himself.

MERKIN: He'll receive a letter this week. It just won't be this one.

DOBBITT: What will it be?

MERKIN: Whatever you choose to write.

DOBBITT: Me?

MERKIN: As unfair as it may be, you know him far better than I do. *(Gets out copies of letters.)* These copies of past letters from the esteemed Mrs. Hanrahan will serve as an excellent guide I'm sure. Your nom de plume will be Jacqueline Hanrahan.

DOBBITT: You're asking me to lie to Hanrahan?

MERKIN: I'm asking you to lie *for* Hanrahan. He'll survive losing his wife, but once the company cuts bait it's a fast drop to the bottom of the ocean, isn't it?

DOBBITT: But Hanrahan treasures honesty more than anything.

MERKIN: More than his own survival?

DOBBITT: I don't know. I'm just…nonplused.

MERKIN: Well I suggest you get yourself plussed and give me your answer right now.

DOBBITT: If I have to answer right now, my answer is no.

MERKIN: Well, there it is, a swift dagger to the heart.

DOBBITT: I've struggled with my decision—

MERKIN: For several seconds.

DOBBITT: You wanted an immediate answer.

MERKIN: You didn't even sit down.

DOBBITT: You told me not to sit down!

MERKIN: I thought you'd want to go off and think about it some more.

DOBBITT: Could I go off and think about it some more?

MERKIN: Alright. But don't go off and think about it some more and then come back here with the same answer.

DOBBITT: You mean if I go off and think about it some more I have to agree to write the letter?

MERKIN: Why else would you go off and think about it some more?

DOBBITT: I might go off and think about it some more and come to the same conclusion that I can't do it.

MERKIN: Then tell me now and save us both the tedium of your going off and thinking about it some more.

DOBBITT: But how can I know the result of going off and thinking about it some more without going off and thinking about it some more?

MERKIN: How will I know you really did go off and think about it some more if you come back in here and still say no? Can you give me the assurance you'll come back in here and say yes?

DOBBITT: I can't assure you I'll come back in here and say yes unless I go off and think about it some more.

MERKIN: Very well then, a simple no would suffice.

DOBBITT: No.

MERKIN: By God, you're something of a sadist, aren't you? Shooting that word at me over and over as if you had a crossbow.

DOBBITT: I'm trying to do what's right. I'd do anything for Hanrahan except lie.

MERKIN: But lying is the one thing that can save him. So you really are saying you'll do nothing for him. Which surprises me.

DOBBITT: Why?

MERKIN: Oh, let's not be coy, Dobbitt. I know what you and Hanrahan are.

DOBBITT: What?

MERKIN: Don't make me say it.

DOBBITT: Say it, Merkin. What are we? *(Advancing on Merkin.)* I demand that you say it! What are we?

MERKIN: Alright, I'll tell you. You're…palsy-walsy. *(Pause.)* There, I've said it.

DOBBITT: Careful, Merkin. That kind of talk hardly dignifies your station.

MERKIN: If Hanrahan leaves his post early, my reference letter will doom him for the remainder of his time on this planet. I need to know what you intend to do.

DOBBITT: In that case…I will try to save him.

MERKIN: That's the spirit! *(Hands Dobbitt the letter.)* With her oath of silence, Dobbitt, these are her last words on this earth. Except for whatever you choose to write.

DOBBITT: I hope I'm doing what's right.

MERKIN: It's you and me, Dobbitt!

(They shake hands as lights fade.)

(Dobbitt crosses to the tractor tire, sits down, sets out the letters, and begins to write as lights fade.)

(Lights up on Merkin in his office. He's carefully folding the letter and putting it in an envelope, which he seals as lights fade.)

(Lights up on Hanrahan on the bridge. He tears open the envelope and begins to read. He does a small, solitary dance of joy. Dobbitt approaches the bridge, and Hanrahan pockets the letter.)

HANRAHAN: What news from Merkin? What malicious little jewel was cast at your feet? What petty slur, what glittering gob of transparent puffery landed in your vicinity?

DOBBITT: He's taking up the animal issue with the powers that be.

HANRAHAN: You've been gone for hours.

DOBBITT: I've been checking the plants. One week to go and we're completely caught up to manufacturing.

HANRAHAN: He said nothing about me?

DOBBITT: No. Nothing.

HANRAHAN: Aha!

DOBBITT: What?

HANRAHAN: I knew the truth would be too much for you to bear. Look at you, eyes averted—

DOBBITT: I tell you, he said nothing!

HANRAHAN: Do you honestly believe you can fool me for an instant?

DOBBITT: Alright! You've got me.

HANRAHAN: I knew it! Tell me everything!

DOBBITT: *(Pause as he considers.)* He said your venomous nature is the reason you excel at checking. You only joy is belittling others—

HANRAHAN: Yes?

DOBBITT: And the very thing that makes you good at your job makes you unfit for human life as we know it—

HANRAHAN: Hallelujah! *(Laughing, he embraces Dobbitt.)* A compliment! I knew you were holding out on me. Now Merkin will have to give me a good report. And with a good report I'll get an in-country assignment and can live with my wife. At long last, my life is beginning! *(Looking at the somber Dobbitt.)* Why can't you share in my happiness, Dobbitt? Must everything be about you?
(Lights fade on Dobbitt and Hanrahan on the bridge.)

(Lights up on Merkin's office. Hanrahan enters.)

MERKIN: Were you and Dobbitt laughing?

HANRAHAN: When?

MERKIN: Yesterday.

HANRAHAN: I don't remember.

MERKIN: Let me help you. I saw the two of you on the bridge. Laughing.

HANRAHAN: Then yes. We laughed.

MERKIN: There you were, outside my window laughing, throwing it in my face like scalding water.

HANRAHAN: We meant no harm.

MERKIN: What were you laughing about?

HANRAHAN: I can't say.

MERKIN: You two must laugh a lot if you can't remember what you were laughing at. Do you know how many times you and I have laughed together, Hanrahan? Do you?

HANRAHAN: No.

MERKIN: Twice. And one of those times you weren't even laughing. I was all alone out there in mid-laugh when I realized you were merely coughing, so it has been just once for us. In a year. And yet you and Dobbitt stand out there on the bridge, flaunting your mirth.

HANRAHAN: I'm sorry if it caused you pain.

MERKIN: I still remember what we laughed at. We were standing over there by the window, looking out at the parking lot. And there was a hard wind coming off the desert which swept the cap off one of the engineers taking his break. He chased after it but as soon as he got near it the wind would dance the little cap away from him again. He kept rushing after it but he was always a step too late, until he lost sight of where he was and with a final burst of speed he smashed face-first into a utility pole. Knocked the poor bastard cold. Do you remember how we laughed, Hanrahan? Tears were streaming down our faces and our insides ached. I'll bet we laughed a damn sight harder than you laugh with Dobbitt. *(Pause.)* You two were laughing at me, weren't you?

HANRAHAN: No, Merkin.

MERKIN: If you know you *weren't* laughing at me then you must know what you *were* laughing at.

HANRAHAN: No, Merkin, it only means we *never* laugh at you!

MERKIN: Listen to you. You speak as though all you and Dobbitt ever do is laugh. Ha, ha, ha, ha, ha. How many times would you say you and Dobbitt laugh in a week?

HANRAHAN: I don't have any idea.

MERKIN: You're such a wizard with figures, come on, over fifteen?

HANRAHAN: I don't know, Merkin.

MERKIN: Then it's over fifteen. More than twice a day. I suggest you put some of that time you spend laughing into your checking.

HANRAHAN: Is our checking suffering?

MERKIN: *Our* checking? Your checking is acceptable. I won't discuss Dobbitt's checking with you.

HANRAHAN: Fair enough.

MERKIN: We're near the end of the order, Hanrahan. It would be a shame to blunder now.

HANRAHAN: Yes. Thank you. *(Hanrahan goes to the door.)*

MERKIN: Hanrahan? Why don't you ever laugh in here? With me?

HANRAHAN: Alright. I will. That would be nice. Thank you.

MERKIN: No need to stand on ceremony. We could laugh together.

HANRAHAN: Now?

MERKIN: Yes, now.

HANRAHAN: Alright. What would you like to laugh at?

MERKIN: I don't know. Dobbitt?

HANRAHAN: Yes. Dobbitt.

(They laugh without conviction.)

HANRAHAN: The truth is, my happiness has nothing to do with Dobbitt. I received a letter from my wife. Do you have any idea what it's like to be truly loved and accepted?

MERKIN: No, of course not.

HANRAHAN: I didn't either. Until I received this.

(Hanrahan gets out his wife's letter. Merkin turns away as lights fade.

(Lights up on Dobbitt typing a report. Hanrahan enters.)

HANRAHAN: My happiness is a problem for Merkin. It's like a terrible rock about to fall on his head and smash him to pieces. He wants it to be gone.

DOBBITT: Perhaps you should temper it in his presence. That's what I do.

HANRAHAN: But my happiness is different from yours, Dobbitt. It can't be tempered. You know I've felt my wife drifting away from me in recent letters, hence my anxiety to go home. Then I received this. *(Reading.)* "When everything else is stripped away, the pain, the hurt, the endless aching years of doubt, the rainy afternoons when the whole world closes in, the desolate lonely nights without comfort, the sudden torturous intoxications of what might have been, the relentless impossible hope that can't be squelched—when all of that falls away, what remains is you and I, the two of us, together, today, tomorrow, and forever, because without you—" *(Stops, pockets the letter.)* Dobbitt, this letter has given me a joy I didn't think possible. Never has she spoken so eloquently to the yearning in my heart. Never before have I felt so needed.

DOBBITT: I'm glad you have this moment of happiness, Hanrahan.

HANRAHAN: It's not a "moment of happiness." It's a lifetime of happiness, it's an eternity of happiness, it's a happiness that won't stop at the grave—

DOBBITT: But things change so quickly. Maybe all we can really trust is what we see before us—

HANRAHAN: See here, Dobbitt, it's a pity you don't have what I have, but I won't let you trample on my happiness.

DOBBITT: I only wish to point out how fleeting one's joy can be. To protect you from whatever hurt is waiting—

HANRAHAN: I won't live my life in fear of what might happen. Do you know what this means? It means I'm not alone.

DOBBITT: No, you're not alone, Hanrahan.

HANRAHAN: And now that my wife has assured me I'm not alone, we're free to be apart.

DOBBITT: What do you mean?

HANRAHAN: With Merkin leaving, you and I could stay on. One tour of duty running the Department and we'll go back to the country at the highest level. We'll be set, Dobbitt, we'll be *them*.

DOBBITT: You'd really stay on?

HANRAHAN: It can all be ours! I can step out of the purgatory I've inhabited since my damnable night of dancing. Oh, I've been haunted, Dobbitt. There I was, a young jackal on his way up the vine, my first company party, sweating through my suit, and you have to understand, this was during my drinking days. My wife and I ended up on the dance floor, a terrifying place for a man who can't dance. And even at the time I knew they were watching, a little cabal of them, laughing, pointing, carrying on. So I didn't disappoint them, I danced as no man has ever danced, flinging my limbs in a multitude of directions, 'til I was the only one out there and the entire party was just a sorry blur around me. And my poor wife, watching me with an awful, stricken smile. It followed me through the company, all these years like a monomaniacal ferret, my dancing was the first sign they had that old Hanrahan wasn't like the rest. Not quite right for the key post. The off-country assignments followed. The lackluster recommendations. I did everything I could think of to lift this curse. I even learned to dance. Not that it ever erased the memory of that grisly night. *(He turns on the radio.)* Come here. I'll prove they were wrong, all of them!

(As the music builds Hanrahan leads Dobbitt in a dance.)

HANRAHAN: I'm not bad, am I?

DOBBITT: You're quite good.

HANRAHAN: Don't patronize me!

DOBBITT: I mean it, you're very good! Not that I'm an expert—

HANRAHAN: Obviously. You're not nearly as good as my wife.

DOBBITT: Sorry.

HANRAHAN: I can stop the whispering forever if I run this Department. And I want you to run it with me, Dobbitt. We'd be a wonderful team, wouldn't we?

(They dance to the music. It's a moment of perfect happiness.)

DOBBITT: Yes. If we could accept each other's shortcomings.

HANRAHAN: Relax, Dobbitt, I can accept your shortcomings and I'm sure you'd do the same if I had any.

DOBBITT: And we can forgive each other's mistakes, however great they may seem?

HANRAHAN: You're forgiven your many mistakes, Dobbitt.

DOBBITT: I must admit, you've taught me a great deal. I'll stay on with you, Hanrahan.

HANRAHAN: Excellent!

DOBBITT: I think your wife is right. Without you I'll never be the person I want to be.

HANRAHAN: *(Stops dancing.)* I never read you that part of my wife's letter. *(Lights fade on the two men looking at each other.)*

(Lights up on Merkin's office. Dobbitt enters.)

MERKIN: Do you know how close I am to the Regional Director? *(Waves a memo.)* He memoed me right back on the animals. Most memos get backed up for *weeks* in that office. You're looking at a 72-hour turnaround. Any closer we'd be tongue-kissing.

DOBBITT: What did he say?

MERKIN: Nothing to worry about. The authorities have ruled that the animals are on this side of the fence. Therefore, they have, in effect, been captured.

DOBBITT: But if they're on this side of the fence then they're in here with us. To do whatever it is they intend to do.

MERKIN: We can't even identify them so I don't think there's any sense speculating about their intentions.

DOBBITT: But if we can't identify them then how can we have captured them?

MERKIN: You're not going to rock the boat are you? Because I'll push you overboard before I let you rock the boat.

DOBBITT: Then you agree with the Regional Director's logic?

MERKIN: He's my closest friend and most trusted ally. I defer to his judgment and I suggest you do the same.

DOBBITT: Merkin, I feel we're in trouble.

MERKIN: See here, Dobbitt, you've just started to make a name for yourself in this company. Don't go out on a limb with this animal issue. What are your plans, anyway?

DOBBITT: I'd like to stay on the compound for the next order.

MERKIN: Well, well, well! This is good news indeed. You've certainly grown as a Checker and as a man under my tutelage, and I'll be sure to note that in your report. With my transfer to Spain, I'll recommend that you run the Department yourselves, if we can talk old Hanrahan into staying around.

DOBBITT: Oh, I think he'll stay.

MERKIN: Ah, yes, I sometimes forget how close you two are. Let's get your paperwork in order. *(Getting out papers.)* Your new contract...and your release papers, soon to be moot.

(Dobbitt signs the new contract.)

DOBBITT: You'll tell Hanrahan about his wife?

MERKIN: Right away. Now that the work is done.

DOBBITT: Because this deception has eaten me up inside. It's very important that he think of me as an honest man.

MERKIN: You wouldn't want him to know who you really are.

DOBBITT: I *am* an honest man. I deceived him for a reason.

MERKIN: There's always a reason for deception, Dobbitt.

DOBBITT: You were the one who talked me into it!

MERKIN: And it was about as difficult as tying my shoe. Now that we'll never see each other again, I can tell you I never much liked you. You've never been comfortable in my presence.

DOBBITT: In that spirit of honesty, I wonder if it's because you have tyrannized me and sought to make every moment of my life a bitter taste of hell.

MERKIN: I'm your boss. It's expected.

DOBBITT: It will be a pleasure to run this Department the right way, with you gone, Merkin.

MERKIN: You've become quite a brave soul, haven't you?

DOBBITT: I learned from Hanrahan the value of honesty and speaking one's mind.

MERKIN: I don't think you were a very bright pupil. Good-bye, Dobbitt. May we go to our graves without ever seeing each other again.

DOBBITT: Likewise, Merkin.

(Merkin slams the "void" stamp on Dobbitt's release papers. It echoes in the silence as lights fade.)

(Lights up on Hanrahan in the room locking up his wife's letters. Two beeps from the intercom. Lights fade.)

(Lights up on Merkin's office. Merkin is on the phone.)

MERKIN: Yes…yes…yes…yes…yes…yes…

(Hanrahan appears in the doorway. Merkin makes a wild waving motion at him. Hanrahan starts to back out. Merkin waves more desperately and Hanrahan comes back in. Merkin hangs up the phone.)

MERKIN: Sit down, Hanrahan.

HANRAHAN: I'd rather stand.

MERKIN: Sit! Please!

HANRAHAN: No, I won't! Dobbitt is conversant with my personal correspondence.

MERKIN: So?

HANRAHAN: I want to know how this is possible.

MERKIN: What happens between you and Dobbitt is outside my bailiwick.

HANRAHAN: He read and memorized what is most precious to me in the whole world.

MERKIN: It's nothing a double lock can't fix.

HANRAHAN: I'm afraid this is beyond fixing.

MERKIN: If it's beyond fixing then it must be a fixation. Have you a fixation on Dobbitt?

HANRAHAN: I have a fixation on honesty.

MERKIN: Which is putting me in quite a fix. But I'll take care of it. I'll bust him down to trainee. Cut off his benefits. Place him on long-term probationary status. I can tie him up in paper so tight he'll never get out. *(Merkin slams his void stamp down ominously.)*

HANRAHAN: I've come for my release papers, Merkin.

MERKIN: I was told you were staying on.

HANRAHAN: My tour of duty is over. I'm leaving.

MERKIN: Where to?

HANRAHAN: I know where I'd like to go. But it's up to you.

MERKIN: Hanrahan, you can't leave. I won't let this happen.

HANRAHAN: Why would it possibly matter to you? You'll be in Spain.

MERKIN: They wouldn't have me.

HANRAHAN: They singled you out. You were a shoe-in.

MERKIN: *(Tosses the award in the trash.)* The Regional Director said my crisis management skills are too valuable to lose. Damn that fire! I almost wish it never happened. He said it would be an insult to send a man of my caliber to Spain. If only I'd acted with cowardice!

HANRAHAN: You certainly seemed frightened and unhinged to me.

MERKIN: I'm afraid it's too late for that. *(Pause.)* Hanrahan. If you go I'll have no one to talk to.

HANRAHAN: You haven't talked to me the entire time I've been here.

MERKIN: I wanted to. I tried to. We just never hit on a topic of mutual interest. Human error.

HANRAHAN: And now it's too late.

MERKIN: Give me a chance, Hanrahan. We'll laugh together, like you and Dobbitt. I'll do whatever it takes to be your friend.

HANRAHAN: Will you?

MERKIN: Yes! I promise.

HANRAHAN: Alright. Then it's you and me, Merkin.

(They shake hands.)

MERKIN: Anything you want, Hanrahan, come to me. My door is frequently open.

HANRAHAN: I want an in-country assignment so I can spend time with my wife.

(Merkin looks helplessly at Hanrahan as lights fade.)

(Lights up on the bridge. Dusk. Dobbitt appears with a bouquet of stunning wildflowers. Hanrahan approaches from the other direction, carrying a suitcase.)

DOBBITT: Hanrahan! Look what's growing in our bog! We've improved on nature.

HANRAHAN: Very nice.

DOBBITT: Where are you going?

HANRAHAN: Home. The helicopter's waiting.

DOBBITT: And you'll return in three days? That's what they give us for Domestic Tragedies, isn't it?

HANRAHAN: My life is hardly a Domestic Tragedy.

DOBBITT: I was under the impression there was no hope.

HANRAHAN: Of what?

DOBBITT: I understood her vows prohibit her from even being in the presence of a man.

HANRAHAN: Whose vows? What the devil are you talking about?

DOBBITT: Your wife joining an Order, the convent—my God, Hanrahan, I thought you knew!

HANRAHAN: I know nothing. Except that you have violated my trust.

DOBBITT: Yes, to save you—

HANRAHAN: From what? My wife has left me and joined an Order?

DOBBITT: The time apart, the endless waiting, the years drifting by, it all became too much—

HANRAHAN: How is it you know all this, Dobbitt?

DOBBITT: I wrote the last letter. So you'd stay 'til the work was done.

HANRAHAN: You wrote the last letter? All those words were yours?

DOBBITT: Merkin was ready to snuff you in the company if you left early. I wrote the letter to keep you here the last week. So all your years of work would pay off. So you'd have what you wanted for so long.

HANRAHAN: Yes. An in-country assignment with my wife. Which Merkin has finally given me.

DOBBITT: My God. Then you really are gone. I'm all alone in this Godforsaken desert.

HANRAHAN: And I'll be all alone in that house. How could you do this to me, Dobbitt?

DOBBITT: It was the hardest thing I've ever done. I gave up my honesty for you.

HANRAHAN: But that was the one thing we pledged each other—

DOBBITT: Which is why it was such a hellish ordeal to lie. It took every fiber of my being. I wonder if you'd have done the same for me.

HANRAHAN: Lied? Of course not!

DOBBITT: Then you'd have sunk me like a stone so you could call yourself an honest man. Tell me you'd lie to me, Hanrahan.

HANRAHAN: Alright, I'd lie to you. I'm lying right now.

DOBBITT: Thank you. That means a lot. *(Pause.)* Hanrahan? These were the most wonderful days of my life.

HANRAHAN: Yes. They became wonderful as soon as they were over.

DOBBITT: Is there a chance our paths will cross again? Perhaps at some other far-flung site?

HANRAHAN: I'm afraid the company doesn't work that way. A brief encounter with a kindred spirit is the most one can hope for. We're the lucky ones, it never happens to most people.

DOBBITT: But we could have stayed on here together! It all could have been ours! This could have been the beginning—

HANRAHAN: Yes. It was ours for the taking. What a pity we didn't take it.

DOBBITT: Running the Department won't be half so much fun without you.

HANRAHAN: I'm afraid you won't be running it. Merkin didn't get the post. His bravery has made him indispensable.

DOBBITT: Merkin is staying on? Then I'm truly alone. What can I do, Hanrahan?

HANRAHAN: What we all learn to do. Drift silently through the void from one assignment to the next, 'til our time is up.

DOBBITT: I don't think I can bear it.

HANRAHAN: You'll be amazed at how fast the years hurtle by. It's the days that last an eternity.

(The sound of a helicopter.)

HANRAHAN: Well.

DOBBITT: Yes. Of course.

HANRAHAN: *(Starts off, then stops.)* Dobbitt? If this helicopter leaves the compound, at least you'll know this is no prison. You'll be free.

DOBBITT: I still have to stay here.

HANRAHAN: But you'll know in your heart you can go.

DOBBITT: Good-bye, Hanrahan.

HANRAHAN: Good-bye, Dobbitt.

(Hanrahan leaves. Dobbitt is alone on the bridge clutching the flowers. The sound of the helicopter lifting off. Dobbitt watches and waves.)

DOBBITT: Hanrahan! I'm free! I'm free!

(The helicopter fades. Dobbitt sees the yellow eyes of the mysterious animals glowing in the gathering darkness. There are more of them and they're much closer. He shivers. Blackout.)

END OF PLAY

Beast on the Moon
by Richard Kalinoski

BIOGRAPHY

Mr. Kalinoski was born and raised in Racine, Wisconsin. He holds an MFA in Drama from Carnegie-Mellon University and is a former Fellow at the American Film Institute in Los Angeles. He has taught in three different public high schools in three states and is presently Director of English Education at Nazareth College in Rochester, New York.

His full-length play, *Beast on the Moon*, has been nominated by the American Theatre Critics Association for best new play of 1995 (outside of New York). *Beast on the Moon* won the 1992 Theatre-in-the-Works National Playwrighting Contest in Amherst, MA, the 1993 South Carolina Playwrights Festival at the Trustus Theatre in Columbia, South Carolina and was named by *The Philadelphia Inquirer* as one of the 10 best productions of the 1995 season in Philadelphia, PA. *Beast on the Moon* was chosen for major production by Actors Theatre of Louisville at the 1995 Humana Festival of New American Plays. The play will also be published by *Dramatics Magazine*.

Mr. Kalinoski's full-length play, *Between Men and Cattle*, was chosen for development at the National Playwright's Conference at the Eugene O'Neill Theatre Company in Waterford, Connecticut in the summer of 1995.

AUTHOR'S NOTE

Beast on the Moon is a play about people who speak what they speak in order to survive. Part of what they say is silent. I hope the reader will look for and hear the silence in the room when these characters speak.

Project Save of Watertown, MA is responsible for providing the haunting photograph that is omnipresent in the lives of these people.

Special thanks to: Ed Golden and Theatre-in-the-Works for the 1992 Equity reading of the play, Jim Thigpen and the Trustus Theatre for the 1993 South Carolina Playwright's Festival production, Mark Hallen and the Venture Theatre for the 1995 Philadelphia production and Jon Jory, Michael Dixon, Michelle Volansky, Lazlo Marton, Ray Fry, Dustin Longstreth, Vilma Silva, and Faran Tahir for the 1995 Humana Festival production.

The author is grateful to Nazareth College for its generous financial support in creating the first draft of *Beast on the Moon* and to David Paar, Marilyn Shaw and the Eureka Theatre of San Francisco for their help in developing the play.

The author is indebted to Stuart Warmflash, Monica Weis, and Deborah Dooley for their steadfast wisdom. To Mary Swanson for ongoing emotional support and uncommon common sense.

ORIGINAL PRODUCTION

Beast on the Moon was first workshopped in April of 1992 in a semiprofessional production at Nazareth College in Rochester, New York. It was directed by Mr. Kalinoski (Holly Valentine, stage manager) with the following cast:

Aram . . . . Mark Almekinder
Seta . . . . Sarah Frank
Vincent. . . . . Ryan Gravelle
Gentleman . . . . William Weyl

PLACE

Milwaukee, Wisconsin 1921–1933.

CHARACTERS

A GENTLEMAN
ARAM TOMASIAN
SETA TOMASIAN
VINCENT: A boy.

BEAST ON THE MOON

ACT ONE

Scene One. Milwaukee. 1921.

An interior space; clean and rigorously spare. To one side an imposing easel. In the space is an old-fashioned wooden camera resting on a tripod. There are uniform pedestals for props that appear later.

A thick and plain wooden table with five hard wooden chairs. The table has four sturdy legs.

In darkness an old Gentleman walks into the space and lights a single candle on the table. The Gentleman holds a large framed photograph (creased and worn) of an Armenian family, circa 1914. The family is a mother, a father, two young teen boys and a young daughter. The heads of the family have been cut out, leaving conspicuous holes. A discreet photo of the head of the youngest son (now 19) occupies the hole made from the cut-out head of the father.

In soft light, the old Gentleman walks slowly toward his audience taking ample time for them to see the portrait he carries. A faint hint of a smile forms on his face and he places the photograph on the easel as he speaks.

GENTLEMAN: *Gar oo chugar.* There was and there was not. Armenian. *(Beat. He looks hard at the picture, then looks out.)* I was born in the year 1921; yes, I am old—it was the aftermath of the Great War; six long years after Turkey, under the roar of guns and fire, began to dispose of some of its people. People we call Armenians. Maybe you know; the Turks distrusted these infidel Christians. Resented their striving and their success; so they pushed them out into the desert. Into nowhere where they starved in their clothes and withered next to their things. Some never made the trip; they were just killed—shot or hanged—or otherwise disposed of. A few of them, through chance, or luck—or will—survived. This play is about two of them. Mr. and Mrs. Aram Tomasian. A boy and a girl. I am their witness.

(The Gentleman sits in an old chair, on a far side. Bright afternoon light pours down. A Young Man enters boldly with a rude suitcase and moves to the table. He is lean and dark. The Young Man stands by the table and calls out.)

YOUNG MAN: Seta! Seta! Come in, please…come in!

(Around a corner, a Young Girl peeks, then giggles.)

YOUNG GIRL: Really? Really?

(She goes out. He pursues.)

YOUNG MAN: Seta. It is all right. Come back. This is where you're going to live.

(She giggles off. He finds her and brings her in.)

SETA: Really, Mr. Tomasian?

MR. TOMASIAN: Yes. Yes, yes, yes. Come in.

SETA: Me?

MR. TOMASIAN: You. Yes, of course, you.

(Seta is dressed formally but her clothes are rough. Mr. Tomasian is dressed in the American fashion of 1921.)

SETA: Here? *(She stares about, her eyes shine.)* Thank you! Thank you! *(She jumps to the floor and kisses it.)* Thank you, Mr. Tomasian. Thank you, thank you, thank you, thank you, thank you.

MR. TOMASIAN: Okay. Okay. Please, Seta.

(She kisses his outstretched hand.)

SETA: I'm just shocked—you must know.

(He moves her to a chair.)

MR. TOMASIAN: Please sit down.

(She sits.)

SETA: Thank you.

MR. TOMASIAN: I have a gift for you. Upon your arrival in Milwaukee, Wisconsin, The United States of America. *(He finds a neatly wrapped package.)* For Mrs. Aram Tomasian.

SETA: Who?

MR. TOMASIAN: You.

(She takes the gift. She weeps.)

MR. TOMASIAN: Seta. It's okay. Seta, you already cried all through the train station in Chicago. You're all right now.

SETA: I don't know…I know…I mean…I don't know…I mean… America, Mr. Tomasian. *(Blowing her nose.)* How is it I came to be this lucky—you chose me, Mr. Tomasian.

MR. TOMASIAN: I think it was a good choice. Your gift, Seta.

(She works at the wrapping.)

SETA: I'm shocked. That's what I think I am. Shocked. Oh. Oh… *(Looking at the wrapping.)* It's so pretty. Everything is. I'm going to save this.

MR. TOMASIAN: *(Smiling.)* Seta, open your gift.

SETA: Yes, Mr. Tomasian. It is a day of gifts, I think. *(She unwraps the bow and puts it around her neck.)* Pretty. Yes. I'm opening. A mirror? A mirror! Oh, look…look. *(She stands with it.)* Oh, isn't it fancy? This is for me? The wood is like glass… *(She has uncovered a fine hand mirror, finished in a shiny hardwood.)*

MR. TOMASIAN: *(Smiling.)* And there's an inscription.

SETA: Oh, yes, Look. (*beat*) I can't read it.

MR. TOMASIAN: I had it inscribed in English. It's from an expensive American shop.

SETA: Thank you, thank you. *(She looks at the writing on the back of the handle.)*

MR. TOMASIAN: *(Beaming.)* It says, 'For my wife, my picture bride from Armenia. 1921. Aram Tomasian.'

SETA: It says all that?

MR. TOMASIAN: *(Cheerfully.)* It says all that.

SETA: I am a picture bride? What's a picture bride?

MR. TOMASIAN: You know, don't you? *(He takes a picture from his suit-coat. He shows it to her.)* This is the picture they sent me from the mission in Istanbul. I chose you from a total of 37 pictures. You haven't seen this?

SETA: *(Giggling.)* Mr. Tomasian. Mr. Tomasian. Oh, oh, please, I apologize. Mr. Tomasian, my…

MR. TOMASIAN: What? Tell me.

SETA: *(Trying to restrain her laughter.)* That isn't me. It isn't.

MR. TOMASIAN: It isn't you? How can that be?

SETA: I'm sorry, that is a picture of a dead girl—she's dead—she died nine months ago of disease, but they must have used her picture. They put my name on the back, I think. Here.

MR. TOMASIAN: But you wrote to me. You said you were you.

SETA: I am me.

MR. TOMASIAN: But this girl looks like you.

SETA: I'm sorry. I'm ashamed. I had my picture taken, but I never saw it. Maybe they used this girl's because of my sores.

MR. TOMASIAN: Sores?

SETA: I had sores on my face from bedbugs.

MR. TOMASIAN: *(Confused.)* They sent a dead girl to me? My bribes went for a dead girl? Who are you?

SETA: Please, please—we look almost the same—but that girl didn't have sores on her face in the picture—so they just sent it—it was over a year ago—I was hardly fourteen years old. All the myrigs, they just wanted to save as many as they could.
(He has turned away.)

SETA: Mr. Tomasian. Mr. Tomasian. I wrote to you. I am the same girl who wrote to you.

MR. TOMASIAN: *(Confused, then pouting.)* I paid a bribe to the mission, to the orphanage—to a man in Istanbul to buy your ticket, to a man in New York at the immigration. I paid everyone. I ordered the girl in this picture and they sent me someone else. We are married. Married. Three months ago, by proxy—you know this.

SETA: Yes. But about the picture, I didn't know...I was just so glad to get your letters. I thought they used my picture. Pictures, names, they mix them up. *(Long pause. She looks at herself in the mirror.)* Thank you for the gift. I can see that my sores are gone.
(He sulks.)

SETA: *(Eager and cheerful.)* I think I am prettier than this other girl. *(She looks at the picture.)* I apologize, Mr. Tomasian. Mr. Tomasian.

MR. TOMASIAN: You didn't know about this picture? About this dead girl?

SETA: I was a girl dying in an orphanage. You wrote to me.

MR. TOMASIAN: Let me see.
(She hands him the picture. He stands next to her and compares. He holds her face to the light.)

MR. TOMASIAN: Okay, okay, open your mouth, Seta.

SETA: Open my mouth?

MR. TOMASIAN: Yes.

(She does. He looks at her teeth, holding open her mouth.)

MR. TOMASIAN: Close.

(She does. He looks at her eyes.)

MR. TOMASIAN: You had trachoma?

SETA: A little bit. I was cured.

MR. TOMASIAN: Okay, good. Good teeth. Clear eyes. Strong face. I see that you are a pretty girl. *(He stands back.)*

SETA: Thank you. *(She waits as he looks at the picture.)*

MR. TOMASIAN: All right, I can forget this picture. I want to take a new one. Sit and try a small smile. Small one. *(He moves to behind the camera.)*

SETA: A new picture?

MR. TOMASIAN: *(A given.)* Our life should be recorded.

(He is busy with the camera. She digs in her suitcase and pulls out a crude doll.)

MR. TOMASIAN: No doll.

SETA: …something to hold. It's…it's what I have. My mother…my mother made it.

MR. TOMASIAN: Seta, no doll.

SETA: Please.

MR. TOMASIAN: Seta.

SETA: Mr. Tomasian, please.

MR. TOMASIAN: We are legally married. Put the doll away. You act like a child.

SETA: It's how I feel…

MR. TOMASIAN: Stop feeling like a child.

(She puts the doll at her feet.)

MR. TOMASIAN: *(Pause.)* Americans…they smile. Smile now—a little, and hold.

(She smiles.)

SETA: Hold what?

MR. TOMASIAN: Hold the smile. The light must soak in. Hold. Hold. Hold.

(Her smile is fading.)

MR. TOMASIAN: Seta, it's gone.

SETA: I don't feel like smiling.

MR. TOMASIAN: Ah! You've ruined it. I must get a new plate. Seta, smile. No grim looking Armenian girls.

SETA: Mr. Tomasian, I apologize, but it doesn't feel natural.

MR. TOMASIAN: Pictures aren't natural, pictures are posed. Now smile.
(She does, and looks like a monkey.)

MR. TOMASIAN: That's too big!
(She withers.)

MR. TOMASIAN: That's too small.

SETA: I don't know. Too big, too small.

MR. TOMASIAN: Look at me. Practice smiling. Smile.
(She does.)

MR. TOMASIAN: Good. Fine. Now stay like that. *(He prepares the camera.)* Stay like that. Stay like that. Okay. Hold!! Hold! Hold, hold, hold, hold, hold, hold, hold, hold, hold, hold hold, hold, hold, hold. Hollllllddddd. Good. *(He presses a bulb.)* Done.
(She grabs the doll. He takes the new plate out and exits. She stands and notices the portrait on the easel. Aram enters.)

SETA: Why are the heads gone? Mr. Tomasian—the heads are gone. Except this one. Your picture is in this one. Who is this?

MR. TOMASIAN: My father.

SETA: You put your head where your father's was?

MR. TOMASIAN: *(Quietly.)* Yes.

SETA: Oh.
(Pause, she waits. Aram has a Bible in his hand. He puts it on the table.)

MR. TOMASIAN: Please sit down. I want you to listen.

SETA: You're still angry.

MR. TOMASIAN: This is the first day of our life together.
(She sits and clutches the doll.)

MR. TOMASIAN: Seta, put the doll away.

SETA: The picture's over.

MR. TOMASIAN: Seta, a man can't have a wife who clutches a doll. Put the doll away.
(She hesitates.)

MR. TOMASIAN: You can put it on the table.
(She looks at him and does this slowly.)

MR. TOMASIAN: You are 15 years old. A woman. A woman doesn't hold dolls. *(Pause.)* Seta, you have no reason to be afraid. Hold my hand then.
(She does this, hesitantly. She looks at his hand, then finally takes it. Awkwardly, they stand together.)

MR. TOMASIAN: There, is that better?

SETA: *(Slowly.)* Maybe. Yes.

MR. TOMASIAN: Good.

(They face out, side by side. She is self-conscious. Long pause.)

MR. TOMASIAN: So. So lucky and such a great day. I have a wife…and she is in America…with me. *(Pause.)* My life can start now. My life…you know…it can start now. *(He breaks.)* My father would never imagine. Milwaukee, Wisconsin. Me, a wife.

SETA: We're both…alive.

MR. TOMASIAN: *(Abruptly.)* So, it's time for reading.

SETA: It is?

MR. TOMASIAN: *(Pleasant veneer.)* Do you have a question about everything?

SETA: It's just that I don't know very much. It's a new country.

MR. TOMASIAN: The man reads. So, I am going to read.

SETA: Umm, Mr. Tomasian, may I be permitted, excuse me, to ask why? Is that what is done with new brides who come from trains?

MR. TOMASIAN: *(A given. Inspecting her.)* My father read at all important events. At meals. At funerals. At weddings. It's in my plan.

SETA: Oh.

MR. TOMASIAN: *(Matter-of-fact.)* Nothing happens without planning.

SETA: Oh.

MR. TOMASIAN: Why do you say 'oh'?

SETA: Mr. Tomasian, forgive me, it's just that things, everything, seems to happen all the time without planning.

MR. TOMASIAN: *(Looking for patience.)* Seta, I am going—

SETA: *(Blurting.)* Here I am in Milwaukee, no one ever planned that I was to live in America—and then the myrigs sent the wrong picture—then the big thing is I'm alive and I certainly didn't plan on being that—because everyone else is just dead—my parents—

MR. TOMASIAN: *(Patiently.)* Stop talking now, Seta.

SETA: Oh. *(She puts her head in her hands.)*

MR. TOMASIAN: What are you doing?

SETA: Nothing.

MR. TOMASIAN: This is from Timothy. Open up your ears.

(She raises her head and pulls on her ears.)

MR. TOMASIAN: *(Simply.)* "Women shall adorn themselves in modest apparel, with shamefacedness and sobriety. I suffer a woman not to teach, nor usurp authority over the man." There, now tell me, say what it means.

SETA: It means…I don't know…it means what it says.

MR. TOMASIAN: Yes, Seta. What is that?

SETA: It means…you're the man and you make the rules. I'm a girl—I mean a woman—and I'm to be quiet and serious. Except I'm not? *(He looks at her.)*

MR. TOMASIAN: What?

SETA: No…thing.

MR. TOMASIAN: Yes—something. Seta, say it.

SETA: I'm not…quiet…I have never been quiet. Mr. Tomasian, I am sorry.

MR. TOMASIAN: It will take training.

SETA: Oh.

MR. TOMASIAN: A lot of training.

SETA: Oh.

MR. TOMASIAN: So…the second reading. You like your mirror?

SETA: I love the mirror.

MR. TOMASIAN: Good. You may hold it.
(She picks up the mirror.)

MR. TOMASIAN: Hand-rubbed. American.

SETA: Yes, Mr. Tomasian.

MR. TOMASIAN: Do this. Hold the mirror out and look into it. I'll read from the Proverbs.
(Uncertain, she does this—but awkwardly.)

MR. TOMASIAN: It concerns the ideal wife. That's you. "Her husband," that's me…*(Smiling.)*

SETA: I know.

MR. TOMASIAN: "Her husband, entrusting his heart to her, has an unfailing prize."
(Mr. Tomasian smiles, and awaits a response. Seta is caught in her pose.)

MR. TOMASIAN: Well? *(He stares.)* Now tell me about Proverbs.

SETA: Well…it says that, that I am your prize. How do I be a prize?
(He regards her.)

MR. TOMASIAN: What did your parents teach you?
(She looks at him. She lets the mirror down.)

SETA: *(Quietly.)* I don't know. They loved me.

MR. TOMASIAN: Good, and what did they teach you?

SETA: They were just…just my parents. My mother sang.

MR. TOMASIAN: She sang…in a theater?

SETA: In the kitchen. *(Wistful.)* When she sang, the whole house shook and the neighbors came out into their yards. *(Glad.)*

MR. TOMASIAN: When my mother married my father she was not allowed to speak for a year. One whole year.
(Seta opens her mouth in awe. He watches her.)

MR. TOMASIAN: You don't understand. You grew up in a city. *(Smiling warmly. speaking gently.)* This one is special and important. *(He sounds it out carefully.)* "She brings him good and not evil all the days of his life." *(He awaits her response.)* Well?
(She is in thought.)

MR. TOMASIAN: Seta?

SETA: Oh, uh, what did she do?

MR. TOMASIAN: What did who do?

SETA: Your mother, Mr. Tomasian, a whole year! She did not speak for a whole year.

MR. TOMASIAN: Haven't I asked you about Proverbs?

SETA: Yes. I'm a prize. I mean, I'm your prize.

MR. TOMASIAN: And the rest?

SETA: I'm supposed to bring good, not evil.
(He tries to discern the intention.)

MR. TOMASIAN: So, you understand.

SETA: I used to read the Bible to my father.

MR. TOMASIAN: You read the Bible? To your father? When?

SETA: Before. Before the Turk. I was a child.

MR. TOMASIAN: He didn't read it to you?

SETA: *(Giggling.)* It put him to sleep.

MR. TOMASIAN: It put him to sleep?

SETA: Oh yes, he loved it. He would start out sitting very straight. *(She postures.)* And I would read and he would go very softly... dead...uh, to the world. It was gentle music for him, I think.

MR. TOMASIAN: In my house the man reads.
(He affects a dramatic pose. She holds the mirror up.)

MR. TOMASIAN: Chapter Six, The Canticle of Canticles. "Your hair is like a flock of goats...
(She spurts.)

MR. TOMASIAN: ...streaming down from Galaad."
(She giggles and then represses it.)

MR. TOMASIAN: This is the Bible!
(She quiets.)

MR. TOMASIAN: "Your teeth are like a flock of ewes which come up from the washing, all of them big with twins, none of them thin and barren."

(Her laugh explodes.)

MR. TOMASIAN: Seta, Seta, Mrs. Tomasian.

SETA: My teeth are like pregnant sheep? *(She laughs.)*

MR. TOMASIAN: These are compliments from the Bible. You laugh?

(She holds herself in.)

MR. TOMASIAN: Seta, the Bible is not funny.

SETA: Yes.

MR. TOMASIAN: The Bible speaks of beauty.

SETA: Yes, Mr. Tomasian. *(She bursts.)* Oh, oh, I'm sorry, but I started to see all the goats, a thousand goats got into my head—they were jumping around and bleating in my hair—Oh, I can't stop! *(Exploding again.)*

MR. TOMASIAN: The Bible is the breath of God.

(She finds control. He watches her, waiting for another burst. He finds the mirror and thrusts it at her.

MR. TOMASIAN: Look at you, Mrs. Tomasian. What do you see?

(She takes the mirror, sobered.)

SETA: Me?

MR. TOMASIAN: Of course you. Who is you? Who?

SETA: I don't...I don't know.

MR. TOMASIAN: When you look, I want you to see a woman.

(She looks.)

MR. TOMASIAN: Well? Seta? *(Slowly.)* Do you see a woman?

SETA: *(Pause.)* I'm sorry. I see me.

MR. TOMASIAN: And who is that?

SETA: *(Looking.)* She's just a girl.

MR. TOMASIAN: 'She's just a girl?' 'She's just a girl?'

SETA: Thank you for this mirror, Mr. Tomasian.

(He fumes.)

SETA: I do very much want to see a woman, but I don't see one. I thank you for the mirror. And for my life.

(He paces. She gets the doll from the table.)

MR. TOMASIAN: In marriage you don't clutch dolls.

SETA: I just want to hold it. Just for now.

MR. TOMASIAN: Do you know the business of a man and a woman? *(Pause.)* Do you? *(Pause.)*

SETA: Yes. I only ask permission for the doll.

MR. TOMASIAN: *(Simply.)* No.

(She fingers the doll. He holds his hand out to take it. Very slowly, she hands it to him.)

MR. TOMASIAN: Good. I am going to wash. You say that you know about marriage. I think it's time for us to realize our marriage.

SETA: Um...I.

MR. TOMASIAN: *(Easily.)* I'll wash, I'll come back. I'll bring you in with me.

(He exits, doll in hand. She looks up, watching him leave. She begins to grasp the meaning of her husband's words. She stands, looking around. She finds her coat and dons it. Finally, she sees the table and the chairs around it. Wary of Mr. Tomasian, she creeps under the table and quietly pulls the chairs around her, forming a barricade. Momentarily, Mr. Tomasian enters, bare chested, carrying a towel. He finds her under the table.)

MR. TOMASIAN: Seta! Seta, come out. Come out. This is embarrassing. You look foolish.

SETA: Please don't make me.

MR. TOMASIAN: Seta, you look like a child.

SETA: I am a child.

MR. TOMASIAN: Seta, this will not hurt you. Did you forget that you are lucky?

SETA: I'm afraid.

MR. TOMASIAN: Okay. Okay.

(He gets an idea. Quickly, he exits. She looks around. He returns.)

MR. TOMASIAN: Okay, Seta. I have something for you.

SETA: What is it?

MR. TOMASIAN: Do you think I will tell you before you come out.

SETA: I can't come out before you tell me.

MR. TOMASIAN: Fine. I am counting to five. One...two...three... four...five.*(Pause.)*

SETA: Why did you count to five?

MR. TOMASIAN: Huh? You don't know why I counted to five?

SETA: No.

MR. TOMASIAN: You are serious? I am giving you a warning.

SETA: What do you have?

MR. TOMASIAN: Okay, okay, it's gum.

SETA: What kind?

MR. TOMASIAN: *(Exasperated.)* Gum. Wrigley gum. Mint. Spearmint.

(There is a pause and then a small voice.)

SETA: May I have the gum?

MR. TOMASIAN: First you come out.

SETA: Can I see it?

MR. TOMASIAN: Huh? Seta, this is a child's game. All right, I'll play. *(He holds it up for her inspection.)* Come out.

SETA: I can't.

MR. TOMASIAN: Come out and you can have the whole package.

SETA: Wrigley gum?

MR. TOMASIAN: Yes.

SETA: Throw a piece to me!

MR. TOMASIAN: You are amazing.

SETA: Forgive me, Mr. Tomasian. I can't come out.

MR. TOMASIAN: What did you think? Before we came here.

SETA: I thought I was safe.

MR. TOMASIAN: Safe? Safe? God in heaven, I am your husband! Seta, you are safe. *(He sits.)* I will wait, then. *(A pause.)*

SETA: May I have the gum?

MR. TOMASIAN: No.

SETA: Mr. Tomasian.

MR. TOMASIAN: Yes.

SETA: I don't...I don't know you.

MR. TOMASIAN: What do you need to know?

SETA: I don't know who you are.

MR. TOMASIAN: I am practicing great patience with you—only because you came to me on a train alone and you don't know America.

SETA: May I have the gum now?

MR. TOMASIAN: Fine. Here. My second gift to you. *(He throws a piece of gum under the table.)* Now will you take your place with your husband? Seta?

SETA: Oh, this is good. This is so good. Thank you. Americans are so clever, I think, don't you think, Mr. Tomasian, so many things they make and all the cars, I can't believe even the toilets they have, even their toilets are pretty—

MR. TOMASIAN: God is not happy, Seta.

SETA: He isn't?

MR. TOMASIAN: God is not happy when a woman hides from her husband.

SETA: Please, I'm sorry.

MR. TOMASIAN: Don't beg. Seta. Fine. I am counting to ten and if you don't come out, I'll come and get you.

SETA: Wait. Mr. Tomasian, Mr. Tomasian, oh, I don't know you, no I don't...

MR. TOMASIAN: One...two...three...four...five...

SETA: I don't even know how you survived, how did you survive, you must have been very brave, yes, brave—

MR. TOMASIAN: six...seven...eight...

SETA: and clever because so few men survived, I know because so few—

MR. TOMASIAN: nine...ten. *(Pause.)*

SETA: No.

MR. TOMASIAN: You are having your last chance. What do you think? Do you expect me to be someone else? Not a man?

SETA: No. No.

MR. TOMASIAN: Do I drag you out then?

SETA: Wait. The picture. The picture!

MR. TOMASIAN: What picture? *(Reaching for her.)* What? What picture?

SETA: Behind me. Up there. That is of your family, right? Of your family?

MR. TOMASIAN: I don't explain that picture.

SETA: The heads, they're gone. Who cut them out? Who cut them out?

MR. TOMASIAN: This is not your business.

SETA: I am your wife. Maybe it is, you see, excuse me. Mr. Tomasian, my business.

MR. TOMASIAN: No, it is my family! Now come! Come! Now!

SETA: No no no no no, please no...

MR. TOMASIAN: Be calm, Seta. I won't hurt you. We have to start, come—Calm, Seta. Calm. Calm.
(He reaches and pulls her by her leg as she grasps a table leg and clings, he pulls and the table comes with her. She gasps from the effort but doesn't scream. Instead, she fights fiercely, kicking wildly.)

MR. TOMASIAN: You don't fight me. Ahh!!!
(She has kicked him, hard. He pulls her with care, evenly, dragging her by both legs. She kicks free. She scrambles and ducks under the table, grabbing a chair as defense, then gives that up and protects her body behind a table leg, clutching it. He lurches after her and in a massive heave, yanks the table away. She tries to escape, but he catches her leg and holds her. She hesitates, looks into his face, and then screams.)

SETA: No!!!

MR. TOMASIAN: Calm yourself, Seta. I won't—

(She wrenches free in a panic, and holds her hands up, and shaking, curls into a ball. He sees her fear and watches her.

MR. TOMASIAN: What? What? Tell me.

(She shudders. Pause. She quiets.)

SETA: A Ttttur...a Ttturk! I saw a Ttturk. Oh no, I saw a Turk.

MR. TOMASIAN: A Turk?! Me?? A Turk! Me? Me? No. No. Seta. It's me, Seta, Aram Tomasian. How could you...How could you?

SETA: It was in your face.

MR. TOMASIAN: Did a...did a Turk...were you...did a Turk???

SETA: No, my sister, my older sister...in my place, she did it for me, for me, but I saw him, I saw him just then, oh I saw him on your face I saw him on you, in your eyes I saw him. *(Shaking.)*

MR. TOMASIAN: You saw a Turk in my face...in my face???

SETA: I'm very sorry. I'm sorry. You are the one who saved me. You saved me, I'm sorry.

(He holds his face. He grabs the mirror. He looks in the mirror.)

MR. TOMASIAN: Me? My face? *(He stares into the mirror. Blackout.)*

Scene Two

Lights reveal the old Gentleman pushing a baby carriage. He stops and looks out. Seta's head now appears in the portrait, where Aram's mother's was.

GENTLEMAN: His father had been a photographer too, the only one in the village. And he was the town clerk and a politician. He signed official documents and took official pictures. He raised goats. His wife, Aram's mother, tended them. His father had been the kind of man on the verge of a smirk all day. Outwardly, he was cheerful even when he disagreed, about the weather, about what the Turkish government might do, about who Aram should be. He was proud and smiling and determined and he seemed to be everywhere. *(The Gentleman places a small American flag somewhere on the outside of the carriage.)* Aram Tomasian, born of Toros Tomasian, was the son. And the endless liquid talk that spilled from the mouths of his mother and father was full of will...and expectation. The future.

Aram Tomasian was the son. Son must follow son. It was understood.

(The Gentleman moves away, leaving the carriage. He is replaced by Aram, in shirtsleeves. He places a huge blue bow and ribbon on the carriage and realigns the camera for a picture. In a moment, Aram stands apart and admires the carriage. Seta enters in a coat, with a hat and dress gloves. She moves cautiously.)

MR. TOMASIAN: You're home. Good. Seta? Seta, tell me. You saw the doctor?

SETA: *(She moves to touch the new carriage, gently.)* Very special, Mr. Tomasian.

MR. TOMASIAN: What of the doctor? Tell me.

SETA: *(Pause.)* He said. *(Pause.)* He said, no. Just no.

MR. TOMASIAN: No?

SETA: I see you have a celebration planned. *(She is wistful.)* Of course the camera. *(Smiling.)* Of course pictures.
(He turns away.)

SETA: Mr. Tomasian, I'm sorry. *(She picks up the flag.)* He said it was the starving. But he doesn't know. He's sorry he said…Mr. Tomasian. He said girls who starve sometimes…can't.

MR. TOMASIAN: Can't? Not can't. Not can't. You aren't starving. This Levine doctor doesn't understand.

SETA: Mr. Tomasian, when I was nine, I starved. I starved.

MR. TOMASIAN: I know. But you have a woman's cycle—and then you missed—you missed—it must mean—

SETA: It means noth—

MR. TOMASIAN: Doctors, doctors. What can they possibly know of you, of me? Huh? What can they?

SETA: The second one—

MR. TOMASIAN: I know. You think I don't know how many doctors?

SETA: And you bought a carriage—was this to be my surprise? Or was it your surprise…Mr. Tomasian, a carriage does not make a baby, I think—*(He speaks over her.)*—a carriage does not bring…

MR. TOMASIAN: He is a foreigner. He is not even American! He is an *odar*…He says he doesn't know? He is a doctor! And he doesn't— God never meant this—he will not…not tolerate this…not this, Aram Tomasian, with…no…it is a joke. A big laugh. *(He laughs.)* Impossible. *(He turns away and is silent.)*

SETA: Dr. Levine is a kind man. He knows you're disappointed.

MR. TOMASIAN: Two years. More than two years. You are seventeen. *(He moves toward the portrait where Seta's face has replaced his mother's.)*

SETA: Yes. Such a lovely carriage, Mr. Tomasian. It makes me so...so sad too. Me. I'm sad. Did you know?

(He turns toward her. She is touching the carriage.)

MR. TOMASIAN: *(Softly.)* Yes. You are.

(They look at each other.)

MR. TOMASIAN: But you are almost eighteen. I see a woman. *(He begins to strip his shirt off.)* And you and me, we have a task. We have work.

SETA: Now?

MR. TOMASIAN: Yes, now, and then again until...our legs ache, because we will, because, my father and his father, their voices are in me...here... *(He points to his head, his shirt off.)* I hear them now. They are a chorus and they demand it. Life after life after life, Seta, so yes, now...now.

(Blackout.)

Scene Three

The lights fade up to reveal first the portrait. Still only the heads of Seta and Aram can be seen. The rest of the portrait consists of children's bodies. Downstage lights reveal Mr. Tomasian at the table, reading from the Bible. Seta enters with a huge cake. She cuts a piece of colossal dimension and places it in front of him.

SETA: I made a new cake. Fudge cake. I got the recipe from Mrs. Binetti. It's an American recipe.

(He looks.)

MR. TOMASIAN: *(Amused.)* This piece is so big, Seta.

SETA: I thought you would like it.

MR. TOMASIAN: It would stuff me.

SETA: It's very special.

MR. TOMASIAN: It's bigger than my foot.

SETA: Maybe you will love it.

(He takes a bite.)

MR. TOMASIAN: *(Cheerfully.)* It's wonderful cake. Thank you.

(They smile at each other.)

MR. TOMASIAN: Delicious. Very. *(He takes a second bite and chews. He remembers the time and looks at his watch.)*

SETA: Don't you want to finish?

MR. TOMASIAN: I can finish later.

SETA: *(Thinking.)* Oh. *(Pause.)* The Binettis are going to start to sell ice cream in their grocery. Mr. Binetti bought a freezer.

MR. TOMASIAN: Good luck. Freezers are expensive. It's about time.

SETA: You don't want to finish the cake?

MR. TOMASIAN: I can eat cake later. You're well? You're not sick? Seta?

SETA: *(Very quickly.)* Mrs. Binetti loves the portrait of her new baby, Nicky. She went on and on, oh, she's funny, she is…her voice is so big and…musical…like big bells. I thought you would like the cake—you do like the cake?

MR. TOMASIAN: Seta, it's time.

SETA: Now? I think I'll eat some cake. *(She starts to gobble the cake.)*

MR. TOMASIAN: I see you like the cake.

SETA: Oh yes. *(With cake in her mouth.)*

MR. TOMASIAN: You can finish the cake later.

SETA: It's so delicious…it has a hint of orange, did you taste that? I added that. That hint of orange is mine.

(He takes her hand. She stops, a huge chunk in her mouth.)

MR. TOMASIAN: Chew.

(She does. The lights fade to near darkness.)

Scene Four

In the dim light Mr. Tomasian and Seta remove most of their clothes and make a pile—shirt, blouse, pants, skirt, shoes—in a stark pool of light. They move toward an unseen bedroom carrying the clothes. A brief pause then a tired Seta returns in her slip, pours a glass of water at the table and drinks. She looks at her tired face in the hand mirror. Aram enters and waits for her. She sees him. She follows him back toward the bedroom as the lights fade…

Scene Five

In the darkness we hear gasps and footsteps. Mr. Tomasian enters. He is in his underwear; his hair is sticking straight up. At the table he pours water and drinks. Seta enters, walking slowly. She sees him in the dim light and laughs.

MR. TOMASIAN: What? What?

SETA: *(Laughing.)* Your hair!

(He picks up the mirror and looks. He sees his hair, and laughs with her. He sits, they laugh. He looks into the mirror again, and the laughter fades. On his face is a vacant stare. Pause. They look away from each other. Pause. The lights fade.)

Scene Six

The Gentleman speaks to the audience.

GENTLEMAN: *Gar oo chugar.* So. There was and there was not. The Armenian and the Turk. On a road, a Turk moving north on his horse. An Armenian moving south on his. The wary Armenian spots the Turk, jumps from his horse, stands still, smiles, even, if he gathers it's required and waits there while the Turk passes. Now how does the Armenian know that what he sees on the road, way away, is a Turk? He doesn't know. But he gets off and waits. Why? It's expected. It's tradition. It's insurance.

(Mr. Tomasian is putting on a massive, very old coat. First he smells it, touches it—then puts it on and stands, Bible in hand. A pause. He hears a noise. He rushes to put away the coat. Seta enters in a hat with gloves.)

SETA: It's too hot for these. *(Pause, looks at gloves.)* April and 81! Do you believe? *(She fidgets.)*

MR. TOMASIAN: Seta. Seta? Yes, all right. You're back. Yes?

(She picks at the fabric of her glove.)

SETA: *(Pause.)* No, Mr. Tomasian.

(He is silent. He walks up and down. He shakes, holds himself.)

SETA: I know. I know.

(He holds his head up.)

SETA: Can you say...something? Anything, Mr. Tomasian. A word? A sound? *(Pause.)* A shout?
(He looks at her. She steps back, then removes her hat and gloves, puts the hat pin in the hat, and places them on the table as the lights fade.)

Scene Seven
The Gentleman speaks to the audience.

GENTLEMAN: Her people were from the city. Her father had been a gentleman and a lawyer. In him, these two were not incompatible. He was a soft man, round at the edges, with huge hands and a big laugh that took up the room. Her mother had been an educated woman, a teacher, lively and important to everyone. Books and stories and music were the daily life of the house. At parties and picnics, her mother sang and the neighbors, some of them Turks, applauded when she raised high that voice. The sound was water clear and whole and for a few moments it was forgotten...that she was a Christian woman, an Infidel, who would one day be crucified on a dust road leading nowhere out of the city. *(The Gentleman produces a newspaper and holds it up.)* In the newspaper, Aram Tomasian kept looking for Americans. He knew Armenians, they were his tribe. But Americans were so often something else— foreigners, Poles, Swedes, Jews, Germans. He was especially fascinated by the photos, staring hard, trying to find the cleanest possible image of an American, the true American. As he learned to read, he read more and more, and found ample uses for the newspaper.
(Mr. Tomasian enters and takes the newspaper and sits. He reads. He is dressed formally, as if he just came from work. Seta comes in with a platter. On it sits a meal: bread, milk, and a lamb stew. She sets the table. Mr. Tomasian reads.)

SETA: Stew. *(Pause.)* Lamb stew. You know, I gave the recipe to Mrs. Binetti. Just imagine that, Mr. Tomasian. I...gave her a recipe. Me. *(She works quickly.)* Maybe I shouldn't tell you this. Oh, I don't know, I suppose I can tell you this. It's about Mrs. Binetti. She thinks you're very...very. She said handsome. She will say almost anything. *(Slight pause.)* She has some shocking opinions I think— and about men. She talks and talks about men, ones I've never seen, from Italy...she knows about men. Now that it's summer, she says the ice cream is very successful. Mr. Binetti can't get the trucks to deliver enough. She said you came in last week and bought some. I hope you enjoyed it. Let me guess what flavor you chose, Mr. Tomasian. The new one. Butter pecan. No? Yes? Probably chocolate. I know you like chocolate. *(Pause.)* So. Yes. I don't think I even told you, Mr. Tomasian. I bought a new bolt of cloth—I thought I would make some new draperies for our room—it was leftover material, just part of a bolt, really but a very royal blue...oh, oh, I have a sample—a dress for my doll—let me show you—

(She finds her old doll, now in a bright dress of blue. She attempts to put the doll in his line of sight, but his gaze is centered on the paper. She holds the doll for a long moment.)

We were talking, Mrs. Binetti and me, we were just talking, you know. She has been working in the grocery for eight years. Eight years. She knows everyone. She knows the Poles, she knows the Italians, of course the Italians, she knows the Greeks, the Armenians, and she knows all the kids in the neighborhood... Just Tuesday she had to break up a fight...several boys...just outside the grocery...tough boys...but they looked scared too.

(Mr. Tomasian puts down his paper and stands. He picks up the Bible. Silence.)

MR. TOMASIAN: Genesis. Chapter One, Verse 28. "Then God blessed them and said to them 'Be fruitful and multiply; fill the earth and subdue it. Have dominion over the fish of the sea and the birds of the air, the cattle and all the animals that crawl on the earth.' " Amen.

SETA: Amen.

(They eat in silence.)

SETA: Is this, Mr. Tomasian, excuse me, please. I mean...just...is this going to be—permanent? Today is July 3rd and tomorrow is the Fourth of July and that will be, that will be ten whole weeks Mr. Tomasian. I wanted us, you know, I thought...this great American holiday, July 4th...a husband and wife, together, America and free- dom...everyone talks about freedom—except the Americans of course. I mean, two Armenian people, lucky Armenian people…I look at you and I see you so unhappy. I do, Mr. Tomasian.

(Mr. Tomasian stops eating and looks at her for the first time. She looks back.)

SETA: It's me. Yes, it's me. Someone would laugh, I think, at this…here a man sits and here a woman sits and day after day they just live, and one talks and the other is a mountain of sadness. I look at your eyes. I talk to your eyes.

(He turns his gaze down and resumes eating.)

SETA: I wait for your eyes. *(Silence.)* Mr. Tomasian. You have, Mr. Tomasian, you have…decided…decided. Yes. It is my fault, you have decided.

(He eats.)

SETA: You. You are my family. *(She waits. She resumes eating.)* Good stew. Very good stew. Delicious, wonderful, full of meat, and rich stew. Don't you think? A special stew, a lucky stew, the day before the Fourth of July. I know! I'll make more, Mr. Tomasian, and we can bring it to the Madha, to the Armenian picnic. An American-Armenian stew…er Armenian-American—

(With a jerk he picks up the Bible. He searches quickly.)

MR. TOMASIAN: *(Evenly.)* Timothy. Chapter Two, Verse One. "Let a woman learn in silence with all submission. For I do not suffer a woman to teach, or to exercise authority over the man; she is to keep quiet."

(She eats enthusiastically. He studies her.)

SETA: *(Slowly, carefully, quietly.)* "Every day is…miserable…for…the…depressed. But a lighthearted man has a continual feast!" Proverbs. Mr. Tomasian, you know Proverbs. "When one finds a worthy wife, her value is far beyond pearls." Chapter 31. And, and… "She opens her mouth in wisdom, and on her tongue is kindly counsel." Chapter 31 also, my father liked Proverbs, Mr. Tomasian.

(He snatches the Bible and stands.)

MR. TOMASIAN: Proverbs Chapter 25 Verse 24. "It is better to dwell in a corner than in a roomy house with a quarrelsome woman."

(He pounds the book shut. Seta stands carefully, slowly.)

SETA: Proverbs Chapter 25 Verse 20. "Like a moth in clothing, or a maggot in wood, sorrow gnaws at the human heart."

MR. TOMASIAN: Genesis! Chapter 25 Verse 21. "Isaac prayed to the Lord for his wife because she was barren!"

SETA: *(Shaking.)* Proverbs—

MR. TOMASIAN: "Isaac prayed to the Lord for his wife because she was barren!!"

SETA: Prov—Prov—Prov—

MR. TOMASIAN: "Isaac prayed to the Lord for his wife because—she... was...barren!"

SETA: Stop! Stop! Please, Mr. Tomasian...stop...stop...stop... st...st...s...

(She sinks slowly to the ground. Mr. Tomasian is startled, surprised. She picks up her plate from the table and brings it with her as she drags her chair across the room.She sits turned away from him. Mr. Tomasian sits, bewildered. He breathes in sighs. A long pause. He picks up the paper and rattles it. He looks at her. He scans the paper. He looks at her. He returns to the paper.)

MR. TOMASIAN: I. Uh...What? Seta. You have never...I have never seen...

(She does not move. He returns to his paper.)

MR. TOMASIAN: Did you see? Here in the paper it says that more than 200 Polish families have come to Milwaukee in 1925 so far. So easy for them, they just get off the boat and like happy puppets they walk into a new country. And the country, Seta—takes anybody, I suppose. Foreigners. They love foreigners. *(He looks for a reaction and finds none.)* Tomorrow the parade will be going down Wisconsin again. I suppose you know. I suppose Mrs. Binetti told you. *(Pause.)* Seta, there's a picture of that fireman hero. He's going to be in the parade. Big white face. Big head. German. I...am... talking...Seta. I am talking? *(He waits.)* This German looks bad. Bad light. Bad picture. Not skillfully done. Here it is American Fourth of July, and they have a German fireman hero. It's funny. Where are the Americans in America? *(He looks at her.)* Seta, isn't it a little funny? A little funny, Seta? *(He quickly eats a spoonful of the stew.)* All right. All right. I will say this. This I will say. Your stew. It's good. Good. There. And the lamb...is...is...just right. Just right, Seta. Seta, won't you look? At your husband? *(He eats.)* Good stew. Seta. Thank you? Thank you for this fine stew. I have never seen...You. You. Like this. *(Pause.)* I think the Greeks are starting. I had a Greek family this week. The first Greeks. They came to me. It's reputation. Fair prices. And I make everyone handsome. Even Greeks. About Nick Binetti and his freezer. How much did he have to pay for that freezer is what I meant. It will be years before it's paid. Pennies for the ice cream and hundreds for the freezer. It's the grocery business. Inventory. Equipment. Money. More money—is what I meant. My business is simple. I take pictures. I have a skill. People pay for the skill. I don't sell, the skill sells.

(She is quiet.)

MR. TOMASIAN: All right. Yes. You are right. I had some of Nick Binetti's chocolate ice cream from his fancy freezer. Yes. I had some. It wasn't so...bad. Yes, I had some. Seta. Seta. You are still my wife. My wife. Seta. *(Slowly he stands, looking at her.)* Maybe. Maybe you can come and finish your meal of lucky lamb stew. Here. *(Pointing.)* With me? No? No? No? Seta, you have never done this. I have never seen you do this. Did I? Did I? I was just frustrate—

(He takes a step toward her. She turns away.)

MR. TOMASIAN: Oh, Seta. How can. How did? How?

(He takes another step. She does not move. Step by careful step he approaches her. Awkwardly, slowly, he puts his hand on hers. She does nothing. He turns and moves away.)

SETA: Aram.

(He stops.)

MR. TOMASIAN: Huh? You said my...? What?

SETA: *(Firmly.)* Just Aram. Nothing else.

(He is bewildered. He looks at her. She looks up and out. Lights fade.)

END OF ACT ONE

ACT TWO
Scene One

The Gentleman steps into a special light, holding the portrait. He carries a blue sweater.

GENTLEMAN: Some of you are sitting too far away to see this. *(He holds it into the light. Long pause.)* Aram and Seta Tomasian. They came from a time that I want to understand. *(Pause.)* I wanted to see this. *(He clutches the portrait to himself.)* You see, in Turkey, in 1893, before Aram and Seta were even born, there was an eclipse of the moon. In villages and towns the Turks came out into the night and shot their cannons and their guns at the 'wild beast' in the sky covering the moon. Their Turkish neighbors shouted at the beast on the moon. The Armenians watched. And then, two years later in 1895, the Sultan, worried about a few upstart Armenians, declared a Holy War, a Jihad, and instantly the Turks came out again into the night and shot their guns. But not at the 'beast on the moon'. They shot their neighbors, the Armenians, who flew into closets, and scrambled into ditches and hid in corners. Shouting, the Turks came out into the streets and shot them. Aram and Seta came from a certain place and a certain time. I am looking for it.* *(The gentleman places the portrait on the case and covers it with the sweater.)*

(Lights reveal a small boy, perhaps 12 or 13. He sits at the table, his mouth bursting with meat and bread. Seta watches him quietly. He eats. Seta is a little amazed.)

VINCENT: Yer shure nice to me fer feedin' me like this Missus Tomasin. I owe ya.

SETA: No, Vincent. You don't owe me anything.

VINCENT: Ya, I do. Nuthin' ain't free. I could carry some messages fer ya somewhere. Like to yer husband at his work maybe. I can scrub yer walls fer ya.

SETA: Vincent, you just enjoy your food.

VINCENT: Fine with me. I can do that.

FOOTNOTE: *If role of the Gentleman and Vincent is played by one actor, the Gentleman's speech should read as follows: "Aram and Seta came from a certain place and a certain time. As an old man, I am still trying to understand. As a boy, I was there. With them.*

(He dives back in. She watches.)

SETA: There is something I would like you to do, Vincent.

VINCENT: Ya? Anything you want.

(Seta finds her hand mirror.)

SETA: Just look. *(She hands the mirror to him.)*

VINCENT: Yeah?

SETA: Vincent, does your face look like other faces you see?

(He looks again.)

VINCENT: Ya, it's an Italian neighborhood.

SETA: Vincent, I want you to take a bath.

VINCENT: Hey, I been livin' on the street. What good's it gonna do I go take a bath. You tryin' ta shame me? I don't want no more shame. *(He starts to leave.)*

SETA: No, no no Vincent. You'll just feel better.

VINCENT: I feel good now.

SETA: Okay. Okay Vincent. You and I—we can make a bargain.

VINCENT: What's at?

SETA: You see, I have a cake. A special cake.

VINCENT: No? Ya? What's it made outta?

SETA: It's a…a magic cake!

VINCENT: Oh, a magic cake. I don't know Missus Tomasin. I never seen no magic cake. You mean you got potions in it?

SETA: It has, I think, special powers.

VINCENT: Noooo!! Ya? *(His eyes widen.)* You mean it puts a spell on you? Ya? Nah—

(She nods.)

VINCENT: I don't believe in magic, cuz I never seen any, 'cept in some phony magic show they took us to one time. What's so magic about it then?

SETA: I think. I think it will make you…happy.

VINCENT: Happy? Oh, shure, happy. Awright, I'll take some. *(He moves toward the table.)*

SETA: First the bath.

VINCENT: Whatsit with ladies 'n baths? My mutha used to sit inna bath for a week sometimes. Then she'd come out all powdered and creamed up like she was posing for a statute. Hey, do I stink? That it?

SETA: You know, Vincent, when I caught you in the Binetti's store?

VINCENT: Ya, I know.

SETA: I smelled you first, then I saw you.

VINCENT: Smell gave me away? God, must be strong. I don't smell it. *(He smells his clothes.)* Well, it's a little snurly.

SETA: Snurly?

VINCENT: Sour. Like a old pickle. Comes from livin' all over the streets. Ya get snurly.

SETA: How many days have you been out on the street?

VINCENT: I don't keep time. More'n a week. They must a stopped lookin' fer me.

SETA: Maybe you will go back.

VINCENT: Sometime, ya.

(Pause. She watches him carefully.)

VINCENT: I hate it there. The Home. *(Pause.)* Saint Bartholamooo! Hey, what's a saint, anyway?

SETA: Someone with a special kindness.

VINCENT: Used to be a guy there like that. Father Christiano. Used to talk to me. Used to listen. They sent him away. Up the church somewhere. Ain't many a those types left at St. Bartholomooos.

SETA: Are they cruel?

VINCENT: *(Quickly.)* Hey, do I get some a yer magic potion cake, or not?

SETA: First the bath.

VINCENT: Awright, but I take my own bath. Hey, wait. Why you doin' this? *(He stares at her.)*

SETA: What?

VINCENT: Fer me? Why you doin' all this fer me?

SETA: Mrs. Binetti—

VINCENT: Missus Binetti. She was gonna call the cops on me. Cuz I picked up some bread. Some bread. Hey, but you brought me here. You don't know me.

SETA: I have seen you, Vincent. I saw you hit a baseball last summer.

VINCENT: Ya, that don't answer it. *(He moves toward her.)*

SETA: Mrs. Binetti told me…She said you were an orphan. I am an orphan.

VINCENT: You? But yer…like a…like a lady.

SETA: An orphan lady. My husband too. He is an orphan.

VINCENT: Gol. Gol. What's it—all Armenians orphans?

SETA: Many.

VINCENT: What, someone just up an kill all the parents?

SETA: Yes.

VINCENT: Gol. Gol. You tell me, who did it?

SETA: *(Pause.)* Turks.

VINCENT: Turks?

SETA: People in a country…called Turkey.

VINCENT: Ya? So whadda they look like?

SETA: They look like Armenians.

VINCENT: They look like you and they killed you? Damn. *(Pause.)* There's lotsa orphans. So you catch one stealin' bread and you bring him home to feed legga lamb to. I don't get it.

SETA: I saw you hesitate when you picked up the bread. You wanted to put it back. You stopped—I caught you.

VINCENT: I just wanted to eat it. That's it.

SETA: You didn't want to steal.

VINCENT: How'd you know?

SETA: I know what it means. To be hungry. To have to steal.

VINCENT: Ya? *(Pause.)* Ya, maybe you do.

SETA: Enough now, okay. You need a bath and I think you should take it before Mr. Tomasian comes home.

VINCENT: Where is he?

SETA: He's working.

VINCENT: Ya, what's he do?

SETA: He is a photographer. Vincent, if you take off your shirt, I'll wash it out while you take the bath. What do you think?
(He begins to take off his shirt.)

VINCENT: Yer husband ain't gonna be mad I'm here?

SETA: I think when you are very clean and fresh—I'm sure he will like a clean boy.
(As he takes off his shirt, a large gold coin pops out. Seta picks it up. Vincent grabs it from her.

VINCENT: That's mine! That's mine! Sorry, I din't want to grab. I forgot.

SETA: That's a shiny coin. It must be important.

VINCENT: *(Pause.)* Ya.

SETA: It must be worth a lot of money.

VINCENT: I bet it's the shiniest one you ever saw.

SETA: Yes it is. *(Sly.)* I see. Now that you have so much money, you can pay for your meal.

VINCENT: Missus Tomasin, I thought you were…I mean…giving it.

SETA: But you are a rich boy—

VINCENT: No—this ain't money. This is more'n money. It's private. It's a part of me.

SETA: Oh. You can't buy things?

VINCENT: I could…I could. But I don't. Never. No matter what. I've eaten garbage next to rats with this coin stuck up under my arm. And nobody at the Home, nobody at Saint Bartholomoos, nobody there knows I got this. I would sew it to my arm if I knew how.

SETA: Did someone give you this?

VINCENT: I din't steal it.

SETA: No.

VINCENT: *(Pause.)* I haven't looked at it for a long time. My…my pop gave it to me.

SETA: Oh good. Fathers should.

VINCENT: When there's nobody around and I'm alone, I rub it on the rug and I hold it up—and in the light, you know, it flicks, it flicks like a piece a fire. My Pop, I wish he could know I got it still.

SETA: Where is Pop?

VINCENT: Huh? *(Pause.)* Uh, he died. He died.

SETA: But, Vincent, maybe he knows.

VINCENT: Oh, like he's in Heaven? Like he's some angel lookin' down and watchin' me? Sounds like a priest. They talk like that around the Home. They got pictures a Heaven. Angels all over. Big 'n fat 'n pink. 'Cept I don't see it. Not around here. My idea is that Jesus is a guy in a striped suit in a big car, and he stops and hands out big shiny coins, millions of um. Jesus in Heaven. A guy in a car in a hat. Anyway, my Pop is no angel. And he don't know I still got it. Ain't we got a deal? I take the bath, I eat the cake, right?

SETA: Yes, I'll run the water and get some towels for you. Okay?

VINCENT: Okay.

(She smiles and exits. Vincent finds the doll. He picks it up and carries it with him and finds the portrait, which is covered with the sweater. Carefully looking around, he peeks underneath. He hears Seta coming. He drops the sweater and holds up the doll. She enters.)

VINCENT: Missus Tomasin, the doll's head is all chopped up—look, it's got half a eye and then here no eye and the hair is yanked out. This doll is dead, Missus Tomasin, but it's dressed up like some princess. You don't wanna get a new head? Get some eyes, some new hair—match the clothes then.

SETA: *(She takes the doll.)* She wouldn't be the same. I dress her up, but she's still the same. I brought you my husband's clothes.
(Vincent takes the clothes.)

VINCENT: Yer husband tall?

SETA: Yes, he is unusual. Armenians are not tall men.

VINCENT: I say somethin' you don't like?

SETA: No.

VINCENT: I didn't mean nothin', bout yer doll, honest, I just thought, you got it dressed all fancy. It's a nice doll, really…really!

SETA: Go.

VINCENT: Ya.

SETA: You can leave your clothes outside the door. Go. I'll cut your cake.

VINCENT: *(Leaving.)* Ya.
(Vincent exits. Seta sits for a time with her doll. She frames the face, holds it away from her. She tries to fix the hair. She fusses with the dress. She returns the doll to its place. She finds the cake and brings it to the table. She cuts a piece of colossal dimension. She hears footsteps. Quickly, she removes the sweater from the portrait and puts it on. Aram enters, beaming energy and carrying a wrapped gift.)

ARAM: Seta. Seta, a big day, yes, a very big day.

SETA: Aram: You're home and it's only the middle of the day.

ARAM: I decided not to wait. I have news and a gift. A big day!

SETA: Good, yes. I just wanted to say—

ARAM: So now we celebrate my news—look, already cake you have out.

SETA: It is just a surprise—only 1:30 in the after—

ARAM: *(Cheerfully.)* Seta, listen to me now—sit down and listen.
(She sits and looks for a sign of Vincent and adopts a little smile.)

ARAM: Good. I…me…I…have a contract. A contract. It's in Racine. And it's with the Jerome Increase Case Company.

SETA: Jerome Increase—

ARAM: J.I. Case. The tractor company. It is big. Oh, it is big. Thousands work there. They want me to take their Christmas pictures for the workers and even for the foremen. And if they like the pictures, if they like them, then I will take…guess. Guess. *(He struts a bit.)*

SETA: Guess?

ARAM: Yes, guess.

SETA: The wives.

ARAM: The wives? Oh, funny. You say the wives. Not the wives. What a guess! *(Laughing.)* No, not the wives, Seta. The Executives. Me, taking pictures of executives. Me, this Christmas, 1933. Me! And so I wanted to come home and give you this gift—a gift to celebrate. A gift of celebration. *(He hands her the wrapped package quickly.)*

SETA: *(Surprised.)* Oh. Oh. Just like that, you buy me a gift. Thank you, Aram. And you just walked in there and they said you could have the contract? Just all of a sudden?

ARAM: I planned it. Vartan Gulbankian—he took me in his new Buick—we went right in and sat in a great office, huge—with sofas and fancy lamps—then they called me in and I laid them out—my pictures—and they looked down, over their noses, and stared at them.

SETA: Aram, I want—

ARAM: Okay, yes. First there were two vice-presidents, Mr. This and Mr. That and then Mr. Big Somebody and Mr. Bigger Somebody Else. You should have seen it! Four of them, Seta. Four. And they stood and laughed in their beautiful blue suits and made loud American jokes while they smoked. And they smiled like happy dogs, and then they shook hands and said 'fine' and 'swell' and my work was rare and clear. They said I had talent. Me. Talent. Americans. My pictures. My contract. You should have seen.

SETA: I am proud.

ARAM: Yes.

SETA: Very proud.

ARAM: The photographer for the Jerome Increase Case Company. My father, you know, was only the village photographer. This is not some small moment.

SETA: No.

ARAM: Seta, your gift. I'll get the camera. *(He goes for the camera.)*

SETA: Aram, you don't have to…to take my picture. We could just celebrate this—together. Private, maybe.

ARAM: Private? No. Not private. I am a photographer, Seta. We have a life. I record the life. *(He is behind the camera.)* Go on. Go on.

SETA: You don't think we could, I mean, take the picture tomorrow?

ARAM: I gave you the gift today. Open.

SETA: I am happy for you, Aram, and the camera—just right now—it gets just a very little, in the way.

ARAM: In the way? It's not in the way. It's here. You're there.

SETA: It's like a third person.

ARAM: *(Amused.)* It's a camera.

SETA: *(Nervously.)* I have so many emotions.

ARAM: *(Smiling.)* Yes, I know. Good. Look at you, Seta. You are proud.

SETA: But the camera, I think it interrupts—

ARAM: How can it interrupt? It's just a camera. Seta, open your gift.
(She collects herself.)

SETA: Yes, right.

ARAM: Good. Open and then as you hold it up, slow… *(He goes behind the camera.)* Just go, Seta. There. You won't even notice Mr. Camera.

SETA: Yes, Aram.
(He buries his head behind the camera. She glances upstage.)

ARAM: Where are you looking? Look here!
(She tears at the paper.)

SETA: Are you staying home this afternoon?

ARAM: Seta, open the gift.

SETA: You've never been home so early on a Monday. *(She reveals a box. Printed on it is a description of an iron.)* Oh. A new iron. *(Chagrined.)*

ARAM: A Westinghouse. The best. Automatic. Better than American Beauty.

SETA: Better, yes. Better than the one I have. *(She glances back.)* Uh, thank you.

ARAM: Seta, hold it up.

SETA: Yes, thank you.

ARAM: Westinghouse. Automatic temperature control—hold it up— even heat, modern—
(She holds it up limply.)

ARAM: Something is wrong?
(Pause, she gains control.)

ARAM: Good. Hold and smile…nice smiling face and there you are— holding a new American Westinghouse on this special day of my contract with the Jerome Increase Case Company—hold, hold, smile, hold, good, hold, smile…
(Vincent comes in, wet and dripping, Aram's clothes draped all over his little body. He is now pink and fresh and his black hair shines.)

ARAM: Huh? What? Who?

VINCENT: Hey, Missus Tomasin, this get up is nuts. Hey, this Mr. Tomasin, the photographer? Hey, I'm Vince—

(Vince steps forward, but Aram avoids him and goes directly to Seta.)

ARAM: Seta, who is this?

SETA: Vincent. This is Vincent. *(Attempting to be confidential.)*

ARAM: He has on my clothes—

SETA: He was taking a bath. Vincent, sit and eat cake now.

(The following overlap.)

VINCENT: This a camera? Holy—

ARAM: Who is this?

VINCENT: Gol. Gol.

SETA: Just a boy.

ARAM: In my house, you bring a boy to my house—just bring him in and give him a bath!

VINCENT: *(Near the camera.)* Hey, Mr. Tomasin, I take my own bath—great bath, too, Missus. You got film in this?

ARAM: Who is this? What did you do, just say come in strange boy—have a bath, eat some cake?

SETA: Yes. He is an orphan.

ARAM: He is wearing my clothes—

SETA: Aram, he is right here, in front of us—His own are filthy.

VINCENT: Some gadget here, mister—

ARAM: Don't touch that please, boy—

SETA: I agree. He should not be wearing your clothes.

(She finds Vincent's rags and holds them up—thrusting them out toward Aram.)

VINCENT: Thanks for these—kinda funny ain't they—I can take 'em off—

ARAM: Where did he come from—I don't want those—do you just bring lost boys home like this—is this your habit?

(End overlap.)

SETA: Not just any boys—

ARAM: This is not the first?

SETA: No.

ARAM: The second? Not the second? The third? Not the third? Not the third?

SETA: Vincent is only the fourth.

VINCENT: Can I eat? Or you want I should take off the clothes, Mister—

SETA: *(Impulsively.)* Aram, he should not be wearing your clothes—I will go wash these—then I can iron them with my new Westinghouse iron. *(She is suddenly gone with Vincent's rags.)*

ARAM: Seta. Seta!

(Aram chases her. He comes back, trapped now by the boy.)

VINCENT: Hey, Mr. Tomasin, you gotta fork?

(Aram inspects the camera, sitting next to it.)

VINCENT: No problem here—I got hands. Feel somethin' like a pig, takin' up your seat. *(He eats.)* Yer a orphan too, that it, Mr. Tomasin? You don't wanna talk it's okay you don't wanna talk. You have stew a lot, Mr. Tomasin? Armenians eat stew everyday? Stew and cake? I'm sorry for bein' here. I mean with you here. I didn't plan it—I ain't been this full for a year. Somebody gave us a bunch of dead gooses last Thanksgiving—at the orphanage, ate half a greasy goose and threw up. Coulda fed six kids with that mess. *(Laughs at his own joke.)* You got maybe a napkin er cloth er anything? *(Vincent's face is smeared with cake and frosting. He holds his chocolate hands up.)* I'm sorry yer a orphan. I don't wanna wipe my hands on yer clothes.

(Aram looks at him for a moment.)

VINCENT: I shure don't. You got some a the finest clothes I seen. Ever.

(Aram finds a cloth and places it on the table not far from Vincent. Vincent wipes his face and hands.)

VINCENT: Thanks. Thanks a lot. *(Vince stands and goes to the portrait.)* Why the heads gone outta these people, Mr. Tomasin? Someone chop their heads off?

ARAM: Yes.

VINCENT: I'm real interested in that camera, you know, in things. People. Places. Stuff. I'd like to have adventures. You're foreign, so I bet anything you had some real adventures. Hey, I can leave soon as I get my clothes. How's it all Armenians are orphans? You got somethin' needs done, I say do it. You don't have to take care a me. I make ya nervous? I ain't really a orphan. I got a mutha. Ya. she's inna place. A institution is what it's called.

(Pause. Aram looks at Vincent. Vincent smiles.)

VINCENT: I ain't a monkey. I can shut up.

(Aram sighs. Aram looks upstage. Aram puts his head in his hands. Very slowly, Vincent also puts his head in his hands. Several beats. Aram looks at Vincent. Aram lifts his head and drops his hands. Pause.

Vincent drops his hands and lifts his head. They are both looking out. Several beats. Aram looks.)

VINCENT: Mr. Tomasin. I can hear your breth. Ever, ever think, where the first one, the very first one come from? The very first breth to ever been breathed on the whole earth—now...listen...hear dat? Hear your breth? I like hearin' yours. Deep. Man breth.

(Aram studies him.)

VINCENT: What I think, what I think is—the breth, just the breth, it's an adventure all by itself, maybe when ya think a all the slimy pipes 'n organs 'n blood the air goes through, like a wet rat through a dark hole. Breathin's a adventure is what I think. Whad you think, Mr. Tomasin? You think breathin's a adventure, Mr. Tomasin?

(Aram looks at the boy. The lights fade as Vincent smiles. A brief pause and the Gentleman speaks.)

Scene Two

The Gentleman speaks to the audience.

GENTLEMAN: I had been off and on staying in St. Bartholomews when she picked me out. She tried so hard that first time to clean me up. Maybe it was to impress him. It was something for her to do; she had no babies and Mrs. Tomasian was somebody with a very busy mind. She stuck me into her life—in the middle of a Monday. What did I know? I thought, okay, funny Armenian lady. Okay. It was time away from scrounging garbage, time away from St. Bartholomews, where I would end up after I ran out of ideas. I hated St. Bartholomews, hated the Crucifixes hanging everywhere and the way a certain priest cooed at me. It was odd sitting there with him, Aram Tomasian. There was something crawling around inside him. Looking for a way out.

(Vincent, the Gentleman, finds a cake box and places it on the table.)

(Several weeks later. At rise, Seta is stacking large cake boxes (cakes inside). She is tired and warm. Flour smudges her apron. A sound outside. Seta removes the sweater from the portrait. Seta follows the sound and a moment later Vincent enters, cold and wrapping himself in his arms.

SETA: Vince. Vince, you're cold. Where is your coat? Vincent?
(*He paces, sputtering.*)

VINCENT: I came for the cakes. Just gimme the cakes, awright, Mrs. Tomasin. I don't wanna talk—just let me deliver…

SETA: And your hair, it's wet—

VINCENT: Ya, ya, it's wet, so it's wet, it's snowing, it's wet…kin I have the cakes? Ya, six cakes two trips. No big deal. (*He shivers, goes for the cakes.*)

SETA: What is wrong, Vincent?

VINCENT: Nuthin' Nuthin' ain't wrong—just lemme go. These ready?

SETA: (*Quickly.*) You have no coat, you're not—

VINCENT: I am! Can't you see? I'm ready. Kin I go? Hey, kin I—

SETA: Your hair is wet—no, you can't—

VINCENT: You want 'em delivered, don't ya? Just lemme go—

SETA: —go, look at yourself, shivering.

VINCENT: Just gimme the—

SETA: —listen, Vincent.

VINCENT: —cake, I kin take three atta time easy—

SETA: —to me. You are cold! Sit now and I'll get you a blanket.

VINCENT: No! Gimme the cakes, we gotta deal, okay? We gotta deal, my part is to deliver, so lemme deliver, Miss Tomasin. Lemme deliver!
(*Shouting, Vincent strains to hold back tears. Pause. Vincent shivers. Seta looks at him.*)

SETA: Now, tell me, what has happened to you? Vincent.

VINCENT: (*Straining.*) Goddam it. You don't wanna hear it. You don't wanna hear it.

SETA: I do. Very much, I do.

VINCENT: (*Pause.*) I hate that goddamn orphanage. Saint. Saint what? Saint goddam what?

SETA: Tell me.

VINCENT: (*Shuddering.*) Fath—Fath—Father Lewinski—I'm inna bathtub and he comes in there with that big cross he's got bouncing around and he don't say nothing', jus' gets a big teethy smile and a giggle and then he tries to yank me outta da tub…so so so I'm bangin' around tryin' to get out and he's grabbin' me but I'm slippery from the soap so I dodged outta der, and he don't want me naked all over da place, so he throws my clothes at me. I don't want no more shame…I don't want no more shame, Missus Tomasin. No more. I gotta mutha inna institution, I gotta father dead, ya know...I never screamed er cried er nuthin'...till now...till now.

(Seta has moved herself closer and closer until she holds him.)

SETA: Okay. Okay. You are good, Vincent. You are good.

VINCENT: My dad, he taught me not to cry at all and here I am, some dinky little boy bawlin'.

SETA: Boys cry. Men cry. If they don't do it outside, they do it inside... many times.

(She holds him and he pulls away.)

VINCENT: Jus lemme deliver the cakes, just lemme take the cakes—

SETA: Are you all right now?

VINCENT: I'm swell. I'm a damn boy scout.

SETA: It's too cold for you to be outside.

VINCENT: I can sneak into da basement at St. Bartholomews. I do it alla time. He don't come down there, Father Lewinski. He might get himself dirty.

SETA: You'll be cold—

VINCENT: I'll hug the furnace, okay, Missus Tomasin? Okay? Jus lemme go.

SETA: Not without a coat—I have a coat for you—my husband's—you just use it—here, let me. Here. *(She finds Aram's father's huge coat.)*

VINCENT: I can't wear that—

SETA: You can—

VINCENT: That coat's for an elephant, Missus Tomasin.

SETA: Vincent, you wear the coat.

VINCENT: *(Laughing.)* I'll be walkin' around inna tent.

SETA: Wear the coat.

(He takes the coat.)

VINCENT: Ya. *(He puts it on.)* Hey, looka me! Looka me!

(She laughs.)

VINCENT: See, you laugh! *(He stomps around.)* Poom. Poom. Poom.

(They laugh.)

VINCENT: I could keep a family in here—this ain't your husband's coat, is it?

SETA: He doesn't use it.

(He pulls the coat above his head.)

VINCENT: Hey. I'm gone—I disappeared— *(He stumbles around, then lunges at Seta and roars.)* Attack of the elephant boy!! Poom! Poom! Poom! Attack of the kid with no head.

(Aram enters.)
ARAM: What are you doing?
SETA: Vincent.
VINCENT: I'll devour all your cakes—Poom, poom—
ARAM: What are you doing?!?
(Vincent stops. He pokes his head out of the large coat.)
ARAM: Stop!
SETA: Aram—he is delivering cakes—-
ARAM: Take the coat off—
(Vincent begins to take the coat off. Aram speaks to Seta.)
ARAM: You ridicule my coat—
SETA: It is 20 degrees outside.
VINCENT: I'm sorry I—
ARAM: *(To Seta.)* You ridicule my father's coat—
SETA: You never wear it, Aram, so I thought—
ARAM: My father's coat!! *(Beat.)* An *odar*?!
SETA: —if you don't use it, Vincent could use it—
ARAM: Give me the coat—
(Vincent hands the coat to Aram.)
VINCENT: I don't need the coat. Missus Tomas—
SETA: You ask him to walk in this cold?
ARAM: I ask him nothing!! I expect my father's coat to be respected. It is
  what survived. It is what I have left.
VINCENT: Good. Right. I don't—
SETA: Aram, I have never seen you wear the coat.
ARAM: Then it is not for wearing, is it?
SETA: You strip a coat off a boy because…because…why? Because your
  father is dead?
ARAM: You raise your voice?
SETA: *(Tersely.)* How is this coat so sacred?…
ARAM: You raise your voice?!!!
  (A silence.)
SETA: I will get a sweater, Vincent.
VINCENT: I don't need it. I'll just go—
SETA: You will have a sweater. That is the least you will have.
  (She looks for a sweater. Aram holds the coat to himself.)
VINCENT: Hey. Hey. I'm sorry. Yer Dad's coat? I din't know. I gotta gold
  coin from my Dad—keep it stuck under my arm. I din't mean to
  make fun ya know—

(Aram sits.)

ARAM: You...you can wear the sweater.

VINCENT: Okay. I'd a brought a coat— 'cept I had to get away in a second—

(Seta returns and grabs Vincent and forces the sweater on him.)

VINCENT: Hey, whad I do? Hey!

SETA: I am going to button every button and I want you to wear this cap... *(She pushes a cap over his head.)* There. And there. Good.

VINCENT: Hey—It's a girl's sweater—this sweater is for a girl—

SETA: *(Hugging him fiercely.)* Shhh! Now you can go deliver my cakes. *(Seta holds on, then releases him.)* You come back with the money and I'll pay you.

VINCENT: Shure. The usual. Ya. Well, bye.

(Vincent leaves. Seta stares at Aram. Aram puts his father's coat on.)

ARAM: *(Pause.)* Do not raise your voice. Ever.

SETA: Yes. *(Pause. Gets hand mirror.)* Now you are wearing two coats. Do you see yourself?

(Holds mirror up to him, he turns away.)

Scene Three

The Gentleman speaks to the audience.

GENTLEMAN: Ya, ya—I remember that coat. Hey, even the feeling of being inside it. It made me feel so small, like a bug in a room. Each of us was clutching at things. I was clutching at life.

(As the lights come up, Aram is sitting at the table reading the Bible. Seta, in the same clothes as the previous scene, is ironing. She pounds the iron into the board with each stroke. After several moments, Aram pounds the Bible on the table. Silence Seta resumes pounding the iron. Aram goes to the portrait and returns with it to the table. He finds something on the portrait.)

ARAM: A piece of yarn. Blue.

(She studies it. Seta pounds the iron a little harder.)

ARAM: Seta, a piece of yarn. A blue piece of yarn. *(Silence.)* Seta, tell me, why is there yarn on my portrait?

SETA: Why?

ARAM: Seta, it is caught here, in a sliver of wood.

(She pounds the iron.)

ARAM: Have you been covering my portrait? Answer.

SETA: Yes.

ARAM: So I go back to work and then you cover my face and your face and my family?

SETA: *(Pounding the iron.)* Yes. I cover your portrait with the sweater Vincent had to wear today.

ARAM: You shun me?

SETA: No.

ARAM: But you cover my family.

SETA: I'm tired.

ARAM: Shunning. It is shunning.

SETA: The portrait is not you. The portrait is a picture with holes in it.

(She continues pounding the iron.)

ARAM: That's all? That's all it is to you? You don't have hope that we will have a child? Begin, begin to fill the holes?

SETA: Right now...right now, I have this iron and this shirt. Your shirt. And it is a great American shirt. So I am lucky. Lucky.

ARAM: Simple then. Simple. Don't cover my portrait.

SETA: *(Evenly.)* I...don't...want...to...look...at...it.

ARAM: Yes. Then don't. Don't cover it; don't look at it.

(She pounds the iron.)

ARAM: Leave it to itself. I am going to bed. *(Pause.)* Will you come soon?

SETA: I have another shirt.

ARAM: After the shirt, then? *(He hesitates.)*

SETA: I am using my Westinghouse iron which you gave me. And I thank you.

(He hesitates for a moment and then leaves. Immediately Seta slumps at the ironing board, taking deep breaths, gasping. She quickly leaps at the portrait, grabs it and holds it, ready to smash it against the table. She stops herself, drops the portrait on the floor and then goes for her doll. She sits with her doll, holds it, looks at it, throws it down fiercely, gets up and paces. She sees the exposed easel, looks at the doll, looks again at the easel, again at the doll, then quickly picks up the doll. She grabs the easel, puts it on the floor. She finds a candle, lights it, places it close to the easel. She finds a hammer, nails. She places the doll against the easel and pounds a nail into an arm and the easel. She

stands back and tries to compose herself; shaking, she puts a second nail into the other arm. Quickly, fiercely, she begins to pound a third nail into a leg. Aram enters and Seta keeps pounding.)

ARAM: Seta? Seta, what—what—

(She pounds.)

ARAM: Seta—listen—what are you doing?

(She pounds.)

ARAM: Are you—you are acting like a cra—

SETA: I am pounding nails.

ARAM: Don't do this.

(He grabs the hammer from her, she fights.)

ARAM: Stop! Now!!

SETA: I am not finished!

(He takes the hammer.)

ARAM: Is this a spell? You take the portrait off its stand—what? A candle? Pounding nails through a doll? You have worms in your brain?

(She picks up the easel, and stands it within his view.)

ARAM: Now I have a crazy wife? Now I have—

SETA: No.

ARAM: No, what no?—Look! You crucify a doll? You light a candle and put spikes through a doll—what, here you make an altar out of a crucified doll, here you kill a doll and then you worship it? It's shame—it is a disgrace!

SETA: It is.

ARAM: You agree?

SETA: Yes!

ARAM: You defile—

SETA: It is a disgrace like your portrait is a disgrace—

ARAM: My—

SETA: A grown man who cuts the heads off his murdered family—

ARAM: You can't—

SETA: I am! I am! A man who shows his murdered family like a trophy, cuts off their heads—

ARAM: Their heads were cut off by Turks—

SETA: And by you! And here sits the murdered family, here sits the dead family, holes for heads, sitting, staring with no eyes, day after day after day after day—

ARAM: A reminder—

SETA: You need a reminder? Of that? Your sister gone, you brother, gone, your mother, gone, your father, gone—but all the more here—

ARAM: Seta, don't—

SETA: Every second, their eyes I have never seen, they stare at me—I fill them in—who would not? I see them now, they are the eyes of mad people, terrible and bleeding and every second in front of me, every second behind me, every second waiting—you are not the only Armenian in all the world to have suffered, Mr. Tomasian. You're not the only Armenian—

ARAM: *(Angry.)* Seta, you can't talk like—

SETA: Yes, you are my husband, and I am grateful, but I am Armenian too, I am a dead person living too—and your parents were be—

ARAM: Don't say this—

SETA: I am going to say it. Your parents were beheaded and my mother was crucified because she would not betray her Bible, her God.

ARAM: I know this.

SETA: No, you do not know this. So some are beheaded and some are crucified and some are slaughtered, and who wins the battle of who died the worst death? Who wins? The one who wins is the one who worships death the best, yes? See this? *(Seta goes to the easel.)* My mother, crucified. I am at the altar of horror in the house of horror. We shall have ceremonies, we shall invite our foreign neighbors, we shall invite—

ARAM: You cannot do—

SETA: I am doing this, I have a stiff husband, a husband living in a casket, who has put all of his grief in a portrait—

ARAM: I can fill the holes!

SETA: How? *(Loudly.)* Your wife is barren, Mr. Tomasian!

ARAM: Not yet, maybe after a time—

SETA: *(Shouting.)* Barren!

ARAM: No!!

SETA: Yes. *(Pause.)* Yes.

    (Aram is quiet. He sits.)

SETA: So this is it. This is me. This is you. *(She indicates the doll, the portrait.)* This is all that we are.

ARAM: I cannot imagine you have said these things to me—

SETA: I cannot imagine I have not—I am your wife.

    (Silence. He looks at her.)

SETA: Now, after these years, years, you have never told me what happened to you—you brought me here—you put this *(indicating portrait)* in front of me and said fill it up, nothing else. And I talked for hours about how they took my father, put him in the Army, took his gun, made him their slave, and my mother, nailed into wood because she would not forsake her God and my sister raped because I was a child…I was left. Did you listen? Did you hear me? Did you hear that the person who is a wife is a person? I do not just do—make cakes! Sell cakes! Cook! Wash! Iron! Sew! Count money! Shop! Make your bed…and make your bed warm. I weep. I feel. I am not just a donkey, excuse me, forgive me, Mr. Tomasian.

(He stands and begins to walk away.)

ARAM: I won't hear any more of—

SETA: A picture with holes in it is not a life—

ARAM: I have never made you a donkey.

SETA: But I am sore like a donkey. I am tired like a donkey.

ARAM: I…give you this burden? Me? No, no.

SETA: *(Quietly.)* Your grief is so great you make me carry it—

ARAM: A lie—

SETA: You have the greatest grief and don't even know what it is—you are like a stone—everyday you live in silence—you have the greatest grief of all Armenians, if there was a contest, you would win it—and you say nothing.

ARAM: You don't know. You don't know me, Mrs. Tomasian. I talk! I talk all day! I am liked. All my customers, I treat them with respect. I give them their families…I am paid to make their children beautiful! *(Long pause.)* When they see their pictures they smile, because they see their children. Their beautiful children…and everyday I see their children…I see…their beautiful children. *(He is frightened.)* …the Italians, the Poles, they have so many—seven, eight children. Four sons, five sons…everyday I look at these beautiful children—and do you ever think of that, Seta, do you? Do you ever think of me there everyday looking at families I don't have? You tell me, Mrs. Tomasian, do you?

SETA: *(Quietly.)* No.

ARAM: *(Looking at the portrait.)* So this is my hope. Hope in a picture.

SETA: I didn't know.

ARAM: *(Trying to continue.)* I did it…I cut the holes…for hope…My father was lucky. He had a family. *(Pause.)* He made a place for me to hide—they put a hole in the floor, and I was to hide under my father's old coat. They told me to go there if anything happened and they stacked old blankets on top. In the night I heard the guns of the Turks. I slid underneath. There were shouts and shots and screaming—they poked at the pile of the blankets. The Turks were clumsy or lazy or drunk. They didn't find me. I lay for a long time, shivering…under my father's coat. When I came out, I was all wet, with urine, and sweat…there was blood…on the floor and the walls…on the ceilings, in the air. Oh, I ran into the backyard… outside…anywhere I thought, and then I saw…My mother had a line outside, for her wash, the Turks they had hung…they had hung…the heads of my family on the clothes…the clothesline. The heads of my family, in my backyard, next to my mother's wash.

SETA: *(Softly.)* Yes.

ARAM: Later, inside the lining of the coat I found the picture—and I carried the coat with me in a sack. I went with the neighbors and they made me dress like a girl. I was a skinny girl for a long time. Just a skinny girl. As a girl I was very ugly. In the lining of the coat—my father had left me some rare stamps—his collection. And later, I bribed some Arabs with one of them and then, later, bribed myself all the way to America…and bought a camera. I sat alone one night and made a new family picture, and wept to see them…coming alive in the chemicals, coming alive, Seta. 19 years old. I sat alone and looked at the picture coming alive in the chemicals and I took out a knife and cut out the heads of my father, Toros, my mother, Vartuhy, my little sister, Karin, and my brother Dickran…I cut out the heads of my family. I thought I could replace them. I really thought that's the way it would be. *(He clutches it.)* I thought…a wife…children…then I would forget. Completely. But I never forget. I never do.
(He falters. Seta crosses to him and kisses him gently, carefully, on the cheek.)

SETA: Okay. Okay, Aram Tomasian.
(She pulls his head to her chest, and he takes her hand as the lights fade.)

Scene Four

Aram and Seta put away the portrait, the easel, the doll. They exit.

GENTLEMAN: *Gar oo chugar.* There was and there was not. Days later, they put these away. Somewhere in the attic, where relics belong. I never saw the coat again. I slipped and dodged around until I settled into school and a life. They took me in. Nothing was said. Later, college—where I studied what people do to survive. After these anxious years of living as I do now, my wife gone, children in this place and that, I still see plainly certain days; each is a whole picture, unframed, but living in my head. As a boy, I was drawn to the man. I found reasons to be there. I won't forget the day I brought back the girlie sweater.

(The Senior Vincent hands the sweater to the Young Vincent, who takes it and bounds toward the doorway. The Senior Vincent stands apart and watches.* Aram sits at the table hunched over, intent on his stamp collector's book. His back is to the doorway and Young Vincent knocks.)

ARAM: Yes. Come.

(Vincent enters.)

VINCENT: Oh…I remembered the sweater.

ARAM: Okay. Put it there.

(Aram indicates the chair. Vincent brings the sweater to the chair.)

VINCENT: Missus Tomasin's not here?

(Aram holds the book to the light.)

ARAM: She went to the Binetti's store.

(Vincent watches Aram, who holds tweezers.)

VINCENT: Oh. Uh, watcha got?

ARAM: It is a book for stamps.

VINCENT: Ya? Hey, you got a hobby?

ARAM: My father did.

VINCENT: So'd my Pop—he collected coins. I still got one.

ARAM: I know.

VINCENT: Ya? Oh ya.

(Vincent has gradually edged himself closer to Aram's work. Aram notices and offers Vincent a look.)

FOOTNOTE: **If one actor plays both the senior and the younger Vincent, the older Vincent simply carries the sweater with him.*

VINCENT: Mr. Tomasin, you ain't got any stamps! Gol. All you got is holes. Just spaces.

(Aram waits.)

VINCENT: Hey, you got all these holes to fill! Wait, no…hey, you got one. Mr. Tomasin, one ain't a collection.

(Aram smiles and Vincent sees the smile.)

VINCENT: Well, it ain't.

ARAM: I have one, and one is a start.

VINCENT: Ya. Kin I see?

(Aram gives him the magnifying glass.)

VINCENT: This stamp really valuable?

ARAM: Yes.

VINCENT: Why's it you have only the one?

(Aram looks at the stamp book.)

VINCENT: I say somethin—

ARAM: I had many, I sold them.

VINCENT: You did? Why?

ARAM: To live. *(Pause.)*

VINCENT: *(Agreeing.)* Shure.

ARAM: There is something for you—there, underneath—on the chair.

VINCENT: Me?

ARAM: You. Go. Go. *(Aram concentrates on the stamp book with the magnifying glass.)*

VINCENT: *(Finding a box.)* Gol.*(Pause.)*

ARAM: It can be opened.

(Vincent scrambles and opens the box to find a coat.)

VINCENT: Wow. This is swell. I'm taking this off. *(He takes off his soiled coat.)* Whew! A whole new coat. Looka me!

ARAM: It should be warm. *(A smile.)*

VINCENT: I'm like a new person.

(He struts. Seta enters with groceries.)

VINCENT: Hey, Missus Tomasin, looka my coat!

SETA: I see. Oh, I see. Very special. *(She beams.)* Very special, Aram.

ARAM: *(Beat.)* Yes.

SETA: *(To Aram.)* I think we could have a picture; what do you think?

ARAM: I think we could. We could.

VINCENT: Ya? Hey, looka me, I'm a swell.

(Aram moves to the camera.)

ARAM: There. In front of the table.

(Vincent and Seta come together.)

ARAM: Okay. Good. Small smile now…and hold—

SETA: Aram, why don't you join?

ARAM: Me? *(Beat.)* Me? *(Long pause, Aram is a little lost.)*

VINCENT: Hey, ya. You can do that?

SETA: Just carry the cord, Aram.

(Aram hesitates, then decides. The Gentleman moves to take Aram's place at the camera. Seta and Vincent smile. Aram starts a very small smile and takes the picture. The lights go black, except a quiet spot on the Gentleman at the camera.* The light fades.)

END OF PLAY

Footnote: **If one actor is playing both the Gentleman and Vincent, the lights fade gradually on all three.*

July 7, 1994
by Donald Margulies

This play, at long last, is for Lynn Street.

BIOGRAPHY

Donald Margulies was born in Brooklyn, New York in 1954. His plays include *Sight Unseen* (1992 Obie Award for Best New American Play, Dramatists Guild/Hull-Warriner Award, Pulitzer Prize finalist, Drama Desk Award nominee, a Burns Mantle "Best Play"); *The Loman Family Picnic* (Drama Desk Award nominee, a Burns Mantle "Best Play"); *Pitching to the Star* (included in *Best American Short Plays 1992-93*); *Found a Peanut*, *Zimmer*, and *Luna Park* (loosely based on "In Dreams Begin Responsibilities" by Delmore Schwartz). *What's Wrong With This Picture?* was produced on Broadway in 1994, and *The Model Apartment*, for which he received a Drama-Logue Award during its world premiere at Los Angeles Theatre Center, will have its New York premiere at Primary Stages in October 1995. His one-act play, *July 7, 1994*, which was commissioned by Actors Theatre of Louisville, premiered in ATL's Humana Festival of New American Plays in 1995. His adaptation of Sholem Asch's Yiddish classic, *God of Vengeance*, will debut in 1996 at Long Wharf Theatre. Mr. Margulies's plays have premiered at Manhattan Theatre Club, South Coast Repertory, The New York Shakespeare Festival, and the Jewish Repertory Theatre. He has won grants from CAPS, The New York Foundation for the Arts, The National Endowment for the Arts, and the John Simon Guggenheim Memorial Foundation. A collection of his work, *Sight Unseen and Other Plays*, will be published by Theatre Communications Group in the fall of 1995. Mr. Margulies is a member of New Dramatists and was elected to the council of the Dramatists Guild in 1993. He has been a playwright-in-residence four times at the Sundance Institute Playwrights' Lab in Utah and a frequent contributor to The 52nd Street Project. His current projects include new play commissions for South Coast Repertory, The Mark Taper Forum, and Actors Theatre of Louisville. He lives with his wife, Lynn Street, a physician, and their son, Miles, in New Haven, Connecticut, where he is a visiting lecturer in playwriting at the Yale School of Drama.

AUTHOR'S NOTE

The one-act play is a beautiful form that, like the best of short fiction, can speak volumes about people and time and place in a concise way. (The stories of Raymond Carver come to mind as models of spareness and specificity.) But despite the pleasures and challenges inherent in the one-act, it has become a fairly scarce commodity; few theaters will produce them so few are written. So, when Actors Theatre of Louisville asked me to write an hour-long play for the 1995 Humana Festival, I leapt at the opportunity.

With rehearsals slated to begin in the winter of 1995, I began writing during the previous summer. The unusually swift course from page to stage (barely six months) inspired me to try something I'd always wanted to do: Write a play that captured the essence of the specific time in which it was written, and create a microcosm of life in America in the desperate, final decade of the millennium.

But being a writer, my days are unmomentous and the view from where I sit fairly bucolic. So I decided to view the world through the experiences of my wife, a physician in a community health care clinic. Through the heartache and banality of a typical day's work, I set out to make a time capsule.

I started writing the play on July 7, 1994. This is what I wrote.

ORIGINAL CAST

July 7, 1994 was first performed at the 1995 Humana Festival of New American Plays, March 1995. It was directed by Lisa Peterson with the following cast:

Kate	Susan Knight
Mark	Kenneth L. Marks
Señora Soto	Miriam Cruz
Ms. Pike	Myra Taylor
Mr. Caridi	Edward Hyland
Paula	Sandra Daley

CHARACTERS

KATE: A general internist in her late 30s, and Mark, her husband, an academic, also in his 30s, are both white.

KATE'S PATIENTS

SEÑORA SOTO: In her 40s, is Hispanic.

MS. PIKE: In her 30s, five months pregnant, is black.

MR. CARIDI: In his 40s, is white.

and PAULA: In her 30s, very thin, is black.

Special thanks to Lourdes Alvarez.

July 7, 1994

The settings are the bedroom and living room of a modest house, and an examination room and waiting area in a community health clinic, both located in a small northeastern city. A television set facing away from the audience is watched by patients in the waiting area.

The play's action takes place on a single day, July 7, 1994.

The play is to be performed without blackouts. As each scene ends the character from the next scene should take his or her place; the transitions should be as seamless as possible, like the way the dissolve is use in film. At the start of each scene, the time of day is projected and soon fades from view.

In the black, a slide is projected: July 7, 1994

When that slide fades out, another is projected: 6:42 AM.

Kate and Mark are in bed. She is having a dream, whimpering in her sleep. Mark is awakened by the sounds and gently shakes her.

MARK: Kate? Honey?

(Kate awakens with a slight start.)

KATE: What.

MARK: You were dreaming.

KATE: *(Still sleepy.)* Oh, yeah, I was.

MARK: Do you remember?

KATE: *(Recollecting.)* I was dreaming about Matthew. Oh, God, it was terrible.

MARK: What. Tell me.

KATE: There was a flood.

MARK: Yeah…?

KATE: The house was flooded. There was water everywhere. It left these red water marks on the walls.

MARK: *Red* water marks? Are you sure it wasn't blood?

KATE: Maybe it *was* blood. Yeah, you're right, it *was* blood. And all the furniture was floating around in it, and all the books. And we were wading through it, you and I, it was kind of fun almost, we were sort of enjoying ourselves, this pool in the living room, and suddenly I got this terrible feeling: Where was Matthew? We forgot about the baby! We'd left him up in the nursery! And the water, the blood, was rising, it was going up the stairs, soon the whole house was gonna be flooded, and I was trying to make it up the stairs to get to him but the current was so strong and I was really panic-stricken, it was awful, I thought I wasn't going to make it up the stairs to save him.

MARK: Did you?

KATE: I don't know; you woke me up.

MARK: Sorry.

KATE: *(Pause.)* Do you have dreams like that?, that Matthew's in distress and you can't reach him?

MARK: Oh, all the time.

KATE: There's some encroaching catastrophe and no matter what you do to protect him, it's no use?

MARK: Sometimes I have these morbid daydreams.

KATE: Really?

MARK: These flashes of dread that something terrible is going to happen to him, something out of my control.

KATE: You really do? You mean it's not just me.

MARK: Oh, no, I imagine him falling down the stairs, cracking his head open in the park, breaking free of my hand and running into traffic…

KATE: What *is* it with us? We weren't always such morbid people.

MARK: We weren't parents before. Oh, God, I just remembered.

KATE: What.

MARK: This dream I had the other night. I was standing, holding Matthew…at the Nicole Simpson murder scene.

KATE: Oh, God! You're kidding.

MARK: No. We were there. Like we beamed-up on Bundy in our pajamas. I was shielding his eyes; I didn't want him to see. I held his face against my shoulder. But *I* could see, very clearly, what was going on. We were invisible; I mean, I saw us standing in that courtyard but they couldn't see us. And it was horrifying. I mean, I saw it all, all the stuff we saw and read about—

KATE: We have to stop watching T.V. Let's get rid of the T.V.

MARK: *(Over "Let's get rid...")* Nicole's standing there barefoot, arguing with him, and O.J.'s completely mad, sweating, shouting...

KATE: You're sure it was O.J.?

MARK: Oh, yeah, and I see he's wearing those gloves, and the fighting escalates, and all of a sudden the knife comes out—it was very fast—and I hear it cut into her throat like, like he's slicing open a melon.

(She winces.)

MARK: And I'm still clutching the baby to me hoping he won't hear or see anything. And then Ron Goldman comes along, he happens up the path to deliver the sunglasses, and stumbles onto this horrible scene going on and he puts up an incredible struggle. I mean, it was fierce. And I'm crying because I'm powerless and it's so upsetting to see. I'm watching these people lose their lives and there's nothing I can do to stop it. Their blood is trickling down the cobblestones like a creek.

(Pause.)

KATE: You know, maybe we really *should* think about getting rid of the T.V. Look what it's doing to our dreams, it's poisoning our dreams.

MARK: I'm not getting rid of that set, we just bought that set.

KATE: Then let's shut it away somehow. Matthew's at that age when kids begin to absorb everything. I don't want him *look*ing at some of that stuff. What's it gonna do to *his* dreams?

MARK: What are you gonna do? There's nothing you can do. It's out there. It's not gonna go away. Unless you want to turn him into the bubble-boy or something. I mean, the kid *is* gonna go to school one day, right?

(Pause. Off, Baby Matthew, announcing that he's up calls, "Momma...Dad-dy..." Mark starts to get up.)

MARK: Well, whataya know...I'll go, you go back to sleep; you've got a long day.

KATE: *(over "...a long day.")* No, no, I'll go, you stay...Stay.

(She kisses him, gets out of the bed and exits for the nursery. Mark pulls the cover over his head and tries to go back to sleep.)

Transition
A slide is projected: 9:25 am.

(As the previous scene ends, Señora Soto, sad demeanor, comes into the examination room, takes off her blouse, hangs it up, puts on a johnny coat and, with her handbag on her lap, sits and waits. Soon, Kate enters. Kate's Spanish is purposely halting and erratic while Señora Soto's is flawless, even poetic. Sentences that are bracketed and printed in italics are projected as surtitles.)

KATE: I'm sorry, Señora Soto, our translator, nuestro translatora, Loida Martinez, ¿conoces Loida Martinez? ¿la mujer que translata aqui?
(Señora shrugs.)

KATE: Well, I thought she was in today but ella es enferma hoy, she's out sick, no aquí, so you're going to have to bear with me, okay? Mi espanol no es muy bien, okay?
(Señora shrugs.)
So, this dolor, tell me about this pain. ¿Cuando dolor? *[When do you feel it?]*

SEÑORA: ¿Cuando?

KATE: Sí. Do you feel it…upon exertion? al exertione…?

SEÑORA: No comprendo.

KATE: Sorry. ¿Tienes dificultad caminando? *[Do you have difficulty walking?]* "Shortness of breath"?
(Señora shakes her head in apologetic uncomprehension; Kate demonstrates shortness of breath.)

KATE: ¿Cuantos cuadros puedes caminar? *[How many picture frames can you walk?]*
(Señora is utterly confused.)

KATE: Outside, afuera how far caminar antes before you get tired? How do you say, ¿como se dice "tired"? Um…*(She thinks.)* cansado. How many blocks? ¿Cuantos cuadros?

SEÑORA: Oh! ¿Cuadras? ¿Cuantas cuadras? *[Blocks? How many blocks?]*

KATE: Sí. Cuadras.

SEÑORA: *(A torrent of words.)* Mi vecindario es bien malo, ¿cuándo camino? *[My neighborhood is so bad, when do I walk?]* Camino a la parada de la guagua y ruego que me dejen en paz. *[I walk to the bus stop and pray to be left in peace.]* Used debería ver lo que está pasando en las calles. *[You should see what's happening on the streets.]* ¡Las cosas que occurren, debajo de nuestras narices! *[The things that go on, right under our noses!]*

KATE: *(During the above.)* Señora…Slow…Slow…Despacio, por favor…

SEÑORA: *(Continuous.)* Yo recuerdo cuando la gente se protegía. *[I remember when people took care of one another.]* Ahora nadie piensa en nada más que sí mismo. *[Now nobody thinks about anyone but himself.]* Te matan antes de saludarte. *[They'd sooner kill you than say hello.]*

KATE: Señora…En la mañana, in the morning, ¿sí?, ¿lavantas con dolor? *[Do you wake up with pain?]*

SEÑORA: Me despierto con dolor, me acuesto con dolor. *[I wake up with pain, I go to sleep with pain.]*

KATE: Cuando diga "dolor," ¿quiere decir "dolor," o quiere…? *[When you say pain, do you mean "pain," or do you…?]*

SEÑORA: ¡Quiero decir dolor! ¡Dolor! ¡Dolor! *[I mean pain! Pain! Pain!]*

KATE: Okay. The pain, el dolor, ¿es un dolor…"sharp"?
(Señora shrugs; she doesn't understand.)
"Sharp?" ¿Como un…cuch…cuchillo? *[Like a knife?]* Or "heavy"… ¿Como una roca sobre su pecho? *[Like a rock on your chest.]*

SEÑORA: *(Another torrent.)* ¡Me siento como que muero! *[I feel like I'm going to die!]* ¡Como que mi corazón va a explotar en mi pecho y me voy a ahogar en mi propia sangre! *[Like my heart is going to burst inside my chest and I'm going to drown in my own blood!]* ¿Es posible eso? ¿Puede eso pasar, Señora doctora? *[Is that possible? Can that happen, Doctor?]*

KATE: *(Over "Como que mi corazón…")* No comprendo. Más despacio. Por favor. Señora, slow down, por favor. No comprendo cuando habla tan rápido. *[I can't understand when you talk so fast.]*

SEÑORA: Sí. Okay. Sorry.

KATE: Let me listen to your heart, okay?, I need to escuchar su corazón. Okay?
(Señora doesn't understand; Kate indicates the stethoscope.)

KATE: May I?

SEÑORA: Oh. Sí, sí.
(Kate listens to her chest, first the front, then the back.)

KATE: Okay. Respira grande. Big.
(Kate demonstrates; Señora complies.)

KATE: Good. Otra vez. Good, bueno. Again. Bueno. ¿Un otro respira grande? Good. *(Listens carefully.)* ¿Otra vez? Bueno. Gracias. *(Beat.)* ¿Señora, hay una historia de enfermedad de corazón en su familia? *[Is there a history of heart disease in your family?]* ¿Problemas de corazón?

SEÑORA: *(Another torrent.)* Mi mamá perdió una hija, una hijita. *[My mother lost a child, a little girl.]* Un ángel. Mi hermanita. *[An angel. My little sister.]* Y mi santa madre se murió en menos de un año. *[And my sainted mother died in less than a year.]* Se le partió el corazón. *[Her heart was broken.]* El doro fué tan tremendo que su corazón no pudo aguantarlo. *[The pain was so great, her heart could not bear it.]* *(She cries.)* ¡Anhelo a mis hijos! *[I miss my children!]*

KATE: ¿Qué?

SEÑORA: ¡Mis hijos! ¡Mis hijos! ¡Extraño a mis hijos! *[My children! My children! I miss my children!]*

KATE: ¿Dónde están tus hijos? *[Where are your children?]*

SEÑORA: En Puerto Rico.

KATE: ¿Por qué son en Puerto Rico? *[Why are they in Puerto Rico?]*

SEÑORA: Los mandé a vivir con mi abuela. *[I sent them to live with my grandmother.]* Mi abuela los están criando. *[My grandmother is raising them.]* Son pobres pero están seguros—más seguros de lo que estarían aquí. *[They're poor but they're safe—safer than they would be here.]* La cuidad no es lugar para los niños. *[The city is no place for children.]*

KATE: ¿Tu esposo...? *[Your husband...?]*
(Señora shrugs, speaking volumes.)

KATE: ¿Por que no regresas? *[Why don't you go back?]*

SEÑORA: ¿A Puerto Rico?

KATE: Sí.

SEÑORA: No puedo. *[I can't.]* Lo poco que gano aquí es mucho más de lo que podría ganar allá. *[The little I make here is much more than I could make there.]*

KATE: What do you do? ¿Qué...haces?

SEÑORA: ¿Conoces el Maritime Center? *[Do you know the Maritime Center?]*

KATE: ¿Sí?

SEÑORA: Limpo oficinas. *[I clean offices.]* Todo lo que gano se lo mando a ellos. *[Everything I make I send to them.]* Quiero que vayan a la universidad. *[I want them to go to college.]* Vivo sin nada. *[I live on *nothing.]* Alguien tiene que trabajar. *[Somebody has to work.]* Mi abuela está muy vieja ahora. *[My grandmother is very old now.]* No puede trabjar. *[She can't work.]* Si yo volviera, nos moriríamos de hambre. *[If I went back we all would starve.]*

KATE: *(Overlap, calming.)* Señora, Señora…*(Beat.)* Creo que está depresada. *[I think you are depressed.]*

SEÑORA: ¿Comó?

KATE: Depresada. "Down." Abajo, ¿no? "Sad." ¿Como se dice "sad"? *(Thinks.)* ¿Triste?

SEÑORA: ¿Triste? Por supuesto estoy triste. Estoy muy triste. Mi vida es triste. *[Sad? Of course I'm sad. I'm very sad. My life is sad.]* ¿Por qué no estaría triste? *[Why shouldn't I be sad?]* No sería humana si no estuviera triste. *[I wouldn't be human if I weren't sad.]* Sería un animal. Un perro. Un perro en la calle. *[I would be an animal. A dog. A dog in the streets.]*

KATE: Señora, I can give you a drug…Te puedo dar una medicina para…animar tus espíritus. *[I can give you a medicine to raise your ghosts.]*

SEÑORA: *(Confused.)* ¡¿Para qué?!

KATE: To raise your spirits. Una medicina para hacerte menos triste. *[A medicine to make you less sad.]* Para elevar tu…"mood." A mood elevator. ¿Comprende? Para hacerte contenta. *[To make you happy.]*

SEÑORA: ¿Una droga para que sea contenta? *[A drug to make me happy?]*

KATE: Sí.

SEÑORA: ¿Una píldora? *[A pill?]*

KATE: Sí.

SEÑORA: ¿Para qué? ¿Por qué tomaría una píldora para estar contenta? *[For what? Why would I take a pill to make me happy?]* ¿Me sanaría el corazón? *[Would it heal my heart?]* Mi corazón está deshecho con razón. *[My heart is broken for a reason.]* ¿Cómo querría olvidarme por qué está deshecho mi corazón? *[Why would I want to forget why my heart is broken?]*

KATE: *(Overlap.)* Señora, estoy tratando de ayudarle. *[I'm trying to help you.]*

SEÑORA: *(Continuous.)* Mi corazón está herido. Tengo el corazón herido. *[My heart is broken. I have a broken heart.]*

KATE: I'm trying to help you, ayudarle, to offer some sort of solution.

SEÑORA: *(Continuous.)* ¡Tengo dolor, Señora doctora! *[I have pain, Doctor!]*

KATE: ¿Quiere ir al hospital? *[Do you want to go to the hospital?]*

SEÑORA: ¡¿Hospital?!¡ No, no, ningún hospital.

KATE: *(Continuous.)* ¿Quiere ir al "emergency room"?

SEÑORA: No, no emergency room.

KATE: Señora, if you go to the hospital, they can do a stress test, "un stress test."

SEÑORA: Nada de hospital... *(Makes ad-libbed rambling protestations during the following.)*

KATE: Señora, I think you may be depressed. ¿Comprende? ¿Señora? Señora, I think you, I think it's possible depression is causing your symptoms but I'm not sure. Pueden hacer un test para ver cómo responde su corazón al "stress." *[They can give you a test to see how your heart responds to stress.]*

SEÑORA: *(Overlap.)* No, no...

KATE: Then what do you want? What can I do? *(Refers to her chart.)* Señora, veo que doctor Leventhal referió tú a la clínica hispánica para "counseling" para depresión. *[I see Dr. Leventhal referred you to the Clinica Hispanica for counseling for depression.]* ¿Fué a la consultación? *[Did you go for a consultation?]*

SEÑORA: No estoy loca. *[I'm not crazy.]*

KATE: Nobody said you were crazy.

SEÑORA: *(Continuous.)* Mi vida es una miseria. *[My life is miserable.]* ¿Es extraño que tenga un dolor en el corazón? *[Is it any wonder I have a pain in my heart?]* Mire a mi vida. *[Look at my life.]* Mire lo que he perdido. *[Look at what I've lost.]* Mire lo que he tenido que sacrificar. *[Look at what I've had to give up.]* Mire cuán duro trabajo por unos centavos, para nada. *[Look at how hard I work for pennies, for nothing.]* Mire a mi vida. *[Look at my life.]* No necesito un psiquiatra para decirme que mi vida es dura. *[I don't need a psychiatrist to tell me my life is hard.]* Lo sé. *[I know.]*

KATE: Señora, es muy importante. You need to follow up on your appointment at the Clínica Hispánica. Okay? I think the psychiatrist can help you. I am not a psychiatrist. Es muy importante. Okay? But if the pain comes back, si el dolor regresa, I mean very strong, muy fuerte, ¿llamas la clínica? *[Will you call us here at the clinic?]*

SEÑORA: *(Shrugs.)* Lo que usted quiera. *[Whatever you want.]*

KATE: It's not what *I* want, it's what you need to do.

SEÑORA: Sí, sí.

KATE: Señora, I'm sorry…Tengo que ver otros pacientes ahora. *[I'm going to have to see other patients now.]* I'm very sorry. I hope you're feeling better.

(Señora nods, turns away from Kate, silently removes the johnny coat, puts her shirt back on. As she goes:)

KATE: I'm sorry.

Transition

A slide is projected: 12:08 pm.

(Kate is now removing stitches from the palm of a woman's hand. Ms. Pike is black, in her thirties, five months pregnant.)

MS. PIKE: Ow!

KATE: Sorry.

(Ms. Pike groans in pain.)

KATE: I'm trying not to hurt you, I'm sorry.

MS. PIKE: How many more you got?

KATE: Just a few. *(Pause.) What* happened exactly?

MS. PIKE: Hm?

KATE: *How'd* you hurt your hand?

MS. PIKE: I told you, I don't know, I cut it.

KATE: How?

MS. PIKE: Kitchen.

KATE: Yeah, I know, how?

MS. PIKE: Accident. You know. Damn! Could you not hurt me so much?

KATE: I'm sorry.

MS. PIKE: This gonna take long? 'Cause I got to pick up my daughter.

KATE: I just need to dress it; there's some infection. *(Silence while she attends to her.)* So, have you been following this O.J. thing?

MS. PIKE: Oh, yeah, are you kidding? There's nothing else on. Day and night. I'm really getting sick of it, too: O.J., O.J., O.J.…

KATE: So what do you think?

MS. PIKE: What do I think?, you mean did he do it?

KATE: Yeah, do you think he did it?

MS. PIKE: Nah, I think it's all a frame-up.

KATE: You do? Really?

MS. PIKE: Oh, yeah. You can be sure, a famous *white* man, they find *his* wife dead, they ain't gonna be all over *him.*

KATE: Oh, I don't know, a history of abuse? I'm sure the ex-husband is the first one they look for, no matter who he is.

MS. PIKE: *(Over "who he is".)* Oh, I don't know about that.

KATE: Who would want to frame him?

MS. PIKE: You'd be surprised.

KATE: No, who? I mean, it would have to be a pretty elaborate frame-up, don't you think? Dripping his blood, planting the gloves?

MS. PIKE: They got nothing on him.

KATE: You don't think?

MS. PIKE: No way.

KATE: The blood in the Bronco?, the blood at the scene?, the blood in his driveway...?

MS. PIKE: *(Over "in his driveway".)* So what? Did anybody see him do it?

KATE: Well...

MS. PIKE: *(Continuous.)* Did anybody *see* him? No. How do you know it wasn't some mugger who did it? Hm? How do you know it wasn't someone out to get O.J.? You don't know that and neither do I. It could've been some Charles Manson thing. You don't know.

KATE: Do you think the judge is going to allow that evidence?

MS. PIKE: She better not.

KATE: Why?!

MS. PIKE: It's illegal! The cops broke the law when they hopped the wall! They had no right!

KATE: Don't you think they had just cause for entering the premises? The Bronco was on the street.

MS.. PIKE: *(Over "The Bronco...")* They didn't have a warrant! They had no warrant! They can't just break into somebody's house...

KATE: But the circumstantial evidence is pretty overwhelming, don't you think? I mean, don't you think there's sufficient cause for him to stand trial?

MS. PIKE: Those L.A. cops, they just want to get themselves one more nigger.

KATE: Why would they want to get O.J. Simpson?

MS. PIKE: Why?! Why?! Honey, what country do *you* live in?

KATE: *(Beat.)* But I think you're confusing the issue; the issue is not about race.

MS. PIKE: Not about race? Sure it's about race. Everything's about race. *This* is about race. *(Meaning their exchange.)*

KATE: *(Beat.)* Maybe I'm hopelessly naive.

MS. PIKE: Maybe you are. Maybe you are. *(Beat.)* I don't know, all I know is, if he *did* do it, if he *did,* you can be sure she pushed him.

KATE: Pushed him?, how do you mean?

MS. PIKE: *Pushed* him. I bet she got him so mad…her with her sexy clothes, waving her titties around, hanging out with those pretty boy models. I bet she got him plenty mad with her ways.

KATE: What ways?

MS. PIKE: Screwing around. She screwed everything in sight, that girl.

KATE: How do you know?

MS. PIKE: She was a tramp. That's what they say.

KATE: Who says?

MS. PIKE: All the papers. That's what you read. She drove him crazy with jealousy. That was her hold on him. I know women like this. That's how they keep their men. My sister is like this.

KATE: But she was trying to break away. She was finally on her own. It's classic, you know, when battered women—

MS. PIKE: Who said she was battered? You don't know. How do you know that? You don't know what goes on in the privacy of their own home.

KATE: *(Continuous, over the above.)* —break away, when they finally break away, that's when their husbands lose it, that's when they get killed. The cops were called to their house on several occasions, she said she was afraid he was going to kill her.

MS. PIKE: Yeah?, if she was so afraid, she should've gotten the hell out of town.

KATE: Oh, come on.—

MS. PIKE: She should've moved.

KATE: *(Continuous, over the above.)* —Take her kids out of school?, away from their family and friends? He would've tracked her down anywhere.

MS. PIKE: Ah, she was too busy spending his money to leave. Too busy shopping Beverly Hills.

KATE: Did you hear that 911 tape?

MS. PIKE: Yeah, I heard it.

KATE: And? What did you think about that?

MS. PIKE: What do I think? I think they had a fight. So what? Lots of folks have fights. Doesn't mean he killed her.

KATE: Yeah, but you heard it. That was rage, pure and simple. She was terrified.

MS. PIKE: I heard the reason he was so mad? He walked in on her and some guy going down on him in the living room.

KATE: Where'd you hear that?

MS. PIKE: Waiting in line Stop 'n Shop, one of those papers. They got sound experts to pick up what he's yelling in the background? He was yelling about her and this guy Keith.

KATE: Who's Keith?

MS. PIKE: *(Shrugs.)* Some guy she was cheating with.

KATE: Wait a second, they were already divorced. She was his ex-wife, she could have sex with whomever she liked. That's not cheating. She was a single woman. And what if she *did* have sex with these guys? Does that mean she deserved to be bludgeoned to death because she was promiscuous?

(Ms. Pike makes a scoffing sound; beat.)

KATE: What are you saying? She deserved it?

(Silence.)

MS. PIKE: All I'm saying…O.J. had no business marrying her in the first place. *If* you know what I mean.

(Silence.)

KATE: When your boyfriend hits *you*, do *you* deserve it?

MS. PIKE: What?! Who said my boyfriend hits me?

(Kate looks at her as if to say, "You can level with me." Long pause.)

MS. PIKE: It's not the same.

KATE: Why not?

MS. PIKE: Oh, man…

KATE: Why isn't it?

MS. PIKE: 'Cause it's not, okay? *(Beat.)* We got into a fight about the kids, that's all.

KATE: What about the kids?

MS. PIKE: I don't know, he started yelling at them about something. I got worried.

KATE: What were you worried about?

MS. PIKE: I was worried he might hit them.

KATE: Why was he yelling at them?

MS. PIKE: What are all these questions?! They were bad, okay?

KATE: Uh huh. What were they doing that was so bad?

MS. PIKE: Yelling and screaming and stuff. *You* know. Talking back.

KATE: Does he hit the kids? I mean, generally?

MS. PIKE: Sometimes.

KATE: Does he hit them hard?

MS. PIKE: Sometimes he'll smack them around, yeah.

KATE: What do you mean by smack them around?

MS. PIKE: Smack them around, *you* know.

KATE: *Does* he smack them? Or punch them?

MS. PIKE: Yeah, smack them, punch them. Just to scare them, you know?

KATE: Uh huh. And does he?

MS. PIKE: Oh, yeah! Sometimes, he'll, *you* know, *use* things.

KATE: *Use* things? What do you mean?

MS. PIKE: Throw things. *You* know, plates, stuff, whatever's there. Once he threw the cat at my son.

KATE: The cat?!

MS. PIKE: *(Continuous.)* Didn't like the way he talked to him?, picked up the cat?, right across the room. I couldn't believe it. You should've seen: scratches all over his face and stuff.

KATE: Sounds pretty bad.

MS. PIKE: *(Shrugs.)* He got the message, though, my son.

KATE: I don't know…Seems to me there are other ways of getting the message across.

MS. PIKE: You got to do *some* thing. I mean, when he hits them, they deserve it. Oh, man, they deserve it alright.

KATE: Why do they deserve it?

MS. PIKE: They're out of control. You should see. They are out of control. They need discipline. They need it. *My* father did it. Otherwise, you know how kids get, they walk all over you. *Some* body's got to take control, show them who's the boss.

KATE: So you were worried he was going to hit the kids, but you say they deserved it? I don't get it.

MS. PIKE: *(Over "get it.")* I was worried he'd get carried away. *You* know.

KATE: Are they his kids?

MS. PIKE: No, no. *This* one's his, though. *(Meaning her pregnancy.)*

KATE: I see. *(Beat.)* So, you got into a fight over the kids, he picked up a knife, started waving it around, and you got cut.

MS. PIKE: It was an accident. He didn't mean it.

KATE: No, you just happened to walk into it.

MS. PIKE: He was mad. He just wanted to scare me.

KATE: "Scare" you? Does he hit you a lot?

MS. PIKE: No! Not a lot. Sometimes. Sometimes he'll, *you* know, give me a punch if I do something he don't like.

KATE: Like what? What could you possibly do to warrant a punch?

MS. PIKE: *(Over "to warrant a punch?")* Could be anything. What I cooked, what I say. He don't like it when I talk back.

KATE: That sounds pretty difficult.

(Ms. Pike shrugs.)

KATE: I mean, you never know when you might set him off.

MS. PIKE: Oh, I have a pretty good idea.

KATE: He just went after you with a knife!

MS. PIKE: *(Shrugs.)* Yeah, well…I interfered.—

KATE: You what?!

MS. PIKE: *(Continuous.)* —I shouldn't've.

KATE: Is that what he told you?

MS. PIKE: No, it's the truth. I should've butt out. It was none of my business. He had words with the kids, I should've butt out.

KATE: *(Over "I should've butt out.")* They're your children! Ms. Pike! This man is abusing you and your children!

MS. PIKE: What, you're gonna lecture me now?

KATE: Why would you, why would anyone deserve to be hit?

MS. PIKE: In his eyes I do.

KATE: I'm not talking about his eyes.

MS. PIKE: I mean, the way he sees it, I do something pisses him off, wham.

KATE: Yeah, but do *you* feel you deserve it?

MS. PIKE: I'm used to it by now.

KATE: That's not what I'm asking.

MS. PIKE: It's the way it is. If that's the way it has to be…

KATE: It doesn't have to be that way, there are people you can talk to, you know, agencies.

MS. PIKE: *(Over "agencies.")* Shit…

KATE: *(Continuous.)* I can walk you over to meet someone right here at the clinic, I can introduce you to someone right now.

MS. PIKE: *(Over "…right now.")* What, so they'd tell me to leave him? Tell me to walk out on him? *Then* what? *Then* what happens to me? What happens to my kids? Look, lady, you don't know *me*. You don't know a *damn* thing about my life.

KATE: True enough.

MS. PIKE: I came for you to take our my stitches.

KATE: *(Nods; a beat; while writing a prescription; back to business.)* Here's an antibiotic for that infection. Three times a day with meals for ten days. And try to keep that hand dry. *(Rips it off the pad, hands it to her.)*

Transition

   A slide is projected: 3:53 pm.

   (Kate is with Mr. Caridi, an unstable, working-class man in his late 40s.)

KATE: What brings *you* here today, Mr. Caridi?

MR. CARIDI: You.

   (She good-naturedly rolls her eyes.)

MR. CARIDI: No, I mean it, I been thinking about you. I *have;* that's the truth.

KATE: *(Over "that's the truth;" keeping her professional cool.)* Mr. Caridi, do you have a complaint?

MR. CARIDI: Only that I don't see you enough.

   (Another disapproving look from Kate: she is not charmed.)

MR. CARIDI: What's the matter, I'm embarrassing you? A beautiful girl like you? *Look* at you, you're blushing.

KATE: I am not.

MR. CARIDI: Don't you know you're beautiful?

KATE: Come on, this is really...

MR. CARIDI: *(Over "this is really...")* Doesn't your husband tell you how beautiful you are? Boy, if you were *mine,* if you were *mine,* I'd tell you all the time, all the *time* I'd tell you.

KATE: *(Over "all the* time *I'd tell you.")* Mr. Caridi, do you have any idea how inappropriate this is? No honestly. Do you? I'm your *doc*tor, Mr. Caridi.

MR. CARIDI: Hey... *(Meaning, "You don't have to tell me.")*

KATE: *(Continuous.)* Do you think you can respect that fact for ten minutes so that I can do my job?

MR. CARIDI: Shoot. *(Meaning, "Go ahead.")*

KATE: Thank you.

MR. CARIDI: *(Beat.)* Can I say one thing, though? You know?, in the beginning I really thought I was gonna have a problem having a lady doctor. But, no, I like it. I really do.

KATE: That's good, Mr. Caridi. I'm glad.

MR. CARIDI: There's something really nice about it, you know? Really refreshing.

KATE: Would you like to tell me what's wrong?

MR. CARIDI: *(Dead serious.)* I really have been thinking about you, you know. I missed you.

KATE: Mr. Caridi, this had got to stop. Okay? Because if you insist on this inappropriate behavior,—

MR. CARIDI: Don't get so worked up!

KATE: —I'm going to have to take you off my patient list and give you to Dr. Leventhal. Do you understand?

MR. CARIDI: Yes, Teacher—I mean, Doctor.

(He cracks himself up; she glares at him.)

MR. CARIDI: That was a joke! Come on! Where's your sense of humor?

KATE: Mr. Caridi, is there a medical reason that brought you here today?

MR. CARIDI: Yeah. What do you think, I make appointments just to see you?

(She says nothing.)

MR. CARIDI: I'm missing O.J. for this! Today's the big day!

KATE: Mr. Caridi, I'm already running twenty minutes late.

MR. CARIDI: Okay, okay, I see you're into being super-serious. I can be super-serious, too. *(He folds his hands like a student.)*

KATE: Well?

MR. CARIDI: I got a few things I care to discuss.

KATE: Alright.

MR. CARIDI: Some personal matters.

KATE: Personal matters or health problems?

MR. CARIDI: Yeah. Health problems. *(Pause.)* You still want me to give up smoking?

KATE: Is that really why you're here? You want to talk about quitting smoking?—

MR. CARIDI: I know, I know.

KATE: *(Continuous.)* —We've talked about this before.

MR. CARIDI: I try. I really do. I just can't. The minute I decide to quit, I can't wait to light up again. Believe me, I'd be so happy to come and see you and tell you I quit. I couldn't wait to see the look on your face when I told you.

KATE: Maybe it's time to think about the patch.

MR. CARIDI: The what?

KATE: The nicotine patch. Remember?

MR. CARIDI: *(Shakes his head, No.)* What's that?

KATE: You wear it on your skin and it releases nicotine into your bloodstream. It takes away the craving.

MR. CARIDI: No kidding.

KATE: Would you like to try it?

MR. CARIDI: Yeah, sure, why not? Does it hurt?

KATE: No, you just wear it on your skin. Like a band-aid. Before you go I'll give you a starter kit. And then you'll need to fill this prescription. *(She writes.)* Okay?

MR. CARIDI: Yeah, Doc. Thanks. *(He watches her write in silence, refers to a framed photo.)* That your kid?

KATE: What?

MR. CARIDI: *(Points to the photo.)* The kid.

KATE: Yes.

(Pause.)

MR. CARIDI: Can I see?

KATE: Mr. Caridi…

MR. CARIDI: Can't I see the picture? I just want to see it. I don't got my glasses. Can I see it up close? I love kids.

(She hesitates, then hands him the frame.)

MR. CARIDI: Thanks.

(He looks at the photo for a long time, which she finds terribly unnerving. She extends her hand.)

KATE: Mr. Caridi?

MR. CARIDI: So: that's your kid.

KATE: Yes. *(Beat.)* May I have it back, please?

MR. CARIDI: That your husband?

KATE: Yes.

MR. CARIDI: Pretty kid. What's his name?

KATE: *(Hesitates.)* Matthew.

MR. CARIDI: Matthew, huh.

KATE: May I please…?

MR. CARIDI: *(Still looking.)* Looks like you, don't he.

KATE: Mr. Caridi, please...Can we get on with this? I've got a whole bunch of patients I've got to see.

(Laughing, he taunts her with the picture frame.)

KATE: Mr. Caridi...Mr. Caridi, please...

(He gives it to her; she puts it back. Pause.)

MR. CARIDI: I wish I had that.

KATE: Had what?

MR. CARIDI: A kid, a family. Maybe if I had a kid...If I didn't have this...disability...Who knows? I might be sitting where you are. Or where your husband sits. You ever think about that? There but for the grace of God?

KATE: All the time. *(Beat.)* Mr. Caridi, have you been taking your lithium?

MR. CARIDI: Why?

KATE: I suspect you haven't.

MR. CARIDI: *(Beat.)* No.

KATE: Why not?

MR. CARIDI: *(Shrugs.)* I hate the way it makes me feel. Makes my mouth taste like shit.

KATE: You can always use a mouthwash if it dries out your mouth. Or chew gum. Mr. Caridi, you've got to be sure to tell your psychiatrist—when's your next appointment?

(He shrugs.)

KATE: Have you been going to your appointments?

MR. CARIDI: I don't like him. Why can't I see you?

KATE: I'm not a psychiatrist. Mr. Caridi, you've got to take your lithium and you've got to take it regularly, do you understand? You have bipolar *disease;—*

MR. CARIDI: Yeah yeah yeah.

KATE: *(Continuous.)* —it's a *disease,* controllable by drugs.

MR. CARIDI: *(Shrugs.)* I got another problem I got to ask you.

KATE: What kind of problem?

MR. CARIDI: It's kind of personal.

KATE: *(Beat.)* Alright.

MR. CARIDI: Kind of confidential.

(She nods, "Okay.")

MR. CARIDI: You're my doctor, right?

KATE: Yes.

MR. CARIDI: I can discuss a personal problem with you, can't I? I mean, that's appropriate, isn't it? Hm? Doctor-patient thing? Like confession, right?

KATE: What's the problem, Mr. Caridi?

(Pause.)

MR. CARIDI: It's my penis.

KATE: *(Beat.)* Yes?

MR. CARIDI: I don't know, something don't seem right.

KATE: Can you be more specific?

MR. CARIDI: Sometimes…Sometimes I have this burning sensation.

KATE: It's painful when you urinate?

MR. CARIDI: I don't know, I think so. Yeah, it is. And sometimes it gets really big and red and swollen; I think you better take a look, Doc. *(He starts to undo his pants.)*

KATE: Alright, alright, that's it.

MR. CARIDI: *(Feigning shock.)* What!

KATE: I did not tell you to take your pants down.

MR. CARIDI: Don't you want to see what's the matter?!—*(His pants fall to his feet.)*

KATE: Mr. Caridi!

MR. CARIDI: *(Continuous.)* —I tell you I got something wrong with my penis, don't you think you'd better take a look?! What's the matter, you shy? You're a doctor!; you've seen naked men before.

KATE: *(Over "naked men before.")* That's right, I'm not your friend, I'm not your girlfriend, I'm your doctor. Now put your pants back on before I call for help.

MR. CARIDI: *(His pants still around his ankles.)* How do you know there isn't something really wrong with me?!

KATE: You're right, I don't.

MR. CARIDI: *(Continuous.)* —How do you know I don't have cancer or a tumor or something?—

KATE: Mr. Caridi, pull up your pants, Mr. Caridi…

MR. CARIDI: *(Continuous.)* —What kind of doctor *are* you? Aren't you supposed to heal the sick? Aren't you?! You and Hillary Clinton! Phony bitches! All smiles and promises.

KATE: *(Overlap.)* I'm setting up another appointment for you with Dr. Leventhal.

MR. CARIDI: What?! Why?!

KATE: *(Continuous.)* I think Dr. Leventhal should be your primary care physician from now on. I think you need to see a male physician.

MR. CARIDI: Oh, come on! What kind of shit is this? What kind of doctor *are* you, anyway? You're no doctor. Where's your compassion? Doctors are supposed to have compassion.

KATE: Excuse me, I'll go get the patch. *(She leaves.)*

MR. CARIDI: Bitch.

(Pause. He picks up the picture frame to look at again, then impulsively hides it in his newspaper. She returns with the patch.)

KATE: Here, let me show you, all you do is...

(He snatches the patch from her.)

MR. CARIDI: *(As he goes.)* Suck my dick.

Transition

A slide is projected: 6:10 pm.

(Kate is with a woman, Paula, black, frail and sick.)

PAULA: *(Brightly, belying its content.)* "Mama, I want to see *Lion King!* I want to see *Lion King!*" I mean, that's all I've been hearing for weeks. "Why can't I see it? Why can't I see it?" You go to *Burg*er King, everything is *Lion King.* You go to the store...

KATE: *How* old is she again?

PAULA: Four and a half, be five in October.

KATE: That's what I thought; that's a little young.

PAULA: Right? I mean, isn't that what everybody's saying? "Well, Ka*ish*a's mother let *her* see it. *Trev*or's mother let *him* see it." Well, I was getting real sick and tired hearing whose mother who see it— I mean, that's all this girl talked about! Day in, day out. I told her, "Lookit, your brother saw it and your sister saw it and they both say you're too young, so forget about it, you're not seeing it, I don't want to hear another word!" Well. To make a long story short... yesterday I get my girlfriend Clarisse drop us off at Showcase in Orange—

KATE: You pushover!

PAULA: *(Continuous.)* —and I take Alexandra to *Lion King.* Yeah.

KATE: And?

PAULA: You see it?

(Kate shakes her head.)

PAULA: *How* old's your boy?

KATE: Just over two.

PAULA: Oh. Well. I don't know who was more upset by it, her or me. You know what happens in it?

KATE: I think so.

PAULA: The father lion dies and Scar makes Simba think it's all his fault?

KATE: Uh huh.

PAULA: Man. Pretty heavy stuff. Well, I'm not sure it was such a great idea. Maybe it was, maybe it wasn't. All I know is, the father dies, right?, and I'm holding my little girl to me, and I'm sobbing my eyes out.

KATE: Oh, Paula...

PAULA: And I mean *sob*bing. Like the dams burst. Whooshh! I totally lose it. I don't know what freaked her out more, me or the stampede. And it's so noisy! It's so loud! It's really scary, it really is, I don't care *what* they say. And I can't stop crying! It's like uncontrollable. Like everything in my life, all the shit, all the disease, everything, is pouring out of my eyes in tears. A flood!, this flood is... And grownups are looking at me funny like "What the fuck *she* on?," and the kids are getting freaked out all around us— "Mommy-who's-that-crazy-lady?"—and I'm squeezing little Alexandra to me and squeezing her and squeezing her with all my might and wailing and rocking and making an all-around *fool* of myself.

KATE: *(Soothingly.)* No...

PAULA: *(Continuous.)* And then, all of a sudden, it stops. Just like that. Like somebody turned off the water, turned off the faucet, you know? And I'm sitting there, so wrecked, so wasted...And it's just a stupid cartoon! A kids' movie! I don't know what the hell set me off like that. Man!
(Long pause.)

KATE: Paula...*(Pause.)* The DDI isn't working.

PAULA: Did I tell you?, at the movies?, she had me getting up for *pop* corn, getting up for *Sprite,* getting up to *pee...*

KATE: Paula?

PAULA: *(Beat.)* So put me back on AZT.

KATE: We can't put you back on AZT.

PAULA: *(Over "on AZT.")* Why not?

KATE: It doesn't work that way. It stopped being effective the first time, it's not going to be effective now.

PAULA: *(Over "effective now.")* How do you know?

KATE: It isn't. *(Beat.)* The sputum and blood cultures we took? Both grew out *M. avium intracellulare.*

PAULA: M. what?

KATE: *M. avium intracellulare.* It's a mycobacterium, a kind of a cousin of TB That's one of the reasons you haven't been able to keep the weight back on.

PAULA: That last pneumonia took a long time, too. Remember? I was sick forever—

KATE: This isn't like that.

PAULA: *(Continuous.)* —and I pulled through.

KATE: Yeah, but it's not the same. You were stronger then. You had more resistance. *(Pause.)* Paula, your T-4 count is down to four. That's as low as it goes; it can't *get* any lower than that. *(Pause.)* Paula...With your T-cell count so low...

PAULA: *(Drops eye contact.)* Yeah...?

KATE: Anything can happen. And it will.

PAULA: Uh huh.

KATE: *(Beat.)* Paula?

PAULA: *(Gets up.)* Lookit, I got to go pick up my kids at my mother's. I'm late, I told her I'd get there at six.

KATE: Paula, please sit down?

PAULA: *(Over "sit down;" enraged.)* You kept me waiting twenty minutes out there!—

KATE: Paula...

PAULA: —My time is valuable, too, you know. May not *look* it to you...

KATE: Please.

(Pause; Paula leans against the chair, carefully.)

KATE: I think it's time to give some serious thought. Remember we talked about this? I think it's time to come up with a plan. *(Beat.)* Did you meet with the social worker?

PAULA: Yeah.

KATE: And?

PAULA: *(Shrugs.)* Her perfume made me sick to my stomach.

KATE: Paula, I know it's hard.

PAULA: You don't know shit. You don't know nothing. When was the last time *you* had to worry what was gonna happen to *your* kids? So don't tell me you know.

(Kate nods. Long pause.)

KATE: What did your mother say?

PAULA: My mother don't want them. Can you blame her? I don't. My mother is 54 years old. What does she want a bunch of kids for? She's tired. She's got diabetes, bad circulation. High blood pressure.

KATE: I know.

PAULA: *(Continuous.)* I mean, a couple of days here and there, when I'm in the hospital or whatever, *that* she can handle. But raising kids that ain't even teenagers yet?! Un-uh. She's done. She's had it. And can you *blame* her with what's going on today? Who needs it? She's tired. She raised kids her whole life. *Her* kids, my sister's kids. My little one? Andre? He's a devil. She can't go chasing him around. How she gonna do that? She can't.

KATE: But they're your *chil*dren. Her *grand*children.

PAULA: You don't understand: She don't want no more children. You understand? She don't *want* them.

KATE: Would she come to a family meeting?

PAULA: I'm telling you she don't want them. Period.

KATE: *(Over "Period.")* If I arranged a family meeting, if I called her and talked to her myself…

PAULA: You don't get it, do you. Forget about my mother. Forget about her. Make believe she's dead. Make believe I don't *have* a mother. 'Cause she ain't gonna take them.

KATE: All I'm asking is, Paula, can you get her down here for a meeting, that's all I'm asking.

(Paula shrugs.)

KATE: You, me, the social worker, your mother, maybe your girlfriend…

PAULA: Clarisse?

KATE: Yeah, have you considered *her?*

PAULA: Clarisse has got four kids of her own! No man, no job, no money, no nothing. How'm I gonna leave my four kids on her doorstep?

KATE: Isn't there somebody else, a friend or a…

PAULA: *All* my friends got problems of their own. Who do you think my friends are? Rich folks? How my friends gonna raise my kids? I can't ask them that. They got problems feeding them*selves.*

KATE: Paula, what I'm concerned about right now are your *chil*dren, what's going to happen to your *chil*dren.

PAULA: And you think I'm not?

KATE: Of course I don't think that. I'm just trying to—

PAULA: I bet you're sitting there asking yourself what business did she have having all these kids for in the first place?

KATE: No...

PAULA: Well, I had no business doing a lot of the things I did. But the thing is I did 'em. Okay? And this is where we're at. *(Pause.)* You just think I'm selfish.

KATE: I never said that.

PAULA: You do. You think I'm too selfish to think about my kids.

KATE: That's not true. I just think there's no time to fool around.

PAULA: Fool *around?* It looks to you like I'm fooling around?

KATE: *(Over "like I'm fooling around;" overly invested.)* You know what I'm saying. This is no time to be passive, Paula, there's no time for that. You *need* a plan. Think about your children. Losing you is going to be hard enough, what if they all get separated from each *oth*er? Hm? Have you thought about that? They'll be shipped all over the place and get tossed around in the child welfare system and maybe get lost forever. Is that what you want for them? You can't let that happen to them, Paula. You've got to plan for it now. Before you get any sicker.

PAULA: You just want to see me dead.

KATE: What?!

PAULA: It's true. You'll be happy when I'm out of your hair forever.

KATE: How can you say that? I've followed you for two and a half years. I care very much about you.

PAULA: *(Over "about you.")* Nah, I'm too much trouble. You'll be happy when I just disappear. One day I will, too, I'll just...poof! and that'll be it. "Bye, bye, Paula. Oh, well, too bad. Next!"

KATE: Paula, let me talk to your mother? *(Pause.)*

PAULA: Look at me. Look at where I'm at. *(She shakes her head.)* My whole life. My whole fucking life: Men. Bad luck with men. Lamar should've just slashed my throat. It've been easier, a lot easier than *this,* that's for sure. A quick knife to the jugular? Sounds good. Sounds good to me. *(Beat.)* Know what it's gonna say on my tombstone? "Fucked over by men." My daddy fucked me over, Lamar finished me off. *(Beat.)* I'm thirty-six years old. Can you believe it? Look at this body, this saggy bag of bones. I look a *hun*dred and thirty-six.

KATE: No...

PAULA: This body used to mean something.

KATE: It still does.

PAULA: *(Shakes her head, then.)* No. No. It was a good body, once. It had value. Now? *(Pause.)* I think back to meeting Lamar? First laying eyes on him? And I think to myself, "Stay away, girl, this man is going to ruin you. This man will make your life hell. This man will poison you and the two of you'll die young and your children'll be cursed forever." *(Beat.)* Did I know, deep down, I was meeting Death himself? Is that what attracted me to him? Did Nicole know when she first laid eyes on that beautiful man? Did she know O.J. was Death and go to him anyway? *(Beat.)* If Lamar was Death, then let me tell you: Death was hot.

(Kate smiles sadly, puts her hand in Paula's; Paula doesn't reject it.)

Transition

A slide is projected: 9:12 pm.

(Kate finishes writing notes on a chart and packs up for the night. She looks at some framed photos, sees that her framed picture is gone and realizes that it was swiped by Mr. Caridi.)

KATE: Sonofabitch.

(Señora Soto appears at the door.)

SEÑORA: ¿Señora doctora?

KATE: Oh, hello.

SEÑORA: Dijo que la llamara. Llamé y me dijeron que podia venir. *[You said to call. I called, they said I could come in.]*

KATE: Sí, sí. Entra. Me voy a casa. I'm going home, terminé por la noche. *[Finished for the night.]* Sólo puedo ver usted por un minuto. *[I can only see you for a minute.]* ¿Qué pasó? *[What happened?]*

SEÑORA: Sentí el dolor otra vez. Volvió el dolor. *[I felt the pain again. The pain came back.]* Dijo que deberia llamar si sentia otra vez el dolor. *[You said I should call if I felt the pain.]*

KATE: Sí. ¿Cuándo paso? *[When did it happen?]*

SEÑORA: Estaba descansador en mi "Lazy Boy." *[I was resting in my Lazy Boy recliner chair.]* Estaba viendo a O.J. Simpson. *[I was watching O.J. Simpson.]* De pronto, me vino una visión. *[Then all of a sudden I had a vision.]*

KATE: ¿Una visión?

SEÑORA: Sí. Mi corazón empezó a latir fuertemente en mi pecho. *[My heart began to pound in my chest.]* La sangre empezó a correr de mi boca *[Blood started pouring out of my mouth]* como un río de sangre *[like a river of blood]* y de los ojos, ye de los oídos y la nariz. *[and out of my eyes, and my ears and my nose.]* La sangre corrio de mi *[Blood gushed out of me]* de alla debajo, de todas partes *[from down there, from everywhere]* llenando el cuarto de sangre. *[filling the room with blood.]* Mi sangre estaba por todo, como un mar. *[My blood was everywhere, like the sea.]* Y pronto los muebles empezaron a bambolear en la sangre *[Soon the furniture started bobbing around in the blood]* el televisor, las sillas, y pronto todo flotó por la ventana. *[the TV, the chairs, and soon everything floated right out the window!]* ¡Y yo oía a mis hijos llorando! *[And I heard my children crying!]* Ellos estaban en algun otro cuarto, llorando, "Mamá! Mamá!" *[They were in another room somewhere, crying, "Mama! Mama!"]* Yo no los oía pero si los veía. *[I could hear them but I couldn't see them.]* ¡Yo no podía llegar hacia ellos! *[I couldn't get to them!]* La olas de sangre eran tan grandes. *[The waves of blood were so strong.]* Que me barraron como una terrible tormenta. *[It tossed me around like a terrible storm.]* ¡Y no podía nadar! ¡Me ahogué! *[And I couldn't swim! The waves overtook me and I drowned!]* ¡Me ahogué en mi propia sangre! *[Drowned in my own blood!]* Señora doctora, ¿puede que el dolor haga que se explote el corazón de una madre? *[Can sorrow make a mother's heart burst open?]* ¿Se puede ahogar uno en su propia sangre? *[Can you drown in your own blood?]* Creo que es posible. *[I think it's possible.]* ¡Creo que voy a morir! *[I think I'm going to die!]* ¡Por favor, no quiero que me lleven de mis hijos! *[Please, I don't want to be taken from my children!]*

KATE: *(Soothing.)* Señora...

SEÑORA: Ya no puede dormir. *[I can't sleep anymore.]* Tengo conversaciones en mi mente con mis hijos. *[I have conversations in my head with my children.]* Les hablo toda la noche. *[I talk to them all night.]* Pienso en ellos todo el día. *[I think about them all day.]* Pienso en ellos ahora mismo. *[I'm thinking about them now.]* Me duele el corazón. *[My heart aches.]* ¡Creo que voy a morir! *[I think I am going to die!]* ¡El dolor! ¡El dolor! *[The pain! The pain!]*

KATE: El dolor es miedo. *[The pain is fear.]*

SEÑORA: ¿Qué?

KATE: El dolor es miedo. Fear. Tienes miedo. *[The pain is fear. You're afraid.]*

SEÑORA: Sí, tengo miedo. Estoy tan asustada. *[Yes, I am afraid. I'm so afraid.]* Señora doctora, ¿que voy a hacer? *[What am I going to do?]* Ayudame, Señora doctora. Ayudame. *[Help me, Doctor. Help me.]* (*Kate and Señora are standing at opposite ends of the room in silence.*)

Transition
A slide is projected: 10:05 pm.

(*Mark is seated on a sofa, his bare feet up, reading* The New York Times. *Kate comes in from work.*)
KATE: Hi.
MARK: Hi. How are you?
(*Kate kisses him, shrugs, a beat. He senses something is wrong.*)
MARK: What.
KATE: (*Shrugs it off.*) Baby sleeping?
MARK: Yeah. He was still flinging himself around the crib a couple of minutes ago but it's been pretty quiet.
KATE: I'm tempted to go in.
MARK: (*Takes her hand to stop her.*) Don't. Please? You'll wake him.
(*Pause. She takes off her shoes, joins him on the sofa.*)
KATE: *Frasier* on?
MARK: Rerun.
KATE: Which one?
MARK: He and Niles take his father out to eat? The steakhouse?
KATE: Oh, yeah.
MARK: I turned it off.
KATE: What about *Seinfeld?*
MARK: That was a rerun, too, but I didn't remember seeing it.
KATE: What was it?
MARK: Elaine's in the ladies' room at a movie theater? And finds there's no toilet paper and asks the woman in the stall next to hers for some and the woman refuses and they argue but can't see each other and of course it turns out the woman is Jerry's new girlfriend.
KATE: Of course...
MARK: And Elaine has a new boyfriend who she's very defensive about because he's supposedly so good-looking. And Kramer and George and this guy go rock climbing and somehow, I don't know, exactly,

I was reading the paper, I think George drops a rope or something and the guy falls and crushes his face.

KATE: *(Winces.)* Ooo.

MARK: Yeah. And then naturally it turns out that Elaine was only interested in him for his looks and has no interest in staying with him if he's disfigured. And also there's this phone sex subplot going on with Kramer where it turns out that the woman he's been calling is Jerry's new girlfriend.

KATE: Was it any good?

MARK: It was alright. *Seinfeld's* getting very, I don't know, there's something very malevolent going on on *Seinfeld.* Something mean-spirited and juvenile.

KATE: Uh huh.

MARK: The attitude toward sex is very screwed up. All this fear and loathing. The women are always portrayed as these alien ciphers good for making out with but there's this underlying ickiness and suspicion. All the women except Elaine all seem to have cooties.

KATE: Mm. Seinfeld seems like a seriously anally retentive guy.

MARK: Right! I mean, anybody who has fifteen cereal boxes lined up like that...You hungry? There's some tortellini left in the fridge.

KATE: *(Shakes her head, No.)* What happened today?

MARK: You heard that the judge ruled that the evidence was admissible?

KATE: I heard that; I meant what's new with *you?*

MARK: Not much.

KATE: Did you talk to many people today?

MARK: You mean besides a two-year-old and the U.P.S. man?

KATE: That's what I thought. How's the writing coming?

MARK: Maybe I'll be done with this dissertation by the time I'm fifty. Maybe. There's an O.J. update on NBC if you're up for it.

KATE: I'm not.

MARK: Are you okay?

KATE: *(Thinks about elaborating.)* Oh...*(But changes her mind.)* Tell me about our boy. What kind of a day did he have?

MARK: I hear he had a good day.

KATE: Tell me. What did you do tonight?

MARK: Well, we ate tortellini—

KATE: Yeah...

MARK: *(Continuous.)* —which he kept popping into his mouth, it was really quite impressive, he can really put it away. And then we went for a walk.

KATE: Where?

MARK: The construction site and then to the park.

KATE: Oh, a serious walk.

MARK: And we saw the backhoe and the crane— biigg crane— and we saw bicyclists and doggies and men running — it was a banner day—and an airplane flew overhead and birdies and later he pointed way up high in the sky: "Look, Daddy, hec-coc-ca" and he was right, there was a helicopter. And we went and got some frozen yogurt which he ate with great abandon and got all over himself. And we ran into Pete closing up which was a source of great excitement. And then we got home and I let him play with the hose while I mowed the lawn.

KATE: You mowed? Excellent.

MARK: So he got soaked and ucky and then we went upstairs and got naked and chased each other around for a little while and he peed on the floor—deliberately—"Look, Daddy, pee"—and I got him into the tub where he peed some more and scrubbed my face with the wash cloth—very hard, I had to take it away from him.

KATE: Did you shampoo?

MARK: Not tonight; I couldn't bring myself to. I couldn't take away the wash cloth *and* wash his hair; that would've been too cruel. And then I got him ready for bed.

KATE: What did you read?

MARK: What did we read. Let's see…we read the bulldozer book. And the truck book. And the piggy book. And the potty book—he now says "I want read potty book," you know, he's fascinated, we'd better go get him a potty, quick, this weekend, before the window of opportunity slams shut forever. *(Pause.)* You know how it is when you turn out the light and you're holding him on your lap and you can see his dark eyes shining and you can smell his milky breath and he seems utterly content and starts getting sleepy and his eyes begin to close but he forces himself awake?

KATE: Mm. He's an angel.

MARK: I sat like that with him in my arms for a while and I said, "In the great green room, there was a telephone and a red balloon," and he crinkled up his face in pure pleasure.

KATE: Say it.

MARK: What.

KATE: "In the great green room…"

MARK: "In the great green room
    There was a telephone
    And a red balloon
    And a picture of—
    The cow jumping over the moon."
    (She is weeping, he becomes concerned.)

MARK: Honey? What is it?
    (She shakes her head dismissively.)

MARK: Bad day?

KATE: That's the thing: it was completely typical; it just got to me today.

MARK: You want to tell me?

KATE: Just finish the story.

MARK: What?

KATE: Finish. Go ahead
    (He hesitates.)

KATE: Please? I want to hear your voice.

MARK: *(Beat.)* "Goodnight room
    Goodnight moon
    Goodnight cow jumping over the moon
    Goodnight light
    And the red balloon
    Goodnight bears
    And goodnight chairs
    Goodnight kittens
    And goodnight mittens"
    (Pause; she is weeping.)

MARK: "Goodnight clocks
    And goodnight socks
    Goodnight little house
    And goodnight mouse
    Goodnight comb
    And goodnight brush
    Goodnight nobody
    Goodnight mush
    And goodnight to the old lady whispering 'hush.'
    Goodnight stars
    Goodnight air

Goodnight noises everywhere."
(During the above, he holds her as lights fade.)

END OF PLAY

Middle-Aged White Guys

by Jane Martin

BIOGRAPHY

Jane Martin's *Middle-Aged White Guys* is her first play at ATL since *Keely and Du* premiered in the 1993 Humana Festival. She received the American Critics Theatre Association Award for *Keely and Du*. Ms. Martin, a Kentuckian, first came to national attention for *Talking With,* a collection of monologues that premiered at Actors Theatre in 1981. Since its New York premiere at the Manhattan Theatre Club in 1982, *Talking With* has been performed around the world, winning the Best Foreign Play of the Year award in Germany from *Theater Heute* magazine. Her other work includes *Cementville* (1991 Humana Festival), *Summer* (1984 Shorts Festival), and *Vital Signs* (1990 Humana Festival).

ORIGINAL PRODUCTION

Middle-Aged White Guys was first presented at the 19th Humana Festival of New American Plays at Actors Theatre of Louisville in March 1995. It was directed by Jon Jory with the following cast:

R.V. . . . . Karenjune Sánchez
Roy . . . . John Griesemer
Clem . . . . Bob Burrus
Mona . . . . Karen Grassle
Moon . . . . Leo Burmester
King . . . . Larry Larson
Mrs. Mannering . . . . Anne Pitoniak

CHARACTERS

ROY: The mayor, 48.
CLEM: The businessman, 47.
MOON: The mercenary, 46.
R.V.: A forerunner, 25.
MONA: A woman in transition, 40.
KING: A messenger.
MRS. MANNERING: Mother to the brothers, 70.

TIME

Present day.

THE PLACE

A dump.

Middle-Aged White Guys

A small-town dump and junk yard, its mounds and valleys of debris slightly steaming in the rose of the sunset. Piles of cans, boxes, barrels, the rusted hulk of an old car, broken bedsteads, refrigerators, garbage, old signs, mounds of the unimaginable. The effect created is a dark, eccentric, contemporary hell.

On top of the junked car, a young woman in a short, red dress, with a snake tattoo coiling up her left arm from wrist to shoulder, sits cross-legged. Heat lightning flashes in the distance. Far away, thunder rolls.

R.V.: Moon? Yo, Moon, can you hear me down there? Down, down, in that river of sleep? Down with one foot in the dark continent? You remember that day, Moon? You know the one I mean. Old guy leans over, touches my tattoo, says, "Hey, Snake, we got a no-hitter goin', woman; we're workin' a virgin top of the sixth."
(Thunder.)
They say there's an hour in everybody's life where all the luck you shoulda' had comes together like drops on the windshield. You ever hear that? State championship high school game, and all the luck we'd never have again just riding your arm through the late afternoon. Roy, he was four for four; Clem caught that relay bare handed for the double play. And there you were, right into the eighth, throwin' smoke and sinkers like Mr. Smooth in the bigs. And then, just then, some tanked-up dickwad on the third base side yells out, "Workin' a no-hitter, Moon!" And you froze stiff in your windup

and looked over there like he woke you up from an afternoon nap, and then you shook your head and threw 14 straight, fat ones up there, and they put *five* runs on the board. I couldn't believe it, Moon. *(Thunder nearer; a dog howling.)* Omens and portents. *(She looks at the sky.)* Read 'em an' weep. *(She knocks on the car top.)* What the hell were you doin', Moon? How come you threw it away?

(Roy Mannering, a man in his late 40s, appears over the ridge of the dump. He is dressed as Abraham Lincoln, including beard and stovepipe hat. Roy carries two six-packs of beer. He looks down and yells a name, apparently not noticing R.V.)

ROY: Clem? You here, Clem? *(To himself.)* What damn color is *that* sky? *(He takes a step forward and falls ass-over-teakettle down the dump's incline.)* Well, that's just perfect. That's just sweet as hell. Clem?

(The girl has disappeared. He wipes at his clothes with a handkerchief.)

ROY: What is this stuff? Oh, that's perfect. *(He pulls out a portable phone and dials.)* Mona? Mona, it's Roy. What's with the voice, Mona? You're not cryin' again, are you? Well, you better not because I'm sick of it, woman, that's why. Listen, Mona, go to the closet...you got any mascara on your hands? Well, you wash them off, go to the closet, get my gray silk summer suit...gray suit...stop cryin', Mona...run that gray suit up to the July 4th reviewing stand... because I got nasty stuff on the Abe Lincoln suit...Mona, I can't give the Gettysburg Address covered in dog shit. Now give that gray suit to Luellen...my assistant Luellen...I am not sleepin' with Luellen, Mona...she is one year out of high school...what the hell are you cryin' about, I put your Prozac right where you could see it. Now I need that suit, woman; you do what I tell you. *(He cuts her off the phone.)* I can't stand that damn cryin'. *(He dials again.)* Luellen, sweetmeat, it's Long Dong Silver. You got any word where those fireworks are? Well, those damn Chinese don't know what U.P.S. means. Well, we'll shoot what we got. Listen, I'll be there... 40, 45 minutes, max. *(Feels beard.)* Yeah, I got it on. This stick-on stuff stings like hell. Look, tell Carl keep the high school band a couple extra numbers 'cause we're missin' those Chinese fireworks. Well, you tell him to do it. I'm the damned mayor!

(Puts phone back in pocket. A man appears above. It is Roy's younger brother Clem. He wears overalls and a work shirt, and carries an umbrella.)

CLEM: That you, Roy?

(Roy startles.)

ROY: Damn, Clem.

CLEM: I tried not to scare you.

ROY: *(Scraping at his pants.)* Look at this? What are we doin' in the dump, Clem? What the hell are we doin' here?

CLEM: We promised her, Roy. It's a sacred trust.

ROY: *(Still looking at his clothes.)* A sacred trust.

CLEM: I get it. You're dressed up as a Smith Brothers cough drop.

ROY: This is Abe Lincoln, Clem.

CLEM: Oh, I see.

ROY: Seventy-five dollar rental, and I fell down the hill.

CLEM: Abe Lincoln, sure. We promised R.V. we'd come down here every 10 years.

ROY: I know that, Clem.

CLEM: Twenty years ago today. You want some Cheezits?

ROY: *(Another matter.)* Clem, I got to talk to you.

CLEM: It's Mama's birthday, too.

ROY: What?

CLEM: I know, you never like to think of her dead.

ROY: Our beautiful Mama.

CLEM: 'Member how she always called you "Tiny?"

ROY: Mama's birthday! Why did she leave us, Clem?

CLEM: She died, Roy.

ROY: I know she died, goddamnit.

CLEM: Our two beautiful ladies in the heavenly choir.

ROY: I miss you, Mama!

CLEM: Mama and R.V. Makes this a sacred trust.

ROY: Alright, Clem. You hear anything from Moon?

CLEM: Can't make it. Wired R.V. a dozen white roses, just like when we did this in '84.

ROY: Well, I knew little brother wouldn't show. Where was the roses wired at?

CLEM: Liberia.

ROY: Well, brother Moon, he's seen the world. Hasn't *built* a damn thing. Hasn't *been* a damn thing. White roses every 10 years. I'm surprised he had the money.

CLEM: R.V. loved him.

ROY: She loved me.

CLEM: Well, Roy, I'd have to say…

ROY: I don't want to hear it! Three brothers, Clem, but everybody thought he was pure gold, didn't they?

CLEM: Oh, they did.

ROY: Well, I'm the gold and you're the gold, an' he's down in Liberia washing out his clothes in a stream full of fecal matter.

CLEM: I miss old Moon. He sure does love to kill people.

ROY: He always killed things. Back in elementary, he'd kill bugs, birds, squirrels, wild dogs…he just grew up, that's all. Clem, I got a time problem…

CLEM: Well, we'll do the toast.

ROY: There's somethin' else, Clem.

CLEM: What, Roy?

ROY: A real bad sign.

CLEM: Bad signs, that's right. You know that palomino horse old Gifford keeps out at four corners? Drivin' over here, seen that horse run mad, goes straight into the barbed wire, tangles himself up, goes to screamin', blood gettin' throwed up into the air, most horrible thing I ever saw, plus everybody's gettin' boils, the creek's turned red, and there's piles a dead frogs right downtown…

ROY: *(Hands him a letter.)* I'm not talkin' about that kind of sign, Clem.

CLEM: There's been three cases of rabid bats…

ROY: Just read the letter, Clem.

(Clem opens it.)

ROY: I'm not worryin' about dead frogs or rabid bats; I'm worryin' about re-election, Clem.

CLEM: *(Referring to the letter.)* So the newspaper guy knows about the chemicals? *(So what?)*

ROY: What chemicals?

CLEM: *(Indicating the barrels stage right.)* Well…these ones.

ROY: They are food additives, Clem, not chemicals.

CLEM: Food additives.

ROY: I got the letter, I went over to the newspaper. Now that pissant editor has a load receipt from Long Island Petrochemical tells him how many barrels of this, how many barrels of that they sent down here.

CLEM: Food additives.

ROY: Food additives, that's right. I explained we have no barrel leakage or groundwater problem on the site. I explained the value of the contract to the city; Hell, it's 37% of the municipal income, you'd think a damn moron could understand the economics, but he reads me a state statute says four of these additives—chloroethylene, hexochlorobenzine, polychlorinated biphenyls and…somethin' else—are prohibited from interstate transport. Too much damn government, Clem, that's what that is. Now where do you think he got that load receipt?

CLEM: Well…

ROY: You gave it to him.

CLEM: Well, he goes to our church, Roy.

ROY: You gave it to him.

CLEM: Well, he said, since it got the town so much money, just how many barrels was it? So I gave him the load receipt, and he was real impressed.

ROY: Now we got to go get it back.

CLEM: Why, Roy?

ROY: So he can't put it in the paper.

CLEM: It's just food additives, Roy.

ROY: Uh-huh, that's one thing, plus you and me set up the haulage company. You ever hear of nepotism?

CLEM: That's a positive word around here.

ROY: Never mind, Clem. Luckily you rent him the building he's in, so you got a key.

CLEM: Sure, but…

ROY: I go get the fireworks started. I got to be there 'cause the new poll says it's a real tight race. You go pick up your key…later on, we go on down to the newspaper, get that load receipt.

CLEM: Walk right in?

ROY: Uh-huh.

CLEM: That's not burglary?

ROY: It's fixin' the problem.

CLEM: I see.

ROY: Clem, there is America and there is not-America. America is the light. Not-America is the darkness. America isn't a place, Clem, it's an idea. Right now Clem, America isn't America, Japan is America. The problem is to get America back *in* America. Now, Clem, this is the idea that *is* America: see the problem, fix the problem, that makes a new problem, fix that problem. Whoever does that the best *is* America, and right now it's *not* America. Not-America, which right now *is* America, has two damn characteristics. Number one: fools. Fools, Clem, cannot see the problem and cannot fix the problem. These people are Democrats. Number two: idealists. These are fools who fix the wrong problem and tell the people who are fixing the right problem that they are short-sighted. For instance, Clem, let us posit this: The world's greatest bomb defuser is defusing a hydrogen bomb planted by Arabs under the Speaker's platform in the U.S. Senate. This is the only man who can defuse this bomb. He has defused bombs like this for years. Because fixing this problem is stressful, he is a chain-smoker. Not-America number two, the goddamn idealists, Clem, pulls that expert defuser off the job because of the danger to United States senators of secondary smoke, and Washington, DC blows up! We are America, Clem—you, me, we fix the problem—but the forces of darkness, the non-America number one and the not-America number two is now America, and these not-Americans are saying the *real* Americans *are* the problem, which of course *is* the problem we, as real Americans, have to fix!

CLEM: We're the real Americans, right?

ROY: That's right.

CLEM: The good ones?

ROY: That's right.

(Clem's face crumples. He pulls out a flask.)

ROY: Don't you dare cry, Clem. You're a big businessman.

CLEM: Then how come Evelyn left me?

ROY: Because you drank her right out of the house.

CLEM: *(Taking a hit.)* I'm a bad person.

ROY: You got a haulin' business, you're into real estate. You run Gunworld, Clem, the biggest handgun retail outfit in a three-state area. You're a big success and you drive a damn Miata, how can you be a bad person?

CLEM: Evelyn still hasn't called, you know. She didn't call you, did she? How the hell am I going to raise those boys? They miss their mama. What kind of woman would run off like that and not even leave a note for those boys? How could she do that?

ROY: *(Handing him his handkerchief.)* She did it because women are a sorry damn lot, Clem. They are neurologically disadvantaged, with the objectivity of a collie dog. They hate all systems, all logic, all authority, and any damn evidence runs contrary to their damn feelings. You take out the sex drive, there isn't one man in a million would stay in a house with 'em for 48 hours.

(Clem weeps.)

ROY: Stop cryin', goddamnit.

CLEM: Jimmy Peaslee...

ROY: What?

CLEM: His mama is the daughter of that woman used to run the Cherokee Diner.

ROY: I got the Gettysburg Address in 20 minutes. I got some colored lawyer dead even in the polls...

CLEM: Jimmy Peaslee took a gun to school, tried to shoot his second grade teacher.

ROY: When?

CLEM: Yesterday. An AK-47. He fired off a burst, but it went wild...

ROY: Down at Lincoln Elementary?

CLEM: Said his teacher was a damn lesbian.

ROY: Was she?

CLEM: I think she just wore a pantsuit.

ROY: We wouldn't have this kind of problem if we had prayer in the schools, Clem. Now let's do the damn toast.

CLEM: *(Heedless.)* That weapon come from Gunworld. It was mine, Roy.

ROY: You sold it to the boy?

CLEM: To the daddy.

ROY: So?

CLEM: I feel real guilty, Roy. *(He weeps.)*

ROY: Clem, I got 1,500, maybe 2,000 people showin' up for my fireworks show, and due to the Chinese I got five, six minutes of fireworks, tops. My wife's on a cryin' jag, I got a little girl on the side is gettin' real pushy, I got to break into the newspaper, I'm runnin' against a damn minority, and my Lincoln suit is covered with dog shit. *You* don't have a problem, Clem. You sold a legal weapon to a legal daddy, and if he is so damn dumb he leaves it where Junior can get it, it sure as hell is not your fault. Democracy honors the individual, Clem, at the cost of givin' him personal responsibility, and if he can't handle the responsibility, the state ought to castrate him so he can't mess up his kid! Plus you don't even know she *wasn't* a lesbian.

CLEM: You explained that real fine, Roy.

ROY: That's right. Now, I got to go to the fireworks. You meet me right after behind the Dairy Freeze. Bring the keys and a ski mask. *(He starts out of the dump.)*

CLEM: What about the sacred trust?

ROY: I don't have time for the sacred trust. *(Starts out.)*

CLEM: She was your wife, Roy.

ROY: That was 20 damn years ago!

CLEM: My wife left me, Roy. *(Weeping.)* My Evelyn left me! *(Roy stops.)*

ROY: Goddamnit Clem, you're gettin' me homicidal. *(Clem weeps.)* If I do the toast, will you stop cryin'?!

CLEM: You'll keep the sacred trust?

ROY: I will keep the goddamn, sonofabitchin' sacred trust. I'm givin' this five minutes, you understand me?

CLEM: You're a prince, Roy. You want some Cheezits?

ROY: Do it! *(He comes back down.)*

CLEM: *(Looking up.)* R.V.? It's me, Clem. I'm here with Roy, in the dump. It's about 8:30. Sky's a real funny color.

ROY: You gonna' do a weather report, Clem?

CLEM: Right, right.

ROY: Four minutes.

CLEM: So, R.V., it's Clem. I'm here with Roy in the dump.

ROY: You're drivin' me apeshit.

CLEM: R.V., we're here like we promised. Roy, me...well, Moon, he's tied up with fecal matter. Boy, I miss your shinin' face. You never loved me. Wasn't your fault. I know you loved Moon. I believe you loved Roy here...mainly. I don't know why you killed yourself, but that was just the worst thing ever happened to me. I still wake up cryin'. You asked in that death note would we hoist a beer ever ten years on the pitcher's mount where we almost got to be state champs an' you sang the National Anthem. See, they sold the field for a dump site when they combined the high school over to Mayberry.

ROY: One minute.

CLEM: *(Quickly.)* I can still hear your beautiful voice. So clear and high. Sounded like Snow White or Cinderella singin' to the mice. Boy, I miss you, R.V....it's just a dump now, but it's a world of memories to me. *(He weeps.)*

ROY: Goddamn it, Clem.

(Clem stops.)

ROY: R.V.? You were a damn fine woman with beautiful breasts and a good sense of humor. We shouldn't have got married with you still stuck on Moon, but that's 20-20 hindsight. You knew what a man is, but you didn't throw it in his face. You were mentally unbalanced, but you never let it show up in bed. That's a good woman in my book.

(A middle-aged woman, Roy's wife Mona, wearing only a slip, high heels and a strand of pearls around her neck, appears on the ridge behind them. She carries a pistol.)

ROY: You are my damn baby, R.V. honey, and any woman since you've gone is just passin' the time.

(At this moment, Mona on the ridge raises the pistol and fires down on Roy. He and Clem scramble. Simultaneously:)

ROY: Hold it.

CLEM: Don't shoot.

MONA: *(Holding Roy's gray suit on a hanger in her other hand.)* You are my nightmare, Roy Mannering! *(She fires again.)* You are a maggot b-b-born in the dung, b-burrowed down in my flesh eating me alive! I hitchhiked out here, so here's your g-g-gray suit! *(She flings it down into the dump.)*

ROY: You hitchhiked in your underwear?

(She fires again.)

ROY: Mona, that's enough now.

CLEM: Jeeminy.

MONA: I c-curse you, Roy. I c-call demons from their d-dank c-caves and crevices the c-creatures of the night to g-give you prostate cancer and Lou G-Gehrig's disease, and make you impotent that one t-time every c-couple of months you can still get it up.

ROY: You've got to relax if you want to stop stuttering, Mona.

(She fires again.)

MONA: Your teenage whore assistant called me up to say you were t-taking her to the Mayor's c-c-c-c-conference next week. She said you b-bought her a sapphire and d-d-diamond ring. Said you were divorcing me and m-m-m-m-marrying her. She said you called me a c-c-corpse with jewelry, Roy. Well, I am. I am eaten up with l-l-loathing for m-myself, and you taught m-me that with your fiendish c-c-c-criticism and little jokes and p-patronizing ways. I looked in the mirror t-t-tonight and I saw my b-bleached b-brain an' my d-dead eyes an' I said Mona, what b-became of you? Where are you, Mona?

(The door of the junked car in the lot opens quietly, and Moon, dressed in jeans and a skull T-shirt with an army field jacket over it, boots and an old kerchief around his head, steps out. He is bearded and in every way piratical.)

MONA: I curse your sons and your sons' sons that they should be b-born without testicles, blind as newts, and they should disinter your corpse and rifle through your pockets for spare change. Now I'm going to shoot your p-puffy head off, and that will make me feel considerably better. *(She raises the gun again.)*

MOON: *(In his left hand, he carries a stubby full automatic as if it were an extension of his arm. As she raises the gun, he speaks consolingly.)* Good evening, ma'am.

(She turns, pointing the gun at him.)

I had a friend used to stutter until his confidence caught up with his heart.

CLEM: Moon.

MOON: How you doin'? Well ma'am, I'd have to agree with you about Roy, untutored as he is, he probably thinks you're a household appliance. He just don't know what a woman is, ma'am, and he's just unteachable as a rooster.

ROY: What the hell, Moon?

MOON: Shut up, Roy. Now ma'am, I'm a brute killer for pay, and they tell me I'm one of the dozen best shots in the world, left-handed or right. May I call you Mona? Mona, what you're holdin' there is a Rossi 518 Tiger Cat Special, accurate up to about 40 feet and, combined with your understandable emotion and inexperience, you most likely won't hit me, whereas, my first couple of rounds will tear off your wrist, leavin' you with one hand for the rest of your life. They tell me the pain's unendurable unless we cauterized it with fire, and by the time we got some kindlin', you'd likely bleed to death. It's strange when you can see right inside your own body like you can when an extremity's gone. We never know what we are because we're covered with skin. Once you find out, you realize we're just walkin' meat. Now I'd feel more comfortable if you'd point that thing at Roy, if you don't mind.

(She does.)

ROY: Damn, Moon.

MOON: Well I feel a whole lot better. Much obliged. Now what can we do for you, ma'am?

MONA: K-K-K-Kill him.

ROY: Moon?

MOON: *(To Roy.)* There's no punishment in death, ma'am. It's over in the blink of an eye. The thing I like least about killin' people is how easy they get off. Hell, he stole your life from you. Wouldn't you say that's the situation?

MONA: I was...I was...I had dreams.

MOON: Sure, I know. You got some place you could go?

MONA: Clem's wife, Evelyn, she called from Arizona.

CLEM: Arizona?

MONA: She says it's n-nice. She l-lives with the Navajos.

CLEM: My Evelyn?

MONA: She said I could c-c-come out there.

MOON: You know what you get out there, ma'am? You get yourself a shadow, so you don't get lonely.

MONA: But I don't have the money. He didn't let me work.

MOON: Well see, he is so small. He is such a small person he could only enlarge himself at your expense.

ROY: Now that's just damned well enough.

MOON: She's going to kill you, Roy, we're lookin' for alternatives.

ROY: She can't hit the side of a barn.

MOON: She isn't stuttering, Roy. Her hand's steady. You ought to hold that with two hands, ma'am. Sort of like this.

(He demonstrates. She changes her grip.)

ROY: Dammit!

MOON: She might get lucky, put one right up your nose.

ROY: I don't know you.

MOON: Ma'am, I believe I'm goin' to take up a collection, how about that? Gimme your wallets, boys.

(They don't respond.)

MOON: I said gimme your goddamn wallets!

(They throw them on the ground.)

MOON: I get real pissed off at myself, the course I've taken. I should have got into robbery, it's just so damn easy. *(Picks them up. He looks.)* You won't mind if your pretty wife goes on a little shoppin' spree, will you, Roy?

(Roy glowers.)

MOON: So now I'm comin' up there, ma'am. Roy, throw me over your car keys, will you?

ROY: I am not givin' you my car keys.

MOON: What are you drivin' these days?

ROY: No way, No damn way.

MOON: Go ahead, ma'am, shoot him.

(She fires. Roy hits the ground. She misses.)

ROY: Goddammit to hell. Son of a bitch.

MOON: That was about a foot left, ma'am. And if you wouldn't mind a little advice, I wouldn't go for the head, I'd go for the gut.

ROY: Alright. Alright. I'm gettin' the keys.

MOON: How are you doin', Clem?

CLEM: Well, Evelyn run off.

MOON: Sorry to hear that. You better have a drink.

CLEM: *(Pulling out the flask.)* Okay, Moon.

MOON: There's a case to be made for finishin' the century blind drunk.

CLEM: Care for a dollop?

(Clem, having taken a hit, passes the flask to Moon.)

MOON: Well, I don't mind. *(Drinks.)* How about you, Mona?

MONA: *(A roar.)* I hate men!

MOON: Me too, ma'am. *(Drinks.)*

ROY: There. *(Tosses the keys.)* This is egregious damn car theft.

MOON: Tell him "Shut up," ma'am.

MONA: Shut up!

MOON: Here I come now. *(Starts up toward Mona.)* Just bringin' the wallets and the car keys. Get you started, you know, before the divorce.

MONA: I was g-good at math.

MOON: Yes ma'am.

MONA: I was better than the boys.

(He nods.)

MOON: Yes ma'am.

MONA: I could have done r-research on the universe.

MOON: Well, you're still young, ma'am.

MONA: No, I'm not. I'm dried out.

MOON: *(Puts the wallets down near her.)* Well, you look a little chilly. You might like to put this around your shoulders. *(He puts his field jacket down on the ground. He looks off.)* Clem, are you drivin' that Mazda Miata or the Chrysler?

CLEM: I'm the Mazda, Moon.

MOON: Good for you, Roy, you bought American made. Hey, Clem, would she still take 79 South and then 64 West? It's been a long time.

CLEM: 64 to 44, then take Interstate 40 west all the way.

MOON: Down to Arizona?

CLEM: Yes sir, headin' west.

MOON: Nice two-day drive.

MONA: I'm too old, Moon.

MOON: Ma'am, Buddha said a good fire can only be made from seasoned wood. The point isn't to end the journey, the point is to make the journey.

MONA: I made the journey with you, Roy. I thought I would rest easy and you would care for me. I knew I wasn't a beautiful, wild creature like that R.V., but I thought we could make a quiet life, Roy. That's a horse laugh. A woman's just disposable goods to you. I gave myself over an' forgot who I was, but those days are over and gone, Roy. I'm makin' my own movie now, and you're just something in the rearview mirror to me. I let your tropical fish go free in the creek; I burned your Louis L'Amour first editions, and I pushed your satellite dish off the roof. I'm an outlaw now, Roy, no one will ever treat me that way again.

MOON: Louis L'Amour would despise you, Roy. *(To Roy and Clem.)* Take off those belts! Do it!

CLEM: I don't have a belt, Moon.

MOON: Lie down on your stomachs. *(Takes off his own belt and, with Roy's, expertly belts the two brothers' hands behind them.)* It took me four planes, an oxcart, and I forded a river on a man's back to get here, boys. Had to sell the gold teeth I'd been collectin' to get it done. See, I wanted to be here for R.V., do a little business, see my big brothers and take a little vacation from gettin' people down on the ground and tyin' them up with their belts. I guess it just shows you're a prisoner of your talents. That isn't too tight, is it?

CLEM: It feels real nice, Moon.

MOON: *(Looking over his handiwork.)* Well, okay… *(Up to Mona.)* You might want to get started, ma'am.

MONA: Are you the worst?

MOON: Beg pardon?

MONA: You have raped and pillaged and slaughtered?

MOON: More or less.

MONA: Are you the worst of men? I need a b-benchmark.

MOON: Well I don't know, ma'am. I guess I'm close enough to be competitive.

MONA: Then I'll k-keep the pistol.

MOON: Good idea. Say, you know what they do all over the world?

MONA: Who?

MOON: Those who have prevailed. Those who have brought their enemies to their knees and made them eat the dust of the road. It doesn't matter if it's Medellin or Kumasi or Kuala Lumpur, they fire their weapons in the air. They empty themselves into the universe in celebration. *(He hands her his automatic weapon.)*

ROY: My God, are you deranged?!

MOON: Go ahead, ma'am.

(Mona looks at him and then fires a long burst in the air.)

MOON: Feels good, huh?

MONA: It feels g-g-g-glorious! *(She hands back the automatic, keeping the pistol. She smiles for the first time.)*

MOON: Well, you might want to get goin', ma'am. Keep your mind real empty and close to hand, that'll let it heal up. You might want to put on some clothes, but everybody's got their own way.

MONA: Good-bye, Moon.

MOON: Adios, babe.

MONA: *(She turns to Roy and Clem.)* Good-bye, Clem. Good-bye, Roy. I'm sorry I was such a bad shot. I'm free now. When I'm out in Arizona, I'm going to take this money and raise b-bees. Millions of b-bees. Then with the aphrodisiac of my freedom, I will lure men to hotel rooms. I will tie them to the b-bed with silk scarves for a g-good time. Then I will place the queen b-bee on their penis and when they are completely covered with the swarm, I will leave them there to figure it out. *(She exits.)*

MOON: Nice night, beautiful stars, minimum of snipers. That's what I call perfect conditions.

ROY: Untie me, you bastard.

MOON: How come you're dressed up like an Amish farmer, Roy?

ROY: Do you know what a divorce is goin' to cost me?

MOON: That's just overhead, Roy, it was comin' on anyway, you just have to amortize it.

CLEM: There's ants in my shirt, Moon.

MOON: I'm goin' to smoke me a Cuban cigar, Clem. They roll these babies on the inside of a beautiful woman's thigh. One of the few luxuries left.

CLEM: My wife left me too.

MOON: Everybody's wife leaves, Clem, it's a shit job.

CLEM: How am I goin' to raise my boys?

MOON: Just tell 'em to do the opposite.

CLEM: The opposite?

MOON: I wouldn't worry about it, Clem. *(Moon lights up.)*

ROY: My own brother robbed me.

MOON: You can get on the phone and cancel the cards, they got all-night service.

ROY: I'm talkin' about my car! You stole my car.

MOON: A Chrysler ain't a car, Roy, it's just upholstery on wheels. *(Suddenly the dump is alive with movement. Small black shapes scurry everywhere.)*

ROY: My God, what's that?

MOON: Looks like the rats are leavin' the dump, Roy.

ROY: Untie me, goddamnit.

MOON: I once saw rats eat a man alive. They ate him in circles like a corn dog.

CLEM: I'm scared of rats, Moon.

MOON: *(Looks up at the stars.)* You both owe me money. *(Silence falls.)*

ROY: Now Moon, this isn't the time to talk about that. This is a time for three brothers, lost to each other by geography, to take hands, kneel down…

MOON: You owe me for the fishing cabin Pop left me that you sold for me in '86.

ROY: Moon, that cabin was in bad shape.

MOON: How much did you get for it?

ROY: …water damaged, rotted out.

MOON: How much, Roy?

ROY: Maybe $1,300, well, no, a little bit less.

MOON: You sold 1.3 acres down on the river for $1,300?

ROY: Hey little brother, this was eight years ago.

MOON: It was appraised 20 years ago at $7,500.

ROY: Are you accusing me of cheatin' my own damn family?

MOON: Yes.

ROY: There is no bond like blood, Moon, and there is nothing so despicable as to doubt it.

CLEM: Mighta been $5,000, Moon.

MOON: That's good, Clem, and when you started your pawnshop I fronted you $5,000, which was ten percent of the capital.

CLEM: Would you care for some Cheezits, Moon?

MOON: You sure that pawnshop didn't grow into your gun store? Because you would owe me ten cents on every dollar of profit.

CLEM: No. No, the pawnshop and the gun shop, that was two completely different enterprises.

MOON: I see. You still located down on the strip across from the Pentacostal Tabernacle of Simple Faith?

CLEM: Well, no, we kind of shifted over toward the water, when I changed over to family security.

MOON: Uh-huh.

CLEM: Riverfront development, you know.

MOON: It wouldn't be located on 1.3 acres of riverfront property, now would it? *(Pause.)* Would it, Clem?

CLEM: *(Pause.)* Come to think of it, Moon, Roy and me might owe you a small sum, and we'd sure like to settle up. Don't you think so, Roy?

ROY: Well, now that we think of it.

MOON: Sounds good to me, boys, because I'm thinkin' of openin' up a chain of coin laundries over in Albania.

CLEM: Albania.

MOON: Clem, those people really need their clothes done.

CLEM: Sounds like a real opportunity.

MOON: *(Rises.)* Well, boys, I look forward to settlin' up.

ROY: There's nothin' that people of good will can't work out.

MOON: There better not be. *(Moves to untie them.)* Say, Roy, there's some barrels in the dump labeled Phinoethylbarmetholine. Don't they use that stuff in nerve gas?

ROY: *(A beat.)* No, actually it's used in barbecue sauce, stuff like that.

MOON: Sure, that must be where I remembered it from.

ROY: We can work the money out, Moon.

MOON: Okay.

ROY: Well, I got a Fourth of July speech to give.

MOON: So.

ROY: I got to go *now*. Gimme your keys, Clem.

CLEM: We got to finish the sacred trust, Roy.

ROY: Goddammit.

MOON: We got to finish the sacred trust, Roy.

ROY: You can't have your community festivities until the mayor speaks to nail down the significance. That is *democracy* which you two wouldn't know a damn thing about.

MOON: Democracy, sure. Hey, I'm out there killin' people for the free enterprise system.

ROY: You're just out there killin' people.

MOON: When you start a democracy you have to kill a few people, if you know your history.

ROY: You don't know squat about history, Moon.

MOON: I was in Nam, man, I *am* history.

ROY: You're history alright, it was the first damn war we ever lost.

CLEM: Now hold on, Roy.

MOON: Are you mockin' my dead buddies?

CLEM: Now hold on, Moon.

ROY: I been workin' 20 years to fix what you and your buddies screwed up!

MOON: *(Starting for him.)* I'm gonna' rip your head off.

CLEM: *(Out of desperation.)* Mama's dead.
(Moon stops in mid-charge.)

MOON: What's that?

CLEM: I didn't know if you knew Mama's dead?

MOON: When?

CLEM: July of '91. We didn't know where you were, Moon. We tried *Soldier of Fortune* magazine.

MOON: How'd Mama go?

CLEM: It was cancer, Moon, it wasn't too bad, she went pretty easy.

MOON: Goddamnit to hell! Was it the cigarettes?

CLEM: I don't know, Moon.

MOON: I told you to get her on to the low tar. I told you to take those Camel cigarettes away from her.

CLEM: I tried, Moon, but...

MOON: Damn! Buried or cremated?

CLEM: Moon, I just don't think...

MOON: Which was it?

CLEM: Cremated.

MOON: Aarrrgh! *(Moon, in a rage, slings trash across the dump.)* A man don't want his mother cremated! You understand that?

ROY: Well, she left instructions.

MOON: Instructions? Piss on the instructions! I want my Mama's grave! Where is she, goddamnit?

CLEM: Scattered.

MOON: *(Sitting down.)* You made bonemeal outta' my Mama.

CLEM: Well Moon, she didn't want to be a bother, see. She didn't want us worried about the upkeep. She just wanted to disperse.

MOON: You two morons went and dispersed her?

ROY: Well, we...

MOON: Dispersed her *where*, damnit?

CLEM: Wendy's.

MOON: Wendy's Fast Food?

CLEM: Well, she stopped cookin' with everybody gone and she liked to go down to the Wendy's.

MOON: You spread our Mama out at a fast food restaurant?

ROY: In the daylily garden.

MOON: I can't kneel down at a fast food restaurant and ask my Mama what to do.

CLEM: Well you could, Moon.

MOON: Never mind!

CLEM: It's a real busy corner though.

MOON: I don't want to talk about it. *(Throws his head back.)* R.V.!? The world's goin' to hell, R.V. Mama's dispersed. You're dead. Roy and Clem cheated on me. Communism wimped out. My trigger hand shakes. Where the hell are we? What the hell's goin' on?!!

CLEM: I'll get the beer.

MOON: *(A moment. He calms.)* I still remember your smell, R.V., the curve of your thigh. I don't know why you killed yourself, but you're sure as hell well out of it. You could gentle me down, I remember that. We never got to say good-bye, so I'm here to do it. Hell, I'm only 20 years late, that's not too bad. You asked for it, an' I'm doin' it, but I tell you what, R.V., I'm tired of dead people. They're piled up, one on top of the other, everywhere you go on this planet. Damn, I'm tired of *that* smell. You an' me were two crazy sons-of-bitches, and that always gave me some comfort. I tell you one thing, R.V., I hope wherever you are you still got that red dress and that snake tattoo.

(R.V. appears again on the car behind them.)
Heaven for climate, hell for company. Let's chug these beers.
(They do. R.V. speaks from behind them.)
R.V.: Did you love me, Moon?
(The men turn, startled.)
R.V.: Holy shit, you got old!
(Clem slumps to the ground in a faint.)
MOON: Is that you, R.V.?
R.V.: It's me, Moon.
ROY: *(To Moon.)* You see her, right?
MOON: I see her.
R.V.: I forgot you would get old.
ROY: Go on now, whatever you are. Go on, shoo! Shoo!
R.V.: Hello, Roy.
ROY: Looks just like the day she died.
MOON: What is it you want, R.V.?
R.V.: I bring the messenger to…say, is Clem alright?
ROY: Damn, but she looks real to the touch.
R.V.: Real to the touch?
(She walks directly to Moon and involves him in a long kiss. Roy talks through it. Clem moans.)
ROY: Shut up, Clem. Is she real, Moon? What's she feel like, Moon? I wouldn't do that, Moon. Hell, she could be a vampire.
(She steps back from him. Their eyes are locked.)
MOON: Your lips are cold.
R.V.: I wrote you 1,200 letters in Nam. I got two postcards.
MOON: It was a bad time.
R.V.: How's the Buddha, Moon?
MOON: I lost track.
R.V.: Where'd you go when you left Nam?
MOON: Angola for awhile, Rhodesia, Ghana, Yemen, Burundi, Salvador, Somalia, a little while in the Seychelles, Afghanistan, Azerbaijan, shacked up for a time in Albania, 26 days in Cambodia, two years near Zagreb, and I was down around Liberia when this came up.
R.V.: You know I married Roy.
MOON: Damn R.V., what's you do that for?
R.V.: I was having nightmares.
MOON: Were you drunk?

R.V.: Some of the time. Shoot, Moon, back then he was the next best thing.

ROY: Thanks a helluva damn lot.

R.V.: Beggin' your pardon, Roy.

CLEM: *(Reviving.)* Roy! Roy!

ROY: *(Annoyed.)* What is it, Clem?

CLEM: *(Not seeing R.V.)* She was *here*, Roy.

ROY: Clem, damn it…

CLEM: No, no, I saw her. I saw R.V. So help me, no kiddin'. Wearin' the red dress just like the last night. I'm not foolin', Roy.
(Roy points. Clem looks.)

CLEM: Oh, my God, the graves are opening. It's the last judgment, Roy, it's on us. My God, humble yourself.

ROY: Will you be quiet, Clem?

CLEM: *(Drinks from his flask, sings.)* "Swing lo', sweet char-i-ot, comin' for to carry me home…"

MOON: Clem, knock that off!

R.V.: What's shakin', Clem?

CLEM: Oh my God, oh my God, oh my God, oh my God.

R.V.: *(R.V. touches him on the cheek. He quiets.)* I had Clem one time, too. I had Clem and Roy 'cause you never answered my letters.

MOON: Come on, R.V.!

ROY: Clem!?

CLEM: Oh my God, oh my God.

ROY: You didn't have Clem? Not while we were married, was it?

R.V.: It was just one time, Roy.

ROY: While we were married?

CLEM: It was just one time, Roy.

ROY: *(To Clem.)* You're my own damn blood and you screwed my wife?!

MOON: That's pretty low, R.V.

ROY: It wasn't in my house, was it?

MOON: You said you were waitin' for me.

ROY: You better answer me, Clem!

CLEM: It was in the garden.

ROY: In the garden? It wasn't near Mama's daylilies, was it?

CLEM: Heck no, Roy, it was over in the phlox. You were sleepin'; it didn't mean to happen.

ROY: I just can't believe this!

R.V.: Roy, you and I were hardly makin' love at all.

ROY: Worst case, we always did it once a week.

R.V.: Yeah, Tuesdays.

ROY: It wasn't only on Tuesdays.

CLEM: We didn't do it on a Tuesday, Roy.

ROY: Shut up. Godawful, R.V., ol' Clem puffin' away in the missionary position.

R.V.: Not quite, Roy.

ROY: What do you mean, *not quite?*

CLEM: Well, I'm double-jointed, Roy.

ROY: Goddamnit!

R.V.: He was the only one of you boys ever loved me. Why the hell are you gettin' riled up? I'm dead, for one thing. He'd bring me coffee, get me car parts, roll my joints, remember my damn birthday, and come down every night to hear me sing at the Holiday Inn. He loved me like a dog; why shouldn't he get laid one time?

MOON: Because it's Clem, damn it!

R.V.: Roy was passed out. I couldn't sleep. The moon was real orange over the hills, so I walked out into the garden and there was Clem sittin' on the bench.

ROY: You didn't go out there naked, did you?

R.V.: I went out there naked all the time. It was 3:00 AM, who cared?

CLEM: I was just out walkin', Roy. I just sat down there for a minute.

ROY: You are a snake in the woodpile.

R.V.: We just sat there on the bench. He told me I looked like a statue in the moonlight. He said he come there some nights when we were asleep, he'd sit there and hope me and him were breathing in and out at the same time. We just sat there, whispering, with our shoulders touching, and after awhile we lay down in the phlox. You did real good, Clem.

CLEM: Thank you, R.V. You want some Cheezits?

R.V.: Sure.

ROY: Why the hell didn't you love me, R.V.? Goddamnit, I'm lovable. I'm a hard worker, ambitious, patriotic; I'm a damn fine provider, like to dance, I got a serious side. Why the hell didn't you love me?

R.V.: You're just too much man, Roy.

ROY: Well, I can't shrivel myself up to win a woman's love. I can't down-size what I am, R.V., I got to let it roll! It's like this country is what it's like. Those pissant third worlds can't stand the sheer magnificent expanse of us. They can't take their eyes off us, but they want to cut us down to size. It's tragic grandeur, that's what I got! Goddamnit, woman, you should have *loved* me!!

R.V.: It's not a function of the will, Roy.

(A moment.)

MOON: You're sure you're dead, R.V.?

R.V.: Deader than hell.

CLEM: There was omens, Roy, the Gifford horse, the frogs, the way the sky was. I must have seen 15 possum in a bunch headin' south on the highway, and a possum he travels alone.

R.V.: How about a beer, boys? A cold one for the road.

ROY: You want a beer?

R.V.: You get pretty dry when you're dead, Roy.

MOON: Get the lady a beer, will you?

ROY: I have got to get over to the…

R.V.: You can't go, Roy, you've been chosen.

ROY: What do you mean, chosen?

R.V.: Chosen, Roy.

(Clem hands out the beer.)

R.V.: How come you were sleeping in the dump, Moon?

MOON: I got in late last night. I can't sleep indoors, it makes me dream.

R.V.: Dream what?

MOON: Things I've done.

ROY: What do you mean chosen?

MOON: Outdoors, I've been dreaming about you.

R.V.: I know. *(She pops the beer and proposes a toast.)* To the white man, God help him.

(Clem, Moon and R.V. drink.)

ROY: What kind of toast is that?

MOON: Where are you, R.V.?

R.V.: Say what?

MOON: When you're not here?

R.V.: Heaven.

CLEM: Oh my Lord, there is life after death?

R.V.: Well, I'm drinkin' my beer, Clem.

CLEM: Moon, Roy, can you believe this. We're sittin' in the dump, and it's been revealed!

MOON: Take it easy, Clem.

CLEM: What do you do there? What's it like, R.V.?

R.V.: It's pure unadulterated longing. It's like you lost a leg but there's still feeling where the leg used to be. The feeling is for the life you didn't live, and you pass the time until you find some way to make yourself whole.

CLEM: Sure, but what's it like?

R.V.: The one you guys have is a celestial theme park with a thousand T.V. channels, continual sex and a 5,000 hole golf course.

ROY: Jee-sus!

R.V.: I go over sometimes for the salad bar.

MOON: Are you kiddin', R.V.?

R.V.: Could be.

ROY: I said chosen for what, damnit?

MOON: How you like it up there?

R.V.: Too damn serene.

MOON: Yeah?

R.V.: I tried to kill myself up there, too. Hell, you know, just for variety. Hurled myself down the cloud canyons. Forget it. Once you're immortal, you're immortal.

MOON: Sounds like a tough gig.

R.V.: It's a perception thing, Moon. See, I only got the perception I took up there, and that just doesn't cut it, you know. I took the messenger gig because I figured you could help me out. I'm locked inside 25 years, Moon. I only get the heaven 25 years can understand. Hell, you must be close to 50. Tell me what you know.

MOON: Shoot low and shoot first.

R.V.: Goddamnit Moon, I'm not jokin'.

MOON: Who said I was jokin', R.V.?

R.V.: Move me on, Moon, don't leave me where I am.

MOON: Got me a limited perspective.

R.V.: You lived all those years and only got smaller?

MOON: I yam what I yam, babe.

R.V.: Well, damn! *(She kicks something across the dump.)* How come this dump's sittin' on the ball field?

ROY: The dump's the whole point, R.V.

R.V.: What point?

ROY: The point. Town was fallin' apart, R.V. The town, the job pool, the tax base.

CLEM: Dollar movie closed down.

ROY: I said to myself, Roy, what is this country based on? And by God it came to me, it's based on garbage. There is nobody in the world has the garbage we do! *(He pulls stuff out of the dump.)* Blenders, TV's, Lazyboys, syringes! We did a little study showed that within one truck day of this town, two billion tons of garbage produced weekly. Bingo! You know where people want to put their garbage? Somewhere else, that's where. And there is no damn town in this country that is more somewhere else than we are. And I sold that idea, by God, and it saved the town. We got the dump here plus nine other locations. I'm not sayin' I can walk on water, but I'll tell you this here is a damn miracle.

R.V.: So the ball field's down there?

CLEM: Down there somewhere. *(Finishes the flask, throws it away.)*

R.V.: How come you started throwin' those change ups, Moon?

MOON: How come you drove off the bridge?

R.V.: You ever been airborne in a Corvette Stingray on a cool night at 145 miles an hour?

MOON: No ma'am.

R.V.: Hang time, it's a real rush. Damn, I love speed. What was I supposed to do, Moon? Stick around, do hair stylin' at Babettes, work part-time at the Seashell Gift Shop, make chocolate chip cookies down at Suzi's Love Oven?! Blow that crap out your ear, man.

CLEM: You could sing, R.V.

R.V.: Good enough for the Holiday Inn Lounge, huh, Clem?

CLEM: I came every night.

R.V.: Bunch of drunks in bad ties, yellin' out "Moon River." Yeah, I could sing that good.

CLEM: You was pearls before swine.

R.V.: Thanks, baby. Ol' Jimmy Dean an' me, we weren't countin' on tomorrow, see? You think I'm gonna drag a broke life behind me down Main Street, like some old rusty tailpipe kickin' up sparks? Hell with that, man! That night I flew the Corvette, I put on my red dress an' I looked fine! I was wearin' the hell out of that thing, you dig? Figured it was time to go out large, so I just slipped my good lookin' legs into some red rhinestone heels and put the pedal to the metal!

CLEM: We could see you go off the bridge from down at Bob's Big Boy parkin' lot. Slow motion right across the moon.

R.V.: Sure, I could see you boys standin' still lookin' up. Hell, 20 years later you're still there. You look sad, Moon. Is it me or the bridge?

MOON: What bridge?

R.V.: Your bridge.

MOON: What the hell are you talking about?

R.V.: The bridge in Liberia. *(A beat.)*

MOON: How do you know that, R.V.?

R.V.: I keep track, Moon.

MOON: Then why ask me?

R.V.: To see if you have the balls to tell me.

MOON: Just a bridge we held.

R.V.: Yeah?

MOON: Yeah.

R.V.: Just a bridge, huh?

MOON: Only way you could still get over into Sierra Leone. We didn't blow it 'cause we had to run transport through there once the town fell.

R.V.: Go on, Moon.

R.V. AND MOON: *(He is unaware that she speaks with him.)* The bridge stretched out like an old rusty skeleton between two hills…

R.V.: Tell it, Moon.

MOON: Those people…

R.V.: Those people…

MOON: Kept tryin' to come across it.

R.V.: That's right.

MOON: Everybody's snipers up in the hills.

R.V.: *(In sync, she sees it too.)* Man in a big brown coat…

MOON: Midday, somebody tried to run it.

R.V.: Uh-huh.

MOON: Looked like a man in a big coat. I was in the hills…

R.V.: Uh-huh.

MOON: I fired a rifle grenade into the coat…

R.V.: It didn't explode…

MOON: Didn't explode, but the coat opened up and it was a woman…

R.V. AND MOON: …carrying a young child.

MOON: *(Hypnotized now by memory's image.)* That rifle grenade nailed the child to the mother's chest…

R.V.: Down there on the bridge…

MOON AND R.V.: …and they lay, mother and child, nailed together on the bridge for two days…

MOON: See, nobody dared try to go out there and get 'em.

MOON AND R.V.: Lay there screaming…

R.V.: On the bridge…

MOON AND R.V.: Screaming.

MOON: Finally I took a rifle, blew up that grenade on the second shot.

R.V.: Then what, Moon?

MOON: I stayed there another day. Then I walked out, following the river. Took me three weeks.

R.V.: How come?

MOON: I figured I'd try something else.

R.V.: Like my bridge?

MOON: Your bridge?

R.V.: Right across the sky.

MOON: No thanks, R.V.

R.V.: What is it you know, Moon?

MOON: A piece of shit doesn't throw a perfect game.

ROY: You threw the damn game on purpose?

MOON: Shut up, Roy.

R.V.: It's getting late, Moon.

MOON: Could be.

R.V.: You don't have somethin' for me?

MOON: Not a damn thing.

R.V.: Well, it's time to get started, boys. *(She raises her arm, one finger pointing up, and there is a shattering crash of thunder. She raises her other arm.)* Spirits of wind, water, earth and fire, enwrap me here! *(Thunder, lightning.)* I am appeared before you, sent by the lord of hosts. She who is both the tumult and the eye of the hurricane. She who throweth up continents and maketh men from the fish of the sea. Hear me. Hear me!

(The rain pours down on everyone except R.V. Clem raises his small umbrella. Roy and Moon are drenched.)

R.V.: I come at her behest to be the harbinger of her great messenger. Through him will the blind see, the broken mend and the heart be made whole. *(A powerful beam of light pours down on her.)* Great spirit, King, right hand of the all-powerful, we welcome thee! Hold onto your seats, boys, he is upon us now!

(A tremendous explosion, as if the stage had been struck in two by a lightning bolt. The rain stops. Smoke, debris and then sudden silence. Elvis appears. He is dressed in his "suit of lights," the famous white sequined performance suit. A driving guitar riff and final chord surround his entrance. He is the same age as at his death.)

CLEM: My God, who are you?

ELVIS: I'm the King of the White Man, asshole, who are you?

CLEM: Elvis?

ELVIS: The Velvet Rocker, buddy, the Hillbilly Cat, the King of Western Bop.

CLEM: You thinned down, King.

ELVIS: I been dinin' on cumulus nimbus.

ROY: Kinda' lost your magnitude.

ELVIS: Well, I'm not dressed up as a Smith Brothers cough drop. I'll tell y'all one thing, boys, there wasn't nobody, nowhere, no time, no way, ever seen a white boy move like me. They couldn't shake it where I shook it or take it where I took it. I was born with a guitar in one hand and the ruination of western civilization in the other. Y'all look a little tight there, boys, so the King's gotta' get you ready to party! Heck, have some Dexedrine... *(He scatters hundreds of pills in a multicolored spray from his pockets as if they were coins for the multitudes.)* Have some Tuinal, Dilaudid, Quaaludes and Demerol! Get up, or get down, get wherever you need to be to hear the *word! (Lightning crackles, framing his figure in its flash.)*

CLEM: *(Picking some up.)* Thanks, King.

ELVIS: Uh-huh! Hit it! *(Another crash and sizzle of lightning.)* The Lord, she stood on the rim of the universe, and she did regard the earth, baby. And wherever her gaze did fall there was real bad doody goin' down. There was a sickly caste, a dread pigmentless, soulless, milky pale fungi suckin' the sustenance right out of the world, man, leavin' things undone, done badly, overlooked, overgrazed, snafued and skimmin' the cream right off the top. And who the hell was in the driver's seat takin' care of business? Buddy, it was a bunch of fat old white men, that's who it was! Greedy ol' farts livin' off the fat of the land while the land fell apart in their hands. They weren't gettin' it there, dudes! You can't rhumba in a sports car, baby. You can't do no Australian crawl in a shot glass. We had it, man, and we pissed it away! Regard me, brethren. I was the most beautiful cat ever rolled into Memphis in a '39 Plymouth. I could sing black boogie and the Mississippi Delta blues. I could shuck and jive like a funky angel. I was the white man triumphant, baby. If I wanted it *now,* I got it *now.* I was the boss, the king, El Presidente Grande, and I ended up fat as a grain-fed hog, down on my knees on the bathroom floor with my head floatin' in a toilet bowl. Hell, you're down in the bowl with me, boys. Y'all had played errorless, no-hit ball goin' into the eighth inning, and you took it from there to the dung heap, poisoned in spirit and your women flee you into the night with whatever they can carry.

CLEM: *(Delighted.)* He's talkin' about us, boys!

ELVIS: She-it, compadres! The last time the Lord saw something' like this, she had the game rained out, man but the Lord wouldn't even trust you cats to build an ark! Huh-uh! She was set to hurl the white man into the eternal dark and see what somebody else could do with it. My people were goin' down, baby, the bell was tollin' the midnight hour, cats, so I had the cherubim and seraphim deliver me to the Lord's right hand an' I whipped out my guitar and shucked out a tune, boys.

CLEM: We love you, Elvis!

ELVIS: *(He throws out his hand and an unseen band crashes into a rock and roll riff. Elvis' voice is now amplified.)* I rocked it, baby, laid down a hot lick, turned it every way but loose, like you know I can, and there amongst the beatific host, the Lord, she got down, she got tight, she got right with my music, and she boogied through the day, and a night, and a day and when I sent that last reverb down through the chambers of her immortal heart, she said, "Elvis, I thought I'd seen it all when I saw Lucifer, but the way you're rockin' tonight, I'm gonna give the white man one *(chord)* more *(chord)* chance. *(chord)*" *(The music ends.)* And I said, "Lord, I'm hip and I'm on it, what's the deal?" And she laid her cool hand on my cheek and asked did I remember what my precious mama said to me when I done wrong and lied about it. And I said, "Yes Lord, I do." She said, "Sonny boy, there ain't nothin' done in this old world so debauched and brought low that you can't get right with your God and your mama with just two little words… *(The big finish.)* and listen here now, those two words, those two paradisiacal confections, sweet as plums or summer cherries, those two words are…I'm sorry!" *(A pause. Distant thunder rolls. The words "I'm Sorry" echo through the heavens.)*

MOON: Hey Elvis?

ELVIS: Yeah?

MOON: The Lord God wants us to say we're sorry?

ELVIS: Uh-huh.

MOON: Just "I'm sorry?"

ELVIS: Well, it's kind of a cosmic thing, man. But you got it, yeah. Otherwise she's gonna' send down the white flu, let it blanket the earth, uh-huh, all you white guys sneeze yourself right into eternity inside of two weeks.

CLEM: The white flu!?

ROY: What the hell are we s'posed to have done?

ELVIS: *(His arms wide.)* This.

ROY: Hey, everybody throws things away, okay?

ELVIS: But who was runnin' the store, buddy?

ROY: Well, it wasn't me, big guy.

ELVIS: Well, who the hell was it?

ROY: Hell, you got your media, your cartels, your multinationals, your big government.

ELVIS: And who was runnin' them?

ROY: How the hell am I supposed to know?

ELVIS: Well, let's just say they weren't purple, how about that?

ROY: I'm damn tired of everybody talkin' trash on the white man. Hell, we thought up about 90% of civilization. It was 12 of our own kind sat with Christ at his table. If these goddamn minorities shoulda' led us somewhere, why didn't they step up to the plate! *(He sneezes explosively.)*

ELVIS: Sounds like you're comin' down with somethin'. Say, R.V., how about some seraphim send us down a milkshake, maybe put an egg in it?

(R.V. snaps her fingers.)

CLEM: Say, King…

ELVIS: Uh-huh?

CLEM: You kinda lost me on the curve, King.

(The milkshake descends from the skies.)

ELVIS: Hell, y'all explain it, R.V., I'm gonna take a load off. *(Takes the milkshake and makes himself comfortable.)*

R.V.: Hear me, fishermen. *(Lightning.)* You, before me, of all those assembled, are the chosen. The bellwethers, the forerunners, you hold redemption in the palm of your hand!

ELVIS: She ain't kiddin'.

R.V.: See Clem, the Lord, she asked me did I know any white guys, and I said sure.

CLEM: How come she asked you, R.V.?

R.V.: I was just standin' there. She touched my snake tattoo, filling me with light, saying I should pave the way and we should proclaim the news.

ELVIS: *(Drinking his milkshake.)* Do it, iridescent one. Attend me, white ones! *(Sizzling lightning crash.)* The Lord God, the First Cause, the Celestial She, the Big Femina, instructs you here to prepare your hearts and set out on foot from this place to great Washington Monument in the city yclept "D.C." and to carry on that journey of the spirit a sign of apology.

CLEM: Gollee Roy, we could do that!

R.V.: Your garments shall you here divest, and your journey shall be unclothed. *(A pause.)*

MOON: Say what?

ELVIS: You got to do it butt-naked, buddy.

ROY: Now just hold on here.

ELVIS: *(Holding out the milkshake.)* You ever try one with an egg in it?

ROY: You want us to strip down and walk 600 miles from here to D.C. with a sign says "I'm sorry?"

ELVIS: Gonna' get a hell of a suntan.

ROY: When hell freezes over, boy! I'm the best damn thing genetics ever come up with, an' that's the American white man, runnin' the most powerful damn nation this world's ever seen, an' we don't strip down for some damn hallucination! *(He sneezes.)*

ELVIS: Have a Kleenex, Roy.

R.V.: Oh man, repent all and regard thee here thy immortal soul.

ROY: Damnit, Moon, listen to this.

MOON: I'm listenin'.

ROY: Clem?

CLEM: Well…

ROY: Stand up for your own blood, goddamnit!

CLEM: I guess God's my own blood, Roy.

R.V.: Lo, the plague will descend, your bodies be consumed and your heart sundered.

MOON: I don't have a heart, R.V.

R.V.: You just never turned it on, Moon.

ROY: R.V.?

R.V.: Sinner, save your kind and rejoice, lest you and all your tribe shall perish from the earth.

MOON: You comin', Elvis?

ELVIS: I'll be just above your head, man.

MOON: You sorry?

ELVIS: I failed my precious mama. I can't sleep the eternal sleep when I done like that.

ROY: The white man shouldn't have to take the rap for this!

ELVIS: Tough nuggies, Roy.

ROY: Who the hell has the moral authority to stand here in this dump and tell me I got to take off my underpants?!

ELVIS: I was you, I'd ask your precious mama.

ROY: How the hell am I gonna' ask my mama.

MOON: You can't ask her, you damn moron, you dispersed her!

(A heavenly chord; a puff of smoke. Their mother appears on the ridge. She is in her early 70s, wearing a housedress. She has a halo.)

CLEM: Holy smoke!

MRS. MANNERING: Hello, son.

ROY AND MOON: Mama!

MRS. MANNERING: Now you do what Elvis says, Roy. I only hope to goodness you took a shower.

CLEM: It's you, Mama.

MRS. MANNERING: Hello Bootsie. I just cannot believe you let an eight-year-old child get hold of an AK-47.

CLEM: I know, Mama.

MRS. MANNERING: I believe you've been imbibing hard liquor.

CLEM: It's only 80 proof, Mama.

MRS. MANNERING: Well, you had better pull up your bootstraps. Moon Mannering, what is that on your face?

MOON: Facial hair, Mama.

MRS. MANNERING: You got something to be ashamed of hid behind that mess?

MOON: Well, Mama...

MRS. MANNERING: You better not let your father catch you like that. Do you have blood on your hands, son?

MOON: I do, Mama.

MRS. MANNERING: I ought to whip your butt off. Thou shalt not kill, do you hear me? Tiny, what in heaven's name are you got up as?

ROY: Abraham Lincoln, Mama.

MRS. MANNERING: Remember the sin of pride, Tiny. Pride goeth before a fall. Look up sinner.

(Roy does.)

CLEM: Gollee Moses.

ROY: Oh, my God, Mama.

(Clem lets out a long whistle.)

ROY: It's the load receipt printed in fire on the sky.

CLEM: Those letters must be a mile high.

ROY: See what you did, Clem?

CLEM: It's real readable.

ROY: Shut up.

CLEM: *(Trying to make up.)* You want some Cheezits?

ROY: *(Ripping them from his hand. Stomps them.)* Arrrrrrgh!

CLEM: You broke my Cheezits. Those were all the Cheezits I had.

ROY: Shut up!

CLEM: *(Suddenly twisted with rage; the straw that broke the camel's back.)* Don't...you...tell me...to...shut up!! You have...humiliated me... for 40 years. *(He reaches down and picks up an iron bar out of the dump.)* If you ever...ever speak to me in that tone of voice... Roy...I will mash you like a potato, tear out your liver and heart and devour them, whole.

MRS. MANNERING: *(Clapping her hands as you do with children.)* Now that is enough, now. You may not eat your brother. That is out of the question.

CLEM: *(Returning to himself.)* Golly, Mama...I didn't mean that.

MRS. MANNERING: Of course you didn't.

MOON: *(Looking at the sky.)* Well, they know what you got in your dump all over North America now, Roy.

MRS. MANNERING: *(With finality.)* People do not eat their own. *(She points up.)* Think of your mama seein' your dirty laundry bein' washed right across the night sky, Roy. You better get right with the deity. *(Roy hangs his head.)* Now have you boys been brushing your teeth?

THE BOYS: Yes Mama.

MRS. MANNERING: Then get undressed.

ROY: I don't want to, Mama.

MRS. MANNERING: It is very, very late.

ROY: I...just can't...Mama.

MRS. MANNERING: Why not, Roy?

ROY: I'm ashamed of the size of my sexual member.

MRS. MANNERING: God gave you that body, there is no reason to be ashamed of it. You think I haven't seen your thing before?

ROY: Yes Mama.

MRS. MANNERING: You have a responsibility to your fellow creatures, Roy Mannering, now I don't want to hear anymore about it. Your sweet Grandpa Abbey, 100 years old, your kind Uncle William always sent five dollars on your birthday, you want them to die of this flu?

THE BOYS: No Mama.

MRS. MANNERING: Well, I would think not. I carried you inside me, boys, and you were, every one of you, breech births. I have cradled your tiny fevered bodies in my arms and sang to you from the opera Aida by the immortal Verdi. I watched you grow from beautiful, tiny, tow-headed perfections into big, splotchy, gangly things who masturbated. I paid your car insurance long after it should have been your responsibility. Yes, Jesus, I have suffered! You could see me draining out into you like a bottle emptying. There wasn't a drop, not a scintilla, left for my thoughts or feelings or dreams. I could have been a supply-side economist or the President of the United States. After you were born, your father was afraid to have marital relations with me because you boys never learned to knock. I dreamed of Mr. Presley drenching my body with scented oils and creamy peanut butter and taking his will with me, but none of you would ever drive me to Memphis! I died as I had lived, a housewife, a mother, a cleaning lady and, when that time came, when I did die, when I was no longer your lifelong wet nurse, you irresponsible sons-of-bitches dispersed me to the wrong place!

ROY: Mama!

MRS. MANNERING: I said Hardee's, goddamnit, not Wendy's! Wendy's Big Bacon Classic is pigeon piss compared to Hardee's Friscoburger! I wanted to be at Hardee's in amongst the begonias, across from the drive-thru!

CLEM: It wasn't Wendy's?

MRS. MANNERING: Never mind! That was then, this is now. You can make it up to me *here, after death*. You can give me what I never had, my dreams, my glory, my *raison d'être*. You three, my spawn, have been chosen by the apogee, the highest of the high, to save the white man! All is forgiven; seize the day, do it for your mama!!
(They stand astounded.)

MRS. MANNERING: Go on, I'm waiting.
(Clem unbuttons his work shirt. Roy and Moon are still. Clem takes off the shirt.)

MRS. MANNERING: Don't make me get the strap, Roy.

(A beat, and then Roy sits and starts taking off his shoes. Moon stands dead still, arms at his side.)

R.V.: Did you ever love me, Moon.

MOON: I did.

R.V.: Then why the hell didn't you write?

MOON: I was ashamed.

R.V.: You damn fool, Moon. Look what became of us.

(He stands for another moment and then starts unbuckling his belt.)

R.V.: Cool.

(She takes a step back.)

MRS. MANNERING: Good night, R.V.

R.V.: Good night, Chlotilda.

MRS. MANNERING: I've still got ironing to do. Good night, Clem.

CLEM: Good night, Mommy.

MRS. MANNERING: Good night, Tiny.

(Roy's hands move instinctively in front of his genitals.)

MRS. MANNERING: Good night, Moon.

(He lifts a hand in farewell. She starts to exit.)

MRS. MANNERING: Everybody sleep tight now.

(Humming a hymn, she disappears. A harmonica, somewhere in the universe, picks up the hymn. R.V. raises one hand and speaks.)

R.V.: And lo, grace descended...

ELVIS: ...and they divested themselves, and the harbinger said to them...

R.V.: As you journey, O chosen ones, men where they stand in the fields will lay down the tools of the harvest and join with you...

ELVIS: Yeah, baby...

R.V.: From far off will men hear your righteous tread and stream weeping from the corporate headquarters...

ELVIS: From the condominiums and nouvelle restaurants...

R.V.: From the universities and the oak-paneled boardrooms.

ELVIS: Outta Wall Street and the Silicone Valley.

R.V. AND ELVIS: See them, this multitude of white guys of a certain age...

ELVIS: CEO's, estate lawyers, congressmen...

R.V.: Pediatric allergists, downsizers, aldermen...

ELVIS: Gettin' on their Harleys and their Swiss Alpine snowmobiles, their longin' palpable...

R.V.: Their eyes regretful, their hands joined.

ELVIS: They are comin', baby!

R.V.: The Catholics, the Jews, the Episcopalians...

ELVIS: The down and dirty Baptists...

R.V. AND ELVIS: And all the lesser faiths!

ELVIS: And Roy, my man, you're in the front, dude.

R.V.: You too, Moon...

ELVIS: And Clem, you swingin' dick, you're drivin' the vanguard forward...

R.V.: Until at last these pale multitudes envelope the Washington Monument, as the muscles surround the heart, and from their throats will spring one single cry...

ELVIS: The cry of sins committed...

R.V.: The cry of sins repented...

ELVIS: The cry of old white guys everywhere...

R.V. AND ELVIS: "I...am...sorry!"

(The word "sorry" echoes through the heavens. Roy's fireworks begin overhead. Three rockets in various colors illuminate those below.)

ROY: Luellen started the show.

(More fireworks.)

R.V.: Oh, boys, you were beautiful that day; your crisp, cream, pin-striped uniforms against that emerald green infield.

(Rocket overhead. The brothers remove their last items of clothing.)

R.V.: You boys, like music box figures, spinnin' and divin'. The endless arching beauty of that final mile-high pop-up.

(Another rocket.)

R.V.: You were gods, boys...

ELVIS: Gods of summer.

R.V.: Think what you might have done?!

(A tattoo of explosions and bursts of color. The brothers are finally naked. They look up at the display. R.V. scribbles on the back of an old "For Rent" sign with her lipstick.)

CLEM: *(A particularly glorious rocket.)* Ooooooo, look at that one!

(A golden light plays down the sequined rope by Elvis. He puts one foot in a loop at the bottom and takes hold of the rope with one hand.)

ELVIS: We've got to get on that resurrection express, boys. *(Making his exit.)* Hail and farewell, buddies. Y'all bring it on home.

(He is gone. A series of sharp explosions. R.V. moves down and hands the sign to Moon.)

R.V.: Let's go, boys.

R.V.: I'd go south on Rural 501 and then east down the turnpike. They'll be comin' that way. Hold it up, Moon. Hold it high, my darlin'!

(He does. It says, "I'm sorry." In the distance the Mayberry High School band strikes up a traditional march, the fireworks redouble. It is the finale of Roy's display. The brothers stare out at us; Moon holds up the sign. R.V., in her red dress, stands on the remains of the car behind them.)

R.V.: Fishers of men! The night is fallen, but the lark yet sings. Oh, you Euro-centric Anglo Saxons, *(They turn front.)* there is still one inning left to play!

(There is a final tattoo of airborne explosions and a dying scutter of fireworks. The Mayberry High School band plays bravely on. The lights fade.)

END OF PLAY

Trudy Blue
by Marsha Norman

Biography

Marsha Norman won the 1983 Pulitzer Prize for her play *'Night, Mother.* The play also won four Tony nominations, the Dramatists Guild's prestigious Hull-Warriner Award and the Susan Smith Blackburn Prize. A feature film, starring Anne Bancroft and Sissy Spacek, with a screenplay by Ms. Norman, was released in August 1986. *'Night, Mother* has been translated into 23 languages and has been performed around the world.

Her first play, *Getting Out,* received the John Gassner Playwriting Medallion, the Newsday Oppenheimer Award, and a special citation from the American Theatre Critics Association. Her two one-act plays, *Third and Oak: The Laundromat* and *The Pool Hall* premiered at Actors Theatre of Louisville. Her play *The Hold-up* was workshopped at ATL as well. *Traveler in the Dark* premiered at American Repertory Theatre and was later staged at the Mark Taper Forum under the direction of Gordon Davidson. *Sarah and Abraham* premiered at Actors Theatre of Louisville in 1987 and was produced at the George Street Playhouse in the fall of 1991.

Ms. Norman received a Tony Award and Drama Desk Award for her Broadway musical *The Secret Garden.* Her play *Loving Daniel Boone* had its premiere at the 1992 Actors Theatre of Louisville Humana Festival, and her latest play, *Trudy Blue,* premiered in the 1995 Humana Festival. She wrote the book and lyrics for *The Red Shoes,* with music by Jule Styne. Her first novel, *The Fortune Teller,* was published in 1987.

Ms. Norman has worked in television and film, including most recently, *Face of a Stranger,* starring Gena Rowlands and Tyne Daly.

Ms. Norman has received grants and awards from the National Endowment for the Arts, the Rockefeller Foundation, and the American Academy and Institute of Letters. She has been playwright-in-residence at the Actors Theatre of Louisville and the Mark Taper Forum in Los Angeles, and she has been elected to membership in the American Academy of Achievement. She serves on the Council of the Dramatists Guild, and on the boards of the New York Foundation for the Arts and the Independent Committee for Arts Policy. She is the recipient of the Literature Award from the American Academy and Institute of Arts and Letters.

ORIGINAL PRODUCTION

Trudy Blue was first performed at the 1995 Humana Festival of New American Plays, March 1995. It was directed by George de la Peña with the following cast:

Ginger.	Joanne Camp
Don.	Leo Burmester
Maria, Admirer	Karenjune Sánchez
Sue	Karen Grassle
Connie, Sales Person, Waitress	Ann Bean
Annie.	Anne Pitoniak
Voice of Swami, Sales Person, Publisher	Larry Larson
James.	Tony Coleman
Beth.	Jennifer Carpenter
Charlie.	Larry Barnett
Waiter.	James McDaniel

A scene from *Trudy Blue* was first presented at the Ensemble Studio Theatre as part of the 1994 Marathon of One-Act Plays.

TRUDY BLUE

Ginger and Don are in bed, propped up on their respective pillows. Reading.

GINGER: How's your mother feeling? Did you talk to her today?
(Don doesn't answer. She closes her book.)
GINGER: I'm going downstairs. Do you want anything? *(She sits up.)* Like a glass of water or anything? *(She looks over at him.)* Don?
DON: I said "No."
GINGER: You did?
DON: There's something the matter with your hearing, have you noticed? Especially on the phone. *(Imitating her.)* What? What?
GINGER: My hearing?
DON: Your hearing. Don't stay up too late. How late were you up last night?
GINGER: I don't know. Three.
DON: Oh. If you'll give me the registration for the Volvo, I'll take it out with me tomorrow and put it on.
GINGER: You're going to the country tomorrow?
DON: I told you that. Jesus, Ginger. Just for the day, though. I'll be back by eight.
GINGER: You told me you were going to the country? What is tomorrow?
DON: Tuesday. Yes. I told you. I rented a workshop.
GINGER: A workshop?
DON: Yes. If you will remember our discussion last weekend, I can

either stop making tables altogether, or just stop making them in the house. So I rented a workshop.

GINGER: It wasn't about the tables. It was about the time you spend making the tables. It was about how I don't see you. About how the first thing you do when we get out to the house is leave.

DON: I'm not leaving, Ginger. I'm getting the mail.

GINGER: Checking on the boat. Going to the hardware store. The liquor store. The bait store. Buying magazines. Getting the cars washed, the oil changed, the tanks filled, the mats cleaned. Buying trash bags. Light bulbs. Tape. Dog food. Bird food. Fish food.

DON: Do you think I like doing those things?

GINGER: I don't know, Don.

DON: If you didn't want any animals, you should've told the kids no.

GINGER: That would have been popular.

DON: Since when did you worry about being popular?

GINGER: What are you going to do in your shop?

DON: Make tables.

GINGER: To sell?

DON: No, not to sell. It would be really stupid to take the one thing I really enjoy doing, and turn it into work.

GINGER: But your tables are beautiful. People love them. You should take one out to Ralph Lauren and—

DON: Just stop it, Ginger. O.K.? I'm never going to make any more money than I do right now. And I'm never going to like what I do. And if that means I'm never going to be good enough for you, then that's just too bad. This is who I am. And this is who you married.

GINGER: I'm sorry. It's just I keep thinking—

DON: Stop thinking. Stop thinking about what would make *my* life more interesting to you. I am not a character in your new novel. I'm your husband. Cut me some slack.

(She gets out of the bed, puts on her slippers and robe. Don looks up.)

DON: Would you bring me a glass of water when you come up?

GINGER: I could be a while. Do you want me to bring it up right now?

DON: That would be great. Thanks.

GINGER: You're going to move all your equipment into this shop?

DON: I have to have a place to go, Ginger. What do you want me to do, hang around the house all weekend and watch you read?

GINGER: Do you want ice in your water?

DON: That would be great. Thanks. I love you.

GINGER: I love you too. Good-night. *(She goes out the door.)*

Scene 1
LUNCH WITH GINGER

Ginger sits at a table for two in a popular lunch spot.

This is actually a series of lunches, in which her conversation remains continuous, but three of her friends rotate into the lunch one at a time, somehow. This change of companions may occur while Ginger looks at the menu, unfolds her napkin, talks to the waiter, or it may be handled with lighting. What is important is that while Ginger does notice that her friends come and go, she seems to accept that this is how things are.

Maria approaches. She is a real estate broker.

MARIA: Ginger, hi. Sorry I'm late. The traffic is terrible.

GINGER: It's O.K. I just got here. You look terrific.

MARIA: What a great little place. How did you know about it?

GINGER: I'm going to an ear doctor in this neighborhood.

MARIA: *(Looking at the menu.)* Nothing serious, I hope.

GINGER: Well. We still don't quite know what it is. My left ear keeps plugging up, like I have water in it from swimming. It doesn't actually hurt, it just makes me feel a little further away. Not that I need to feel any further away. If I get any further away, sooner or later, someone will realize I'm actually gone.

(Lights go out on Maria and come up on Ginger's best friend, Sue.)

SUE: This day. Lord. Oh well. What's good?

GINGER: I like the omelets. You know, eggs in time of stress.

SUE: *(Reaching for her bag.)* Oh here. I brought you the new Anna Quindlen. How's *your* book coming?

GINGER: Good. God knows who's going to read it, but. Hey.

SUE: What do you mean? Everyone who reads will read it. How close are you?

GINGER: Actually, I'm stuck. I can't seem to figure out...whether...what she should...

SUE: *(Seeing the waiter.)* Know what you want?

GINGER: *(Looking up as if at the waiter.)* Swiss and bacon, I think. And a small salad. And some juice. Can you make a mix of orange and pineapple?

(Lights go out on Sue, and come up on Ginger's friend, Connie, a nurse.)

CONNIE: Everything O.K. at home?

GINGER: The kids are good. Don's good. Except he thinks he's too fat. *(She has to laugh.)* I had this weird thought the other day about how different the world would have been if Darwin had called it, "The Survival of the Fattest."

CONNIE: You're so funny.

GINGER: But then I thought, maybe that's why diets don't work.

CONNIE: None of them work.

GINGER: Well, what if the reason they don't work is that diets are about individuals, you know, what individuals want. Whereas what the *species* wants is for people to have enough fat on them to survive. And the more fat you have, the better your chances are of survival. So even though *you* want to be thin, your body takes its direction from the species, and the species says eat. You know?

CONNIE: The bread looks great. Want some?

GINGER: Thanks. I mean, what if the species is really in charge of everything? What if the things we *think* we need, love and children and a place to live, are really just things the species needs, to keep itself going. But the only way the species can get these things is to trick us, with hormones mainly, into thinking *we* need them.

MARIA: Well, I know what I need. A new coat. I've looked all over town, and I can't find what I want.

(Ginger knows she's said too much, and tries to take a lighter approach.)

GINGER: Well, the species would certainly like for you to be warm. What are you looking for?

MARIA: Oh, you know, black, soft, something I can wear everywhere.

GINGER: Like something a species would put on a big black Lab.

MARIA: Exactly.

GINGER: Or a lot of little rabbits.

MARIA: You're so funny.

GINGER: You'll find it. Did you try Bergdorf's?

MARIA: I'm waiting for the sale. You should try this dill butter. Now tell me. What's the new book about? Anybody I know?

GINGER: No, no. It's just about some people who can't figure out why they have the lives they have. Not that they don't like their lives, just that the thrill that made them choose this particular man, or this particular kind of work, they don't feel that thrill anymore. All they feel is guilt that they're not taking good enough care of them.

MARIA: Oh good. The food is here. Yours looks wonderful.

GINGER: Want to trade?

MARIA: No, no.

GINGER: I mean, maybe the reason people don't change more than they do, is the species likes for you to stay put. So. After it gets your children out of you, the species just cuts you loose. And without the species to tell you what you want, you really don't want anything.

MARIA: *(To the waiter.)* Could I have some ketchup please?

GINGER: I'm sorry. I should know not to talk about something before it's finished. It's just...well, did you ever look at your family and think, "Who are these people?"

SUE: But you love your family.

GINGER: I know. My work too. I don't know what it is.

SUE: Do you believe this Michael Jackson thing?

GINGER: I know. It's crazy. But obviously, the species doesn't want us to know it controls us like this. Because nobody will talk about this with me. Nobody.

SUE: How's your ear doing?

GINGER: About the same. Thanks for asking, though. I'm seeing this new doctor Mary told me about tomorrow. Are you reading anything?

SUE: Just *Anna Karenina*. Again.

GINGER: Well. We all know what that means.

(A moment.)

SUE: You?

GINGER: The new Marquez is good. The last story is unbelievable. About three pages in, I got this incredible sense of dread about what was going to happen. Worse than any horror story I ever read. And all I wanted to do was turn to the last page to see if I was right. My hand actually went up to turn to the end, and I literally had to put my hand under the covers to keep reading the page I was on. You have to get it.

CONNIE: And what happened? You can tell me. You know I won't read it.

GINGER: Oh nothing. Just this amazing girl died, and this boy she was so in love with didn't know about it til after she was buried.

CONNIE: How are the kids?

GINGER: They're good.

CONNIE: Want any dessert?

GINGER: Does anybody ever ask you a personal question?

SUE: What do you mean, personal?

GINGER: Something they're not supposed to ask. Something you'd tell them if they asked, but they don't ask.

SUE: I don't think so.

GINGER: But why is that? Does the species not want us to get personal, so we won't realize how bad we feel and won't go around tearing things up?

SUE: You don't think people know how they feel?

GINGER: I don't. I think after a certain point, people put these huge sections of their lives on auto, you know. Like there's this big switchboard and people go through and... *(Mimes flipping switches.)* this is my family, and this is where I live, and this is what I do, and this is what I eat, and these are the people I have lunch with, and these are the books I read, and this is my radio station, and here's what I think about this and this and this. And they don't think about it any more. So they never try anything else.

SUE: But if you know you like something, why should you try something else?

GINGER: Because if you don't, then all you are is comfortable. Is that what we're doing here, trying to get comfortable? Do you think it's even possible? O.K. Say you actually *got* comfortable. *Then* what would you do? Go to sleep? Die? What?

SUE: Would you like to come to the gym with me some day?

GINGER: You don't feel silly exercising with all those young people?

SUE: I think they're cute, actually.

GINGER: Anyone in particular?

SUE: I wish. It's really been a long time since I've been attracted to anybody. It used to happen all the time.

GINGER: I know.

CONNIE: Like in college.

GINGER: It's not us, I can tell you that.

MARIA: Oh good.

GINGER: It's the species. It doesn't need us to find mates any more, so it just doesn't turn us on to anybody. Or them to us.

MARIA: I can't believe how cold it is out there. I don't know what I would've done if I hadn't found my coat. I love my new coat. So what are you up to?

GINGER: I'm taking a painting class.

MARIA: I didn't know you were interested in painting.

GINGER: Maybe I'm not. Maybe the species just needs me to find some little hobby so I'll stay out of the way til I die. You know, so it can save all the jobs for the people who are having babies.

SUE: How's Don?

GINGER: He's good. He's rented a little woodworking shop in the country.

SUE: Is he any good at it?

GINGER: No. He says it soothes him.

SUE: How's your ear.

GINGER: It's O.K. I can hear enough.

SUE: You seem a little down.

GINGER: Put your money away. I've got it.

SUE: *(Getting up.)* Did you tell me what your new book is about?

GINGER: Yes, but I gave up on it. Just…threw it away. I've never done that before.

SUE: You're not working on anything?

GINGER: No, I am. It's an old idea, actually. But I'm thinking I might know how to do it now. It's about…well, it's about pleasure.

SUE: *(Stricken.)* Pleasure? What's that?

CONNIE: Do you mean erotic pleasure, or like cooking?

MARIA: Well. I can't wait to read it. Thanks for lunch.

SUE: Pleasure? Really? Are you serious?

GINGER: *(With a smile.)* I could be. *(A moment.)* I know. *(A smile.)* How odd.

(Blackout.)

Scene 2
TRANSITION
Ginger's Mother and Husband

Lights come up on a peaceful woman sitting in a chair. This woman need not leave the stage as the piece continues. Lights can simply go out on her.

ANNIE: Ginger was a happy child. So happy. Happy all the time. Singing and dancing and playing by herself. I kept telling her how nice it was outside, but I have to admit it was sweet that she wanted to stay down in the basement with me. None of the other neighborhood children were well...good enough to play with her, really, so I would iron and she would play school, making little books, writing things. Even before she knew how, she was writing, scribbling on the paper and then hiding her little messages behind the runner on the stairs. She didn't know I knew, but I did. But I didn't read them. *(A moment.)* If she had wanted me to know what she thought, she would've just told me.

(A moment. Don enters the area defined by Annie. He is reading a magazine.)

ANNIE: Her husband, Don, is...it's hard to say. I didn't know him very well.

(Don is not talking to Annie, but he is not unaware of her presence.)

DON: I met Ginger's father a few times. I liked him. She always called him the original unknowable man, but hey. What's to know? He was friendly.

ANNIE: Don designed their house. I don't know why he doesn't get more work as an architect. He's a very smart man.

DON: The house doesn't work. Not for me, it doesn't. I tried to tell Ginger it wouldn't, but she kept having all these ideas. And the thing ended up so personal that we'll never be able to sell it. The kids like the fireman's pole, though. I'll give her credit for that. So fine. We'll just plug it up when they leave.

Scene 3
Dawn with Ginger

Curtain rises on a beautiful outdoor deck, furnished comfortably, but exquisitely. Hanging baskets of fuschia and ivy are everywhere. It is just dawn. And it looks like it's going to be a stunning day. The air will be cool and clear, and the sun will be warm. A eucalyptus-scented candle is burning. It is a safe world.

Ginger enters from the house, closing the glass door behind her. She is brushing her hair. She wears a loose pair of white silk pajamas, over which she wears an unbelted kimono. On her feet are Chanel-type bedroom slippers.

She puts down her hairbrush, takes her yoga mat from the baker's rack in the corner, unfolds it and places it on the deck. She takes off her kimono and slippers, then walks to the tape player in the corner, inserts a tape and pushes Play.

As the New Age music of the tape begins, Ginger stands on the mat, relaxed and serene, and rolls her head slowly from side to side.

VOICE OF THE SWAMI: The chariot of the mind is drawn by wild horses. These horses have to be tamed.

(She brings her hands into the prayer pose.)

VOICE OF THE SWAMI: Standing erect, feet together, bring your hands in front of your chest in the prayer pose. Keeping your body completely still, breathe slowly through the nostrils. Bring your mind into a state of quiet awareness, concentrating only on your breathing. In. Out. In. Out. *(A moment.)* And now, when you next exhale, join me in the Salutation to the Sun.

(Ginger now performs the Salutation to the Sun chanting with the Swami.)

GINGER AND THE SWAMI'S VOICE: Om Namo Suryaya

Om Namo Bhaskraya

Om Namo Divaya

(James, a lean, handsome, mysterious man comes up the steps, wearing loose pants, but no shirt. Ginger bows to him, and he to her. He might be a wizard.)

GINGER AND JAMES: Namaste.

GINGER AND THE SWAMI'S VOICE: Om Namo Tajaya

Om Namo Prkashaya

(James does a few stretches, then joins Ginger for the second repetition

of the Salutation to the Sun, chanting with her. She is happy to see him, but not surprised.)

GINGER, JAMES AND SWAMI'S VOICE: Om Namo Suryaya

Om Namo Bhaskraya

Om Nama Divaya

Om Namo Tejaya

Om Namo Prkashaya

(Ginger and James smile comfortably as the Swami's voice on tape begins again. Something about the voice sounds slightly different.)

VOICE OF THE SWAMI: The goal of tantric yoga is to transform your lovemaking from a brief and entirely genital encounter, to a transcendent sensual meditation, leading to an union that transcends the boundaries of everyday experience.

(The glass door slides open and Ginger's daughter, Beth, sticks her head out. She doesn't seem to see James.)

BETH: Mom?

GINGER: Right here.

BETH: O.K.

(The girl, apparently happy just to know where Ginger is, closes the door and the voice on the tape comes back up.)

VOICE OF THE SWAMI: You begin by sitting quietly together, *(Ginger and the man sit.)* meditating or praying or simply opening to the sounds around you.

(Ginger and James follow the Swami's instructions.)

VOICE OF THE SWAMI: As you embrace and kiss, align your throats, hearts and bodies, and breathe as one. In and out. Easily. Freely. Now, begin to touch one another with utmost sensitivity. Reveal to each other those places where you feel fear or shame.

(The door opens and Ginger's son sticks his head out. He doesn't seem to see the man.)

CHARLIE: Mom?

GINGER: Hi.

CHARLIE: What's today?

GINGER: Thursday.

CHARLIE: Damn.

(He leaves quickly, as though it being Thursday means he had to do something right away. The Swami's voice continues on the tape.)

VOICE OF THE SWAMI: Return to the Butterfly Pose and sit calmly for a moment, feeling centered and at peace.

(Ginger and James sit up now, facing each other in the Butterfly pose.)

VOICE OF THE SWAMI: Today you will learn the Set of Nines. In which you will discover a powerful current of energy connecting you at the genitals, rising up to the heart, bridging the space between you, and dropping back to the genitals again.

(They are amused.)

GINGER AND JAMES: O.K.

VOICE OF THE SWAMI: As you listen to the instructions, place your hands on your breasts in order to feel the heat from your hands entering the skin.

(The door opens again and Ginger's husband, Don, comes out. He doesn't seem to see the man lying next to her.)

DON: Honey?

GINGER: Hi, Don.

DON: It's almost seven.

GINGER: Thanks.

(Don goes back inside as the Swami's voice begins again. James may reach across to Ginger and take her hands in his.)

VOICE OF THE SWAMI: To begin the Set of Nines, the man enters the woman with nine shallow thrusts. He withdraws and pauses before entering again, this time for eight shallow thrusts followed by one deep thrust.

JAMES: I think I know where this is going.

(But it sounds so good to Ginger that she can't really respond.)

VOICE OF THE SWAMI: Again he withdraws, pulling back briefly from the edge of orgasm.

BETH'S VOICE O.S.: *(Calling out.)* Mom?

VOICE OF THE SWAMI: Now the man takes seven shallow thrusts and two deep thrusts, and withdraws.

(James nods and begins to speak with the Swami.)

JAMES AND SWAMI'S VOICE: Six shallow, three deep, withdraw; five shallow, four deep, withdraw; four shallow, five deep, withdraw; three shallow, six deep, withdraw...

CHARLIE'S VOICE O.S.: *(Calling out.)* Mom!

JAMES: *(To Ginger.)* Do you want to stop?

GINGER: No.

JAMES AND SWAMI'S VOICE: Two shallow, seven deep, withdraw. One shallow, eight deep,...withdraw...

DON'S VOICE O.S.: *(Calling out.)* Ginger!

VOICE OF THE SWAMI: Until…

GINGER: *(Calling to them.)* Just a minute!

SWAMI'S VOICE: Until the man brings his lover to orgasm with nine deep thrusting strokes.

(There is a silence.)

GINGER: Probably worth a try.

JAMES: I'm in.

(And after a moment, James helps Ginger stand up, and facing each other once again, they assume the prayer pose as the Swami signs off.)

VOICE OF THE SWAMI: O Life-giving Sun, offspring of the Lord of Creation—

(Don enters, but waits through the Swami's blessing. Ginger joins in with the Swami.)

GINGER AND THE SWAMI'S VOICE: —let me behold they radiant form, that I may realize that the Spirit far away within thee, is my Spirit, my own inmost Spirit.

(Ginger and James bow to each other as before.)

GINGER AND JAMES: Namaste.

(James leaves and Don starts talking as Ginger folds up her mat and blows out the candle.)

DON: Are we still on with Jerry and Sue tonight?

GINGER: Yes, but I haven't talked to her yet, so I don't know what we're doing.

DON: Just so it's not Mexican.

GINGER: O.K.

DON: And for God's sake, not at *their* house.

GINGER: Are you going to be this way tonight?

DON: What way?

GINGER: If you don't like them, why don't you just say you never want to see them again?

DON: Because it wouldn't do any good.

GINGER: Don. They're the only friends we have.

DON: They're not my friends.

GINGER: They could be.

DON: Oh sure. If I liked them they could. If I were somebody else who liked them. Well, believe me, if I could be somebody else, I would.

GINGER: You would? Who would you be?

DON: I don't know. What difference does it make? I can't be anybody else, can I. So why should we talk about who, exactly, I could never be?

GINGER: Because I want to know. Who is it?

DON: I don't know. *(A wild idea.)* Mohammed Ali.

GINGER: Please.

DON: Or you.

GINGER: Me?

DON: Of course you. Isn't it everybody's dream, to make a living by not going to work?

GINGER: Writing is work.

DON: Come on. You don't work the hours lawyers work. Or salesgirls even. You talk on the phone, and have lunch with your friends.

GINGER: That's not all I do.

DON: Are we still on with Jerry and Sue tonight?

(This seems familiar to Ginger, like maybe she's had this conversation before, but maybe not, so she continues bravely on.)

GINGER: Yes, but I forget what we're doing.

DON: Just so it's not Mexican.

GINGER: I remember now. She's cooking.

DON: Oh for Christ's sake. You can't even sit down in their house without some bird flying over your head, or some handicapped cat jumping in your lap.

GINGER: Why do you have to be this way? They have pets because they can't have children. She's my oldest friend.

DON: She's not older than I am. Nobody is older than I am. I've asked you not to say "old."

GINGER: Don, please.

DON: I'm sorry, honey. I'll see you tonight. Are we still on with Jerry and Sue?

GINGER: We're going to that Chinese place you like.

DON: Does *Jerry* have to come?

GINGER: He's Sue's husband!

DON: But they're so terrible to each other. If I'm going to watch a fight, I'd rather see one on TV. Why don't you girls just go out by yourselves?

GINGER: Could you pick up the dry cleaning?

DON: No problem. What are we doing tonight?

GINGER: I'm having supper with Sue.

DON: Great. There's a fight on TV I want to watch.

GINGER: Bye, hon.

(He kisses her on the cheek and leaves. The son comes by and kisses her.)

CHARLIE: Mom!

GINGER: Charlie!

CHARLIE: You hair looks funny.

(The daughter runs to catch up to him. She poses for Ginger.)

BETH: Mom?

GINGER: *(Still thinking there's hope.)* Beth!

BETH: How do I look?

GINGER: Great. You look great.

(Blackout. Ginger remains on the stage.)

Scene 4
Transition
Ginger, Her Mother, and James

Lights come back up on Annie still sitting in her chair.

ANNIE: I don't know why these girls today wait so long to have their children. Why if Ginger had had hers when I told her to, they'd be so much older by now. They'd be in college. They might even have jobs. At the very least they wouldn't still be children. But she said no. She had plenty of time to have children. Girls that age think they have their whole lives in front of them. But…at least she had her children. A girl and a boy. And I have to say, in spite of everything, she was a perfect mother.

(Ginger approaches Annie and responds.)

GINGER: That's not true.

ANNIE: She was a perfect daughter.

GINGER: There's no such thing as perfect.

ANNIE: Everything you *do* is perfect!

GINGER: It is not! I don't even *want* it to be. I'm not trying to live a perfect life.

ANNIE: You could.

GINGER: Stop it. Just stop it.

ANNIE: What do you want, my permission not to live a perfect life? My congratulations on not living a perfect life? Well, listen here, young lady. If you're not living a perfect life, I don't want to hear about it.

GINGER: What *do* you want to hear about? How I'm planning the perfect Christmas? Perfect for whom? The whole purpose of perfect is to make us feel bad. Like we don't measure up. Well I'm sorry, but could we go find whoever this is who's measuring us all the time, and take away their goddamn stick?

ANNIE: Their stick?

GINGER: *(Really irritated now.)* Their measuring stick. You know, the one that's marked…Really Bad, Bad. Not Good, Not Good Enough, Perfect. It's killing us. *(A small smile.)* I found that once I quit trying to put on the perfect outfit, *(A moment.)* …I could actually get dressed.

ANNIE: The last Christmas I spent with you was perfect.

GINGER: I'm glad you thought so.

ANNIE: You didn't?

GINGER: Christmas to me feels like a happiness test. One I have failed for years now.

ANNIE: What is the matter with you today?

GINGER: You think it's just today?

ANNIE: Are you sick? You seem a little flushed.

(Ginger suddenly wishes her mother would understand, is suddenly willing to try.)

GINGER: I can't seem to fit in anywhere. I don't know the rules.

ANNIE: You know the rules because I told them to you. You just broke the rules.

GINGER: No, I didn't.

ANNIE: You talked to strangers. Didn't you?

(James appears on the other side of the stage, cleaning his sax.)

GINGER: That was a real rule?

ANNIE: Very.

(Annie exits. Sue appears.)

SUE: Are you seeing someone? I think you're seeing someone.

GINGER: No. I'm not.

SUE: Then why do you look so happy?

GINGER: I'm flirting with someone. But he started it.

SUE: Is he married?

GINGER: No.

SUE: How long has he not been married?

GINGER: Stop it.

SUE: How long has he not been married?

GINGER: Two years.

SUE: O.K. That's long enough. Does he have children?

GINGER: They live with their mother.

SUE: What does he do?

GINGER: He plays the sax.

SUE: *(Suddenly very sober.)* How well does he play the sax?

GINGER: Like a dream.

SUE: I see.

GINGER: It's not just that.

SUE: Oh, sure.

GINGER: Sue. I told you. We're flirting. Oh, I don't know. What do I do?

SUE: Well. I don't think you have to stop flirting.

(Sue exits. Ginger picks up the phone on her desk, and hears the message on James's machine.)

JAMES ON TAPE: Hi. This is James. You can leave me a message at the tone, or you can come to Mabel's and buy me a drink between sets. Up to you. Bye.

GINGER: *(Leaving him a message.)* James. My name is Ginger Andrews. My agent said you would be willing to talk to me about Morocco. About oases, actually, for a book I'm thinking about. Well, it's about pleasure in general, but he seemed to think you were my best bet. So. My number is— *(A moment.)* Why do I think you don't return calls? O.K. I'll come find you at Mabel's on Thursday night. I'll be wearing…I have red hair and a notebook. Bye.

(James begins to play the saxophone. Lights down on Annie's area.)

Scene 5
GINGER AT WORK

Ginger is working at her computer. Don appears.

GINGER: Hi. *(She continues to type.)*

DON: Hi.

(Ginger looks up while typing a sentence.)

GINGER: Yes?

DON: If you'd had an affair, would you have told me?

GINGER: You think I'm having an affair?

DON: That's not what I asked I asked...

GINGER: ...if I had had an affair, would I have told you.

DON: Yes.

GINGER: I don't think so, Don. No. Probably not.

DON: Right.

GINGER: Why would I?

DON: No. That seems right to me too. I was just checking. I'll see you later. *(He starts to leave.)*

GINGER: You don't want to know?

DON: I don't want to look stupid.

GINGER: Why would my having an affair make you look stupid?

DON: Because it would mean I couldn't keep you from having them.

GINGER: My affairs would have nothing to do with you.

DON: That can't be true.

GINGER: It's not.

DON: Would they have anything to do with the fact that we don't have sex?

GINGER: No.

DON: Really?

GINGER: No.

DON: So they do.

GINGER: They could.

DON: That can't be all of it though. Don't tell me. You're afraid of getting old.

GINGER: I'm not getting old.

DON: I didn't say you were.

GINGER: No. I'm not. I'm not getting old. I thought I would by now. But I'm not.

DON: You don't think you're immortal.

GINGER: No. Thanks, though.

DON: But wouldn't having affairs make you feel bad?

GINGER: I wouldn't have them if they made me feel bad.

DON: O.K. They'd make you feel great. Then what?

GINGER: Then I would come home, I guess.

DON: But what if I found out? What if I saw you going into wherever it is you'd go with them?

GINGER: I would try to explain, I guess.

DON: And what if I left you because of it?

GINGER: Then you would be gone.

DON: But I could take the children away. Accuse you of being an unfit mother—

GINGER: I'm a great mother.

DON: —and take the children away.

GINGER: A lot of things could take my children away, Don. Drugs, or TV, or a terrible disease, or bad luck with a car or, God, what if they grew up?

DON: Would you talk to your lovers?

GINGER: Yes, Don. Lovers like to be talked to. *(A moment.)* Some more than others, of course.

DON: And what would you talk about?

GINGER: About ourselves, mainly. About when we first knew we were going to make love, and how long we waited, and how it wasn't fair that we couldn't see each other whenever we wanted.

DON: And what would they say? Would they ask about me?

GINGER: No, Don. They would say that I was beautiful.

(The phone rings.)

GINGER: *(Picks it up.)* Hello?

(Don walks out of the room, as Ginger erases something on the computer.)

GINGER: Hi Sue. *(Listens.)* I'm just working. No. It's O.K. *(Listens.)* I don't know *what* it is. Maybe it's not even a book. Maybe it's a nervous breakdown. *(Then quickly.)* It's a joke, Sue. I'm fine. I'm obsessed. I don't want to be here. *(Changing the subject.)* So. Where shall we eat tonight? Is Jerry coming? *(Listens.)* No, no. Don's still in Chicago. Yeah. So first we'll go look for your coat and then we'll decide where to eat. If we find something at Barney's we can just eat there. O.K. Say six-thirty? *(Listens.)* Very funny. See you then, honey bun. *(Ginger hangs up the phone, opens a soda and studies the computer screen.)* About when we first knew we were going to make love, and how long we *(Changes a word.)* resisted, and how it wasn't fair we couldn't see each other whenever we wanted.

(Don walks back in.)

DON: And what would they say? Would they ask about me?

GINGER: No, Don. They would say that I was beautiful.

(The phone rings.)

GINGER: Hello. *(Ginger practically swears into the phone hearing who it is.)* I'm sorry. Was I supposed to call *you? (Listens.)* Oh good. O.K. No. I haven't thought about it. I agree to phone interviews and then I forget to write them down, so…Yes. I remember that it was just one question. I just don't remember what that question was, exactly. *(Listens.)* Oh that's right. Of course. *(Stating her answer.)* What is most helpful for writers to hear, is…how fabulous they look and how everybody wants to go to bed with them. *(She laughs.)* No. That's the real answer. *(A moment.)* You're welcome. Yes, please. Send me a copy. *(Ginger hangs up the phone. Quickly.)* Bullshit, bullshit, bullshit.

(Ginger unwraps a stick of gum. She looks up and sees Don standing there.)

DON: Surprise!

GINGER: Don!

DON: I'm early.

GINGER: Why didn't you call?

DON: This is my home. Do I have to call before I come over?

GINGER: What's up?

DON: I read this new…whatever this thing is that you're writing. About having these affairs. Is this me, this Ron character?

GINGER: Where did you find it?

DON: On your desk.

GINGER: I didn't leave it on my desk.

DON: O.K. It was under a big stack of papers on the floor. But I found it. So you must have meant for me to find it.

GINGER: Maybe I did.

DON: Are you telling me you've had affairs?

GINGER: It's not about me. It's about—

DON: Don't insult me, Ginger.

GINGER: It doesn't say she's had affairs. Just that she's—

DON: Thinking about it?

GINGER: Yes. She, the main character, Trudy, is thinking about it.

DON: And you're not.

GINGER: Are you asking me if I'm having an affair?

DON: *(After a moment.)* No.

GINGER: *(After a moment.)* Is there anything else you don't want to know?

DON: Not that I can think of. No.

GINGER: I'm going to keep working a little longer, I think.

DON: I'm going to bed.

GINGER: All right.

DON: Goodnight, hon.

GINGER: Goodnight.

(Don turns to leave, then turns back.)

DON: I just want you to know that if anything ever happens to you, if you die...the first thing I'm going to do, after I stop crying, is go into your study and read everything you've ever written. Not just your short stories and books, but your notes, your journals, your letters...everything you've ever written.

(Ginger nods and Don leaves. She waits a moment, then turns back to the computer and types.)

GINGER: "Ron turned away." *(She looks up at the door, as though waiting for him to come back in.)* "Ron turned away, took one step, and fell into the bottomless pit." *(Then going on, apparently unable to stop herself, speaking as though reading to a child.)* "Poor Ron. Didn't he see the pit? Hadn't she *told* him there was a pit? Hadn't she told him every day she had to work so hard *not* to fall into that pit? Well, he should've listened to her. The pit is there, all right. Only now, it has a man in it. And he is really pissed off." *(A smile.)* Will Ron get out of the hole? Will Ginger get out of her study? Tune in tomorrow for another episode of... *(Her anger coming through.)* "Trudy Blue, Girl in Love."

Scene 6
TRANSITION
The phone rings again.

GINGER: Hello.

(She hears the voice, recognizes who it is, is thrilled to hear it's him, but lowers her voice.)

GINGER: Oh Hi! Where are you, are you here? I was afraid you wouldn't get in. *(Listens.)* You do *(Listens in rapture.)* I'm sorry. Maybe I did-n't hear that right. *(Having heard it perfectly.)* Would you say that again? *(Listens.)* I have missed you so much. I've never missed anybody like this. It's getting to where seeing you is just some kind of break between these bouts of missing you. So? Where shall we meet? *(She listens. Trying not to convey her disappointment.)* Oh. All right. No, no. You sound exhausted. It would be a little tricky to out of here anyway. O.K. Good. *(Listens.)* I love you too. Goodnight, sweetie. *(She hangs up the phone.)*

Scene 7
GINGER IN THE SPY SHOP

Ginger walks into a Spy Shop. There are several other shoppers. A clerk comes up to her. He is dressed very neatly, and though he is probably a neo-Nazi, he tries to conceal that.

CLERK: May I help you?

GINGER: Yes. *(She is very nervous.)* I was just walking by, and saw the lie detection phone in the window and I—

CLERK: Certainly. *(Getting it out of the case.)* What kind of businesses are you in?

GINGER: It's…very small. We—

CLERK: You'll be pleased with this. It's the top of the line in vocal stress measurement devices. Someone is lying to you? *(He looks up, as though he must maintain a constant surveillance over the front door.)*

GINGER: I don't know.

CLERK: What security measures do you currently employ?

GINGER: *(A moment.)* None.

    (He shakes his head reprovingly, looking around the store again.)

CLERK: Well, then. The first thing you have to know is that there's no such thing as perfect security.

GINGER: I wondered.

CLERK: There is only effective security.

GINGER: That might be enough.

CLERK: We'll talk about that later. Now. *(Showing her the phone.)* When the subject is under emotional stress, his vocal chords will, as you have no doubt noticed, tremble.

GINGER: *(After a moment.)* Quiver. Yes.

CLERK: *(A moment.)* The Model 862 gives you a baseline readout here…for the subject's normal voice, usually somewhere around 20.

GINGER: And I establish this baseline by—

CLERK: By first asking questions the subject would have no reason to lie about, such as

GINGER: What day is this, what year is this…

CLERK: Exactly. Then once you have a baseline, any response which produces a reading significantly higher than the baseline, is clearly a lie. I didn't get your name.

GINGER: Trudy. Trudy Blue.

CLERK: Bill Evans. Now. It usually takes about five responses to establish the baseline. After that, you simply ask what it is you really want to know. What kind of business did you say you were in?

GINGER: I didn't.

CLERK: Please. Trudy. Come with me. I have something I want to show you.

(Ginger follows him to another room.)

CLERK: This is better. In this area, nothing we say can be heard by anyone else in the store.

GINGER: Really?

CLERK: Try it. Scream if you want.

(Ginger looks around, then screams…)

GINGER: Help!!!!!!!!!

(No one turns around. She smiles.)

GINGER: That's good. And we can't hear them either. That's really good. How do you do it?

CLERK: It's our business, Trudy. Now. Let's talk about the chances of your private information falling into the wrong hands.

GINGER: All right.

CLERK: Do you conduct sensitive discussions in your office?

GINGER: I do. Yes.

(That's what he was afraid of.)

CLERK: But not on the telephone, I trust.

(She indicates yes.)

CLERK: Not in your car too.

(She indicates yes.)

CLERK: In public?

GINGER: I'm sorry.

CLERK: *(Stunned.)* Trudy, if this information were used to your disadvantage, wouldn't the consequences be inconvenient?

GINGER: I'm sorry.

CLERK: Don't apologize. Just take care of it. I'm sorry. *(Realizing he went too far.)* That's why you're here, isn't it.

GINGER: Can I try the phone?

CLERK: *(He begins to plug things in.)* Of course. What makes you think they're lying to you?

GINGER: There's nothing in particular. It's just—

CLERK: They usually are. Go ahead. Dial the number.

(The phone rings. Ginger picks it up. But instead of the clerk on the phone, we hear James' voice. The Clerk is monitoring over a set of earphones, as if from a surveillance van. James picks up the phone.)

JAMES' VOICE: Ginger!

GINGER: James

JAMES' VOICE: What's up? You don't sound like yourself.

GINGER: I don't feel like myself either.

(The clerk signals to begin the baseline check. Ginger remembers what she's doing. James enters, taking his saxophone out of its case.)

GINGER: What day is this?

JAMES: Thursday.

(The clerk nods. James wipes off the sax.)

GINGER: The 10th, the 11th?

JAMES: The 10th. This is a terrible connection. Why don't I call you back on—

GINGER: No. You can't. I'm trying out phones. Only I realized I couldn't know what they sounded like unless I called somebody. I hope I'm not interrupting anything.

JAMES: No, no.

(The clerk indicates this may be a lie.)

GINGER: Well, I'll let you go then—

(The clerk indicates she must keep talking.)

JAMES: Any chance we can get together later?

GINGER: About five I could.

JAMES: Is six too late? There's something I have to take care of.

(The clerk indicates this is a lie. Suddenly, Ginger is nervous.)

JAMES: I miss you, Ginny.

(The clerk indicates this is the truth. She is very relieved.)

GINGER: I miss you too. I'll see you at six.

JAMES: Six it is. Same place. I love you.

GINGER: I love you too.

JAMES: Bye.

(*Ginger hears the click then looks at the phone. The clerk unplugs the telephone and looks at her. She did not look at the clerk for affirmation that James loves her.*)

CLERK: So it's personal.

GINGER: (*Watching James.*) Deeply.

CLERK: Why don't I come to your office tomorrow and do a silent sweep, just so we know what we're up against. Or if you can't wait that long, I could lease you a jammer to take home with you right now.

GINGER: No, I think I know what to do.

CLERK: No. You don't. You're an amateur. I like you, Trudy. I don't want to read your name in the paper one of these days.

GINGER: No. Neither do I. Thank you very much.

(*Ginger sees James waiting for her at a table. She moves toward him and starts to speak, but lights come up on Annie first and she speaks.*)

Scene 8
GINGER, HER MOM, AND CONTROL

ANNIE: What did you want, Ginger?

GINGER: I wanted to be taken away.

ANNIE: Any place in particular?

GINGER: Just away. I wanted someone to know where I was, come find me and take me away.

ANNIE: And bring you back later?

GINGER: No. I wanted to live my other life.

ANNIE: Somewhere else.

GINGER: I know how it sounds.

ANNIE: And so do I. It sounds like something you said as a ten-year-old when you didn't want to take out the garbage. "Oh, I can't take out the garbage, mother, there are kidnappers in the alley and they'll come and take me away." (*Pretending to be scared.*) Ooh—Kidnappers. (*Shaking her head.*) You weren't afraid of those men.

You were *hoping* there was somebody out there, weren't you. You *wanted* to be taken away.

GINGER: Didn't I just say that?

ANNIE: Ginger. I told you this when you were a girl and I'm telling you again now. These fantasies are *not* the answer.

GINGER: What fantasies? What answer? There isn't any answer. Not to these questions there isn't. *(Listing them.)* If I have never been happy, is there any reason to think I ever could be? If I have never felt safe, is there any reason to keep longing for a place where I will feel that way?

(James appears.)

JAMES: Yes.

GINGER: *(Softly, to him.)* What did you say?

JAMES: I said yes.

GINGER: Is that the answer? Yes?

JAMES: Is that so hard?

GINGER: Yes!

JAMES: All right, it's hard. *(A moment.)* It's still the answer. *(A moment.)* Yes. Yes, ma'm. Yes, sir. Yes.

(Lights down on Annie. Ginger walks over to James.)

Scene 9
DRINKS WITH GINGER AND JAMES

James is seated by himself, perhaps cleaning his saxophone. Ginger enters the bar, sees him, pauses a moment, as if gathering her courage, then walks toward him. He looks up and, seeing her coming, smiles and motions her over.

JAMES: Ginger. Is that you?

GINGER: Ginger Andrews, yes. Did you get my message?

JAMES: It made me laugh.

GINGER: I'm sorry.

JAMES: But I like to laugh.

GINGER: Thank you for meeting me—

JAMES: The pleasure's mine. Sit down.

GINGER: I won't take long.

JAMES: Take as long as you want.

GINGER: Well, I'm a writer, and

JAMES: I know.

GINGER: —a novelist, mainly, but I've been thinking about doing a book about pleasure.

JAMES: Ginger. I can see who you are.

(Ginger hears more in his response than he meant. Or exactly what he meant. She drops her pen. Or in some ways betrays herself.)

GINGER: You can?

JAMES: Sure I can. What does your hat say?

GINGER: It doesn't say anything. That's why I...My hat say I hate my hair.

JAMES: Could I see it?

GINGER: You want to see my hair?

JAMES: I do. But if it makes you uncomfortable, please. Go on. If I've upset you I'm sorry. I tend to do that.

GINGER: On purpose?

JAMES: It's beautiful hair.

GINGER: Do you upset people on purpose?

JAMES: Well, I don't stop myself, if that's what you mean.

GINGER: *(Beginning to relax.)* And do you have this effect on everybody?

JAMES: People should affect each other. Now. *(A moment.)* I'm hungry. Are you hungry?

GINGER: I am, actually.

JAMES: Then let's go eat. What are you hungry for?

(A waiter appears.)

WAITER: What would you like?

GINGER: Just a Chardonnay, I think.

JAMES: What kind of beer do you have?

WAITER: Bud. Bud light. Bud dry. Bud wet.

(Ginger laughs. They are better acquainted now. More playful. It is another day. But the passage of time is indicated more by their attitude than by change in lighting or staging.)

GINGER: How could you ask me that?

JAMES: *(As if innocent.)* Ask you what?

GINGER: If I was hungry. What was I hungry for. You knew what I was hungry for from the moment you saw me.

JAMES: *(Remembering the subject.)* Actually. I wanted to say angry. Were you angry. But that didn't seem like a good way to start, so I decided to try something harmless like...feeding you.

GINGER: Harmless.

JAMES: But now I have to know.

GINGER: All right.

JAMES: What do you do with your rage?

(There is a moment.)

GINGER: I sell it.

JAMES: Ah.

GINGER: I do. I sell it. I make things out of hurt and loss and I sell them. Books and things. *(She laughs.)* Isn't that what everybody does? Isn't that what you do with yours?

JAMES: No. I let mine eat me up. *(He has to laugh.)* Keeps the weight down.

GINGER: I thought the music just washed yours away.

JAMES: Washed what away?

GINGER: I don't know. I don't know what we're talking about.

JAMES: Your mouth. Does everybody tell you about your mouth?

GINGER: No.

JAMES: Are they blind?

GINGER: Maybe they are. That would...

JAMES: Explain a lot.

(The waiter appears.)

GINGER: Do you know what you'd like?

JAMES: What would I like.

GINGER: We could do that.

JAMES: God, you're beautiful. I'm away from you all week, and I think of you as smart and sexy, and I forget how beautiful you are.

GINGER: James. James. Tell all these people to go away.

JAMES: Do you think they can see us?

GINGER: I believe they can. Yes.

JAMES: Well, then. *(Turning to talk to them.)* Excuse me, ladies and gentlemen, but my Ginny here wants to be kissed, and if I'm going to kiss her the way she wants to be kissed, you're just going to have to look the other way for a moment. *(A thought.)* Or if you wanted to leave, that would be even better.

GINGER: *(Looking away.)* How do you know how I want to be kissed.

JAMES: Are you saying I don't?

GINGER: *(Quietly.)* No. I'm asking you how you know.

JAMES: I need more time with you. This once a week thing is no good. Want to join the band?

GINGER: I do actually. What can I play?

JAMES: Whatever you'd like.

(The waiter appears.)

WAITER: Anybody know what they want?

GINGER: I lied to you, James.

JAMES: You don't love me?

GINGER: No. I do. I lied to you about what I do with my rage.

JAMES: Well.

GINGER: I think it's the best question anybody ever asked me. I just didn't know the answer so I made one up.

JAMES: That's all right. I'll ask you again. What have you done with your rage?

GINGER: I buried it.

JAMES: Where?

GINGER: I forgot. *(Amused in spite of herself.)* Right?

JAMES: *(Like in a horror movie.)* But will it stay dead? No! Here it comes. The Rage of the Living Dead.

(And suddenly, they are like two children, playing monsters.)

GINGER: *(Running away.)* Help! Help!

(He chases her.)

JAMES: *(In another accent.)* Every day I will eat a little part of you…

GINGER: Mother!!!!!

(As they fall to the floor wrestling.)

(A waiter appears. Ginger and James stop and look up at him. James is supremely annoyed.)

JAMES: You want to know what we want.

WAITER: I do.

JAMES: *(Getting up.)* Can't you tell? Jesus Christ.

(The waiter leaves, and James pulls some folded pages from inside his jacket pocket.)

JAMES: This is wonderful, Ginny.

(He hands her the pages. She makes her way back to the table.)

GINGER: How much did you read?

JAMES: Everything you gave me. I love it. I love your Trudy Blue. She's a lot like you.

GINGER: She's me off the leash. A girl I'd like to play with.

JAMES: Me too.

GINGER: Somebody I'd like to know.

JAMES: I liked her joke about the hundred year old couple.

GINGER: It was Beth's joke actually. But you know writers. If you don't want us to take it, you better not say it in front of us.

JAMES: What's she going to do?

GINGER: Beth?

JAMES: Trudy.

GINGER: Solve the mystery, I guess. Isn't that what detectives usually do? (*A waiter walks through. For once she is glad to see him. She flags him down.*)

GINGER: I'll have a kir on the rocks.

JAMES: Answer my question, Ginger. What is Trudy going to do with this man, this lover. I forget his name. Jason, is it?

GINGER: She doesn't know yet.

JAMES: Then can you tell me what you're doing next week.

GINGER: Next week?

JAMES: Yeah. We're playing in New Orleans again all next week. Why don't you come down with me?

GINGER: Why don't I come to New Orleans with you next week?

JAMES: It's a great city.

GINGER: It certainly is. Dear Don. I have gone to New Orleans with James. You don't know him. It's a great city.

JAMES: No?

GINGER: I can't.

JAMES: That's too bad. All right, then. Drink up, Ginny my girl. Your cousin James is going to play for you. What would you like to hear?

GINGER: Please. Just sit with me. (*He nods and she takes the conversation into what might be safer territory.*)

GINGER: Why do you call yourself Cousin James? You're not my cousin.

JAMES: No. But if I were, that would be even more reason not to do what we do. Does it bother you?

GINGER: I like it.

JAMES: I could be your Uncle James, if you like, or your brother James. Just so we're related somehow.

GINGER: All right, cousin.. (*A woman comes up to the table now. She is wearing a silky short black trenchcoat.*)

FAN: I hate to interrupt you, but I heard you play last week at Mabel's. You made me cry.

JAMES: Thanks.

FAN: *(To Ginger.)* I'm sorry.

GINGER: That's all right.

FAN: I don't have any paper for an autograph. Would you…

GINGER: *(Offers her a matchbook.)* Here.

(But that isn't what the fan wants.)

FAN: Would you sign my hand? *(She unbuttons her cuff.)* Or maybe my arm?

(Ginger is embarrassed. James laughs.)

JAMES: Sure.

(Ginger watches as the Fan pushes her sleeve up further and James signs her arm.)

JAMES: What's your name?

FAN: Trudy. *(A moment.)* Trudy Blue.

JAMES: Sit down, Trudy.

(Ginger is upset. Her imagination has led her someplace she doesn't exactly want to go. Suddenly, Don enters. He is surprised to see Ginger.)

DON: Ginger.

GINGER: Don.

DON: What are you doing here?

GINGER: What do you mean?

DON: I thought you had a meeting with your editor.

GINGER: We finished early, so I came—

(Beth appears, laughing. Her nose in a book.)

GINGER: —home.

(And we realize we are not in the restaurant. We are in their house.)

DON: What's so funny?

GINGER: We don't allow laughing in this house?

DON: I thought she forgot how.

GINGER: Don.

BETH: *(Very silly.)* O.K. Tell me if you've heard it. It's the Divorce Court, and there's this hundred-year-old couple standing in front of the judge, and they've been married for eighty years and they are really miserable. And from the looks of them, they have been this miserable for the whole eighty years, and the judge leans over and says, "You poor old people. Why in God's name, did you take so long to get a divorce?"

DON: I've heard this one.

GINGER: Don...

DON: I have.

GINGER: Well, I haven't. Beth. Why did the poor old people take so long to get a divorce?

BETH: They wanted to wait 'til the kids died.

(Don grabs the book away from her.)

DON: I don't want you reading this stuff.

GINGER: Don. It's a joke book.

DON: Divorce is not a joke. Kids dying is not a joke.

BETH: Don't fight. I hate it when you fight.

DON AND GINGER: We're not fighting.

BETH: You are too. The only time you're not fighting is when one of you isn't home.

DON: I give up.

GINGER: Where are you going?

DON: To the basement.

BETH: I hate this.

GINGER: Where are you going?

BETH: Girl Scouts.

GINGER: You're not a Girl Scout.

BETH: Mom. It was a joke.

(Beth and Don exit, and Ginger turns back to James and Trudy.)

GINGER: I better go. I'm meeting Sue at Barney's and then we're having supper.

TRUDY: Bye.

JAMES: Do you have to leave?

GINGER: Do you want to meet at Sam's later?

JAMES: I want to. But I don't know if I can. I have to make a call.

(Ginger doesn't want to leave at all now. This Trudy person seems to be staying here with James.)

GINGER: All right, then.

JAMES: Good bye, gorgeous.

GINGER: Bye, sweetie.

(Ginger kisses him, then takes a few steps backward, then stops to watch. Trudy looks at him.)

TRUDY: She's not happy.

JAMES: She could be.

TRUDY: *(A little giddy.)* In this lifetime?

> *(James looks at her a moment.)*

JAMES: How old are you, Trudy?

TRUDY: We can talk on the way, James. Are you ready?

JAMES: Where are we going?

TRUDY: Someplace warm, that's all I care about. If we leave right now, we can wake up on the beach.

> *(She pulls a tiny bathing suit out of her pocket.)*

TRUDY: Yes no?

> *(Ginger can't watch any more. She leaves. A waiter appears. He speaks to Trudy and James.)*

WAITER: Anybody know what they want?

TRUDY: I do.

JAMES: *(Standing up.)* Me too.

> *(James leaves. Trudy looks up at the waiter.)*

TRUDY: What kind of beer do you have?

Scene 10
TRANSITION

JAMES: You're absolutely right, Ginny. Humans are always going to feel incomplete, always going to be looking for our other half. It's who we are. We have to mate. And we're not amoebas or something that can mate by themselves, so we have to find somebody that fits with us. Only if we don't know too much about ourselves, how can we know what we're looking for. We shake hands, "Is it you?" We kiss, "Is it you?" We try. But it's so hard, that sometimes you tell yourself you don't need anybody else. But it's no use. All you do then is just end up filling your empty half with something else, like work, or your children, or you know, chocolate bars...

Scene 11
SHOPPING WITH SUE

Ginger and Sue walk through a very chic department store.

GINGER: What are you looking for?

SUE: Something to make me feel good.

GINGER: This is nice.

SUE: God. What would I do if for some reason I couldn't shop.

SALES PERSON: Hi.

SUE: Hi.

SALES PERSON: *(Very friendly.)* Would you like to be helped or ignored?

SUE: I don't know yet.

GINGER: *(To the sales person.)* Just let us wander a little.

SUE: Oh. I almost forgot.
> (She reaches in her purse. And something makes us think she hasn't "almost forgotten" at all. In fact, this letter might be the point of this whole trip.)

SUE: Look what came to my house today. *(She produces an envelope.)* Mail for you.

GINGER: What is it?

SUE: How should I know? It's from a real estate agent in Montana. What are you doing, Ginger?
> *(Sue hands Ginger the letter.)*

GINGER: I don't know anything about this. They must have gotten my name from a—

SUE: Ginger, when they send you junk mail, they send it to *your* house. Not mine. Now what is this? And don't tell me it's research. I want the truth here.

GINGER: I was feeling sorry for myself.

SUE: Yeah, yeah.

GINGER: And thinking about the last time I was deeply happy.

SUE: Why the hell would you want to do that?

GINGER: It was at Lolo Hot Springs.
> *(The sales person comes out with a stack of beautiful scarves.)*

SALES PERSON: Look what just came in.

SUE: Wasn't that the hot springs in that Redford movie, what was the name of it, *A River Runs Through It?*

GINGER: Yes. It's in Montana. My friend Stu took me there one winter. With a couple of his friends.

SUE: This almost looks like a Fendi.

GINGER: Why don't we go to Fendi?

SUE: No, no. I'm not dressed.

GINGER: They don't care.

SUE: I do. *(Putting on a coat.)* So that last time you were happy you were in a hot tub in Montana? *(Picking one for Ginger.)* This one looks like you.

(Ginger takes the scarf, but just holds it. Sue tries on several as Ginger talks. The scarves are all very amusing. Some fluffy, some brightly colored, but all very tempting one-of-a-kind creations. Nothing ordinary in sight.)

GINGER: Not a hot tub. A hot springs. A geothermal...never mind. We drove down this incredibly dark mountain from skiing. And there was snow up to here on both sides of the road and a fair amount of snow actually *in* the road, and the sound of the tires was really loud, you know that squishy sound of tires driving over snow, and my knee really hurt where I fell, but the supper Stu packed was good. Cold beer, and roast beef on dark rye bread with sweet butter, and for dessert these huge brownies—

SUE: You were stoned.

GINGER: We were stoned. And there were these slippery sweet plums somebody's aunt put in a jar at the end of summer, and finally I wondered more or less out loud where we were going, and Stu said Lolo Hot Springs.

SUE: The plums were slippery? What were you eating them with, your fingers? *(To the sales person.)* They're not quite right. Thank you. *(To Ginger.)* Shall we try jewelry? The buyer finds wonderful gold here. Please. Go on.

(They walk toward another department, as Ginger continues her story...)

GINGER: Well finally, we pulled off the road but there were still no lights. Lights hadn't really caught on yet in Montana. And then I saw it.

SUE: Maybe a charm bracelet. Remember charms? Remember charm?

GINGER: The building looked like a bar, like a roadhouse. But we went in anyway. And it *was* a bar. An old bar. With old wood and old signs, and pictures of miners and moose heads and some stuffed fish...

(The sales person come up to them with a tray of jewelry.)

SALES PERSON: Hello, Mrs. Parker. What are we looking for today?

SUE: I wish I knew. Is that a Piaget? I love old Piagets.

(Ginger drifts further into her memory. As Sue and the sales person look at watches.)

GINGER: And we went up to the bar and got our Margaritas. Big margaritas in big paper cups. And Stu opened the back door and there it was. Like a great big swimming pool, only with steam rising up from it, and snow sprinkling down on it, and right in back of it, a sheer wall of solid rock like a mountain rising straight up into the night. Black sky. Billions of stars. The smell of juniper and wood fires...

SUE: *(Putting a watch on Ginger's wrist.)* Please try this on. I want to see how it looks on somebody else.

(Ginger tries on the watch, but in an absent sort of way. She is only aware of the weight of it. As though she must remember to take it off before she gets in the water.)

GINGER: And nobody had to tell me what to do next. I just seemed to know. Went right into the dressing room and put on my bathing suit, and came back out with my clothes in a little wire basket, and put the basket in the rack, and it was cold, maybe twenty degrees, maybe not, and we took our Margaritas and stepped into the pool. *(A moment.)* And it was so hot. And it felt so good.

(Sue takes the watch off Ginger's wrist.)

SUE: *(To the sales person.)* It's stunning. Where did it come from, do you know?

GINGER: And then we just paddled around, swimming away from our Margaritas and then swimming back to them. Thinking how happy we were. Not thinking. Just happy. *(A moment.)* And we forgot about everything except the water and the air and just floated around, and drank our drinks, and talked about nothing, and kissed each other, and came out later after everyone left and made love, and what I have wondered ever since that night, was why none of those vocational counselors in high school ever told me I could grow up to run a hot springs.

SUE: *(To the sales person.)* Well. Good. Have it cleaned and I'll come back and try it again on Friday.

(Ginger and Sue wander off into another area.)

GINGER: That was a beautiful watch, Sue.

SUE: Let's look at cashmere. You like cashmere, I know. Maybe they've got some cashmere longjohns for when you move to Montana.

GINGER: Did I say I was moving to Montana?

SUE: You didn't have to. *(To the sales person.)* I'd like to try a wrap, I think. Or a stole, maybe. Am I old enough for a stole?

SALES PERSON: Certainly.

(Sue wants to know the truth now.)

SUE: No, no. The black. *(Then to Ginger.)* You get a letter from a real estate agent and you obviously know it's coming because—

(Ginger opens her letter but doesn't read it yet.)

GINGER: All right. Yes. I found a real estate agent and called to see if there was a cabin or something I could rent for a…month. And I gave the agent your address so I didn't have to talk with Don about it before I knew what I wanted to do.

(Ginger reads the letter. Sue puts on a cashmere wrap.)

SUE: And?

(Ginger scans the letter looking for the answer. Sue waits eagerly.)

GINGER: They say they have a few things I might be interested in.

SUE: Ginger. It's Montana.

(Sue drapes a wrap around Ginger.)

GINGER: What's wrong with Montana?

SUE: You hate the cold.

GINGER: Maybe I've changed.

SUE: What do you mean, you've changed? Does Don want to go to Montana? Do the kids want to go to Montana?

GINGER: I didn't say maybe *they'd* changed. I said maybe—

SUE: Do they want to go to Montana?

GINGER: No. They don't. I tried it out on them the other day. I said, "I'm going to run a hot springs in Montana." And Don said "Well I'm going to run a dive shop in Key West."

SUE: Oh great. And the kids?

GINGER: Charlie said he was going to run Disneyland, and Beth said she was too.

SUE: So.

GINGER: So at least the kids can live together.

SUE: I'm sorry. I didn't realize it had gotten that bad. *(Sue turns to the sales person.)* Can you hold this for me til tomorrow?

GINGER: It's beautiful, Sue.

SUE: I don't know. Let's look at coats. Do you mind?

GINGER: What do you mean, do I mind? I'll go wherever you want. *(Ginger realizes how upset Sue is.)*

GINGER: What?

SUE: I don't want you to leave me. *(Trying to lighten up.)* Who would I talk to? Do you have a lover?

GINGER: No...

SUE: Because if this is about a man, if this is just about running away with some man and living happily ever after, I am really going to be pissed off. Who do you think you are, goddamn Snow White?

GINGER: Jesus, Sue.

SUE: I'm sorry. I don't know what I'm so upset about.

GINGER: Yes, you do. It's becoming very clear why women used to die in their forties.

SUE: Don't tell me.

GINGER: Because it was easier. Now, please...

(A sales person appears.)

SALES PERSON: Mrs. Parker. Did you decide on that coat? Would you like to try it on again?

SUE: Yes, please. *(Then to Ginger.)* Why can't you just be happy with Don? You have nice kids, and a great job, and a house that you like, and terrific friends, and you have spent a lot of time and energy getting all that stuff together. And now you want to be happy too? O.K., O.K. Maybe I do too. But how happy do you have to be?

GINGER: *(Stunned by this.)* You're *afraid* I'll be happy.

SUE: I am not.

GINGER: You are. *(Her anger growing.)* You're afraid I will find something that will actually make me happy, while you, who have given up on happiness, will be miserable for another forty-five years.

SUE: I will not be miserable for another forty-five years! Jesus, I hope I don't live another forty-five years. But I promise you, a new man will not make you happy. A new job, a new house, a new car, a new hair color, or running a goddamn hot springs will not make you happy.

GINGER: You don't know that. *I* don't know that.

(The sales person appears with a beautiful short white fur coat.)

SALES PERSON: Here we are.

(Sue puts it on. It is stunning. She wraps herself up in it.)

SUE: Don't do this to me, Ginger. Please don't do this.

GINGER: I thought you were my friend.

SUE: It's a man. It has to be. You wouldn't be ready to leave everything if there weren't somebody waiting for you. Is it Stu? Who is it? Tell me his name.

GINGER: How do you know I'm ready to leave?

SUE: This is a big mistake, Ginger.

GINGER: I've made them before.

SUE: Why won't you tell me his name?

GINGER: I can't just leave on my own? I have to have a man waiting for me?

SUE: What is his name?

GINGER: I don't like this. I don't like this one bit.

SUE: You don't care about anybody in your life except you. Why did you even come here tonight? Why aren't you gone already?

GINGER: I have to go. I can't go to dinner. I'll call you tomorrow.

SUE: I've seen you do some selfish things in your life, Ginger, but this is the worst.

GINGER: How do you know what I'm going to do?

SUE: You'll do whatever you feel like doing. Do you have any idea the pain you're about to cause? No. You don't, do you. And you don't care.

(Ginger cannot answer her. She leaves. The clerk comes out with Sue's coat in a bag.)

SALES PERSON: If you'll just sign here, Mrs. Parker.

(Sue takes the coat, signs the bill, nods to the woman and leaves.)

Scene 12

HER CHILDREN'S BEDTIME

In Annie's Area Beth and Charlie, Ginger's children, appear in their nightclothes. It may seem as if they are lying in their beds.

CHARLIE: I don't know where she went, and I don't know why she went there, and I don't care.

BETH: Charlie…

CHARLIE: And I hope she stays there and never comes back. I hope she gets hit by a truck.

BETH: That could happen.

CHARLIE: She didn't even say good-bye.

BETH: She said good-bye to me.

CHARLIE: Did not.

BETH: Did too.

CHARLIE: What do I care? Half the time she was here she wasn't here, so what else is new?

BETH: She's gone, Charlie. Get over it.

CHARLIE: Leave me alone.

BETH: Leave you here by yourself and go out with my boyfriend? O.K. Bye.

(Lights come up on Annie. We were not aware she was here.)

ANNIE: Does Charlie talk in his sleep?

BETH: Every night of my life.

CHARLIE: She wouldn't have left me if she liked me.

BETH: That's right.

ANNIE: Who is he talking about?

BETH: His teacher. *(A moment.)* His teacher moved away.

ANNIE: Why are you so mean to him?

BETH: He's my brother.

ANNIE: And why are you so angry?

BETH: What do you care?

ANNIE: I'm your grandmother. You're supposed to tell me things.

BETH: Yeah, and you're supposed to make me cookies and send me money. Where's mother? Do you know?

ANNIE: No, I don't. Did she say where she was going?

BETH: Sure she did. That doesn't mean that's where she went.

ANNIE: All right. Where did she *say* she was going?

BETH: She said she was having supper with Sue.

ANNIE: If you don't think she's having supper with Sue, what *do* you think she's doing? Do you think she's out having fun?

BETH: Is there life after death?

ANNIE: No, dear.

BETH: Then how am I talking to you?

ANNIE: Well, you do notice I mainly say things you've already thought of.

BETH: You're in my mind?

ANNIE: I'll leave if you want me to.

BETH: That's all right. I like talking to you.

ANNIE: You're not talking to me, dear.

BETH: Right. If I was talking to the real you, when I asked if there was life after death, you'd have said, "Yes, dear." Right? You'd have lied.

ANNIE: That's right.

BETH: So I'm talking to myself here?

ANNIE: It runs in the family.

BETH: Do people like me?

ANNIE: They love you. Your father loves you. Your mother loves you.

BETH: Then where is she?

ANNIE: Beth, your mother is just having dinner with her friend.

BETH: Why?

ANNIE: She'll be back soon.

BETH: When?

(Lights go down on them and come up on.)

Scene 13
DINNER WITH A FRIEND
Ginger sits on the bed in a hotel room. She picks up the phone, dials, then listens as the Concierge answers.

GINGER: *(Listens.)* Oh. I'm sorry. I wanted room service. *(Listens.)* Thank you. *(Waits to be connected.)* Yes. Hi. Could I get some coffee and juice. Yes. For two. Orange. And some kind of water, what kind do you have? O.K. One fizzy, one non. And I want a smoothie, too. Banana. No. Yes, all right. I'll take two. And I'm sure there's a wine list here somewhere, but what's the best Chardonnay you have? No, I like the New Zealands, actually. Is there a Cloudy Bay? There is? Amazing. All right. No. No food. I'm just thirsty. Thank you.

(James comes out of one of the other doors wearing a thick white terry bathrobe.)

JAMES: The Jacuzzi is great. You should try it.

GINGER: I don't want to get my hair wet.

JAMES: They have a dryer.

GINGER: I don't want to dry my hair. I want to not get it wet. *(Then recovering.)* Maybe this wasn't a good idea.

JAMES: You look sad.

(James opens his arms and she walks into them. He begins to rub her back.)

GINGER: My friends hate me.

JAMES: How could they?

GINGER: Because I don't want what they want. *(A moment.)* But *they* don't want it either. They just don't want me to *say* I don't want it.

JAMES: I think they're envious of you.

GINGER: Why?

JAMES: Because you're not afraid to know what you know.

GINGER: What do I know, James? Is there something I know that I'm not telling myself? *(A moment.)* And if I'm so brave about the truth, how come I'm afraid of the Jacuzzi?

JAMES: You're avoiding me.

GINGER: *(A little irritated.)* I'm avoiding a bath.

JAMES: Why?

GINGER: Because it will make me want you.

JAMES: And you don't want me?

GINGER: No. I do. Want you.

(There is a knock at the door.)

WAITER: Room Service.

JAMES: Saved by the bell.

(The waiter enters, carrying the tray of liquids. He has been wondering about all these liquids all the way up to the room. And indeed, the tray does look strange. It looks like a bar set up.)

WAITER: Don't tell me. Did you guys just get back from the desert?

(After a moment. James answers. Looking at Ginger. None of this is directed at the waiter.)

JAMES: Actually, no. We just stopped in here on our way *across* the desert.

GINGER: We still have the last half to go.

(James signs the check, and the waiter leaves. James is very careful with her now.)

JAMES: What would you like?

GINGER: A glass of wine.

(He pours them each a glass of wine, takes hers to her, then offers a toast.)

JAMES: To us. To happiness.

GINGER: To happily ever after?

JAMES: Why not? Wait right here, Princess. I'll go put on my doublet and tights.

GINGER: Nobody has ever lived happily ever after. *(Walking away from him.)* If we had a shred of courage, we'd tell our kids the truth. "And after they married, the prince and the princess lived for fifty years, and some days were better than others, and for the most part, they could stand it."

JAMES: What's going on, Ginger?

GINGER: *(Not answering.)* No. I get it. Maybe there wasn't any prince. Maybe the poisoned apple actually killed Snow White. And the prince was just some happy little hallucination she had right before she died.

JAMES: What do you want, Ginger?

GINGER: I don't want to want *anything*.

JAMES: I see.

GINGER: I want to be a Buddhist.

JAMES: It's a peaceful life they say.

GINGER: You're no help.

JAMES: Don't be mad at me. You're the one saying it's all so impossible.

GINGER: Is that what I'm saying?

JAMES: Yes. Well, maybe it's not impossible. But the odds on true love are very long.

GINGER: Even with you? Is that what I feel about you? That's not what I feel about you, is it?

JAMES: Well, of course not. But that's because I'm perfect.

GINGER: *(Laughs, teasing him.)* You're not perfect.

JAMES: I'm not? Then tell me something that's not perfect about me.

GINGER: *(Giving in, flirting.)* All right. You're perfect. You're the man of my dreams.

JAMES: That's right. I am. But that doesn't mean there isn't someone out there who—

GINGER: What do you mean, someone out there?

JAMES: A real man who could—

GINGER: A real man? What are *you*, a ghost?

JAMES: More like a wish.

GINGER: *(Quietly.)* Oh no.

JAMES: A longing. A need.

GINGER: You're in my mind. *(He doesn't answer.)* Please don't let this be true. You're not real.

JAMES: Ginny, Ginny, the things in your mind are as real as can be.

(Ginger is stricken almost dumb with sadness and despair.)

GINGER: I can't live with you? I can't wake up next to you?

JAMES: You always have. I thought you knew.

GINGER: You're a part of me.

JAMES: A part of you that adores you.

GINGER: What are you telling me? That I've given up? That I've fallen in love with myself?

JAMES: Ginny. That's not giving up.

GINGER: *(Her fury beginning to burn.)* I was so stupid. I was so lonely.

JAMES: I'm never leaving you, Ginny.

GINGER: *(Pulling away from him.)* Get away from me. You're not enough. If I'm going to have a lover, I at least want one I can see. *(Not looking at him.)* I can't believe this. I see you in the bar, I hear you play, something happens between us, and yes, I'm attracted to you, but then. Then you say something wonderful, something I'd always wanted to hear someone say, something I thought nobody thought but me, and before I know it, I'm saying all kinds of things to myself. You know who I am. You know when I'm lying. You know why I'm sad. You know what I want. You know what I really want. What I don't even *know* I want. You know what I need. *(A moment.)* The only problem is— *(Throws something.)* I'm not talking to you any more. I'm standing there talking to my idea of what would make me happy.

JAMES: Don't do this.

GINGER: This will teach me, all right. It's good to know what you want, Ginger. And very brave to ask for it. *(Her fury peaking.)* But next time, why don't you try asking it of someone who actually has it to give. *(A cry of grief.)* Oh James...

JAMES: Ginny. Don't be so—

GINGER: Don't tell me what to do.

(He moves in front of her.)

GINGER: Get out of here. And don't even think about telling me I might never find you again, because right at this moment, that is my fondest dream. I hope to God I never see you again.

(He doesn't move.)

GINGER: Leave me alone!

JAMES: Whatever you say.

(He takes off his white robe, hands it to her and walks through the door to the Jacuzzi. Holding the robe to her face, Ginger slowly sinks to the floor.)

Scene 14
AFTER DINNER

Ginger walks into the children's bedroom to say goodnight. She kisses Charlie, then Beth.

GINGER: Goodnight, sweetheart. I love you so much.

BETH: Where were you?

GINGER: I had supper with Sue.

BETH: Then how come Sue called here looking for you?

GINGER: When was this?

BETH: She wanted to say how sorry she was you had a fight, and see if you would come back to the restaurant and have supper with her.

GINGER: All right. I'll call her.

BETH: That was five hours ago, Mom. Where were you?

GINGER: I was so mad at Sue. I walked around. I stopped in a bar. I met a man. We went dancing. I left the country with him and now I'm living in Madagascar making necklaces to sell to the tourists.

BETH: Where were you, Mom?

GINGER: I was walking around thinking. I know it sounds weird, but that's where I was. Where's Daddy?

BETH: Your Daddy or mine?

GINGER: Why are you so mean to me? What did I do?

BETH: You gave me a home, in which I am now trapped.

GINGER: You'll be leaving soon enough.

BETH: Yeah, but you can leave whenever you want.

GINGER: Can I get that in writing?

BETH: *(Very angry.)* So go if you want to go. I don't see anybody trying to stop you.

GINGER: *(Very quickly, very irritated.)* Fine. I'm leaving. Do you want to come with me, or stay here?

(Beth sits up in the bed and grabs Ginger.)

BETH: No! You can't leave! Where are you going? Mom! You can't go.

GINGER: Beth, Beth. It's all right. I'm not going anywhere. I'm right here.

(As Ginger holds Beth, lights come up on Annie.)

ANNIE: She's a very disturbed child.

GINGER: She's fourteen.

ANNIE: You've told her too much.

GINGER: Could you just shut up?

ANNIE: *(Answering honestly.)* I don't know.

(Ginger puts Beth in her bed and pulls the covers back up over her.)

GINGER: Good-night, sweetheart. I love you to the end of the earth. *(A moment.)* Did you brush your teeth?

BETH: Yes, Mom.

GINGER: Good. Now tell me good-night.

BETH: Good-night, Mom.

(Ginger kisses Beth, then they repeat a poem they wrote together when Beth was little.)

GINGER AND BETH: Good-night to all the Birds above
And all the Fish below.
Good-night to all the Ones we love,
And all the rest, Yo-ho.

Scene 15
BEDTIME WITH GINGER

Ginger enters the bedroom. Don is sitting in bed, balancing the checkbook.

GINGER: You're awake.

DON: You noticed.

GINGER: What are you doing?

DON: Balancing the checkbook. When I do it in the morning, I stay mad all day. So I thought I'd try it at night.

GINGER: Isn't that what we pay Michael for?

DON: I'm supposed to take his word for how much money we have? It's not his money. What does he care? How was dinner?

GINGER: You didn't miss anything.

DON: Where did you go?

GINGER: O'Neals.

DON: I know where you were, Ginger.

GINGER: Where was I, Don?

DON: You got in a fight with Sue and you walked out on her.

GINGER: She said some terrible things to me. I don't want to talk about it. I went to the movies.

DON: I don't believe you.

GINGER: Don't believe me, then. What I really did was meet my lover in a hotel and made mad passionate love. I'm going to bed.

DON: Did you know you went to see seventeen doctors last month?

GINGER: Yes, I did, Don. Good-night.

DON: All right, but the hypnosis isn't deductible unless it's both pre-scribed and administered by a real doctor.

GINGER: You mean an M.D.

DON: By an M.D., yes. So maybe you could get Bruce to prescribe it for you the next time. Assuming there is a next time. I didn't know hypnosis was so expensive.

(Ginger doesn't answer, but begins to change into her pajamas.)

DON: How is your hearing?

GINGER: It depends on which doctor you believe. The first one said there was nothing wrong, the second one said there was nothing wrong, and—

DON: Does your therapist know about this?

GINGER: And the third one said I just didn't want to listen to my hus-band and kids screaming all the time.

DON: We don't scream all the time.

GINGER: I'm just telling you what he said. *(Notices the list.)* You made a list? Fine. Who's next?

DON: The gynecologist.

GINGER: She said I looked great. But it seemed like I had lost faith in you. And maybe I should get more exercise, or maybe meditate. She said basically I had to decide what I wanted out of life.

DON: And the herbalist?

GINGER: He said my body wasn't producing enough heat.

DON: No kidding.

GINGER: What does that mean?

DON: Well, let's see. How do we put this in layman's terms? Someone whose body is not producing enough heat is…oh, I know, cold..

But how could we tell if she was cold? Well, feeling the temperature of her skin would be a good way, but she doesn't want to be touched, so that's a problem. But it's common knowledge that cold people don't want to be touched. Yes. Cold fish, they're often called. So that's it. You should've come to see me sooner. The problem with you, Ginger, is that you are a cold fish.

GINGER: I'm definitely out of my element. I'll give you that much.

DON: *(Finding another check.)* Now what the hell is soul retrieval?

GINGER: You think I don't want to be touched?

DON: Not by me, you don't.

GINGER: Not the way you touch me, no. You're right.

DON: I wasn't asking for a lesson.

GINGER: You weren't going to get one.

    (A moment.)

DON: I'm worried about you, Ginger.

GINGER: Don't be.

DON: You're sick.

GINGER: I'm not.

DON: You're not sleeping, you don't care what you say, you're not yourself. I think you should check yourself into someplace for a few weeks and go get some help. Don't worry about the kids. We'll be fine.

GINGER: I'm not sick. I'm angry.

DON: You've always been angry.

GINGER: Maybe so. But now, I'm angry at you.

DON: No. You're not mad at me. You're mad at men. But I shouldn't have to take the blame for all the bad men you've known. Why don't you call Dr. Sterling and ask her for the name of a treatment center. Maybe there's a new medication you could take that—

GINGER: *(Stunned.)* Maybe there's a medicine that would make me love you?

DON: Are you telling me you wouldn't take it?

GINGER: I think we're about through here, Don. I think it's getting real clear that nobody loves anybody. Except the kids. The kids love us and we love them. We just don't love each other. And sooner or later the kids will see that we don't love each other, and I really don't want them thinking that it's O.K. to sleep and eat and celebrate Christmas with someone you don't love. So.

DON: I love you, Ginger. And I want nothing more than to spend the rest of my life with you.

GINGER: No you don't.

DON: How do you know whether I love you or not? Isn't that something *I* know, not you? We all know you're a very smart woman, but couldn't there be one tiny little thing that had escaped you?

(Ginger is suddenly released. Suddenly very calm.)

GINGER: Actually, Don. If it doesn't feel like you love me, then you don't.

(Don realizes something has happened, but instead of regrouping, he goes more on the attack. Ginger gets out of her pajamas and puts her clothes back on.)

DON: I don't love you unless you *believe* I love you? I have to convince you I love you? Come on.

GINGER: Good-bye, Don.

DON: What are you doing? *(No answer.)* Ginger. *(No answer.)* What the hell are you doing? *(No answer.)* Talk to me.

(She goes to his wallet. Takes out all the cash and puts it in her purse.)

DON: That's *my* wallet. *(He grabs her as she walks past.)* Ginger!

(She breaks away from him.)

DON: What are you doing?

GINGER: I'm leaving.

DON: Where are you going?

(She doesn't answer.)

DON: You're not going to say good-bye?

GINGER: I already did. You weren't listening.

(And she walks out the door. Don sits up straighter in the bed.)

DON: Ginger!

(He hears the door slam downstairs. He waits a moment, then picks up the phone, dials, and leaves a message on the machine. For all that has gone on, he seems quite calm. Even a little irritated.)

DON: Hi, Dr. Sterling, this is Don Wilson, Ginger Andrew's husband. She's just left the house very disturbed, and she didn't take any of her medication with her. I'm afraid she might be...well, suicidal. I've never seen her this way. Would you call me if she calls you? *(A moment.)* Sorry to bother you about this. It's probably nothing. If she shows back up here, I'll let you know.

(Don hangs up the phone.)

Scene 16
THE BOOK PARTY

This feels like a combination book party and memorial service. Her new book is out. But Ginger is gone. Don, her three friends, Annie, and her publisher are here. A waiter circulates as if among a crowd.

EDITOR: *(As to a larger group.)* Ladies and Gentlemen. I know you want to say hello to Ginger's husband and friends, so I won't take long. I'm Kate Morgan. I was Ginger's editor here at Herald Books. I know she would be pleased that so many of you could be here today. *(Holding up the book.)* I want to personally thank all those who helped bring her wonderful book to life. I feel her presence with us here, I do. So if you will, please join me in raising a glass to the publication of… *Trudy Blue, Girl in Love.*
(There is applause and we find Sue talking to Don.)
SUE: *(Holding a copy of the book.)* Did you read it?
DON: Yes, I did.
SUE: What did you think?
DON: What do you think I think? Ginger took my life and made it into a goddamn novel.
SUE: It was her life too, Don. I think she had the right to do that.
DON: It wasn't the truth.
SUE: It wasn't you?
DON: Of course it was me. But she didn't have to tell everybody. O.K. Sure. I said that stupid thing about running the dive shop, but I was kidding. Besides, what she was really mad about was about how much money I spent on dive gear and dive trips, but do you know how much money she spent on doctors? I got a lot more good out of diving than she ever did out of those doctors. I'm not the one who ended up in therapy.
SUE: She thought her therapist was very good.
DON: She was all right. I mean, I never met Dr. Sterling, but since Ginger started seeing her, she actually seemed to be, you know, present, about half the time.
SUE: Excuse me, Don. I have to—
DON: You know what I think? I think Ginger was still pissed off about that time she had pneumonia and I went on a dive trip the day of her cat scan. But I knew she didn't have cancer. She knew she did-

n't have cancer. And anyway, I asked her if she wanted me to stay home and she said no.

SUE: You did?

DON: I'm sure I did.

SUE: Well. *(Looking around.)* I'm sorry she's gone, Don.

DON: I know. Thanks.

(The other two friends from the Lunch scene appear.)

MARIA: Isn't it Ginger's birthday tomorrow?

CONNIE: No, it's the sixteenth.

SUE: It's the eighteenth.

MARIA: What's Don going to do now?

SUE: I don't think he's decided yet.

CONNIE: How could she do this to us?

(A light comes up on Annie.)

ANNIE: I'm not surprised, actually. It was just like Ginger to do something like this. I suppose I could tell her friends that they would get over losing her, but I don't think they will. I certainly haven't. And I lost her a long time ago. *(A moment.)* I could also tell them she might come back. But I don't think she will. I just hope that wherever she is, she can find some way to be happy there.

(The editor comes up to Don.)

EDITOR: Don, the publicity department was wondering if you would like to do some interviews for us.

DON: Interviews about what?

EDITOR: If you're uncomfortable talking about your relationship, we understand, of course. I didn't think you would go for it, but I promised I would ask. So don't worry about it. I'll just tell them you were unavailable.

(Don has no idea how to respond to this.)

DON: Thanks.

(Lights fade out on the party and come up on:)

Scene 16
LOLO HOT SPRINGS

Steam rises from the magnificent hot pool at the base of the mountain. The night is clear and cold, four zillion stars glitter in the dark sky. It smells like eucalyptus and rosemary. A single large paper cup sits on the rocky edge of the pool. Suddenly, Ginger bursts out of the water in the center of the pool, as though she swam the length of the pool underwater and her lungs are now desperate for air.

GINGER: Ah! *(We notice, however fleetingly, that Ginger is not wearing the top of her bikini. She sinks back into the water in complete surrender to the hot water and cold air and then paddles over to her Margarita at the side of the pool. She takes a sip. She rests her head on the edge of the pool. She sees the moon.)*

GINGER: Dear Sue, My happiness is in orbit around me like the moon. Not really mine, but rather like something I glimpse on many nights in various forms. Full. Half. Waning. Waxing. Usually seeming quite familiar, but sometimes so startling, I can't remember ever seeing it before. Because it circles me, if I don't see it tonight, that will only mean it's on its way back. I'll call you one of these days. But it could be a while. As to the questions in your letter, no, my ear hasn't bothered me at all since I've been here. And yes, the kids are fine. I'm glad you liked Trudy Blue. She likes you too. *(She looks at her Margarita. She smiles. She raises her glass in a toast. To herself. To the night. To the mountain.)*

GINGER: Love, Ginger.

END OF PLAY

Cloud Tectonics

By José Rivera

For Heather

BIOGRAPHY

José Rivera's play *Marisol* premiered at the 16th Annual Humana Festival of New American Plays at the Actors Theatre of Louisville and was produced off-Broadway at the Joseph Papp Public Theatre (1993 Obie Award for Outstanding Play). His other plays include *Each Day Dies with Sleep* (Berkeley Rep. and Circle Rep. Theatres), *Giants Have Us in Their Books* (The Magic Theatre), *The Promise* (Los Angeles Theatre Center), and *The House of Ramon Iglesia* (Ensemble Studio Theatre). *Cloud Tectonics* premiered at the 19th Annual Humana Festival and was produced at the La Jolla Playhouse. Honors include grants from the NEA, the Rockefeller Foundation, and the New York Foundation for the Arts. In 1989 Rivera studied screenwriting with Nobel Prize winner Gabriela García Márquez at the Sundance Institute. In 1990 he was writer-in-residence at the Royal Court Theatre, London while on a Fulbright Arts Fellowship in Playwriting. In 1992 he received the Whiting Foundation Writing Award. Television and film credits include NBC's critically acclaimed "Eerie, Indiana" series; "The House of Ramon Iglesia" which was adapted for PBS's American Playhouse series; the Ace Award–nominated "P.O.W.E.R.: The Eddie Matos Story"'" for HBO; the pilot for Fox's "Goosebumps" series; and the Interscope screenplay "Lucky."

Cloud Formations: Musing On the Act of Creation by Gregory Gunter

On a dark and stormy night, as all good stories begin, José Rivera passed a pregnant hitchhiker on a street in Los Angeles. "I didn't stop because traffic was heavy and I'm not given to picking up hitchhikers," says the playwright. But he could not stop thinking about her. "I've become obsessed with what that women's story might have been. How she arrived at that place. What happens to bring a life to that point?" At the same time José was obsessing, as he calls it, about love. "How do you know when you've fallen in love with someone? How does that feel and what does it mean? If you were to describe that to a person from another planet what would you say?"

José's hitchhiker and ruminations about love collided with a view of clouds from an airplane window. "I was flying one day, looking out at the clouds going by and marveling at the incredible chaos. I was thinking about this quest to define the parameters of the experience of love. Defining love seemed as do-able as defining those shapes in the air. It's impossible to put a formula to that chaos and it struck me that the emotional connections between people are similarly undefinable, mysterious, and chaotic. And maybe that's what the charm is." This freewheeling rumination led to inspiration. "Suddenly these varied ideas weren't fractions of unrelated experience—they were really part of a bigger picture that was beginning to take shape. And I think the picture became the play."

José's relationship with his four brothers also found its way into *Cloud Tectonics* in the relationship between Aníbal, a delivery man, and Nelson, his brother in the military. "My brother Julio is an ex-marine who served in the 1980 mission to free the hostages from Tehran. He lost several friends when the helicopters crashed. My brother Charlie is a former sergeant who served in the army during the Persian Gulf war. Tony is currently an army sergeant at Fort Irwin and Hector works in Sacramento as a marine recruiter. All of them chose the military as a way out of the poverty we grew up in."

"I'm the black sheep of the family. My brothers are very conservative. My worldview is completely different. Nevertheless, we are very tight as brothers. There isn't anything we wouldn't do for each other or any place we wouldn't go for one another. I respect my brothers because they have found a way to survive."

Part of his exploration was precipitated by seeing the hitchhiker during the storm and part of it was José's need to examine his relationship with the love of his life, his wife, to whom the play is dedicated. Heather Dundas and José met when she was twenty and he was twenty-four. "This was quite a long time ago," he laughs, "We went through every minute of the eighties together…as hellish as they were. She really made me believe in somebody that you would commit your life to. One of the biggest elements in love," he muses, "is luck. Sometimes you are lucky enough to find someone early in life. We're really committed to doing this as a lifetime journey. I spent time contemplating what a lifetime journey means and how that effects you biologically. It's a central part of the play."

The character of Celestina, the hitchhiker, transcends time itself in her quest for love. She lives outside of normal time, so it is possible for her to observe profound changes in the people around her. "I wanted her to have a condition that was beyond time as we know it. Beyond what any human could possibly experience." In creating a new language for time, José hopes the audience will be moved by the possibility such alteration of time provides. "Camilia Sanes, the actress who plays Celestina, told me this wonderful story. She had a boyfriend when she was very young and she said she got to see him go through puberty. They stopped seeing each other but they're still friends. Now when she sees him, he's gray. How incredible it is to have been audience to those lifetime transformations in a person you care about."

"We are in a perpetual state of what is possible. Things don't ever actually become...they are always in a state of becoming. We never get there. Celestina's freezing time is a way to theatricalize that feeling. To me, when I think about my life and various relationships that I've had and the people whom I've encountered—I always see that I'm in a state of potential with almost everyone I meet. You are forced by life to make choices, you have to close off potential avenues all the time. I always wonder, What would those avenues be like if I didn't?"

Gregory Gunter is Literary Manager of La Jolle Playhouse and Dramaturg for the West Coast premiere of Cloud Tectonics.

ORIGINAL PRODUCTION

Cloud Tectonics premiered at the 19th Annual Humana Festival of New American Plays at the Actors Theatre of Louisville, Jon Jory, Producing Director, on March 1, 1995. It was directed by Tina Landau with the following cast:

Celestina del Sol . . . . Camilia Sanes
Aníbal de la Luna . . . . Robert Montano
Nelson de la Luna. . . . . Javi Mulero

Special thanks to Alice's Fourth Floor, New York, and to the Wilton Project, Los Angeles, for the development of this play. Extra special thanks to Ivonne Coll for the Spanish translation of Celestina's speech.

"Ah déjame recordate como eras entonces, cuando aún no existías."
—*Pablo Neruda*

"…love was the promised land, an ark on which two might escape the Flood."
—*Julian Barnes*

"The mystery of what a couple *is,* exactly, is almost the only true mystery left to us, and when we come to the end of it there will be no more need for literature…"
—*Mavis Gallant*

"…the discovery that the speed of light appeared the same to every observer, no matter how he was moving, led to the theory of relativity—and in that one had to abandon the idea that there was a unique and absolute time. Instead, every observer would have his own measure of time as recorded by a clock that he carried; clocks carried by different observers would not necessarily agree. Thus time became a more personal concept, relative to the observer who measured it. When one tried to unify gravity with quantum mechanics, one had to introduce the concept of 'imaginary' time."
—*Stephen W. Hawking,* A Brief History of Time

"Todo me parece como un sueno todavia…"
—*Danny Daniel*

CHARACTERS
CELESTINA DEL SOL: 20s.
ANÍBAL DE LA LUNA: 30s.
NELSON DE LA LUNA: 25.

PLACE
Prologue. Los Angeles. The present. Night.
Scene. Same. Later that night.
Epilogue. Same. Forty years later.

CLOUD TECTONICS

Los Angeles. Night. A bare stage with:
  A floating bed, high in the air, tilted so the upstage headboard is slightly higher than the downstage footboard.
  A glass wall. Water drips down the side of the glass wall. It represents a city bus stop during a rainstorm.
  A pair of microphones on C-stands, downstage, a few feet apart.

Prologue
  The Prologue begins with bolero *music: Los Panchos singing "Por El Amor De Una Mujer."*
  Celestina del Sol is standing at the bus stop. There's the sound of rain. Celestina is soaking wet. She carries a small shopping bag. She wears a thin maternity dress and she shivers. She looks exhausted, as if she's been wandering on foot for days. It's impossible to tell her actual age. It's impossible to tell if she's rich or poor. She's very, very pregnant.
  As the bolero *plays, Celestina holds her thumb out, hoping to catch a ride, but there doesn't seem to be any traffic in Los Angeles tonight. She reaches into a pocket, pulls out some saltine crackers, and eats them hungrily, savoring each bite.*
  Car lights wash over Celestina. She sticks her thumb up higher. The lights cruise past her and disappear. Disappointed, Celestina eats another cracker.
  We wait for the bolero *to end or fade out.*
  A moment's silence, then another car's headlights pass over Celestina. This time they stay on her. She holds her thumb up expec-

tantly. The car's horn beckons her and she happily leaves the wall and goes to one of the microphones.

The microphones are suddenly awash in red light.

Aníbal de la Luna enters and goes to the other microphone. Aníbal is a pleasant-looking man, 30s, dressed in an American Airlines ground crew uniform. Aníbal and Celestina perform the following scene into the microphones. At no time do they pantomime being in a car.

During the Prologue, Aníbal's house in the Echo Park section of Los Angeles is loaded in. This takes as long as the Prologue takes to perform, please.

CELESTINA: *(Shivering.)* Thank you so much for this.

ANÍBAL: Jesus, you're soaked. There's a jacket in the back seat.

CELESTINA: *(Putting on jacket.)* Thank you.
(Short beat.)

ANÍBAL: I can't believe anyone's out in that deluge. They're calling it the storm of the century.

CELESTINA: Where am I?

ANÍBAL: Los Angeles.

CELESTINA: *(Troubled.)* Los Angeles?

ANÍBAL: Corner of Virgil and Santa Monica.

CELESTINA: *(Means nothing to her.)* Oh.
(Celestina says no more. She just rubs her pregnant stomach and stares ahead. Her silence makes Aníbal a little nervous.)

ANÍBAL: Can you believe this rain for L.A.? *Coño!* Raging floods on Fairfax…bodies floating down the L.A. River…LAX closed…if the Big One came right now, forget it, half this city would die. But that's L.A. for you: disasters just waiting to happen. *(Aníbal laughs. No response from Celestina.)*

ANÍBAL: I lived in New York. Lived in every borough except Staten Island. And Brooklyn. And Queens. And the thing is, New York kills its people one-by-one, you know? A gun here, a knife there, hand-to-hand combat at the ATM, little countable deaths. But this? This L.A. thing? *Mass* death, *mass* destruction. One freak flood at the wrong time of year and hundreds die…the atmosphere sags from its own toxic heaviness and thousands perish…the Big One is finally born, eats a hundred thousand souls for *breakfast.* And I'm not even talking fire season!

(Celestina looks at Aníbal for the first time.)

CELESTINA: Why don't you go back to New York?

ANÍBAL: Are you kidding? I love it here. I have a house here. I have gorgeous fucking incredible-looking women falling outta the sky here! *Coño,* I've made a commitment to that!
(No response from Celestina. She eats a cracker quietly, her mind far away. Aníbal looks at her a long moment.)

ANÍBAL: You alright?

CELESTINA: The trucker that dropped me off kept touching my knees and I screamed.

ANÍBAL: How long were you out there?
(Beat.)

CELESTINA: I don't know.

ANÍBAL: You don't know?
(Beat.)

CELESTINA: I don't have a watch…I don't keep a watch…I don't keep "time"…"Time" and I don't hang out together!

ANÍBAL: *(Not understanding.)* Oh. Where can I take you?

CELESTINA: I don't know. Away from the rain?

ANÍBAL: Tough luck; it's everywhere. Where were you hitching to?

CELESTINA: Nowhere. I'm not going anywhere. I don't know where I'm going, I'm sorry.

ANÍBAL: You're just out there hitching? In a hurricane? Pregnant? For fun?

CELESTINA: Are you going to ask me a lot of questions?

ANÍBAL: Why don't I take you to a hospital? Get someone to check out your baby.

CELESTINA: No! No! Don't do that! I don't want doctors asking me a lot of questions!

ANÍBAL: Maybe the police could…

CELESTINA: No police! Please! No police! I don't want to go to the police!

ANÍBAL: No friends or family in L.A.?

CELESTINA: No one. I have no one. You're the only one I know!

ANÍBAL: *(Choosing to ignore that.)* Well, you're in my car, I gotta take you somewhere…

CELESTINA: Take me to this baby's father. I'm looking for this baby's father. His name is Rodrigo Cruz. Do you know him? He's a very handsome and dishonest man.

ANÍBAL: No, I don't think I…

CELESTINA: Nobody knows him. I ask everybody. That trucker took me to every state looking for Rodrigo Cruz!

ANÍBAL: …I'm sorry…

CELESTINA: I started my journey on Montauk Point: A room in a house, very small, my Papi sailed boats for tourists, it was some distance back—but I—I lost all track of "time"—I hate to use that word—"time"—but it's the only word I have, isn't it?

ANÍBAL: *Coño,* I'm not following this…

CELESTINA: I can give you *details* of Rodrigo Cruz. He worked for Papi repairing the boat. His eyes were ocean-green. His back was wrinkled. But I can't tell you *when* he was like that, okay? He might have *changed,* you see? I can't tell you his *age.* Do you know how hard it is to find someone when you can't tell anyone their age?

ANÍBAL: Well, it's not a problem I ever…

CELESTINA: All this traveling has been a blur! It's a huge country! I never should have left my house in Montauk! I was safe in my house! Papi and Mami had it all worked out for me! They took away all the clocks!

ANÍBAL: *(Completely lost.)* The clocks?

CELESTINA: But I was sleeping when that gorgeous son-of-a-bitch Rodrigo Cruz came into my room! He knocked me up! He left! Now look at me! I'm starving and lost and sick of these soggy *fucking* crackers…and I'm just so tired of being *pregnant!*

ANÍBAL: *(Worried.)* Take it easy…

CELESTINA: You can let me out right here, I'm sorry!

ANÍBAL: But we haven't moved. Light's still red.

CELESTINA: Oh. Right. *(Celestina cries and stuffs her mouth with crackers.)*

ANÍBAL: You alright?

CELESTINA: Please, I don't want to bother you anymore.

ANÍBAL: I don't want you sleeping outside. Not with a baby coming.

CELESTINA: I've done it before!

(The relentless rain slaps the car as Aníbal contemplates his options.)

ANÍBAL: *Coño,* okay, listen: if you promise me you're not an ax-murderer …I promise you *I'm* not an ax-murderer too, okay? You can stay in my house tonight, okay? Just tonight, okay? I'm right up here in Echo Park, okay?

CELESTINA: I can? I can't.

ANÍBAL: I promise not to touch your knees, okay?

(Celestina looks at Aníbal.)

CELESTINA: What's your name?

ANÍBAL: Oh I'm sorry. Aníbal de la Luna. Nice to meet you.

CELESTINA: I'm Celestina del Sol.

(She reaches out her hand. Aníbal and Celestina shake hands. She smiles.)

CELESTINA: Okay. Let's go to your place.

(The light turns green The lights go down on Aníbal and Celestina. The crew finishes assembling Aníbal's house. Aníbal and Celestina exit. The microphones are struck.)

END OF PROLOGUE

Scene One

The lights are dark in Aníbal's house, a modest pre-W.W.II wooden bungalow, working class, not Hollywood.

The living room, kitchen, and small eating area are basically one room full of sentimental family pictures, and second- and third-hand furniture. The door in the living room leads to the front porch. Another door leads to the bathroom.

There are a couple of subtle plaster cracks on the walls from a recent earthquake.

Everything—sink, television, stereo, refrigerator, microwave, VCR, telephone, O'Keefe & Merritt stove, etc.—should be fully functional. There's a Sparkletts water dispenser in the kitchen: the bottle is empty.

The only light in the house comes from the glowing digital clocks on all the appliances. It's 8:05 PM.

The glass wall has been incorporated into the house. Two ladders have been placed next to the floating bed to make it accessible to the living room.

We hear footsteps. The sound of keys unlocking the front door. The door opens. Suddenly all the digital clocks turn off and come back on blinking a new time: 12:00. It stays 12:00 for the rest of the scene.

Celestina and Aníbal enter from the porch. Both are dripping wet. Celestina now wears a thin suede jacket. Aníbal carries in a five-gallon bottle of Sparkletts water.

With the door wide open we hear distant police, ambulance, and fire truck sirens. Celestina closes the door and the sirens stop.

ANÍBAL: Watch your step.

CELESTINA: It's a pretty house.

ANÍBAL: It's a craftsman. Built in the forties.

CELESTINA: Is that old?

ANÍBAL: In L.A. it's the Middle Ages.

CELESTINA: *(Not understanding.)* Oh.

(Aníbal puts the water bottle on the kitchen floor as Celestina takes off the wet jacket. They both take off their water-logged shoes.)

ANÍBAL: *(Re: her shoes.)* Just leave them anywhere.

CELESTINA: *(Looking around, smiles.)* I'll never forget this as long as I live.

ANÍBAL: Let me turn up the heat. Get some light going here.

(Aníbal turns up the heat and turns on some lights.
Aníbal looks over at Celestina—getting his first full view of her. She's much more pregnant, and much more beautiful, than he realized. She smiles warmly at him.)

CELESTINA: You have the most beautiful house, Aníbal.

ANÍBAL: It's dry at least. More than I can say for you.

(Aníbal goes to the bathroom and comes back with a towel, which he tosses to Celestina. She dries her face, arms, and feet.)

CELESTINA: You're the kindest, most beautiful man in the world! And this is the happiest night of my life!

ANÍBAL: *(Smiles.)* Can I get you anything to drink?

CELESTINA: *(Eager.)* Water. Please.

(Aníbal goes to the kitchen.)

ANÍBAL: So please make yourself at home. Sit. Relax.

(Aníbal puts the full Sparkletts bottle on the dispenser. He takes the empty bottle out to the porch; again, as he opens the door, we hear distant sirens which stop when he closes the door.
Too happy to sit still, Celestina starts exploring the house, checking out pictures on tables, books on bookshelves, etc.)

CELESTINA: Everything is so beautiful. Everything in order.

ANÍBAL: Debbie does that.

CELESTINA: My little room in Montauk had no order. It wasn't big, but it was my whole world. Things were everywhere, on top of everything: I'd sleep in my clothes, and eat in bed, and read detective novels, hardly ever sleep, dream wide awake, make plans that were never fulfilled, watch storms coming in, the moon's neurotic phases, hear stars being scraped across the sky, dance, sing *boleros,* make

love to myself over and over, live a whole life in one room!
(*Celestina laughs as she holds herself and does a little dance around the room.*)

ANÍBAL: (*Giving her a look.*) You want a *quesadilla*?

CELESTINA: And my Mami and Papi worked so hard for me. They loved me so much. They thought I was cursed! They really did! They put everything in its proper place for me!
(*Aníbal looks at Celestina a long moment, not sure what to make of all this.*)

ANÍBAL: Your parents thought you were cursed?

CELESTINA: Yeah. They're dead. I'd love a *quesadilla*.

ANÍBAL: Wait.

CELESTINA: Papi used to cross himself when he looked at me. Mami wouldn't breast feed me. They kept eighteen statues of Jesus Christ in my room!

ANÍBAL: Wait. Why did you live in one room...?
(*Celestina looks at Aníbal, aware of his look. She laughs.*)

CELESTINA: I hope I don't sound...I hope I don't sound...I'm not a lunatic. Hey. You're in no danger, Aníbal. It's just hard for me to tell a story. Straight.

ANÍBAL: (*Worried; re: her baby.*) Just take it easy. For both of you.

CELESTINA: (*Touching her stomach.*) This baby must think I'm a lunatic too!

ANÍBAL: But I don't—.

CELESTINA: I wonder what this baby hears. Oh God! This baby must've heard me talking to that trucker, and all his dirty words! Ugly, filthy man!
(*Celestina suddenly gets a fierce contraction that doubles her over. Aníbal goes to her and takes her hand.*)

ANÍBAL: Celestina, please...if you...if you sat down, I'd feel a lot better...

CELESTINA: (*Pain.*) Why?

ANÍBAL: 'Cause if you get too agitated, you might...I mean, I don't want you having that baby all over my floor tonight...

CELESTINA: And your floor is so clean!

ANÍBAL: Yes...I mean, you're not, like, *coño, due* tonight, are you?

CELESTINA: (*Pain subsiding.*) I don't know.

ANÍBAL: You don't know?
(*The discomfort goes away and Celestina straightens up again. She smiles as if nothing happened.*)

CELESTINA: I don't think so.

ANÍBAL: Well, wait. How pregnant are you? Exactly.

CELESTINA: *(Defensive.)* What do you mean?

ANÍBAL: How far along are you?

CELESTINA: I'm not really sure.

ANÍBAL: You're not *sure?*

CELESTINA: This is the warmest, most enchanting house I've ever…

ANÍBAL: Wait. Isn't knowing how pregnant you are…a little basic? Like knowing your age?

CELESTINA: Yes…yes it is…but you should never ask a woman's age, you might not like what you hear! *(Smiles at him.)* Can I have my water?

(Aníbal looks at Celestina—then goes to the Sparkletts dispenser and pours Celestina a tall glass of water. He gives it to her. Celestina drinks the water very fast, almost choking on it, like she hasn't had water in a long time. Finished, she holds out her empty glass for more. As Aníbal takes Celestina's empty glass and goes back for a refill, Celestina finds a framed picture of a Young Woman on a table.)

CELESTINA: So do you have a lot of "gorgeous fucking incredible-look-ing women" in your life, Aníbal?

(Aníbal hands Celestina the glass of water.)

ANÍBAL: *(Re: photograph.)* Well, no. Well, one. That one.

CELESTINA: She's beautiful.

ANÍBAL: That's Debbie.

(Celestina looks at the photograph a long time. Aníbal waits for her to say something.)

ANÍBAL: She's at her office now. She sleeps there a lot. She works for Disney. She answers phones. She's gorgeous. She's Puerto Rican too but she changed her name from Epifania Niguayona Gonzalez to Debbie Shapiro. They still don't respect her. She thinks they do. But she's deluding herself. I can tell. I know guys. I know when a guy is thinking pussy and every guy she works with at Disney is thinking pussy. She thinks they're thinking brain cells. They're not going to make her an executive like she thinks. She's going to remain a receptionist until she turns thirty, then they're gonna fire her and get a younger, prettier, whiter-looking Latin girl to replace her.

CELESTINA: Will she mind my being here?

ANÍBAL: She'd hate it except you're pregnant. Deb doesn't believe in friendship between the sexes, she believes in sex between the sexes. Being pregnant makes you safe.

CELESTINA: *(Surprised.)* I'm safe?

ANÍBAL: Guess so.

(Celestina puts the photograph down, finishes her glass of water, and looks at Aníbal.)

CELESTINA: What do you believe? Sex or friendship?

ANÍBAL: I believe friendship between the sexes is not only possible, it's preferable. Makes everything cleaner. But then I don't work in the movie business. I load luggage at LAX. There's no sex in that job.

CELESTINA: *(Shocked.)* None?

(Beat. Aníbal isn't sure how far he wants this conversation to go, but there's something about Celestina. He can't help but open up to her.)

ANÍBAL: The closest is…I look up at an airplane sometimes and it's full of people going to New York and sometimes I make eye contact with a woman at a window seat in First Class. And she's looking down at me, daydreaming, maybe she's afraid of the flight, thinking this could be her last hour on earth, wondering if she's done enough, dared enough, eaten enough, and everyone around her seems dead already. And that fear of crashing is bringing all her latent sexual dreams up from their deep well, and she's getting all excited by her own images—and there *we* are, making split-second eye contact and suddenly that faceless male in her dreamworld has a pair of eyes…and they are vivid eyes, and they are Puerto Rican eyes, and they are my eyes, Celestina.

(A short silence. Celestina goes to Aníbal. She gets close to him—so close her huge belly gently touches his stomach. She looks into Aníbal's eyes. The intensity of this makes Aníbal a little nervous.)

ANÍBAL: What are you doing?

CELESTINA: Can I see?

ANÍBAL: Can you see? What? Can you what?

CELESTINA: Your vivid, Puerto Rican eyes, Aníbal, can I see them?

ANÍBAL: *(Nervous.)* Why? No.

CELESTINA: Just because. Let me.

ANÍBAL: *Coño*, I brought you here on faith, now. That you're not a killer. Not a psycho. Not a hypnotizing, blood-drinking Scientologist…

(Celestina looks deep into Aníbal's eyes.)

CELESTINA: I think about sex all the time, though I've only had one lover in my life, only one time. Rodrigo Cruz. And I almost had two! That despicable trucker who kept touching my knees. But I ran away from him. I took my chances in the rain. But even he couldn't stop my endless daydreaming and nightdreaming about sex: about Rodrigo's wrinkled back, my legs wrapped around his face…this obsession of mine…this tidal wave that started some-time when I was younger, when I lived in that one room…when Papi bought me a bicycle to give me something else to think about beside my body, and one glorious day I was allowed to ride around and around the house, because my Papi wanted me to count num-bers, count numbers, over and over; he said it would teach me about the nature of "time," and I tried and tried, I really did, but I didn't learn anything, I was just so grateful to be outside my little room for once! *(Beat.)* Then Papi hired Rodrigo to work on his boat "The Celestina." And I would stare at him from my window as he worked. He was beautiful. I wondered if I was in love. Is that what it felt like? And he would look back at me and stare and his hair was so long and black. And I wondered is that what love looks like? And I don't know how many years passed…(I didn't know the word "years" then. I learned it on the road when the trucker taught me all kinds of words like "years" and "now" and "yesterday" and "minute" and "century")…and it must have been years…because years are longer than days (I learned this!)…and Rodrigo's hair was long and gray and he snuck into my room and did his dirty thing and left me…and my parents died in the other room and I went out to see because the house had grown so quiet and there they were in their little bed, holding hands, the green bedspread half-covering their wrinkled bodies, naked and pale and covered in long gray hairs and very, very dead. That's the one time I stopped dreaming of sex when I called the police and told them Mami and Papi were dead, then I got dressed, and I lost all track of "time" and I got scared, and I ran out into the rain because I was sure they'd blame me and in my endless stay in my one room I didn't learn much, but I learned by reading detective novels that when some-body dies the police always come to take you away and kill you with a lightning chair. That's when I hit the road, pregnant, look-ing for Rodrigo Cruz, angry and excited because he was the only man I ever had sex with and I keep thinking about sex with

Rodrigo and I love the word sex and if I could fuck fuck fuck all day I would!

(Aníbal impulsively, quickly kisses Celestina. She gasps. Aníbal turns away.)

ANÍBAL: Let me start those *quesadillas* for you! *(Aníbal quickly turns on the griddle and busies himself in the kitchen.)*

CELESTINA: I should leave. *(Celestina starts to go to the front door.)*

ANÍBAL: I don't want you to leave.

CELESTINA: You don't think I'm strange?

ANÍBAL: I do think you're strange. But I don't want you to leave.

CELESTINA: But I don't know how long I've been here. I don't know if it's been too long! I should go!

ANÍBAL: *(Re: the kiss.)* I'm sorry I did that! I never do that!

CELESTINA: Have I been here minutes? Days?! Shit! I knew this would happen!

ANÍBAL: A half hour at the most! Twenty minutes. Not days.

CELESTINA: Are you sure?

(Aníbal looks at his watch.)

ANÍBAL: My watch stopped.

CELESTINA: *(Knew this would happen.)* I really have to go before Rodrigo turns into an unrecognizable old man and dies!

(Aníbal looks at all the digital clocks in the house—all are blinking 12:00.)

ANÍBAL: The clocks have stopped…

(Celestina goes to put on her shoes and the wet jacket.)

CELESTINA: I can't miss my chance to make that bastard do right by me!

(Celestina goes to the door, opens it. We hear sirens.

Aníbal grabs Celestina's arm, physically stopping her from running out.)

ANÍBAL: Celestina, wait a second—.

CELESTINA: *I can't wait a second; I don't know what you mean!*

ANÍBAL: Listen! You can't go out into that fucking typhoon, *do you understand me?!*

CELESTINA: But—.

ANÍBAL: You've been here only a few *minutes.* Just minutes. Tomorrow morning, when the sun comes up, it'll be only a few *hours*…

(Beat. She looks at him.)

CELESTINA: Hours? Is it a lot? Is it long?

ANÍBAL: *Coño*…I think you're…I think something has happened to you, Celestina, something really bad, I don't know what, but it's some kind of trauma, and you're not making any *sense*...

CELESTINA: *(Offended.)* I have not lost my mind.

ANÍBAL: Please, just stay a little longer, okay? Eat dinner. Sleep on the sofabed. In the morning, we'll have a big breakfast and I'll give you some money. Drive you wherever you want, okay?

(Aníbal goes to the kitchen and comes back with another glass of water. He holds it out for Celestina. Still thirsty, Celestina comes back in and takes the glass of water.)

CELESTINA: Your beauty is overwhelming, Aníbal.

(Aníbal closes the door. The sirens stop. Keeping a watchful eye on Celestina as she drinks the water, Aníbal goes to the kitchen, opens the refrigerator, and takes out packets of tortillas, cheese, salsa, and guacamole. As Aníbal prepares dinner, he can't help but look at her in wonder.)

ANÍBAL: Who are you, Celestina?

(Celestina smiles at the inevitable question, then thinks a moment. She starts setting the table for dinner as Aníbal puts the tortillas and cheese on the hot griddle.)

CELESTINA: How do you know what "time" feels like, Aníbal? In your body? You feel it, don't you? Pushing at your heart muscles. Pricking the nerves in your brain, turning some on, turning some off. Is that what "time" feels like? And where *is* "time?" Is the organ for "time" the heart? Is it the spinal chord, that silver waterfall of nerves and memories: Is "time" in there? Is it the gonads? Does "time" have a sound? What bells, Aníbal, what vibrating string played by what virtuoso accompanies the passage of "time?" Is "time" blue? Does it taste like steak? Can you fuck it? Or is it just the invisible freight train that runs you over every single day... breaking you into smaller and smaller pieces...pieces so small they can't hold your soul to the earth anymore, and *that's* why you die? C'mon, Aníbal, help me out here!

ANÍBAL: We just know. Commonsense tells us.

CELESTINA: Well, then...what if there are people who don't have that sense? Don't have that inner clock telling them when a moment has passed, when another has started, how a day feels different from a year. What would you say to such people?

ANÍBAL: *Coño:* your imagination...

CELESTINA: And what if these people don't progress through space and "time" the same way you do? They don't age smoothly. They stay little far longer than they should. Then, all of a sudden, they change into an old person overnight? Or the rhythms of the day mean nothing. So they sleep for weeks at a "time." They stay awake all winter scaring the shit out of their parents! They can make love for two weeks straight without a break!

ANÍBAL: I don't know.

(Beat.)

CELESTINA: No. Of course not. How could you?

(Dinner is ready. The table is set. Celestina looks at the table appreciatively.)

CELESTINA: I should wash my hands.

ANÍBAL: *(Re: bathroom.)* That way.

(Celestina starts to go off. Then she looks at Aníbal. She goes to him, kisses him on the cheek, and embraces him. He holds her close.)

CELESTINA: Papi told me he was twenty-five when I was born. Before he died, we celebrated his seventy-seventh birthday. When the trucker picked me up outside Montauk Point, I was pregnant and starting to show. When we crossed the frontier into Los Angeles, before he touched my knees, he put two candles on a little cake and said we were celebrating two years together. *(Beat.)* So that's who I am: I'm a fifty-four year old woman, Aníbal, and I've been pregnant with this baby for two years.

(Celestina goes to the bathroom and closes the door. Aníbal is alone. Aníbal goes to the telephone in the living room. Picks it up. It's dead. Aníbal slams it.)

ANÍBAL: Shit.

(Aníbal goes to the TV and turns it on. All he can get, in channel after channel, is static. He turns on a radio. More static. Aníbal goes back to the kitchen and hides all the knives. There's a knock at the door. Aníbal looks at the door, worried. A second knock. Aníbal goes to the door and opens it. Sirens. Aníbal's younger brother, Sgt. Nelson de la Luna, is there. Nelson (25) is taller, broader than his older brother: He has a sweet baby face, short hair, and a little mustache. Nelson wears an army issue raincoat and army boots.)

ANÍBAL: Nelson?

NELSON: *(Big smile.)* Brother!

(Nelson laughs and scoops up Aníbal in a big bear hug. The brothers kiss and pound each others' backs.)

ANÍBAL: Son-of-a-bitch, Nelson, what the fuck are you doing here?!

NELSON: Surprise! Nice *house!*

(Nelson comes in, takes off his rain coat. Underneath he wears army issue T-shirt, khakis, dog tags, etc. Aníbal still can't believe his brother's there. He closes the door. Sirens stop.)

ANÍBAL: Look at you. Fucking amazing. Are you alone?

NELSON: No, I got half the company out in the Grand National, asshole. Man look at you. You old.

ANÍBAL: Fuck you too. What an asshole; you didn't even *call* me...

NELSON: Surprise, surprise, how much you pay for this dump?

ANÍBAL: What a dickhead! So what's up? I thought you were in Germany.

NELSON: Not any more, bro. They shipped my ass to Fort Benning, Georgia, six months ago. Then they sent my ass out here for two days.

ANÍBAL: Are you in training for something? Getting ready to invade some hapless third world country?

NELSON: "Hapless." What a homo. You got a beer? *(Nelson goes to the refrigerator and helps himself to a beer.)*

ANÍBAL: Have a beer.

NELSON: I'm fucking out in Death Valley now. It's a fucking *lake.* I thought you lived in sunny Southern California, jerk-off.

ANÍBAL: It rains out here too, asswipe. *Coño,* it's great to see you, Nelson.

(They embrace exuberantly again, pound backs.)

NELSON: So yeah, got my ass shipped to Death Valley, I'm good to go, bro, desert training for the Middle East or some towelhead shithole with oil underneath it...fucking tanks all over the place, blow up anything stupid enough to get in our way—mostly stray sheep and coyotes—'cause we're *men,* Aníbal, not pussies like you: men, *men!*

ANÍBAL: *(Laughs.)* Get outta my face with that shit.

NELSON: Yo, it beats jerkin' off all day like you, so this is your *house* finally, I gotta get me one of these, I guess loading luggage really pays, what: You helpin' smuggle drugs-'n-shit?

ANÍBAL: *(Laughs.)* How long are you staying?

NELSON: Man, I'm hosed. I gotta be back in Death Valley oh-five-hundred tomorrow morning for a fucking dipshit meeting with my C.O. that's only supposed to last five *minutes.* So I can only hang 'bout an hour, 'cause the roads suck tonight.

ANÍBAL: *(Disappointed.)* An hour? Nelson, I haven't seen you in six years.

NELSON: Time flies, motherfucker!

ANÍBAL: So why can't you call the guy—?

NELSON: No way. Gotta *be* there. They gotta *see* my ass in front of the C.O., in person. It's really fucking stupid.

ANÍBAL: The army's perfect for you.

NELSON: *(Re: Aníbal.)* What a waste of a human being. Man, you get uglier and stupider all the time.

ANÍBAL: You're just pissed my mother loved me and she didn't love you.
(Nelson starts looking for the bathroom.)

NELSON: Aw shit, where's the head, man? All I've eaten is beef jerky and I gotta take a massive dump.

ANÍBAL: You're a poet, Nelson, you know that? A poet of our time.

NELSON: Yo, eat me!

ANÍBAL: There's somebody in the bathroom. A woman.

NELSON: *(Surprised.)* You got a woman in your bathroom, Aníbal?

ANÍBAL: Her name is Celestina. I picked her up tonight.

NELSON: *(Big smile.)* Brother! You're *not* a total waste!
(Nelson high-fives Aníbal.)

ANÍBAL: No, she's pregnant, Nelson, and she's…I think…mentally disturbed or something…or she's living in a dream world, I don't know.

NELSON: Women.

ANÍBAL: She looks like she's twenty-five years old but she *says* she's fifty-four.

NELSON: That's fucking L.A., bro.

ANÍBAL: And she says she's been pregnant for two years.

NELSON: And you picked her up? *You're* not an asshole!

ANÍBAL: She was hitching. In this storm. I can't drive by somebody like that.

NELSON: A total fairy. What a liberal. Is she cute?

ANÍBAL: She's gorgeous.

NELSON: Oh well, that's cool. I could fuck an insane pregnant girl if she's gorgeous.

ANÍBAL: Don't be a pig, Nelson—.

NELSON: What? I'll have that bitch howlin' at the moon!

ANÍBAL: She's not—.

NELSON: Hey, I've been in a *tank* nine *weeks,* bro, I'm ready to seduce *goats.* Swear: My mother must've been exposed to radiation when you were born.

ANÍBAL: *(Laughs.)* Fuck you through the head.

NELSON: *You're* the fucking poet of our time! Asshole! Liberal! I'mma fuckin' bodyslam you!

(Nelson lunges at Aníbal. Aníbal fights him off. They wrestle around the living room, knocking furniture around, laughing. Nelson catches Aníbal. Nelson lifts Aníbal over his head and prepares to bodyslam him.)

ANÍBAL: Nelson—*dooooooon't!!*

(Celestina comes in. She's got a gun. She aims it at Nelson's head. Both men freeze.)

NELSON: Oh shit.

ANÍBAL: Celestina…?

NELSON: *(Already admiring her.)* Training and instinct tell me that's a gun.

CELESTINA: Put him down.

(Nelson quickly puts Aníbal down. Celestina continues pointing the gun at Nelson.)

ANÍBAL: Celestina. Could you please put that away—it's fine…

CELESTINA: Who is he?

ANÍBAL: —this is my brother—Nelson—this is Nelson, it's okay…

(Celestina reluctantly puts the gun in a pocket. Both men are greatly relieved. Nelson laughs nervously.)

NELSON: Whoa. Fuckme. I love L.A.!

ANÍBAL: *(To Celestina.)* I didn't know you were armed, Celestina. *Christ.*

CELESTINA: I stole it from the trucker while he was sleeping.

NELSON: Whoa.

ANÍBAL: *(Still shaken.)* Jesus.

CELESTINA: I'm sorry, Aníbal, I…

ANÍBAL: It's cool. It's just—*coño.* Heart attack.

CELESTINA: I wanted to protect you.

NELSON: *(To Aníbal.)* She wanted to protect you, asshole!

ANÍBAL: *(To Nelson.)* I'm not crazy about guns.

NELSON: *(To Celestina.)* I am. *(Sotto to Aníbal.)* She's gorgeous, man. Introduce.

ANÍBAL: *(Wary.)* Fuck. Nelson, this is Celestina. Celestina, this is my little brother, Nelson.

(Celestina goes to shake Nelson's hand.)

CELESTINA: *(To Nelson.)* Nice to meet you.

NELSON: *(Big charming smile.)* So Celestina, what's *up?!*

ANÍBAL: *(Sotto to Nelson.)* Nelson...slow...

NELSON: *(Sotto to Aníbal.)* Step back or I'll bodyslam you...

ANÍBAL: *(Sotto to Nelson; re: Celestina.)* ...disturbed...?

NELSON: *(To Celestina.)* ...I'm married, okay? But. I'm separated from my wife. Bitch left me. Got drunk one night, said: "You know, Nelson, deep inside o' my heart, I just don't like you fucking little greasy Puerto Ricans!" I said, "Fuck you, ho'" and threw a hand grenade at her.

CELESTINA: *(Amused.)* You threw a hand grenade...?

ANÍBAL: *(Horrified.)* You threw a hand grenade...?

NELSON: *(Defensive.)* It didn't go off! We filed for divorce. That little baby got a father?

CELESTINA: I'm looking for him. His name is Rodrigo Cruz.

NELSON: You married to him?

CELESTINA: No but I'm going to make him!

NELSON: You love this man?

CELESTINA: I don't know.

NELSON: Well, if you don't find him, let me know. I love children. I understand children. You have beautiful eyes, Celestina.

CELESTINA: Thank you.

ANÍBAL: I may vomit.

NELSON: I can't stay too long, Celestina. I'm serving our country in the armed forces of the U.S. Protecting us from...uhm...not communists...uhm...illegal aliens, drug king pins, and Arabs. It's dangerous work. My life is on the line each and every day. But I'm good to go! And the thing is, I gotta be back in Death Valley tonight— *Death* Valley, so appropriate, huh?—I have very important meetings with high ranking officers—then I go to Fort Benning, Georgia, Monday to finalize my divorce from my cracker wife. And then, in about two years, I'll be getting my discharge from the army. What I'm saying is...I won't be back this way for awhile. But I'm gonna come back in two years and look you up, okay? And if you ain't found that baby's father, I just might ask you to marry me, 'cause no woman should raise her baby alone. You understand? This cool with you, Celestina? Can I ask you?

CELESTINA: *(Not knowing what to say.)* Uhm. You can ask me.

NELSON: Yes! Good! Well, my work is done here. Bye. *(Nelson goes to his raincoat and starts putting it on.)*

ANÍBAL: What do you mean? What are you doing?

NELSON: I gotta get back to Death Valley. Duty calls.

ANÍBAL: Right *now?*

NELSON: *(Looking at his watch.)* No! My watch died! Fuckit. Yes. I gotta go. I'll take my dump on the road. I'm fucked I'm not there.

ANÍBAL: This is happening too fast—

NELSON: What's life? A fucking *blink*. Get used to it. And thanks for introducing me to the woman of my dreams, homeboy.

(Celestina smiles. Then she gets another pain in her belly.)

CELESTINA: Ohhhhhhhh.

(Nelson and Aníbal quickly go to Celestina.)

ANÍBAL AND NELSON: You okay?

CELESTINA: *(Still in pain.)* It's okay. Thank you. *(Another jolt.)* Why is my baby doing this? Why is he tapping my spine with his fingers? What code is that? What words?

(Nelson looks at her pregnant stomach.)

NELSON: May I?

(Celestina nods yes and Nelson kneels at her feet and rubs her belly. The pain slowly subsides. Celestina smiles with relief.)

CELESTINA: Thank you, Nelson.

(Nelson puts his head on her stomach, listening to the sounds inside.)

NELSON: Check it out. I can hear the ocean! Stars being scraped across the sky!

CELESTINA: *(Delighted.)* You can?

NELSON: I hear a little body searching for the way out. Little bones. *(To her stomach.)* Yo in there. I'mma wait for you, little man. Be the father of your dreams. You come outta this deep night you're in, *hijo de mi alma,* see my big-ass smile, you're gonna know what sunshine is! That cool? And you tell your beautiful mami to wait for me, okay *mijo?*

(Nelson kisses Celestina's stomach. Moved, Celestina gently kisses the top of Nelson's head. Nelson gets up. Nelson and Aníbal have a long embrace.)

ANÍBAL: Six years, Nelson. Six fucking years.

NELSON: This is the happiest night of my life!

(Nelson opens the door. Sirens. He disappears into the rain. Aníbal goes to the door.)

ANÍBAL: You'll never get to Death Valley in that rain…

NELSON: *(Off.)* A *man* would!

(Aníbal watches Nelson driving away, his back to the audience. Aníbal sadly waves good-bye. Celestina looks at Aníbal. Aníbal closes the door. Sirens stop. Celestina is watching Aníbal who is quiet a long moment, his mind far away.)

CELESTINA: You okay?

(Beat. He tries to smile. He starts clearing up the kitchen table.)

ANÍBAL: Are you really going to wait for him? Two years?

CELESTINA: I don't know what "two years" means, Aníbal.

(Aníbal rubs his tired eyes—then looks at his watch—then realizes it's not working.)

ANÍBAL: I don't even know what time it is. It could be next week. I don't remember this morning. I don't remember kissing Debbie good-bye or working or eating or driving from LAX or finding a hitch-hiker in the storm of the century. And was my fucking little *brother* really here? I can't believe he's a *man* already! Ten minutes ago, *I* was bodyslamming *him!*

CELESTINA: Why don't we eat?

ANÍBAL: *(Trying to focus.)* Eat. Yeah. Eat.

(Aníbal and Celestina sit at the kitchen table. Celestina can hardly wait and immediately stuffs her mouth with food, eating with the passion of a starving person.)

CELESTINA: This is the best food!

ANÍBAL: *(Concerned.)* Easy…Celestina…easy…

(Aníbal and Celestina continue their dinner. This should take it's natural time—despite the speed with which Celestina attacks her food—and should happen in silence. All the while Aníbal and Celestina may make periodic eye contact—smile—look away—sometimes Aníbal finds himself staring—sometimes Celestina does. Suddenly the house is rocked by several claps of harsh thunder. The lightning outside lights up the house through the windows brighter than could possibly occur in nature. Celestina looks at Aníbal.)

CELESTINA: *Me pregunto…me pregunto como será haberte amado en cada etapa de tu vida, Aníbal.*

(Beat. He looks at her and she continues in Spanish.)

CELESTINA: *Amar al niñito que fuiste, y tomarte de la mano, y ayudarte a cruzar la calle, y besar tu barriquita gordita de bebé, y peinar tus greñitas de chiquillo. Y luego, mas adelante, amar al anciano en que te*

convertiste, y besar tus arrugas profundas, y suavizar tu pelo canoso, y deleitar tu sabio y cansado corazón, y mirar fijamente hacia adentro de esos ojos misteriosos, mas allá de las cataratas, y muy adentro de tí, hacia los verdes prados donde uno nunca envejece. No te parecería lindo tener ese tipo de amor, Aníbal? El amor de toda una vida?
(Beat. Aníbal smiles nervously.)

ANÍBAL: What?

CELESTINA: What?

ANÍBAL: I didn't know you could speak Spanish.

CELESTINA: *(Smiles) Solamente hablo Espanol cuando estoy enamorada.*

ANÍBAL: What?

(Beat.)

CELESTINA: Don't you speak *any* Spanish?

ANÍBAL: *(Sad.)* I don't.

CELESTINA: You don't?

ANÍBAL: I don't.

CELESTINA: Why not?

ANÍBAL: Sometimes...I don't know...you forget things...

CELESTINA: But how do you forget a *language?*

ANÍBAL: It happened, Celestina. It's not nice and I'm not proud of it, but it happened.

CELESTINA: I'm sorry.

ANÍBAL: All I know is *"coño!"*

CELESTINA: *(Laughs.)* Well, *"coño's"* useful.

(Celestina laughs sadly. Aníbal laughs with her. He looks at her. She reaches out a hand. He takes it and holds it a moment.)

ANÍBAL: *(Pulling away.)* I'll get the sofabed ready for you.

CELESTINA: *(Beat.)* Okay. I'll help you set up.

(During the following, Aníbal goes to the sofabed, pulls it out. He goes to the closet and comes back with pillows, blankets, and sheets. Together he and Celestina make the sofabed. If necessary for timing, Aníbal could go through whatever bedtime ritual he needs: turning off lights, locking the door, turning on the security system, taking out the trash, etc.

Toward the end of the speech, while Aníbal is deeper in his memories, he stops looking at Celestina. Behind Aníbal, facing upstage, Celestina takes off her maternity dress and slips into a nightgown she keeps in her shopping bag. She lets her long hair down. She looks more unearthly, more angelic than ever.)

ANÍBAL: I made love with Debbie just last night. Or was it this morning? *(Beat.)*

I had to talk her into spending the night, instead of sleeping in her office again. It seems like a million years ago. *(Beat.)*

I know Debbie from high school in the Bronx. We went out. Then she went out of state for college and I couldn't afford college so I stayed behind and worked. She married her English professor and moved to Ohio. I wanted to kill myself. I spent the next five years getting into these other relationships. The first one, I was twenty-two. The woman I fell in love with was thirty-nine. We had a great time together. But I took her home to meet my parents and my father made a pass at her and it was over. Then I fell in love with a blonde. She was a real beauty. But she came from this fucked up home and she had a drug problem and she drank too much and the night I told her I didn't love her anymore she tried to throw herself out of a moving car on the Belt Parkway. Then I fell in love with a series of lesbians. Every woman I liked turned out to be gay! Then one night, New Year's Eve, I'm living in the Lower East Side, the phone rings, it's Debbie. She left her husband. She left Ohio. She was staying at her sister's in Harlem. Would I like to get together. I said sure. *(Beat.)*

I went to her place. I didn't know what to expect. She was staying in one of those worn out tenements with the steam heat up too high and the steel radiators that clamored all night, and Willie Colon and laughing and partying and loud kissing coming at you from all the apartments all over us. People just exploding! Going nuts! I remember the smell of *tostones* and beans and garlic and oregano and *lechon asado*. You know: everything cooked with a lot of *manteca!* *(Beat.)*

And I held Debbie all night long. We didn't fuck. I kissed her a lot. We touched all over. But we didn't go to bed. We were starting over. I was figuring out this new body. She seemed richer. All the years we hadn't seen each other, miles she's traveled, all this married wisdom and experience she had that I didn't have. I felt like a *boy*, a child, in the arms of this mature *woman*. We decided that night to go to Los Angeles together and start over. Be in that one city where you can really re-make yourself. Pan for gold in the L.A. River. She wanted to get rich on the movies. I wanted to get away from the racists who thought of me only as a spik. *(Beat.)*

As we were holding each other, touching each other, I started to remember something I thought I had forgotten. It was when I was a little boy. I don't even remember how old. We were living in Newark, New Jersey. We were visiting my cousins who lived in a big house in Patchogue, Long Island. My child's memory makes that house enormous, like a Victorian haunted house, but maybe it wasn't. They had thirteen kids. We used to watch *lucha libre* together, professional wrestling, all the time. One time my cousin Ernesto got carried away watching Bruno Samartino on TV and he punched me in the stomach. Ernie liked to inflict pain. He had long, black curly hair and a thin black mustache, freckles, large, red lips, crooked teeth: He was the cousin that looked most like me. Another night, after a party, my cousin Cheo told me how he could feel his balls flapping around in his pants when he danced to American music. His balls went flap-flap-flap when he danced to rock-'n'-roll. I liked Cheo. He never punched me like Ernesto did. Cheo taught me about exponents and square roots. He went to Vietnam. Everybody thought Ernesto would get into drug dealing. *(Beat.)*

One night I was on the second floor of my cousins' house. I remember walking past a dark bedroom: the door was open. I thought I heard a voice inside calling my name. I went in. My cousin Eva was there. She was older than Ernie or Cheo. Much older than me. I remember her standing by the window. I could see her face lit up by a streetlight—or was it the moon? I remember there was a heavy smell in the room. And I don't know how I eventually got there…but I ended up lying in bed with Eva. I was on my back, looking at the ceiling. Eva was kneeling next to me. Then Eva lifted her dress and she was straddling me and pressing her pelvis into me. I think she had her underwear on. I had my pants on and I didn't know why she was doing this to me, though I knew I had to do this because she was my older cousin, therefore she had authority. I remember her legs being smooth. I remember her face. She was looking out the window. I don't remember how long this lasted. I don't remember if anyone came in. I don't remember if anyone ever knew about this, though, later on it seemed that everybody knew. I liked Eva on top of me. I remember her weight. I liked her weight. I don't remember if I got hard or not: I was only a little boy! I liked watching Eva's face, the way she looked out the window. How the light struck half her face. I wish I could remember her mouth! I think it was open. But I don't remember. Was there a smile? Did she bite her lower lip? Was she talking to me? Did she say something in Spanish? I remember her eyes. *(Beat.)*

So I fell in love with Eva. She was all I thought about. And I think my mother suspected something and she was worried about us, though first cousins had married several times in my family. One night my mother and I were washing dishes together, side-by-side. And we had the only conversation about sex we were ever to have. Without looking at me, she said: "Aníbal, remember: There is some fruit you are not allowed to eat." And that's all she said. And I knew *exactly* what she meant. And it was all she had to say to me. *(Beat.)*

I've never forgotten Eva. Even in Debbie's arms after five years of missing her and wanting her, I thought easily of Eva. It's like... the space around my body was permanently curved—or dented—by Eva's heaviness. I wonder if love sometimes does that to you. It alters the physics around you in some way: changing the speed of light and the shape of space and how you experience time.

CELESTINA: What do you think made you fall in love with those women?

ANÍBAL: Do you think I know?

(Aníbal turns around to look at Celestina who has changed into her nightgown. She smiles at him. Beat.)

CELESTINA: Would you rub my feet?

ANÍBAL: What?

CELESTINA: Would rub my feet?

(Beat.)

ANÍBAL: Uhm, sure.

(Beat.
Celestina sits on the sofabed and puts her bare feet up expectantly. Aníbal sits with her, her feet on his lap. He gently rubs her feet. She closes her eyes in bliss.)

CELESTINA: Hmmmmmm...yeah...

(Celestina seems to fall asleep, a look of peace and serenity on her face. Aníbal looks at her a moment and can't help but smile.)

ANÍBAL: *Buenas noches.*

(Aníbal starts to get up. Celestina opens her eyes.)

CELESTINA: Kiss my toes.

ANÍBAL: …What?

CELESTINA: Just once?

ANÍBAL: Kiss your—what—?

CELESTINA: Please? Just once?

>   *(Beat.)*

ANÍBAL: Okay.

>   *(Aníbal kisses her toes one by one. She smiles with each little kiss, try-*
>   *ing not to giggle, eyes still closed. Aníbal finishes and starts to leave.)*

CELESTINA: No you don't.

ANÍBAL: Now what?

CELESTINA: Higher.

ANÍBAL: …Higher?

CELESTINA: Up the body.

ANÍBAL: Okay.

>   *(Aníbal kisses her knees. Celestina sighs deeply, stretching out.)*

CELESTINA: Little higher.

>   *(Aníbal kisses her thighs. Celestina whispers.)*

CELESTINA: Up.

>   *(Aníbal kisses her enormous stomach.)*

CELESTINA: More up.

>   *(Aníbal kisses her breasts.)*

CELESTINA: Keep going.

>   *(Aníbal kisses her neck.)*

CELESTINA: …Home, traveler. You're home!

>   *(Aníbal kisses Celestina lightly once on the lips. They hold each other a*
>   *long moment. We hear the sound of the rain beating against the house.*
>   *They don't look at each other as they talk.)*

ANÍBAL: I'm afraid.

CELESTINA: Don't be.

ANÍBAL: Not about bodies. I'm afraid we're going to be mixing my sad
dreams with your wild ones.

CELESTINA: *(Smiles.)* Maybe they'll have beautiful children, Aníbal.

>   *(Aníbal kisses her gently on the lips She opens her mouth to him and*
>   *takes him in, kissing him back with all the passion in her body.)*

ANÍBAL: Celestina.

>   *(Celestina speaks to Aníbal as she holds him.)*

CELESTINA: Sometimes, Aníbal, sometimes there's no "time"—only an
endless now that needs to be filled with life. To be rescued from
habit and death. *(Beat.)* C'mon.

ANÍBAL: Okay.

(Aníbal takes Celestina's hand and leads her to the ladders which go up to the floating bed. As they climb the ladders, the rest of the house seems to disappear and be replaced by vague twinkling stars and crescent moons and dark, silvery clouds. As they reach the bed, there's another knock at the door. The house instantly changes back to its normal state, like a spell broken. Aníbal looks at the door.)

CELESTINA: *(Sotto.)* Who's that?

ANÍBAL: *(Sotto.)* Stay.

(Aníbal climbs down the ladder. Celestina stays up on the bed, partially hidden from view by the downstage footboard. Aníbal opens the door. Sirens. Aníbal is surprised by the sight of hundreds of Sparkletts water bottles covering the porch. Nelson is there. Nelson looks different. His hair is slightly longer. His mustache is gone. His army clothes have been replaced by blue jeans, sneakers, and an old jeans jacket. He walks with a cane. But that's not the only thing that's changed. Something childlike and happy has been taken away from Nelson. Though he mouths some of the same old lines, they lack his spirit.)

ANÍBAL: Nelson?

NELSON: *(Tired smile.)* Brother!

(Nelson scoops up Aníbal in a bear hug and pounds his back.)

ANÍBAL: *(Confused.)* What are you doing here?

(Nelson holds Aníbal for a long time. Aníbal has to pull away. Nelson won't let him.)

NELSON: Look at you! You get older and uglier all the time!

ANÍBAL: Everything okay?

NELSON: Fucking just wanna hold you, man.

(Aníbal, worried, pulls away from Nelson.)

ANÍBAL: What happened? Couldn't you get back to Death Valley? Are the freeways closed?

NELSON: Death *Valley?* What are you talking about? Everything's great. Hey, I'm a free man! I can do whatever I want now!

ANÍBAL: *(Noticing.)* Hey, what happened to you? Why's your face like that?

(Nelson comes into the living room, closing the door behind him. Sirens stop. Nelson looks around.)

NELSON: Fuckme, the old place hasn't changed at all. Everything's just the way I remember it!

ANÍBAL: Wait. Wait a minute. What happened to you? You look totally—why are your clothes like that?

NELSON: Jesus, will you get over my appearance? What are you, gay? I'm lucky to be *alive,* motherfucker. I need a beer. *(Nelson goes to the refrigerator to get a beer.)*

ANÍBAL: *(Still confused.)* Have a beer.

NELSON: I was pissed at you, bro. I don't mind telling you. All my letters to you came back, your phone's been disconnected, I thought, "that asshole moved without telling me! He makes me drive cross-country—three fucking days—and he's not there, I'mma kill him!" *(Beat.)*

ANÍBAL: You've been driving three days?

NELSON: Hello? From *Georgia?* Have you gone *stupid?* You have no *memory?* What did I tell you two years ago? Soon's I get to Benning, get my discharge and my divorce from Mein Kampf, I was comin' back here, find that girl, and ask her to marry me. *(A short beat as Aníbal looks at Nelson.)*

ANÍBAL: Two years? Nelson are you drunk? That was only a few minutes ago you left here and said that.

NELSON: *(Laughs.)* You gotta get outta L.A., bro. Your *brain!*

ANÍBAL: A half hour—.

NELSON: Maybe to *you!* Mr. Lalaland! You still got on the same boring clothes you had that night! And wasn't it raining then?

ANÍBAL: *(Nervous, worried.)* Cut the shit, Nelson...

NELSON: *You* cut the shit or I'll bodyslam you! Where's Celestina? You hiding her? Did she have her baby? Does the baby know who I am? Does he ask about me? I bet he loves me!

ANÍBAL: *(Trying to focus.)* She...she uh...

NELSON: And you! You fuck! Why did all my letters come back? You think it was fun being out in fucking Bosnia and not hearing from you all that fucking time!? Fuck you!

ANÍBAL: Bosnia?

NELSON: Yo, the *war?* The Battle of Mostar? Are you stoned or what? Don't they get the news in L.A.? *(Nelson reaches into his raincoat and pulls up a handful of medals. He throws them across the room, one-by-one.)* R-com with two oak leaf clusters! Army Achievement Medal! Bronze Star with three oak leaf clusters! Silver star with two oak leaf clusters! Bosnia Liberation Medal! *(Nelson laughs and digs into another pocket and pulls out a dozen letters he wrote to Aníbal, all of which were returned to him. Aníbal looks with amazement at their postmarks.)*

ANÍBAL: These letters are from Bosnia, Nelson.

NELSON: Beautiful land. I met a pregnant girl, too. Man, I really wanted to marry her—broke my heart to leave her—but "No," I said, "I have the most beautiful girl named Celestina waiting for me in the States!"

(Aníbal, shaking, puts the letters down.)

ANÍBAL: How can one night be two years...Celestina?

(Celestina sits up in the bed and climbs down the ladder to the living room during the following:)

NELSON: They had to fucking put me in a fucking army hospital Æcause I have a fucking nervous *breakdown?* I thought: I gotta live through this so I can see my bride and my child again! And I said this to myself, over and over like a prayer, and *that's the only thing* that kept some fucking Serbian sniper bullet from finding the back of my head or some land mine from erasing my legs. The unbearable luck of her *name!*

(By the last line of Nelson's speech, Celestina is in the living room, face-to-face with Nelson who can't believe his eyes.)

CELESTINA: Hi Nelson.

(A long pause as Nelson just takes her in with his eyes and smiles.)

NELSON: That's really you.

CELESTINA: It's really me.

(Nelson starts to cry. Celestina goes to him.)

CELESTINA: Hey, hey, what is it?

NELSON: Nothing. It's nothing. No problem.

(Celestina wipes Nelson's eyes.)

CELESTINA: I heard what happened to you in the war. I'm really sorry.

NELSON: It's over. I lived. I'm gonna forget it as soon as I can.

CELESTINA: *(Touching her stomach.)* I have a lot to tell you...as you can see...

NELSON: Oh yeah! Uh-huh! I can see a lot has happened in your life, Celestina!

ANÍBAL: *(To Celestina.)* Do you know what's going on here?

CELESTINA: *(Torn.)* Don't be afraid, Aníbal, please...

NELSON: *(Not listening.)* But what's weird? I'm looking at you. It's like you never aged a day!

CELESTINA: That's because I haven't!

NELSON: And you're pregnant again. Just like that night!

CELESTINA: It's not—Nelson—that's what I have to tell you—and you know I'd only tell you the truth. This baby. Is not a different baby. You left Los Angeles. You went to war…

ANÍBAL: *(To Celestina.)* Is this something you did?

CELESTINA: …but here, in this house, time didn't pass; it's still the same night; you only left a little while ago. And this baby is the same baby…it's Rodrigo's baby…do you understand that…?

NELSON: *(Laughs.)* Fuck you!

CELESTINA: It's the truth!

NELSON: I can't believe you would lie to me!

CELESTINA: And Aníbal—two years have passed—whether you want to believe it or not!

ANÍBAL: How is that possible?

CELESTINA: It's me, Aníbal. I've infected you! I've changed the "time" around you—.

ANÍBAL: But—who's been paying the light bill?! Who's been paying the rent?! Where's Debbie been?! What happened to my job?!

NELSON: *(Overlapping with Aníbal.)* Look, I *know* that's Aníbal's baby! Okay?! I can see what happened!

CELESTINA: Nothing happened!

NELSON: You two fell in love! It's cool! And I guess we didn't make any promises to each other, huh Celestina?

CELESTINA: I'm sorry, Nelson…

NELSON: So I just want to see that little baby before I go! Where is he? Where's that little boy I talked to? Did something happen to him?!

CELESTINA: He hasn't been born—!

NELSON: *(Angry.)* Man, I don't need to hear this double-talk *bullshit* any more! Fuck you both! I don't give a fuck if you two fell in love with each other! I was stupid to think you would wait for me! But you didn't! *You didn't wait for me, did you!?*

(Nelson makes a move toward Celestina. Aníbal tries to protect her. Nelson grabs Aníbal, lifts him up, and bodyslams him to the floor. Celestina goes to Aníbal and holds him. Aníbal writhes in pain, speechless. Nelson is breathing hard, instantly sorry he hurt his brother, but still frozen by anger. Silence. Nelson quietly cries.)

ANÍBAL: *(In pain.)* Oh my God.

NELSON: I'm sorry, bro. I'm not myself. Something in myself got taken out sometime as I was looking through the sights of the tank, lining up targets, watching things blow up. Jesus shit! I got so much I gotta forget!

ANÍBAL: Jesus Christ, bro...

(Nelson goes to Aníbal, lifts him, and puts him gently on the sofabed. He holds Aníbal.)

NELSON: I'm sorry, bro, you know I fucking love you, man! I'm a total asshole! I shouldn't have come here! You got something good with your woman, man, that's cool, that's great! I gotta step aside and let your happiness be, man! Fuck me! I'm sorry! You're my fucking brother and I'm sorry!

ANÍBAL: Nelson...

(Nelson wipes his eyes and goes to the door. He opens it. Sirens. Nelson runs out into the night.)

ANÍBAL: Nelson? Nelson!

(Aníbal gets up to follow Nelson.)

CELESTINA: Aníbal—don't leave me alone!

(Aníbal goes to the door.)

ANÍBAL: I gotta talk to him!

CELESTINA: I can't be alone!

(Aníbal runs out into the night to chase down Nelson, closing the door behind him. Celestina is alone. She goes to the door and waits for Aníbal. She closes the door. She opens it again. She closes it again. She sits. In moments she has no idea how much time has passed since Aníbal left. For all she knows it could be days, weeks later. She's getting more and more nervous. Nervousness gives way to panic. She shakes. She looks around. Unable to bear the pain of waiting any longer, Celestina gets quickly dressed. She puts on her shoes and Aníbal's suede jacket. She goes to the door. Celestina runs out into the night, leaving the door open. The digital clocks stop blinking and a new time comes on: 8:06. Aníbal comes in. He's got his arm around Nelson, who is soaking wet and looks disheveled. Aníbal helps Nelson sit. Nelson sits with his face in his hands. Aníbal closes the door behind him. Sirens stop. Aníbal looks very shaken.)

ANÍBAL: *(To Nelson.)* ...it's okay...it's okay, bro...you're home...

NELSON: Thanks, man.

ANÍBAL: Celestina! I found him! Bet you thought we'd never get back! Took all night but I got him!

(No answer. Aníbal goes to the offstage bathroom.)

ANÍBAL: Celestina?

(No response. Aníbal goes back to the living room.)

ANÍBAL: Celestina!

NELSON: Celestina!

ANÍBAL: Goddammit.

NELSON: Where is she?

ANÍBAL: Her shoes are gone...the jacket...all the clocks are going...she's taken off...*shit!*...stay here... *(Aníbal grabs a coat, and runs out into the rain. From offstage:)* Celestina!
(The door closes with a slam! Nelson is left alone on stage. Lights start to go down on him.)

NELSON: Celestina.
(Lights to black. The sound of the rain stops. Nelson calls out in the dark, silent house.)

NELSON: Celestina!
(Black out.)

END OF SCENE ONE

Epilogue

In the dark, the bolero *from the Prologue starts again, though quieter, distorted if possible. Lights come up downstage. During Celestina's speech, the crew comes on and disassembles the house. By the end of Celestina's speech, there should be nothing left of Aníbal's house in Echo Park. The ladders next to the bed are removed and the bed is lowered to the stage. The glass wall is removed from the house and left freestanding, to the side. Water drips down the side of the glass wall, as in the Prologue. A microphone on a C-stand is placed downcenter. It's forty years later. Celestina enters and goes to the microphone. She's no longer pregnant. Her clothes are nicer than before. But otherwise she looks the same. She could be wearing a slightly futuristic costume. She's pushing a stroller. She wears Aníbal's suede jacket. She's talking to the baby. She's in mid-conversation.)*

CELESTINA: Can you believe this rain for L.A.? *Coño! (Beat.)* The last time I was here it was raining just like this, right before you were born, and Los Angeles has changed so much, *mijo.* I can't get over it. The Big One was finally born—a monster with seven epicenters—releasing unimaginable waves of energy and killing many unprepared people—the six active oil fields on Pico exploded—glass came down from the towers in Downtown and Century City and Burbank like floating guillotines—there were fourteen million refugees—and Los Angeles died for a while. People went back to New York and the Midwest. There was a long sleep. *(Beat.)*

But people came back. They came back for the things they loved about L.A. the first time. They rebuilt the city. And the city was reborn—and now it's better than ever! Look, *mijo*, you see? That building over there? That's the White House. They moved it from Washington, D.C. and put it on Wilshire Blvd. And there's the United Nations building and the World Trade Center. All of it is here in the new L.A. The new capitol of the United States. The capitol of world culture and trade. The capitol of the Third World. Boy, they really fixed this place up, Aníbal! The largest subway system in the world is here, connecting everything from Catalina Island to the Angeles National Forest. The air is clean! It's chic to read! All the street signs are in Spanish! They integrated all the neighborhoods! There are no more poor sections! No more big earthquakes for another one hundred and fifty years! In L.A., that's forever!

(The house has been completely dismantled and removed from the stage. It looks like the opening of the play. The bolero *ends or fades out. In the dark, Aníbal enters and lies on the bed. Celestina pushes the stroller to the bed. Lights on the bed go up. We can see clearly that Aníbal is an old man in his 70s. Aníbal lies in bed, reading a book. The light around the bed goes very dark, leaving the bed in limbo. The vague twinkling stars, crescent moons, and dark, silvery clouds of the earlier scene return: It should seem as if once again the bed were floating in space. Celestina goes to Aníbal's side and she looks at him a long moment.)*

CELESTINA: *(Big smile.)* Is that really you, Aníbal?

ANÍBAL: *(Looking up from his book.)* Huh?

(Aníbal looks at Celestina a long moment. He doesn't remember her.)

CELESTINA: It's me, Aníbal! I'm back! I just got into L.A.! I didn't think I'd remember how to get to Echo Park—but that bus stop at Virgil and Santa Monica is still there—and your house is exactly the same—the earthquake didn't hurt it—I can't believe my luck!

ANÍBAL: Are you the new nurse?

CELESTINA: It's me.

ANÍBAL: You're not the new nurse? Who's going to give me a bath?

CELESTINA: I'm Celestina.

ANÍBAL: Who is Celestina?

CELESTINA: Aníbal, stop.

ANÍBAL: Who are you?

(Beat.)

CELESTINA: Celestina del Sol.

(Celestina waits for the name to click in Aníbal's memory. It doesn't. Aníbal holds out his hand.)

ANÍBAL: I'm Aníbal de la Luna. Nice to meet you.

(Disappointed, Celestina shakes hands with Aníbal.)

CELESTINA: Nice to meet you.

ANÍBAL: Are you here for the house? It's a craftsman. Built in the last century. In the forties.

CELESTINA: Don't you remember me?

ANÍBAL: Well, I'm sorry. I'm afraid I don't.

CELESTINA: C'mon, Aníbal, think, you have to remember me.

ANÍBAL: When did we meet?

CELESTINA: I think it was forty years ago, but I can't be sure.

ANÍBAL: Forty years! *Coño!* Memory doesn't go back that far!

CELESTINA: It's just like yesterday for me! You picked me up by the side of the road. I was pregnant. You took me to this house. We had *quesadillas!* You rubbed my feet!

ANÍBAL: I did?

CELESTINA: I remember every moment of that night! I never stopped thinking about you! And I meant to come back sooner, but I just lost track of the "time!"

ANÍBAL: It couldn't have been forty years ago. Eyesight isn't so hot—these fucking cataracts, you know?—but—you're a kid. What're you, twenty-five? Twenty-six?

(Slight beat.)

CELESTINA: I'm not really sure.

(This response seems to jog something in Aníbal's memory, but he isn't sure what.)

ANÍBAL: Well, if you're here for the house, make yourself at home, look around—it's a craftsman!

CELESTINA: I know it's a fucking craftsman, Aníbal!

ANÍBAL: *(Laughs; re: baby.)* And who's that little guy?

CELESTINA: My son. I think I was in labor with him for six months!

ANÍBAL: Why do I feel like I've had this conversation before?

CELESTINA: His name is Aníbal. Aníbal del Sol y la Luna. His father's dead. Rodrigo's body was pulled out of the L.A. River in the storm of the century.

ANÍBAL: *Coño!*

CELESTINA: It was the night that we met, Aníbal. Your brother was in the army. You had a girlfriend named Debbie.

ANÍBAL: Debbie? You're a week too late. We buried her last week in Anaheim. Disney did a fucking hell of a job burying my wife, let me tell you. Those people know how to throw a funeral! They are true merchants of death!

CELESTINA: So you married her, huh?

ANÍBAL: Had to. Knocked her up.

CELESTINA: And Nelson?

ANÍBAL: He's a war hero, you know. Lives up the street. Married a beautiful girl many years ago...a Bosnian.

CELESTINA: *(Smiles.)* Good.

(Aníbal stares at Celestina a long moment.)

ANÍBAL: You look...*coño*...you look so familiar. You look vaguely like...there was a young woman...on a night that seemed to last forever...she was...crazy...and very fat...

CELESTINA: I was pregnant!

ANÍBAL: ...but it was some forty years ago...before the Big One... before they moved the capitol...something happened to me back then...I woke up and it was two years later! I had dreams in my coma that made no sense! *(Laughs.)*

But you know what? It was so long ago and so much has happened since then, so much life, so much dying, so many changes, it just gets buried under all the time between now and then, you know? It's like, somewhere in my mind is a ditch, a very dark and deep hole, and time keeps filling this hole with all the debris of my fucking life, the *details*—every name, face, taste, sound—gone! Down the hole! Outta reach! *Coño!* What's the point of that, huh? Does that make any sense to you?

CELESTINA: No.

ANÍBAL: No. You're very beautiful, though. Kind. It would be nice to remember you. To have been in love with you.

CELESTINA: We were in love, Aníbal.

ANÍBAL: How do you know we were in love?

CELESTINA: We lived together for two years, didn't we?

ANÍBAL: We did?

CELESTINA: They were the happiest two years of my life.

ANÍBAL: You sure it was me?

(Beat. Celestina wipes her tears, then reaches out, touches his hands, and kisses it.)

CELESTINA: I should probably let you get some sleep. It's been great seeing you again, Aníbal.

ANÍBAL: Yes.

CELESTINA: You take care of yourself, okay?

ANÍBAL: Thanks for dropping by. Listen, this house is a steal at this price! Great place to raise a family!

CELESTINA: I'll keep that in mind.

ANÍBAL: Yes. Good.

CELESTINA: Is there anything I can do for you before I go?

(Beat.)

ANÍBAL: Yes there is.

CELESTINA: What?

ANÍBAL: Would you rub my feet? They're freezing.

(Beat.)

CELESTINA: *(Smiles.)* Okay.

(Celestina gets into bed with Aníbal. He puts his feet up on her lap. She rubs his feet gently. The feeling of her hands on his feet has an instant and electrifying effect on Aníbal. When he talks, he sounds like a young man again.)

ANÍBAL: I searched Los Angeles for days and days after she left me. I went to that bus stop on the corner of Virgil and Santa Monica and waited there day and night. I called every hospital and went to every police station in L.A. County. *(Beat.)*

   I imagined finding her. Living with her forever. I imagined long moments of silence between us when we didn't have anything to say. I imagined enduring the terror of a Los Angeles gone out of control because these quiet moments would be like iron wings and we'd be sheltered inside them. We wouldn't hear the noise of the earthquakes or the screams of a dying culture. But she never came back to me. I never saw her again. All I kept were memories of that extraordinary woman and a night that had that dream feeling to it, you know that feeling: there's a sound like suspended music, air that doesn't move, time that doesn't add to itself. It took me years but I finally understood that I had encountered a true mystery that night, that I had taken a living miracle into my house. That Celestina del Sol was from a world I would never understand. That sometimes Nature improvises. That Nature created a woman that lived outside the field of time and may never die. That someday everyone who ever knew her and remembered her would be gone. That she would live forever in that physical perfection like some kind of exiled and forgotten goddess. And that trying to understand such a life, and why love matters to it, why a god would need to be loved too, was like trying to understand the anatomy of the wind or the architecture of silence or cloud tectonics. *(Aníbal laughs.)* Yeah. What better way to respond to a miracle than to fall in love with it?

(During the following, lights start to go down on the bed. The sound of rain comes up.)

ANÍBAL: And at one point in the evening, I heard the sound of Spanish, as love assumed the language my parents spoke the night I was conceived, the language I had forgotten...

(Celestina kisses Aníbal. Celestina leaves the bed, takes the baby out of the stroller, and starts walking to the bus stop with the baby in her arms.)

ANÍBAL: Celestina said to me: *"Me pregunto como será haberte amado en cada etapa de tu vida, Aníbal..."*

(Aníbal continues the speech in Spanish, quietly, underneath Celestina's simultaneous, and louder, translation:)

CELESTINA: *(To the baby.)* ...I wonder what it would be like to love you in every age of your life, Aníbal. To love the little boy you were, and hold your hand, and lead you across the street, and kiss your fat little baby stomach, and comb your little boy's hair. And then, later, to love the old man you've become, and kiss your deep wrinkles, and smooth out the gray hair, and delight your wise and tired heart, and stare into those mysterious eyes, past the cataracts, and deep into you, to the green landscapes where you never age. Wouldn't it be sweet to have that kind of love, Aníbal?

ANÍBAL: *"...El amor de toda una vida."*

(Celestina has reached the bus stop with the baby.)

CELESTINA: ...The love of a lifetime.

(Aníbal smiles sadly at the sweet memory. Then he forgets it again and goes back to his book as if nothing happened. Lights slowly to black on the bed. At the dark bus stop, Celestina holds her thumb up, hoping to catch a ride out of Los Angeles. She reaches into a pocket and pulls out saltine crackers. She gives one to the baby and eats the other. Rain. Headlights. Blackout.)

END OF PLAY

Between the Lines
by Regina Taylor

BIOGRAPHY

Regina Taylor's writing and performing credits include her one-woman show, *Escape from Paradise*, which premiered at Circle Repertory in New York. She made her ATL playwrighting debut in the 1993 Humana Festival with *Jennine's Diary* and *Watermelon Rinds* (two one-acts titled *Various Small Fires*). Another pair of one-acts titled *The Ties That Bind* was produced at the Goodman Theatre. Other writing credits include *Mudtracks* and her adaptation of Franz Xavier Kroetz's *Ghost Train* and *Sty Farm*. As an actress, Ms. Taylor won a Drama-Logue Award for her "Ariel" in *The Tempest* at La Mama and a Golden Globe Award and NAACP Image Award for "Lilly Harper" in television's *I'll Fly Away*. Upcoming films include Spike Lee's *Clockers, Losing Isaiah* with Halle Berry and Jessica Lange and *Children of the Dust* with Sidney Poitier. Currently Ms. Taylor is writing the book for a musical based on the Fisk Jubilee Singers, commissioned by the Alliance Theatre, and she is an associate artist at Chicago's Goodman Theatre.

ORIGINAL PRODUCTION

Between the Lines was originally produced in the Humana Festival 1995 at Actors Theatre of Louisville. It was directed by Shirley Jo Finney with the following cast:

Nina	Ellen Bethea
Becca	Dee Pelletier
Mother, Angela Davis	Lizan Mitchell
Jonathan, George Jackson	Jacinto Tara Riddick
Rufus	Gordon Joseph Weiss
Mercedes	Ashley Savage
Pam, Nancy, Nadine	Denise Gientke*
Supervisor, Marcus	Andrew Pyle
Ensemble	Jamison Newlander*, Leah Price*

*Members of the ATL Apprentice/Intern Company

TIME AND PLACE

From the late 1970s to the present, between an American metropolis, memory and a dream. Each scene overlaps, spilling into the next scene. Nina is a constant on the stage.

BETWEEN THE LINES

Scene One
NINA'S APARTMENT

Nina awkwardly holds the crying child. We hear sirens.

Scene Two
INTERROGATION ROOM

Blaring light comes up on each speaker.

MOTHER: Is she accused of something here? *(Pause.)* I'm responsible.
(Light out. Light up.)
NINA: Am I guilty? *(Pause.)* Who's on trial here? Is this a trial?
(Light out. Light up.)
MERCEDES: I confess.
(Light out. Light up.)
JONATHAN: I believe in a commitment. Is something wrong with that?
(Light out. Light up.)
RUFUS: *(Humming.)*
(Light out. Light up.)
PAM: *(Holding a knife.)* She pointed me like a loaded pistol.

Scene Three
NINA'S APARTMENT

Nina awkwardly holding a baby as if she might drop it. The baby is crying. We hear sirens and then knocking at the door.

Scene Four
INTERROGATION ROOM

Slide: Interior/Interrogation Room. *The Interrogation Room looks like a confession box.*

NINA: *(In bright spot.)* Commitments, my commitments. Do you mean what am I committed to? I don't believe I understand the question. *(We see slide of Becca.)* Yes. We were roommates. In college—she— *(Pause.)* No. I was not aware of her involvement... *(Pause.)* No. I don't know how she came to...commit such an act... No. Not since college. *(Pause.)* No. Not since college. *(Pause.)* She wrote me letters. I'd hold my breath waiting for her letters. I saved them. Reading them over and over. Always lined stationery and she never wrote inside the margins. Small. Large. Sideways—boldly across— around borders. She was barely legible... *(Pause.)* Me? I *live* between the lines.

Scene Five
COLLEGE DORM

Slide: Flashback. *Slide:* Interior/Dorm 1979

BECCA: It didn't hurt.
NINA: How did it feel?
BECCA: I thought it would hurt. It didn't.
NINA: Was there any blood?
BECCA: No.
NINA: Did you look?
BECCA: There was no blood.
NINA: I always read about the blood-stained sheets. White. Satin.— What kind of sheets?
BECCA: You don't want to know. It was a cheap hotel.
NINA: You should have gone somewhere nice.
BECCA: It was either the hotel or his roommate's bug.
NINA: You could have gone to the lake. Laid down by the edge of the lake. Ducks...
BECCA: Everybody's at the lake on a Friday night. You can trip over half the student body trying to get to the edge of the fucking lake.

NINA: How was he? Passionate?

BECCA: Steve? Yeah. I don't think he's done it much. We were both nervous. We didn't know what to hold onto first. I thought he was going to pull my ears off.

NINA: Your ears?

BECCA: And it went kind of fast. There wasn't much time to think about what we were doing. It was passionate. Fast and passionate. I thought—Oh my God—this is going to hurt so much—and the next thing you know—it was—over. It was passionate—yes. It was nice. It wasn't such a big deal, really. It wasn't what I had expected. Another kind of passion. Not like what you hear about—or read about. But maybe that's it. I don't know. — I can't wait to do it again. Maybe it will be different. More like what I had expected. Or maybe this is it.

NINA: Are you sure he did it right? Maybe you should try someone with more experience.

BECCA: We did it right.

NINA: Are you OK?

BECCA: Yeah. But—different now.—What a relief. *(Then.)* I thought I was bleeding. I felt...like I was bleeding. I thought—Oh my God—I'm going to bleed to death now—But it wasn't blood.

Scene Six
DORM ROOM
Nina studying. George Jackson and Angela Davis appear.

GEORGE: This shit is
starting to thicken.
Two in Jackson.

NINA: He wrote
her—June 21st,
1970.

GEORGE: Hard hats,
counter-demonstrations.
Much like Germany in
the 1930s.

NINA & GEORGE: *(In unison.)* Demonstrations.

ANGELA: *(Reading.)*
It has taken me a
long time to convince
myself that you are not
a dream.

NINA: is not a
dream…
—She writes him.

GEORGE: That thing in
Georgia and the one in
Jackson were like turkey
shoots.

ANGELA: A wish
dream which evapo-
rates when it comes
down to hard realities

NINA: evaporates

…hard realities

GEORGE: We die
altogether too easy.

ANGELA: But you are
those realities and
everything else.

GEORGE: Each one of
those brothers has
fathers, blood brothers,
sisters and mamas.
Something very wrong
has swept over us.
We've grown so
accustomed to seeing
murder done to us
that no one takes
it seriously anymore.

NINA: *(Reading)*
Something very
wrong

ANGELA: I wish I could
touch you. We could
touch each other here,
now.

NINA: We could
touch each other.

GEORGE: We've grown
numb, immune to pain.

ANGELA: Something in
you has managed to
smash through the
fortress I long ago
erected around myself.

*(Light change—as
Nina watches.)*
ANGELA: I didn't know how to
respond.

(Angela is now facing George.)
ANGELA: Until I saw you.

ANGELA: And stunned—I stared
like a love-struck girl.

GEORGE: You may never read this.

GEORGE: And I may never touch you

GEORGE: I feel better than I have
for many seasons. You do know
that I live and hope that by some
means you may have discovered
that I love you deeply and I would
touch you tenderly, warmly, fiercely,
if I could, if my enemies were not
at present stronger. I'm going to
stop here and do something
physical, pushups, finger stands,
something quiet and strenuous.
I love you woman.—George

*(As music comes up, Angela
begins to move—Nina watches,
begins to respond, touching herself.)*

(Music suddenly stops. Light change.)

Scene Seven
DORM ROOM
Becca enters carrying a sign.

BECCA: Oh man! It was just incredible. Just fucking incredible. I tell
you—you should have come Nina. What a rush.
NINA: Your folks have been phoning for the last three hours.
BECCA: Yeah, they must've talked to Gran—she put up bail for me and
a couple of the others. No sweat. It was great—you know. We were
out there singing and then when the cops came we linked arms and
got up and got into the paddy wagon. We sang all the way there—
"Where have all the flowers gone...long time passing...where have

all the flowers gone…long time ago…" *(She hums.)* I don't know all the words—but we sang all the way to the hoosegow. Finger-printed—strip search—man. Slammed into the old clinker. Singing—"Kumbabya" and shit. Old stupid Rita started a round of "Puff the Magic Dragon"—I was going like—Oh man—Where's my harmonica or a comb—you know—it felt like—felt like we were grooving like way back when—like with Joan Baez and…and you know we were partying. It was a party.

NINA: And what about the park?

BECCA: What?

NINA: The park. Are they closing it down or what?

BECCA: We'll be out there again tomorrow. The best part was lying down in front of the bulldozers. What a rush. We'll be out there again—We ain't finished. You should come. There were about 25-30 today. We could use some more numbers. It'll be a party.

NINA: Midterms.

BECCA: We were hoping for some press. We sent out letters. Nobody showed.

NINA: When was the last time you used that park?

BECCA: What?

NINA: No one uses that park. You never heard of it before last week.

BECCA: So? That's not the point. *(Pause.)* Screw you, Nina.

NINA: Somethings have become obsolete—dashikis, Afros and hula hoops.

BECCA: You got Lit notes from yesterday and today?

NINA: Sure. *(She hands her notebook.)*

BECCA: How about French?

NINA: Yeah—and Trig and History.

BECCA: You're swell, Nina.

NINA: Sure.

BECCA: We're almost done with this crap. Soon's I graduate, I'm out of here. I'm taking off—maybe France. Maybe the Riviera—Find myself—on some beach with a bottle of champagne. Come with me, Nina.

NINA: I have to get a job.

BECCA: Get a job when you come back. I'll finally have my grubby hands on my trust fund. We can travel all over Europe.

NINA: I can't.

BECCA: You're such a stick in the mud. Study, study…study. Where's Nina? Studying in her room.

NINA: Some of us have to—we all aren't so privileged…

BECCA: Oh stuff a sock in it.

NINA: Ms. my daddy only donated a law library to this institution…

BECCA: My daddy—

NINA: Miss—I'm going to gallivant all over Europe and drink up my trust fund then come home and marry the son of one of my daddy's friends.

BECCA: And daddy will take him into the company and groom him to take over the business—me being his only and female child—And I'll stay home and give dinner parties and host charity functions and pick up little Hank junior from little league batting practice and little Mary from ballet and I'll be the perfect little Mother. That's what I've been groomed for—birthing and sacrifice. Gag me. Gag me. Gag me! Save me from great expectations. And you— Miss Honor Roll Student—over-achiever…What do you dream — Nina?

NINA: Get a good job. Pay the bills. Live in the burbs—happily ever after.

BECCA: Come on.

NINA: I'm going to be a prize-winning journalist. I'm going to expose corruption and explode the minds of the masses. I want to make a difference—change an individual's perspective of the world…The power of putting pen to paper…I was reading the letters of Angela Davis and George Jackson. You know they never touched…but with their letters…They never had to… *(Nina stops shyly.)* *(Pause.)*

BECCA: Oh yeah. You had a call. Forgot to write it down.

NINA: Who?

BECCA: *Allan.* What's with you two?

NINA: Nothing.

BECCA: He's really cute.

NINA: We've been out a few times.

BECCA: Did you and him *do* it?

NINA: Becca.

BECCA: Sure? He's really cute.

NINA: He's very nice. We went out a couple of times.

BECCA: And?

NINA: And that's it.

BECCA: That's it.

(Nina shakes her head "Yes".)

BECCA: I think he's really cute.

NINA: Shut up.

BECCA: Virgin.

NINA: Shut up.

(Freeze Frame: Becca freezes in place. Becca examines her.)

Scene Eight

George does Kata. Angela touches Nina's face and exits. We see images of assassinations, Martin Luther King, Malcolm X. Overlap with...

Scene Nine
DORM ROOM

Slide: ...and exited through his brain. *We hear French lesson tape playing. George mimes action as...*

NINA: *(Studying.)* ...at approximately 3 P.M. the authorities said that George Jackson had been shot to death by guards in the prison yard at San Quentin while trying to escape. A bullet it was reported later entered the lower part of his back and passed upward along the right side of his body and exited through his brain...

Scene Ten
DORM ROOM

Slide: Interior Dorm 1981 *Light change. French tape is playing louder. Becca conjugating "to go": Je va, tu vas, il va, nous allons, vous allez, ils vont — Her French is bad.*

BECCA: We won't lose each other, will we?

NINA: We'll keep in touch.

(Becca exits. Light Change. Slide: Two years later.)

Scene Eleven
ANGELA'S KITCHEN

ANGELA: Chocolate souffle—you will need the following ingredients.

NINA: Do you mind if I use a tape recorder—

ANGELA: As a matter of fact—

NINA: —So that there is no discrepancy between my notes and memory.

ANGELA: There should be no need...

NINA: I'm new at this—If you don't mind—

ANGELA: It's a simple recipe—I could write down—

NINA: But some details—nuances—if not recorded— *(Pause. Nina puts away the tape recorder.)* Thank you for granting me this interview, Ms. Davis.

ANGELA: Angela. Shall we begin?
(Nina pulls out camera.)

ANGELA: $1/3$ cup light cream.
(Nina snaps picture.)

ANGELA: 3 egg whites. 3 egg yolks.
(Nina snaps another picture.)

NINA: I have to admit that I'm an admirer. I read the letters in college—

ANGELA: $1/4$ cup sifted confectioners sugar.

NINA: —and dreamed of one day meeting—talking with you.

ANGELA: $1/2$ cup semi-sweet chocolate pieces.

NINA: So when this assignment came in, I literally begged the editor for this opportunity.

ANGELA: In saucepan blend cream cheese over low heat.
(Short pause.)

NINA: I wanted to talk to you about your present stance on communism—Reagan—What are your current issues—projects?

ANGELA: My cookbook is my latest project. I'm traveling—promoting my new cookbook. The subject of this interview, I was assured, would be this cookbook...I've added chocolate—I'm stirring to melt—Let cool.
(Pause. On Screen, we see: June 4, 1970, Dearest Angela, This is the fifth one of these...I hope one reaches you soon...Very discouraging. But I'll never stop trying...)

ANGELA: Beat yolks with dash of salt till thick and lemon-colored.

NINA: George's letters—Soledad Brothers—the prison letters of George

Jackson, were printed in 1970 with a foreword by Jean Genet, you never printed yours.

(Short pause.)

ANGELA: Slowly blend into cool chocolate.

NINA: I know this interview was set up about your book—your cookbook—but the letters are of great political and historical significance. In them we get a sense of the temperature of the times—

ANGELA: ...beat whites...

NINA: Two minds that met and melded. A book of your letters it seems is owed.

ANGELA: Owed.

GEORGE: I promised not to be bashful with you...

ANGELA: They were confessions—

GEORGE: It's crazy—all women even the very phenomenal want at least a promise of brighter days—

ANGELA: They were confessions—

GEORGE: Bright tomorrows. I have no tomorrows at all.

ANGELA: Confessions—of the heart.

NINA: Used against you at your trial. *(Writing furiously.)* The D.A. intended to argue that you were driven by political fanaticism.

ANGELA: The "newly enlightened" public didn't buy it.

NINA: So he embellished the other side of this case—irresistible passion.

GEORGE: The worst thing that could have happened to the woman in the dream—

ANGELA: —credible motive—

GEORGE: —was letting me touch her.

ANGELA: He lacked credible motive.

NINA: Violence by reason of passion. He introduced your letters into the trial to support—

ANGELA: Shrouding me in the age old white mystique of Black sexuality.

NINA: —Blind passion—

ANGELA: A black woman's motive—not political ideology—not social reform—*motive*—Base animal craving.

NINA: You met George once—your only physical meeting.

ANGELA: How old are you?

NINA: —at the men's mess hall at San Quentin. There was a guard present who witnessed that meeting.

ANGELA: They couldn't make the case—

NINA: What happened at that meeting?

ANGELA: Very young.

NINA: The guards claims were deemed—

NINA & ANGELA: —inadmissible.

ANGELA: A matter of public record. I was exonerated.

(Nina rewinds, then steps back into altered reality. Note: The following underlined words are spoken as main thoughts and should be heard above the overlapping sections. The words should be spoken like an operatic jazz riff. George is percussive, keeping a steady beat. Angela's voice is the horn. Nina is the main soloist—whaling sax. The actors must listen and play off of each other to make the music work.)

GEORGE: I have like most people a recurring dream.

ANGELA: Innocent.

GEORGE: In this dream is a great deal of abstract activity.

ANGELA: Where was I?

GEORGE: Have you ever seen the pig they named General something or other? I don't know why my mind locked on him but part of this dream is a still-shot of me trying to fit a large steel boomerang into his mouth.

NINA: I always believed...I always wanted to believe... What I'm trying to understand— to ask is—as a woman...as an African-American—

ANGELA: *(Softly:)* Add sugar—beat to stiff peaks—fold small amounts of whites into chocolate mixture—Fold chocolate half at a time into whites.

GEORGE: It switches to a scene where me and two other brothers are holding hands to form a circle. In the ring—Inside the ring is this guy wearing top hat and tails— stars and stripes— beard and bushy eyebrows.

NINA: What I'm trying to say is—because of women like you— I have choices— I have these options— and I want to follow my...In what direction do I?...or—do I?

ANGELA: Pour into ungreased one-quart soufflé dish.

GEORGE: The action part goes like this: Old Sam tries to break out of the circle. *We stop him.*

ANGELA: Bake 300 degrees for 50 minutes or *(Angela makes stabbing motion to Nina's heart.)* till knife inserted halfway between center and edge comes out clean.

GEORGE: It goes like that, scenes running into each other. Overlapping—all very gratifying stuff,

NINA: I wanted to *believe* in your—

ANGELA: *Guilt.*

NINA: *Conviction.*

GEORGE: But the high point, the climax…

ANGELA: You want a confession—

GEORGE: Well—a tall, slim African woman—firelight and the beautiful dance of death didn't become part of my dream until last year sometime. I knew that things could never be good with me without her.

NINA: It's just— I want—

ANGELA: —a scoop with your byline.

NINA: I just want to know—

(Music stops.)
NINA: There were others. You weren't the only one he wrote.

ANGELA: My recipe made of air and hope.

Scene Twelve
OFFICE

Slide: Two years later. *Nina is in the same light as the Interrogation Room.*

SUPERVISOR: Quite an impressive resume, Ms. Avery. KCET Intern, Investigative Reporter for *The Morning News.* Good recommendations. Impressive awards. Your career, Ms. Avery, to this point has been—impressive. *(Then:)* What we're looking for—I believe, is someone who will fit in—if you know what I mean. *(He winks.)*

NINA: Fit in?

SUPERVISOR: I mean that in both the broad and specific sense. I find you highly qualified for the position—perhaps overly qualified—wouldn't you say?

NINA: I think I'd do a good job.

SUPERVISOR: You're being modest. Many people I've seen today would do a good job. An excellent job. The question has been—would they fit in?

(Nina looks back on previous scene, and then turns attention to next scene.)

Scene Thirteen
MOROCCO

Slide: Postcard from Morocco. *Rebecca cuts her hair.*

BECCA: I've been moving around a lot lately and haven't had the chance—to write—keeping one step ahead of the country club. In case you didn't know—camels stink—they're honery and they spit in your face. Other than that, Morocco is the best. Some great hash and moonshine that will blind you. I've been reading about this Russian woman—I know, I

NINA: *(Reading.)* —to write—

NINA: —camels stink—

graduate from college and *then* crack open a book.

NINA: I graduate from college and then crack open a book.

ANGELA: She traveled across the desert disguised as a man. She looked like a boy—Had several male lovers—who never discovered she was a woman. Can you figure?

NINA: Never discovered she was a woman

(Slide: Time passes.)

Scene Fourteen
EDITING ROOM

Slide: Interior/Editing Room. *Nina works as Supervisor hovers. We see Nancy in a square of light—as if her image were being projected onto a screen. She lip syncs her dialogue.*

NANCY: We had been married twelve years. I said—enough. I'd left him before but I'd always end up coming back. I mean—where would I go? I'd been with him since I was sixteen. What'd I do? I mean, he paid the bills. What do I do? Get a job? Please—or move back in with Ma. Couldn't stand that stankin' bitch.

NINA: Edit that.

(Nancy rewinds.)

NANCY: Been with him since I was sixteen—Sure he was mean. Had a temper. Haul off—hit me. Drop me like a sack of potatoes. He was a scrawny little something. Hell, I coulda beat him down easy— Sometimes I did. We'd be wrestling on the floor. Hell, he'd cry like a baby...

NINA: Edit.

(Nancy rewinds.)

NANCY: ...like a sack of potatoes. Got tired of it—that's all.

NINA: *(Voiceover.)* He beat you.

NANCY: Yeah. *(For the camera.)* Yes. He beat me repeatedly. He wasn't no good in bed neither.

NINA: *(Voiceover.)* He forced you when you didn't want to have sex with him?

NANCY: Oh I never wanted to— *(She laughs.)* Not with him anyways…

NINA: Edit.

NINA: *(Voiceover.)* So you're saying your abusive husband beat and raped you.

NANCY: Uh huh.

NINA: *(Voiceover.)* For the camera please.

NANCY: Yeah repeatedly. Finally I said enough—That's why I'm here. To tell how I got my life together…

NINA: *(Voiceover.)* —And when he raped you—What would he do?

NANCY: You mean how'd he like it? Sometimes I'd be in the kitchen frying up some eggs—eggs over easy—that's all he ate. I'd be in the kitchen and he'd just bend me over.

NINA: *(Voiceover.)* Bend you over—

NANCY: *(Demonstrates.)* Like this?

NINA: *(As she bends over editing unit.)* Edit that.

SUPERVISOR: *(As he bends over Nina.)* Keep it.

> *(Pause.)*

NINA: Keep it.

NANCY: *(Bends over.)* Like this?

> *(Everyone freezes—as Nina steps out of time.)*

NINA: No. That didn't hurt…

> *(Everyone freezes. Aloud.)*

NINA: Let's move on…

> *(Lights out.)*

Scene Fifteen
SCREEN

> *We see images of atrocities—the starving, the murders, the wars…in graphic detail. One after the other as we hear an announcer rattling off horror statistics over Marvin Gayes' "Let's Get It On."*

Scene Sixteen
THE STOOP

Slide: Exterior/Nina's Stoop. *Rufus sits on the stoop drinking T-bird and listening to Marvin Gaye's "Let's Get It On."*

RUFUS: *(Singing with Marvin.)* ... "We're all sensitive people. So much to give. Understand me sugar..."

NINA: *(With bag of groceries.)* Hello sweetheart.

RUFUS: Hi honey. How was work today?

NINA: Same old grind.

RUFUS: How about I fix you a martini? Help you to unwind.

(Nina gives Rufus some spare bills.)

RUFUS: You a sweet sugar mama. You gonna let your sweet papa in tonight?

NINA: Not tonight, dear. I got a headache.

RUFUS: You change your mind, you know where to find me. Right here waiting. For you and only you. You're gonna break down one day, sweetheart, and I'm gonna be sitting right here—waiting.

NINA: Thanks Rufus. That's good to know. You get yourself something to eat. Don't drink up my money.

(Nina picks up her mail and hands Rufus a bag of chips.)

NINA: Good night, Rufus.

RUFUS: Good night, baby.

(Nina enters her apartment.)

RUFUS: You ain't got no Bar-b-que. Like 'em with the ridges—man could starve to death on these thin things...

Scene Seventeen A
NINA'S APARTMENT

Slide: Interior/Nina's Apartment. *Nina turns on answering machine and starts getting comfortable.*

MESSAGE 1 *(Marcus' voice):* Hey sweetheart—can't wait until Friday.

MESSAGE 2 *(Supervisor's voice):* Nina, say the dailys on the Baby Killer piece. Fantastic stuff.

(Nine unpacks groceries...chips, sodas, TV dinner-type stuff.)

MESSAGE 3 *(Mother's voice):* Nina,
just calling to see how you are.

Figured you were busy. We've been
thinking about you. It's been
awhile since you called.
Three weeks. /Figured you   NINA: *(Ad-libs.)* /Four weeks
were busy. We were hoping
you'd come down this weekend. Your father went fishing—
caught a "whole mess of perch."
His back...you know your father/   NINA: /You know your father
and his back...went out on him
day before yesterday. Climbing up
on the roof to do repairs. I told
him not to—but you know your
father. Fortunately, he landed in
the bushes. It was a miracle. I told
him so. I'm doing fine. Just thought
I'd call to talk to you—but you're
not in. Figure you've been busy./   NINA: /Busy, busy
My busy baby girl. I'm sure other
people want to call you—and leave
messages, so let me hang up./   NINA: /Please hang up
Call me when you get a free
moment. Or I'll call back.
And don't eat out all the time.
Take some time for yourself and
have a home-cooked meal.   NINA: Yes Ma'am.
   (Nina pops a TV dinner into the microwave.)
MOTHER'S VOICE: Well, we were
thinking of you. Bye now sweetheart.
   *(We hear three beeps signaling end of tape. Nina flips through her
   mail. She stops at Becca's letter.)*

Scene Seventeen B
FRANCE
   Slide: Postcard from France. *Rebecca sits at a table with Claude and
   Jeanette.*

REBECCA: The Eiffel Tower,   NINA: *(Reading.)* The Eiffel Tower

the left bank, music…I met a
street painter. His name is
Claude Le Fauvere. *Intense* colors.
Muscular brushstrokes.   NINA: *(Reading.)* brushstrokes
I bought one of his paintings—
hung it on the wall of my hotel
room—and daydreamed.   NINA: *(Reading.)* daydreamed
At six he takes me out to the
clubs. Dancing till four.   NINA: *(Reading.)* dancing
We drink coffee and smoke
till noon. He says he's an
anarchist or the anti-christ—
I'm not sure. He speaks no
English—and you know my
French…But now I am enjoying
learning foreign tongues.
    (Claude kisses Rebecca then Jeanette. Rebecca then kisses Claude then
    Jeanette.)

Scene Eighteen
EDITING ROOM
    Nadine is celluloid, flickering on the screen.

NADINE: I stabbed her sixteen times.
NINA: Why sixteen times? You started by stabbing her five times in the
    head—
NADINE: Each time I stabbed—I spoke *his* name. I became a chant—a
    prayer. A prayer over the dying. How many times…They told me
    later how many times I stabbed her. That I started with her head.
    Five times in the head. Her eyes. Her mouth. Her nose. Twice in
    her mouth. I can still hear her screaming. Even now. I've been bap-
    tized since I've been in. I've at last found the true savior. Still I can
    hear her screaming. I just want to say—I'm sorry—
    (Freeze frame.)
NINA: Edit that. Edit the whole thing. We've done it. The Manson fam-
    ily. The Son of Sam. The Mother of Sam. Sam's cousin. Sam I Am.

Now—speaking *dead* from the necropheliac hotel, it's Jeffrey Dahmer.
(Nadine rewinds and edits.)

NINA: Fresh. I need fresh bodies, fresh victims, fresh blood. Our audience is tired of the same old stew. God. *(Pause.)* Open up your heavens and give me a sign. *(Pause.)*
(We hear Mother's laughter.)

Scene Nineteen
NINA'S APARTMENT
Slide: Interior/Nina's Apartment *Mother and Rufus are laughing as Nina enters.*

NINA: Mom. Rufus...

MOTHER: Hello sweetheart. I figured if Mohammed wouldn't come to the mountain...

NINA: How did you get in? How did Rufus...

MOTHER: Picked the lock? Didn't we Rufus? I thought I'd come up—surprise you—wasn't until I got off the train—I thought—I don't even know when you'll be home—I called your office—they said you were out on assignment. Wouldn't tell me where—like...I told them I'm your mother not some dreaded stalker. Well, I'm not to be deterred. I decided to camp on your stoop till you came home. That's where I met Rufus. *(Mother is preparing to cook.)*

NINA: You let Rufus in. *(To Rufus.)* You picked my lock?

MOTHER: Calm down dear. There's no damage. I picked the lock. We got tired of sitting out there waiting on you. *(To Rufus.)* I used to pick locks all the time. Back in the 60s. Break into the dean's office—sneak into public buildings at night—set off stink bombs. Nothing serious...

NINA: You broke in and let a stranger into my house, Ma—

MOTHER: Rufus here would have remained a perfect stranger—if it were left up to you. My daughter always has been secretive. Everything is a mystery. When was the last time you brought a young man home to meet me and your dad?

NINA: Two years ago. He left screaming from the house before we got to dessert.

MOTHER: Dessert? It was the first course. I made a tuna casserole.

NINA: Perhaps the spam pate appetizer didn't set well with him.

MOTHER: It's all the herbs—pick them fresh. *(To Rufus.)* You like crab cakes?

(Rufus nods "Yes".)

MOTHER: You buy 'em frozen—pop them in the oven—microwave's ruin one's childbearing possibilities—I believe that…They're done in 15 minutes. They come with its own packet of sauce—but you add fresh herbs…delicious. *(To Nina.)* Your daddy's favorite if he ain't caught it himself. I don't go for that cleaning business—It's your daddy goes in for that blood and guts. Carp—you stab in the heart—*(She makes stabbing motions to Nina's heart.)* right between the gills—and bleed it. Bleed out all the toxins so it's good to eat. Says it makes him feel like a man… Three and a half years ago was the last time you brought a man home—and he was as nervous and highstrung as a catfish on the line.

NINA: You scared him off.

MOTHER: Who? Asked him two simple questions—He started wiggling and flapping—Two simple questions make him nervous—throw him back in—But Rufus here…

NINA: Rufus?

MOTHER: Rufus—the answer to a mother's prayers. He said yes to both my questions.

RUFUS: Yes and yes.

MOTHER: Does he want to marry you? Does he want a big family?

NINA: Mama, I don't believe you. Look at Rufus—Rufus is…Rufus is a…

MOTHER: A white man. I'm not blind. Times are changing. Nothing to be ashamed of. Your Aunt Altricia's baby girl married a white boy just last year—sent you an invitation…Broke Altricia's heart. But it was a beautiful wedding. Nobody fell out over it. As long as he treats you right—makes you happy—I'm happy.

NINA: Rufus—

MOTHER: He has a good job too—Investigative Reporter. Undercover doing a story on the homeless. He's doing a story on the *homeless.*

RUFUS: City Shelters are a breeding ground for crime. Safer sleeping on the streets—so much red tape—waiting lists miles long for decent shelter—and women and children are on the top of the list. Illegals taking all the crap jobs. You do better panhandling. Once you trip in this system it's a fast tumble down to a slippery bottom. Most people stingy with kindness. Forget it. Ain't worth nothing unless it's given.

(Pause.)

NINA: So you staying for dinner sweetheart?

RUFUS: Of course, pumpkin. But got to hit the streets again afterwards. A journalist's work is never done.

MOTHER: I admire that, Rufus. You're doing stories of human value. You talk to my daughter—maybe you'll be a good influence.

NINA: What does that mean? I'm always doing warm human interest stories.

MOTHER: "Elvis is alive and well living on Mars with Jimmy Hoffa."... Give me a hand with this macaroni and cheese.

NINA: We have the number one show in syndication.

RUFUS: Love that macaroni and cheese Father Mason at the 12th Street Mission does: Macaroni and cheese and hamburger patties on Tuesday nights. It's the Hamburger Helper that does it.

MOTHER: You'll love mine—We're having hot dogs, the Hormel chili and Campbell's chicken noodle soup...cucumber salad.

RUFUS: Sounds delicious.

MOTHER: That's a can of water to each can of soup, Nina. Girl is always eating out. Thought you might enjoy a home-cooked meal.

NINA: Just last week we featured the seven-year-old girl kidnapped by drug dealers. Turned out her father had sold her for crack. She was returned alive.

MOTHER: Um hum...needs garlic.

NINA: I worked hard to get where I am mother.

MOTHER: Where are you?

(Freeze frame.)

NINA: Sshh...

Scene Twenty
RUSSIA

Slide: Russian postcard. *Light comes up on Becca in Russia. Nina undresses.*

NINA: Ssh—

BECCA: Kruschev   OFFSTAGE CAST: Ssh
      Chernynko   Ssh

Breznev	Ssh
Andropov	Ssh
Gorbachev	Ssh

Yelt-sssin

(Becca begins stomping, cast off-stage also stomps in Russian army cadence.)

BECCA: Baklanov/Yanayev

Kryuchkev/Boldin

Tizykov/Moiseyev

Lukianov/Pugo

Yazov/Komar

Papov/Pankin

(Stomping ends.)

BECCA: Walls fall.

(Becca flashes. An automatic rifle is revealed inside her fur coat. Nina has to turn the letter around and upside down to read it. Becca and then Nina laugh.)

Scene Twenty-One
HOTEL ROOM

Slide: Interior/Hotel Room. *Nina in a robe at barred window. Marcus remains in bed—We see him in the shadows with a lit cigarette.*

NINA: You should give that up.

MARCUS: Ex-smokers make the best crusaders. When is your mother going home?

NINA: Never.

MARCUS: I miss your bed. Something about a four-poster bed.

NINA: I like hotel rooms. Something about cheap hotel rooms with worn sheets.

MARCUS: I wish would've known that. There was a place just off the highway...next to the hamburger joint.

NINA: That would have been perfect.

MARCUS: Whatever turns you on—cupcake.

(Pause.)

NINA: You called my name.

MARCUS: What?

NINA: You called *my* name tonight.

MARCUS: Whose name was I supposed to call?

NINA: Baby dove, sweetheart, Have mercy Honey Lamb! You never call out my name.

MARCUS: I don't?

NINA: No.

MARCUS: What does that mean?

NINA: What *does* that mean?

(Pause.)

MARCUS: I missed you real bad. How long has it been?

NINA: Two months.

MARCUS: Two and a half months. I was in Chicago two and a half months. Gets real chilly in Chicago, Sweet flower.

NINA: Say my name, Marcus.

MARCUS: Nina.

NINA: See, that wasn't so hard.

MARCUS: Nina. It's a beautiful name. So is my angel, doe eyes, sugar pie. You used to like my nicknames.

NINA: Yeah. (Then.) This time you slipped and said *my* name. You're not going soft on me—are you?

MARCUS: Next thing you know I'll be asking you to take me home to meet your folks.

NINA: Then I'll know you've gone mad.

MARCUS: I mean, what's the big deal? I called your name. What's the big deal? Why are you making such a big deal? It's not like the first time I called our your name—Is it? (Pause.) I mean, what are you getting at? You want me to admit something. Like I'm guilty of something. Like…It's not like I'm guilty of anything. You want me to admit something here. I don't feel guilty about anything.

(Pause.)

NINA: You know, Lamp Chop—It's fine. It's OK when we don't say anything.

(As she takes off her robe, a shaft of light pierces her—she is transparent—a bird—beating against the bars. Light change: Nina dresses. Light change: we hear TV laugh track.)

Scene Twenty-Two
NINA'S APARTMENT

Nina enters. Mother watches TV.

MOTHER: It's late.

NINA: What're you doing still up?

MOTHER: Can't sleep. *(Pause.)* You have a nice time tonight?

NINA: Finishing up some details.

MOTHER: Ummm.

NINA: Deadline is next Wednesday.

MOTHER: Ummm. You could've spent the night. Could've called—just so I don't worry—Gone and spent the night. You're grown.
(Pause, as Nina turns off TV.)

NINA: I go to bed with him. I don't sleep with him. *(Pause.)* His name is Marcus. He travels a lot. He comes through town, once—ever other month. If I'm not too busy, we get together. When we're in bed he calls me nicknames. My peach. My pumpkin—cauliflower…Afraid that in the heat of the moment he might call me by some other women's name. We've been seeing each other 3 years now. He's good in bed. I like him when he doesn't talk too much. He's a nice guy. Fits into my life without making things too complicated. I don't care who he sees when he's not with me. I don't think I'd miss him if he didn't call. I'd miss the convenience.

MOTHER: You know I always wanted a boy.

NINA: I know.

MOTHER: I always thought—boys are no trouble. Don't have to worry about raising them. They pretty much raise themselves. Less to worry about. Push them out—They run around conquering. Shoving, pushing—They fall down, they get right back up. No tears. Lots of mess. But strong, independent. Not needy. They don't need…My first and only child. I was afraid. Didn't know what to do. If I would do it right. A boy would've been less worry. And he would grow up and be just like his daddy. You know your daddy. Mr. Rock of Gibraltar. You know I've never seen your father cry. Never. Never. 36 years. You came out. So small. I didn't know how to hold you. Didn't know what to do. I thought something was wrong with me. A mother's supposed to know how to hold her own baby. And you grew so fast. Tearing around in those jeans. That's all you ever wanted to wear was jeans or overalls. Tough lit-

tle thing. Fight with the best of them. Remember little Freddy—
Oh... No sitting on mama's lap and putting ribbons in your hair—
baking cookies in the afternoon. Somehow I was relieved. Never
had to wipe any tears from your eyes. Just like your daddy—He
has a hard time saying what he feels. What he needs. He doesn't
have to. Because he has me. I know from a gesture, a look. And he's
the same with me. That comes from 36 years. *(Pause.)* 36 years. I
was so innocent. I thought men had it so much easier. *(Pause.)*
Want to bake some cookies?

NINA: It's late Mama.

MOTHER: They're frozen. All you have to do is cut them up. And put
them in the oven. Takes 20 minutes to bake. While they bake you
can put on your jammies, we'll switch on the Late Show and I'll
braid your hair.

(Nina shifts awkwardly. Freeze Frame—Nina steps out of time.)

NINA: How would you describe yourself?

Scene Twenty-Three
EDITING ROOM

PAM: Misunderstood—yes—misunderstood. The world is full of people
lying to themselves—avoiding themselves. They don't want to
make contact—but they do. They crave intimacy but they deny
that—cut it out in themselves. I don't lie to myself. I'm in love
with love. Have to have it. I'm honest, who says otherwise is a liar.
And I don't want intimacy for just intimacy. I want something
that's all consuming. Something that I could die for. I don't consider myself obsessive. I know what I want.

*(Light Change. Pam steps off the screen. We are in the Interview Room.
Cameraman and boom operator enter.)*

PAM: He smiled at me.

NINA: That's how you knew?

PAM: Yes. It wasn't just a smile. It wasn't just a casual smile. He was
speaking to me with his smile. I knew everything about him. His
pain. His longing. He gave all of that to me when he smiled. He
chose me out of everyone else in this world.

NINA: That was in the subway?

PAM: yes. I was sitting next to him. Our bodies almost touching.

NINA: And you followed him home.

PAM: He got off at 86th and Lex. And I followed him.

NINA: Did he speak to you?

PAM: I told you, he spoke his heart with his smile. His eyes told me everything. Sometimes you know, you just know. And I followed him.

NINA: To his apartment.

PAM: Yes. Not inside. Not the first time. I just wanted to see where he lived. Then I waited outside his apartment until morning. Then I followed him back to the subway. He got off at 14th. Followed him to his job. I applied for work there. It was a publishing firm. They needed a receptionist. I brought him coffee every morning. Screened his messages...ran errands...picked up his laundry. He appreciated my attentions. He needed me.

NINA: When you first saw him on the train—When he spoke with his eyes—

PAM: His smile spoke to me.

NINA: Yes. Why didn't you simply ask him to go out with you then? Wouldn't that have been easier?

PAM: It would have been vulgar. Much too vulgar. When we first saw each other we knew this was something special. Ron wouldn't have wanted it that way. He didn't even know my name. He's too sensitive to ask a woman on a subway...He wanted us to first get to know each other. I know it sounds archaic. *(She giggles.)* I guess what we had was an old-fashioned romance. We wanted it to be pure.

NINA: I'm sorry, Pam. We lost audio on that. I loved that last part. Could you repeat that? Make sure we get it this time, Rosanne. OK? From the old-fashioned part...Pete, could we get in tighter for this part? *(Nina points at Pam.)*

PAM: It was pure, old-fashioned...

NINA: I'm sorry, Pam. The first time you said it—You seemed almost embarrassed. You sort of blushed—the way you said it the first time. Take your time.

PAM: It was an old-fashioned romance. We wanted it to be pure.

NINA: Great.

Scene Twenty-Four
NINA'S APARTMENT

MERCEDES: I slapped him. Threw that ring out the window. I don't know who he thought he was dealing with. Told him to try again when he could offer real diamonds. Trying to pass off some zirconian chips. I can smell the real thing. He cried. I slapped him again—sent him on his way. Tears don't bother me.

NINA: She's been here 8 days. Tuna casserole. Eggplant casserole. Casserole surprise. She's out there now—potting plants.

(Mercedes notices a cart full of junk.)

NINA: Rufus's things. He's been over every night for dinner—bringing things.

(We hear Rufus singing in the shower.)

NINA: He shaves here now. He likes it better than the train station men's room.

MERCEDES: Men are like that. You invite them over for dinner—They come, carrying a toothbrush in their pocket—leave it in the bathroom next to yours. That's the first step. Next thing they want a drawer and a little closet space. Next thing you know he's sitting up in his underwear watching TV. "Honey—get me a beer…Oh geez, were we supposed to go out tonight? Sweetie—there's a great game on. Let's stay in. And—Oh, by the way, I invited a few of the boys over. Whip us up some sandwiches, would ya, hon?" That's men. They pee on their territory. I'm not having it. I don't even let a man set foot in my house. No home-cooked meals. He buys me dinner. The Four Seasons every night—if that's my taste. If he wants some coochy-coochy time—it's at his place—If he has the *right* address—otherwise, it's the penthouse suite. The Ritz.

(Rufus enters in a towel.)

RUFUS: So, what time's dinner?

(He sits and flips on the TV. The TV continues its images of mind-numbing atrocities.)

MOTHER: *(Voice from outside)* You're gonna love these azaleas, Nina.

RUFUS: *(Flipping channels.)* Chipped beef on toast. Father Harrigan makes good chipped beef on toast—Thursday nights.

MOTHER'S VOICE: And peonies—white and red.

MERCEDES: *(To Rufus.)* You're a scum sucker. You know that, don't you?

RUFUS: You talking to me?

MERCEDES: You're one of those bottom feeders. Hog wallowing—

RUFUS: What a mouth on you. The rest ain't bad either.

MERCEDES: You make me sick.

RUFUS: What do you want for me to do?—What, for you?—I'm a guest in this house—just like you. Here's my invitation. Nina invited me—

(He looks over at Nina—she says nothing.)

RUFUS: Et tu? Maybe I've overstayed my welcome?

NINA: Rufus—I barely know you.

RUFUS: What? We've known each other four years now. Everyday on the stoop. We talk, you give me something—keep me in my T-bird. We make contact, you know? You could have pretended I'm not here. I'm the invisible man. People walk by—I don't exist. We have a four-year relationship going on here. I just thought we could get to know each other better. In a respectable way. The boyfriend stuff—that was for your mother's benefit, you know. But, you want to know something funny? I sit there every day, morning—noon—night—waiting for you. Like if you don't see me I'll disappear. Wait—that's not the funny part. I think it's the same for you—If I don't see you—POOF. Make me feel needed. Like it's a reciprocal relationship.

Scene Twenty-Five
NINA'S APARTMENT
A few minutes later. Mother enters.

MOTHER: *(To Mercedes.)* Are those real? You didn't have those the last time I saw you.

MERCEDES: I wasn't complete then.

MOTHER: Built like a Buick.

MERCEDES: The name is Mercedes.

MOTHER: Mercedes—? That wasn't your name last time I met you. Didn't you tell me your name was Sophie?

MERCEDES: I was trying it out.

MOTHER: *(Checking her over.)* And those...and that...and...open your mouth. Is any part of you real?

MERCEDES: Men prefer fantasy. That's me—head to toe. Got tired of women hypnotizing men and passing me over. Then when I got everything done—I figured it out—I don't have to work—ever again. Men work for me. Sometimes I might give them a little something in return. Most times I don't.

MOTHER: Where's Rufus?

MERCEDES: Thursday night. Chipped beef on toast.

MOTHER: *(To Nina.)* You kicked him out. He was a good man—just down on his luck.

NINA: You knew?

MOTHER: I ain't daft.

NINA: And you let him in?

MOTHER: Why not. He was harmless. Besides, I enjoyed his company. Me and your daddy went through some hard times. Wish somebody would've let us in the door. *(To Mercedes.)* All those fixtures and attachments—You got something that will snag you a husband?

MERCEDES: Husbands are my specialty. What would I do with one of my own. I have a pet chow—His name is Tom Tom. When I get home he's sitting there waiting faithfully for mommy to arrive.

MOTHER: Well, at least you have a dog. *(To Nina.)* At least she has a dog.

Scene Twenty-Six
NICARAGUA
Slide: Nicaragua Postcard. *We hear castinets.*

BECCA: Someone told me that the dangerous part of traveling alone is that after 2 weeks you begin to lose sense of self. I told him that didn't sound like such a dangerous notion. In these five thousand one hundred, ten some odd days of doing just that—I have lost myself repeatedly and found many other selves along the way that I never imagined. My letters to you have acted like a divining

NINA: the dangerous part of traveling alone...

rod. Pointing my compass back to
where I came from. Like leaving a
trail of bread crumbs on this journey...
Giving me a sense that someone
familiar is watching.

> *(As she speaks,* someone *is watching. She slowly takes out a gun. Ready in case of ambush. The Watching Figure moves down from shadows— as lights go down on Becca taking aim. Light Change. We see that the Watching Figure is Jonathan. He has been staring at Nina.)*

Scene Twenty-Seven
PARK
> *Jonathan approaches Nina and trips.*

JONATHAN: I'm sorry. I was staring. *(He sits next to her on the bench, rustling his newspaper for attention.)*
NINA: Can I help you?
JONATHAN: You just did. *(Then.)* I didn't mean to disturb you. You are alone this afternoon?
NINA: No.
> *(Pause.)*
JONATHAN: You're waiting for someone?
NINA: Yes.
JONATHAN: I hope it's not your boyfriend—or husband. That would break my heart.
NINA: I'm waiting for a friend.
JONATHAN: A friend.
NINA: Yes. She—
JONATHAN: *(Pleased.)* She. Aha.
NINA: Ah.
JONATHAN: You have a beautiful mouth—when you said "Ah"— I...well. I apologize. I'm going too fast. You don't even know my name. I'm Jonathan, Jonathan Lawson. *(Pause.)* And your name is? *(Nina looks at him.)*
JONATHAN: And your name must be Nina. ...Your paper. I read upside down. That is your name isn't it? Nina?
NINA: Yeah.

JONATHAN: Nina. Beautiful. Like Nina Simone. Do you like Nina Simone? I love her voice. Deep, sultry... I'm not good at this—I'll admit. I'm clear about what I want. That is, what I like. I saw you sitting there and found myself attracted to you and wanted to strike up a conversation. How are you? How's the weather? What movies do you like conversation. We talk, maybe we make each other laugh or think or remember. Maybe we have things in common. Maybe there's nothing. Maybe we find that we hate each other. We go on about our lives. Maybe we never see each other again. Gee. I think I'm sweating. You're making me sweat, Nina. And I see you're a busy person. I don't want to take you away from your business.

NINA: Avery.

JONATHAN: Hm?

NINA: Nina Avery.

JONATHAN: It's a pleasure to meet you Nina Avery.

NINA: I am seeing someone.

JONATHAN: But nothing serious.

NINA: Not quite. No. I'm more married to my work.

JONATHAN: I see.

NINA: I'm very good at what I do. *(Pause.)* I produce an issue show...for T.V. *(Pause.)*

JONATHAN: I'm just visiting from Utah. *(Pause.)* I like old movies. Bette Davis.

NINA: I've seen all her movies.

JONATHAN: I loved when she played Queen Victoria. And—

NINA: She came down the stairs—

JONATHAN: With that hairdo. And when she played the sister—the crazy sister of the other actress.

NINA: Yes—what was her name?

JONATHAN: The Coca-Cola...she married Mr. Coca-Cola.

NINA: Mommy Dearest—Oh...it's on the tip...

JONATHAN/NINA: *(Together.)* "Whatever Happened to Baby Jane..."

NINA: And the other one—where she cut off...

JONATHAN: ...his head—"Hush Hush...

NINA: ...Sweet Charlotte"

JONATHAN/NINA: *(Singing.)* Charlotte don't you cry.
  Hush, Hush sweet Charlotte
  I'll love you 'till you die.

NINA: And the one where—
JONATHAN: Yeah—
(Laughing together. Pause.)
JONATHAN: The weather was nice today. Warm.
NINA: Very nice. *(Pause.)* I like things flexible.
JONATHAN: I wouldn't want you to leave in the middle of the night.
NINA: Slow down, Jon.
JONATHAN: Jon already. *(Pause.)* I'm just warning you.

Scene Twenty-Eight
INTERVIEW ROOM
Boom and camera operator enter.

PAM: What we had was so strong. It was true love.
NINA: If it was true love, why did you slash his tires? Why did he issue a restraining order? Didn't you go to jail?
PAM: *(Ignited.)* He didn't know how to express what he felt. He had never experienced a love so profound. He had never felt…allowed himself to feel much of anything. He avoided commitment. He had a job which he worked hard at but he didn't love. He had nothing in his life that he really connected to until he met me. He was afraid. He rejected what he really felt. I wanted to wake him up—shake him— *(She breaks down.)* I would have hooked him up to electric wires and turned up the current—if that's what it took to make him feel how much love was between us.
NINA: We'll go with that take.

Scene Twenty-Nine
RESTAURANT
Slide: Interior/Restaurant

MERCEDES: She looks like she's lost a lot of weight lately. All that loose flesh. She hasn't toned yet. Her ring keeps slipping off. She's having it adjusted. He's the type that finds excuses not to wear his. That's why she lost the weight. She thinks it's her fault. He keeps patting her hand with assuring— "You know little wifey I'm here right beside you with no one else on my mind."—pat, pat, pat. While he's gobbling me up with his eyes—in between mouthfuls of filet mignon. If I give him the right look at the right time—just a quick glance—he'll take his wife home tonight and fuck her loose flesh and dream about me. Tomorrow morning—he won't rest until he's tracked me down. The mighty hunter will track me down and we'll begin the mating dance. I'll waltz him around for months. It's the tits. Since I got them done—I don't feel a thing. After a few months—he'll earn the tits. "Oooo-ooo baby. Now that's enough tiger—You *are* a married man—and I just *can't*. I'm just not ready—yet." And give him my Catholic girl smile.

NINA: I can't imagine—

MERCEDES: In the meantime, his wifey is getting it three—four times a night. She hasn't had it like this since—not even their honeymoon. Not even before... —So afterwards, she's munching down soda crackers and celery going—wow—this diet's really working— While he rolls over dreaming— "Ooooo-ooo baby." When I tire of him, I'll hide my bra in his pocket. An earring in the cuff of his pants. Smear my lips under the flap of his lapel. "Hi honey, I'm home—" She's always known. She's just waiting for the unavoidable evidence. Then she gets the house, the cars, bonds—a *nice* cash settlement, child support. He forks it over and comes running knocking on my door—Nothing stands between us now— Knocking on my door. Knock, knock, knock. Knock, knock, knock. The way I look at it—I'll be doing her a favor and him—he deserves me. The way I look at it—It's a war—The lines are drawn—and either way, I'm on the winning side.

NINA: Sometimes you scare me Mercedes.

MERCEDES: Why? Because we're so much alike?

NINA: You're too cynical.

MERCEDES: *(Laughs.)* Why did you invite me tonight?

NINA: I wanted you to meet Jon.

MERCEDES: *(Dryly.)* Why?

NINA: ...We're friends. I wanted to know what you think.

MERCEDES: Because you're as cynical as I am. He'll sit in the middle. And you can check while he's holding your hand if he's playing with my knee.

NINA: I think I've been out on my own too long.

MERCEDES: Sounds serious. Is this serious?
    (Pause.)
NINA: No. Not really.
MERCEDES: OK.
    (Jonathan enters with flowers.)
JONATHAN: Am I late?
MERCEDES: Right on time. *(Offering him the seat in the middle.)*
    Jonathan.
NINA: *(Introducing.)* Mercedes
    *(Jonathan sits. He looks at Nina, then looks at Mercedes, then back to
    Nina. Nina and Mercedes look at Jonathan, then look at each other,
    then back at Jonathan. Light change. Mercedes exits. We see Nina and
    Jonathan embrace—Freeze Frame as…)*

Scene Thirty
AFRICA
    Slide: Postcard of Africa. *Becca dressed in combat gear and camou-
    flage—hacking her way through the jungle.*

BECCA: …did I tell you I'm earning my own way these days. The trust
    fund was spent a while ago—I gave the last of it to feed the hun-
    gry…They kept dying. The children—they kept dying Nina…The
    things I've seen. Done. In the name of different causes. I keep
    searching for something I can commit to. I used to think commit-
    ment had something to do with a strong belief. I've grown too cyn-
    ical. Today I saw a protester bow down and pray to the east, and
    then he poured gasoline on himself and struck the match. A rare
    breed. Nearly extinct. Now I think true commitment has to do
    with the suspension of belief.
    (We hear jungle noises mixed with sounds of lovemaking.)
JONATHAN'S VOICE: Nina…Nina…
    (Then silence:)
NINA: Say it again.
JONATHAN: Nina…
    (Jungle noises.)

Scene Thirty-One
NINA'S APARTMENT

MERCEDES: He's a regular Prince Charming.

NINA: I don't know if we should lead in with the serial killer interview—

MERCEDES: You have to admit, he's a hunk.

NINA: Or the earthquake victims.

MERCEDES: And he's got money to boot. He never takes his eyes off you or his hands.

NINA: We have some great footage of rescue workers reclaiming bodies. Some close-ups of body parts...weeping survivors.

(Mother enters from terrace carrying ferns and geraniums.)

MOTHER: I think these ferns should go in the bathroom...

NINA: There's no room to breathe—

MOTHER: Plants purify the air and they're great listeners. I talk to my plants all the time.

NINA: *(Her tone is sharper than she expected.)* I have a deadline. I need some room here.

MOTHER: *(Hurt.)* Am I in the way? I never intended...

NINA: It's not that...You've come here now, I don't know what you want from me. I've never known.

MOTHER: *(Overlapping.)* I just want...

NINA: Nothing I do is ever good enough.

MOTHER: No, that's not...

NINA: We've never been close.

(Pause.)

MOTHER: Your dad called—The dinners I put up in the freezer for him are just about gone.

NINA: Mom, don't—it's just...I need some room...I need to make some decisions.

MOTHER: Remember to water the hibiscus every other day. The iron plant doesn't need much handling. It grows strong even with neglect. And the cactus—it blooms bone dry. Maybe Mercedes would like the geraniums. *(Mother exits.)*

(Pause.)

NINA: He asked me to marry him.

(Pause.)

MERCEDES: *(Smiles.)* My cheeks are numb—from the silicone—when I smile.

NINA: I'm no good with these things. She knows. *(Indicates plants.)* They'll die. By the end of the week.

MERCEDES: There are other parts. I don't feel a thing.

NINA: *(Frustrated.)* Is this how it feels?

MERCEDES: What?

Scene Thirty-Two
NINA'S APARTMENT
Cameraman enters, hits clapboard, says, "Take One."

NINA: No.

JONATHAN: *(Kissing her.)* Utah is beautiful. Peaceful—

NINA: What you're asking isn't fair.

JONATHAN: Why don't you believe in us, Nina?

NINA: That's not the point. I can't just pick up and leave everything behind.

JONATHAN: You love what you have here more than what we could make together?

Scene Thirty-Three
Clapboard: "Take Two."

NINA: *(Lipsyncing to Pam's Voice:)* I know it's a bit archaic. *(She giggles.)* I guess what we had was old-fashioned. And old-fashioned romance… *(Nina and Jonathan embrace as romantic music swells…The music repeats itself like a broken record.)*

SceneThirty-Four
Clapboard: "Take Three."

NINA: It has taken me a long time to convince myself that you are not a dream—a wish dream which evaporates when it comes down to hard realities—

GEORGE/JONATHAN: We die altogether too easy.

Scene Thirty-Five
NINA'S APARTMENT

Nina puts TV dinner into microwave. We hear ticking of microwave timer. The telephone rings and rings and rings. Nina doesn't answer the phone. She waits for her dinner.

MESSAGE #1—JON'S VOICE: Nina. Nina. What's wrong. Nina. I just want...I know you're home. Nina...

MESSAGE #2...MARCUS'S VOICE: Nina Avery, Nina Avery, Nina Avery. Is that better, sweet peach?

Scene Thirty-Six
NINA'S APARTMENT

Nina with her TV dinner watches the horror images on TV. The phone rings and rings.

T.V. ANNOUNCER'S VOICE: We think the Bomber is someone with strong religious or moral views.

Scene Thirty-Seven
EDITING ROOM

Horror images continue.

PAM: *(Lipsyncing.)* The world is full of people lying to themselves... avoiding...they don't want to make contact—but they do.

NINA: Edit that.

ANGELA: ...and stunned I stared like a love struck...

NINA: Edit that.

BECCA: I've grown too cynical...

NINA: Edit that.

Scene Thirty-Eight
JONATHAN'S APARTMENT

Jonathan answers the door in a robe. Nina enters. She is disheveled.

NINA: I'm sorry…Jon, I need to talk to you. I needed time to think.

JONATHAN: I called you for two weeks.

NINA: I know. I'm sorry. I needed to try and figure out…Look, maybe we can work something out. There has to be room for compromise. I just felt…It was just to fast…see…with you. You come on like— It felt like you were saying it was all or nothing.

(Mercedes enters from Jon's bedroom in a robe.)

MERCEDES: Got that straight.

NINA: What are you doing here?

JONATHAN: Nina, when you didn't answer my calls…

NINA: But Mercedes—

MERCEDES: He called me trying to contact you. You told me it was over with you two./   NINA: /This is insane.
You told me you didn't want to see him again.

JONATHAN: I'm sorry Nina.

MERCEDES: We were going to tell you. It just happened—
last night./   JONATHAN: /We were going to tell you.
You dumped him—
I didn't think you'd
mind if I picked him up.

NINA: I thought you were real.

JONATHAN: I am. I loved you.

NINA: And now you love Mercedes?

JONATHAN: Yes.

NINA: *(To Mercedes.)* And does he know who he's dealing with?

MERCEDES: He knows. He sees right through me.

(Jonathan looks at Mercedes, then to Nina.)

JONATHAN: You two…excuse me. *(Jonathan exits.)*

NINA: What are you up to Mercedes? This one of your games? Drive him crazy, so he'll run back to me? So he'll see…

MERCEDES: I love him. He sees me for who I am. Beyond the tits, the ass, the legs, the hair, the nails, the ears, lips, eyes…He sees

through all my bull—through the games. He made me feel some-
thing. Scary…scary. *(Then:)* Be happy for me Nina.
(Pause.)
NINA: Fine. That's fine.

Scene Thirty-Nine
STOOP

*Nina trips on an empty Thunderbird bottle. As Rufus' boombox plays
Marvin Gaye's "…We are all sensitive people…So much to give…"*

NINA: What?—No martini cocktail?…Rufus?

Scene Forty
NINA'S APARTMENT
The plants are dying.

NINA: Fine. Just fine. No blood. …Is this what it feels like? No. No
blood.
(Blackout. In the blackout, we hear thud.)
NINA'S VOICE: Mom? Mama is that you?
(Nina turns on the light. Rebecca is standing in the room.)
NINA: Becca?
BECCA: Nina—sorry. I didn't want to wake you. Let myself in.
NINA: How—
BECCA: It's a long story. You should get an alarm system. The latch on
the window popped right open. Been traveling the last three weeks
up from Africa through Germany, Bosnia, Ireland.
(The baby starts crying.)
BECCA: It's a long story. Feeding time.
NINA: It's a baby.
BECCA: Did you get my postcards?
NINA: Whose baby, Becca?
BECCA: She's my little fuzzy headed chocolate fudge bar. Mine. Her
name's Benin. Her father was a student. Murdered before Benin

was born. "Radical cleansings"… Just passing through…I needed to see you. Nina. Mind if we crash here a couple of days.

NINA: Becca.

(Becca curls up on the couch with her baby. She rocks and sings.)

Scene Forty-One
NINA'S APARTMENT

BECCA: Terrorist sounds so extreme.

NINA: You plant bombs.

BECCA: I blow things up. Sure. Facades, empty buildings, useless monuments. At first it was for the thrill—Now it's for the Pampers, the doctors bills, daycare, the college nest egg—stocks, bonds, real estate. Benin's developing a pretty impressive portfolio. Listen to me. You know what I fear? I fear becoming jaded. As jaded as the ones whose cages I rattle. Maybe I have become a little jaded since the last time I saw you—14 years?

NINA: Jaded? You're a terrorist Becca! In your letters I always imagined you…

BECCA: The cockeyed idealist—running away from the confines of society—shattering the boundaries of race, creed and sex.

NINA: I always believed that at least *you* would find…

BECCA: I have—many times—and now—I have this child. Beautiful, healthy child—and she'll grow strong and brave. And she's so charming.

NINA: But this is what you ran away from.

BECCA: Ironic huh? This motherhood thing is so empowering—from one perspective…my life has been guided by my passions. Letting life in. See what I created? Feel her. Her little heart beating.

(Nina holds that baby awkwardly as if she would drop her.)

BECCA: Do you feel the possibilities—beating inside the tight skin?

NINA: Why did you come back?

BECCA: I've gone too far out to come back. Just passing through.

(Nina puts her ear to the baby—listening. The baby ticks like a bomb.)

Scene Forty-Two
NINA'S APARTMENT

Becca busily waters plants. Nina dials the phone. The phone rings in Jonathan's apartment. It continues ringing as Jonathan puts engagement ring on Mercedes' finger. They kiss. Nina covers her mouth. Becca notices the TV—the images flicker by—she covers her mouth. In the blackout we hear—

RADIO: ...She was smartly dressed...
(Lights up on Nina. She puts on makeup/warpaint. In her mirror is reflected Becca, Mother/Angela, Mercedes.)
RADIO: ...Carried a shopping bag and packed enough high explosives in the trunk of her car three days ago to wreck part of the Embassy. Police said that although the woman did not appear unusual—She attracted the attention of two security men—When she left the car in a parking lot near the Embassy. As they approached, the car blew up and she disappeared in the confusion...

Scene Forty-Three
NINA'S APARTMENT
We see Angela mixing a souffle.

NINA: I appreciate you two agreeing to meet with me here. I just wanted you to know that there were no hard feelings.
MERCEDES: I knew you'd understand.
NINA: I do.
ANGELA: A black woman's motive...
MERCEDES: We've always been friends.
ANGELA: —not political ideology—
NINA: Why should things be different. *(Raising glass in a toast.)*
ANGELA: —not social reform—
JONATHAN: To friendship.
ANGELA: Motive—
NINA: To passion.
ANGELA: Base animal craving.

(They clink glasses as lights come up on Becca putting together a bomb. Pam enters.)

PAM: Nina—am I late?

NINA: Right on time. *(Introducing.)* Pam, this is Mercedes and Jonathan.

PAM: Jonathan, such a nice smile. *(Pam sits.)*

MERCEDES: Pam?

NINA: A friend…

(Pam smiles at Jonathan, Mercedes looks at Pam, Jonathan looks at Pam, then Nina, then Mercedes.)
(Overlap…)

Scene Forty-Four
NINA'S APARTMENT

Becca tests timer. We tear ticking. Ticking overlaps…

Scene Forty-Five
EDITING ROOM

ANGELA: My recipe—

NINA & PAM: *(Lipsyncing Pam's voice.)* …I would have hooked him up to electric wires…

(As Becca straps the explosive around her waist. She puts on a wig— Afro and mask, looks like Angela—and a nondescript dress. She looks very pregnant. As ticking continues.)

ANGELA: —made of air and hope.

Scene Forty-Six
INTERROGATION ROOM

Nina in cab, holding screaming child.

NINA: When I got home, the child was crying.
(Lights up on Mercedes.)

MERCEDES: He saw right through me. That's why I loved him.
(*As Jonathan does Kata.*)
NINA: *(In cab.)* She left the child behind.
(*Becca passes through. Lights up on Pam.*)
PAM: She pointed me like a loaded pistol.
MERCEDES: She would call all hours—day—night. Calling for him. He swore there was nothing between them. Swore he loved only me. She followed us. At night—standing on the corner looking at our rooms.
RADIO: Police said that although the woman did not appear unusual...
MERCEDES: He said he never encouraged her. Gave no signals. Denied all accusations. At a restaurant she'd be seated across the room. He pretended not to notice.
NINA: *(In cab.)* Pam called—She told me what she was planning to do. I hurried after her.
MERCEDES: She didn't know we'd broken up. Jealous—she followed me down an alley. When she pulled the knife—I thought—my heart—exploded.
NINA: On the way I heard the explosion.
PAM: Her breast just popped. I didn't touch her. It hissed—
MERCEDES: S-S-Silicone.
PAM: I ran. Ran into his arms.
RADIO: ...In an apparent terrorist attempt...
MERCEDES: At last Prince Charming has found his perfect love.
(*Mercedes is dismantled—her heart in her hands—she exits as Pam, knife still in hand rushes toward Jonathan—they struggle/waltz off stage in an uneasy union.*)
RADIO: The unidentified woman had strapped a bomb to her body which exploded before she reached her destination...There were no other known...*casualties.* (*Nina watches as Becca explodes.*)
NINA: Can we edit that and start from the beginning?
(*Nina rewinds—it is a wordless choreographed fast rewind, highlighting turning points for Nina—departing Rufus, Mother wanting to braid Nina's hair, Supervisor bending over Nina, meeting Jon in the park, setting Jon up with Mercedes, interview with Pam, interview with Angela, as Angela makes stabbing movement ot Nina's heart. Camera operator acts as a witness, while Nina relives these moments. Back to Becca's telling Nina about the first time: "It wasn't blood." The dance stops. Nina is left alone on stage.*)

NINA: No blood. No...Feels like I'm bleeding to death, but no...*No.*
*(Facing a blank screen. She holds fast to herself/newborn. She steps
through into light. Nina retracing her past—runs headlong into her
future. Slow Fade. Blackout.)*

END OF PLAY

Helen At Risk

by Dana Yeaton

BIOGRAPHY

Dana Yeaton is the winner of the 1995 Heideman Award from the Actors Theatre of Louisville. His full-length play *Kin Deep* was the winner of a New Play Fellowship at the Shenandoah International Playwrights Retreat and is scheduled to premiere next season in Washington, D.C. In 1993, his satire of contemporary American life, *To Bed With Betsy*, was produced at the Volkov in Yaroslavl, Russia, that nation's oldest professional theatre. He has received three fellowships for playwriting from the Vermont Council on the Arts.

His plays for young adults include *Alice In Love*, *The Garden of Needham*, and *How the Schools Was Won*. Dana is Playwright-in-Residence at the Vermont Stage Company in Burlington, Vermont, where he directs the Vermont Young Playwrights Festival. He is now collaborating with independent filmmaker Jay Craven on a screen adaptation of Garret Keiser's *No Place But Here*.

AUTHOR'S NOTE

For a while I worked in a small prison, making videos with the medium security inmates. A friend and I would go in every Saturday night with a camera and a few ideas for improvs — How about you play a real estate agent taking us on tour of the facility? Or what if everyone tells about the last time they saw their dad cry? Or how about we're a video dating service and you have to describe yourself to your perfect woman? ... Week after week we'd come back with increasingly foolish ideas and the guys *would actually do them.* At Christmas, while Nat King Cole sang, "He's The Little Boy That Santa Claus Forgot," the inmates took turns punching the heavy bag and telling about the best present they ever got.

One of the prisoners, a tall, well-spoken man named Tom, was particularly game. He was always the first to volunteer, encouraged others to do the same, and had some of the better technical ideas. At ten of ten he would start packing up our equipment and coiling extension cords to help us get out on time. He didn't want to anger the authorities and risk not seeing us again.

Tom had been working with a cabinetmaker and was just a few weeks from being released. One night I was waiting for the security guard to check me out and got talking to one of the guards who'd actually joined in that night. I mentioned how great Tom was and how glad I was he'd be getting out.

"I've been here for eight years," the guard said, "and Tom is the most dangerous inmate I've ever met." In fact Tom wasn't making cabinets and he wasn't scheduled to go anywhere. "He came in as a killer and he hasn't changed a bit," the guard assured me. So much for *my* ability to judge character.

And for my good intentions. Lately I find myself more willingly to believe that some people *are* beyond redemption, that there is such a thing as Evil. Whether that's a sign of wisdom, or just age, I don't know, but Helen and I could both stand to get better at recognizing the devil when he's staring back at us.

ORIGINAL PRODUCTION

Helen at Risk was first performed March 1995 at the Humana Festival of New American Plays, Actors Theatre of Louisville. It was directed by Frazier W. Marsh with the following cast:

Helen . . . . Adale O'Brien
Ronnie Guyette . . . . V Craig Heidenreich
Guard. . . . . William McNulty

CHARACTERS

HELEN: An attractive middle-aged woman, dressed sensibly but with an artistic flair.
RONNIE GUYETTE: An inmate.
GUARD

PLACE

A prison rec-room. A long table centerstage; downstage and to one side, a chair.

HELEN AT RISK

AT RISE: *Ronnie is lying on the table, a kerchief covering his hair, while Helen applies the final touches to his white plaster mask. Guard sits facing audience.*

HELEN: *(To audience.)* Now this last piece, the little triangular, Vermont piece, or…*(Turns it upside down.)* New Hampshire-shaped piece, depending…*(She dunks it in a small tupperware container of murky, white water. Throughout the play, she continues to shape and smooth the mask with her hands.)* This will go between the nostrils, not over the nostrils or your partner will no longer be able to breathe. Now in your kits you will find that I have pre-cut all the pieces, which I do not like to do but I had all I could do to get plaster and paint supplies in here and they definitely were not going to let me hand out scissors. So now really, I'm just smoothing, the forehead's already hard, of course the nose will be the last to dry. *Do not hurry the mask,* it should be completely hard before you try to take it off. I will show you how to do that in a minute— *(To man whose mask she is making.)* How ya doin' there Ronnie? Happy? No complaints, right? Yes it was an education just trying to get in here, the Arts Council had warned us about belts, so I knew to come beltless, and no gum to stick in the locks, I can understand that, but pens? Ball point pens? Apparently you boys start tattooing yourself is that right?…*(Responding to an inmate.)* No I don't mind tattoos, one of my friends has a lovely little tattoo…I'm not tellin' where! You just pay attention to what I'm doing because in a minute *you* are gonna be up here doing the same thing…Now doesn't Ronnie look peaceful? And look at those cheek bones…*(To another inmate.)* No, you are not allowed to say anything to people who are having their masks done. Especially…

(Ronnie gives the finger.)

HELEN: Especially…this is the time when the slightest little move can…good now the jaws are fully dry and the chin is coming. *(To guard.)* How we doin' for time?

GUARD: Nine twenty.

HELEN: And we can go 'til when?

GUARD: We got room check at ten.

HELEN: Ooh. Okay. That's gonna be a little tight. *(To guard.)* Sure you don't wanna join in?

GUARD: I'm sure.

HELEN: Okay…*(Shrugs.)* Well we gotta keep uh, lemme see, why don't I tell you a little bit about what we do once the mask is dry…um… we may end up cutting some of the decoration time short. What I usually do in the schools is set out two or three tables of materials. Beads, feathers, ribbon, paints, glitter, knick-knacks—I love yard sales—and I ask that you find some colors or objects, any combination of paints and materials that will make the mask express who *you are.* Now today, as I said, we're going to use, I was only allowed three brushes, so we're going to have to share. I'm not quite clear on what the danger of a paint brush is but…What have we got here? *(Inspecting another tupperware container, full of paints.)* Black, blue, um yellow, peach, I hope y'all won't use a lot of the peach, though I don't actually…I don't see my red. Pardon? *(To an inmate.)* Well, no, you *can* use the peach, I just think, you know, I want to encourage you to experiment, use your imagination and not feel like your mask has to be the same color as you…though I can see that, well we, if you would *like* to use black, some of you, or anybody, that's up to you. We're looking for something that expresses *you,* how you feel as a person, how you feel today, right now.

GUARD: *(In response to an inmate.)* Pearson!

HELEN: *(To guard.)* No that's okay. *(To Pearson.)* If that's how you really feel then try to imagine how that shapes your face and let that be the mask and later before you do any decorating—we're all dry through here now *(chin),* we're just waiting on the nose—before you paint or do anything, make sure that you have an image in your mind, in your mind's eye, of what your mask should finally be...Yes I suppose you could. Sure, sort of a fantasy of what you'd *like* to be. That would be equally valid. Now we just keep—

(Ronnie is pretending to masturbate.)

GUARD: *(To Ronnie.)* Guyette!

HELEN: *(Placing Ronnie's hand at his side.)* We'll just put this over here...Ronnie doesn't seem to understand how simple it would be for us to place another piece of plaster right along here. *(Pretending to cover the nose completely.)* I should tell you that for some people having your eyes completely covered can be very...disorienting, very frightening. A man once, I was out in Colorado, at this convention, and this man had volunteered to be the guinea pig, and all of a sudden about ten minutes into the demonstration he let's out this blood-curdling—

(Ronnie grabs Helen by the arm, shaking as if terrified.)

HELEN: *(Pulling him down to flat again.)* DO NOT MOVE until the mask is off or you will—

GUARD: Guyette you're gonna be outa here.

HELEN: Ronnie will be good, won't you Ronnie?...There now lie back...Good. For some reason the nose always takes the longest to dry... *(To Pearson.)* Yes I am. Are you?

GUARD: Pearson! ...Yeah, I heard what you asked.

HELEN: I don't like to wear my ring when I'm working with plaster.

GUARD: Look, these guys don't have to be in here. Anybody you want out, say so.

HELEN: We're fine. Look, I appreciate, I mean *(laughs)* for God's sake, I have worked in junior high schools!

GUARD: Okay.

HELEN: *Then* it would have been nice to have a guard.

GUARD: Your call.

HELEN: If I need you I can always just scream, right?

GUARD: Whatever.

HELEN: Y'all promise to be good don't you? *(In response to Pearson.)* I'll bet you are. Um...one thing we *may* want to do since we will be a little short on time is use *warm* water for soaking because this will speed the drying process *however* warm water *will* mean that we have to work a little faster to keep it from setting before we're... *(To Pearson.)* Pardon?...You mean today?...I just thought it would be fun...Well, *that* and I think it's important for people to learn more about who—Yes, I am...Well I'd rather not...A hundred and fifty dollars, not including the materials, which of course here don't really amount—Because that's *not* why I'm here. If I wanted to make money I'd go do that. I think people deserve a chance to, this always sounds stupid, but I *do* think there is a basic human need to create and to express yourself. See you think I'm an outsider, I don't think I'm an outsider. What happened to you *before*, what your parents did, I don't know the particulars but...I mean I think I know what it's like to grow up with no one caring what you think or feel. You're just some piece of furniture. And finally you blow up, of course! Thank god. You're alive! Do you ever look at other people and really think about being *them?* Which would mean everything about them, their families, their genes, every experience, but you're still *you,* you still know that you're only visiting. There was a little boy, maybe one of yours, waiting to get buzzed out while I was waiting to get buzzed in, and his mother was doing something at the front desk and through the glass, he couldn't see me I guess or didn't care but he was opening, he seemed to be practicing opening his mouth as wide as he could. And he wasn't saying anything but I could see way back in this throat.

(Ronnie taps her arm.)

HELEN: Oops, I think our guinea pig is telling us it's time. *(To Pearson.)* And by the way, I *do* need the money. *(Touching the mask.)* Okay, does it feel hard all over?

(Ronnie does a spectacular mock orgasm.)

HELEN: That is not what I— *(Trying to restrain him.)* I can see I have to be careful what I say to *this* man. Now stay still. STOP! ...There. *(To guard.)* See how well he minds? *(To all.)* Now, what I was going to say is that when you are having your mask made you'll notice how as the plaster hardens it cools. So you should be able to tell *from the inside* when it's ready to come off. Now I want to demonstrate how we remove the mask. You in the back, make sure you can see this. First you v-e-e-ery gently slip your fingers up under here *(the cheeks)* and you just keep working your way around, under the chin. Careful not to pinch. Nice and gentle. Back and forth. Ronnie you can start to make little faces under there, maybe try a little smile, open your mouth a bit. Good—this is where you find out if you used enough vaseline. And ready?...Voilà.

(The mask is off. Ronnie sits up, bits of plaster on his face. He pulls off the kerchief.)

HELEN: *(She hands the mask to Ronnie.)* And that, my friend…is you.
(Ronnie stares, unimpressed.)

HELEN: Most people have only a two-dimensional image of themselves which is what a mirror gives you or a photo. But. Here…*(Helen turns the mask to show Ronnie his profile.)* What you're looking at right now, maybe for the first time ever, is your third dimension…Now before you say anything, here's your paint brush. Kinda big but do your best—Oh first we need to get your name written on the inside so we don't get 'em confused. Don't want any arguments over whose face is whose…'Course I don't have a pen.

GUARD: *(Pulling a pen from his pocket.)* I can do it.

HELEN: Great. You don't mind?

GUARD: *(To Ronnie.)* C'm'ere.

(Ronnie crosses, hands mask to Guard, who writes in it.)

HELEN: See, I knew we'd get him participating. Now before we all get started I just want to remind you that with the vaseline, do a good, thorough job, remember that beards and mustaches will have to be covered with *tissue* paper and make sure to go way up into the hair line. There's no such thing as—

RONNIE: *(To Guard.)* Try it on.

GUARD: No.

RONNIE: Come on. Just try it. *(To inmates.)* Don't ya think he should try it on? *(After an enthusiastic "yeah".)* All right. Let's see.
(Guard holds mask to his face.

Ronnie looks to the inmates, then turns and drives the large, wooden paint brush deep into the eye of the mask. He slashes side to side. Guard falls to the floor, thrashes for a moment, then lies still.

Ronnie pulls the mask from Guard's face. He uses the paint brush to wipe blood from the back of the mask, then flips it, and paints a trail of blood descending, like a tear, from the eye hole.)

RONNIE: Hey look. *(Holding the mask out to Helen.)* It's me.
(They stand facing each other, motionless.)

RONNIE: Aren't ya gonna try it on?
(Beat. Blackout.)

END OF PLAY

Smith and Kraus *Books For Actors*
THE MONOLOGUE SERIES
The Best Men's / Women's Stage Monologues of 1994
The Best Men's / Women's Stage Monologues of 1993
The Best Men's / Women's Stage Monologues of 1992
The Best Men's / Women's Stage Monologues of 1991
The Best Men's / Women's Stage Monologues of 1990
One Hundred Men's / Women's Stage Monologues from the 1980's
2 Minutes and Under: Original Character Monologues for Actors
Street Talk: Original Character Monologues for Actors
Uptown: Original Character Monologues for Actors
Ice Babies in Oz: Original Character Monologues for Actors
Monologues from Contemporary Literature: Volume I
Monologues from Classic Plays
100 Great Monologues from the Renaissance Theatre
100 Great Monologues from the Neo-Classical Theatre
100 Great Monologues from the 19th C. Romantic and Realistic Theatres
YOUNG ACTORS SERIES
Great Scenes and Monologues for Children
New Plays from A.C.T.'s Young Conservatory Vol. I
Great Scenes for Young Actors from the Stage
Great Monologues for Young Actors
Multicultural Monologues for Young Actors
Multicultural Scenes for Young Actors
CONTEMPORARY PLAYWRIGHTS SERIES
Romulus Linney: 17 Short Plays
Eric Overmyer: Collected Plays
Lanford Wilson: 21 Short Plays
William Mastrosimone: Collected Plays
Horton Foote: 4 New Plays
Israel Horovitz: 16 Short Plays
Israel Horovitz Vol. II: New England Blue
Terrence McNally: 15 Short Plays
Humana Festival '93: The Complete Plays
Humana Festival '94: The Complete Plays
Women Playwrights: The Best Plays of 1992
Women Playwrights: The Best Plays of 1993
Women Playwrights: The Best Plays of 1994
EST Marathon '94: One-Act Plays
EST Marathon '95: One-Act Plays
Showtime's Act One Festival '94: One-Act Plays
Showtime's Act One Festival '95: One-Act Plays
GREAT TRANSLATION FOR ACTORS SERIES
The Wood Demon by Anton Chekhov, tr. by N. Saunders & F. Dwyer
The Sea Gull by Anton Chekhov, tr. by N. Saunders & F. Dwyer
Three Sisters by Anton Chekhov, tr. by Lanford Wilson
Mercadet by Honoré de Balzac, tr. by Robert Cornthwaite
Villeggiatura: The Trilogy by Carlo Goldoni, tr. by Robert Cornthwaite
Cyrano de Bergerac by Edmond Rostand, tr. by Charles Marowitz
CAREER DEVELOPMENT SERIES
The Job Book: 100 Acting Jobs for Actors
The Smith and Kraus Monologue Index
What to Give Your Agent for Christmas and 100 Other Tips for the Working Actor
The Camera Smart Actor
The Sanford Meisner Approach
Anne Bogart: Viewpoints
The Actor's Chekhov
A Brave and Violent Theatre: 20th C. Irish Scenes, Monologues, & History
Cold Readings: Some Do's and Don'ts for Actors at Auditions

If you require pre-publication information about upcoming Smith and Kraus books, you may receive our semi-annual catalogue, free of charge, by sending your name and address to *Smith and Kraus Catalogue, P.O. Box 127, One Main Street, Lyme, NH 03768. Or call us at (800) 895-4331, fax (603) 795-4427.*